100 GREAT AFRICANS

by
ALAN RAKE

The Scarecrow Press, Inc.
Lanham, Md., & London

Other works by Alan Rake from Scarecrow Press:
Who's Who in Africa: Leaders for the 1990s, 1992.

British Library Cataloguing-in-Publication data available

Library of Congress Cataloging-in-Publication Data

Rake, Alan.
    100 great Africans / by Alan Rake.
        p.   cm.
    Includes index
    ISBN 0-8108-2929-0 (alk. paper)
    1. Africa--Biography. I. Title. II. Title: One hundred great Africans.
DT18.R34   1994
920.06--dc20   94-25934

CONTENTS

WITHDRAWN

11. Living Greats

> **Note:** Some dates are marked r., indicating length
> of rule or reign, where dates of birth are not known.
> Many of the above dates are approximate, marked c.
> (see specific chapters for explanation).

Preface

This book is an attempt to choose and tell the stories of the hundred greatest Africans of all time. I have scoured the pages of history and have considered every country within the geographical continent of Africa. These catholic parameters allowed me to consider all great men and women from the time of the pharaohs to the present day. Yet problems of definition remain.

Many might argue that Egypt is not really Africa, and that the early Egyptian civilisation is too self contained and too distant in time to be compared with other parts of Africa.

But Egypt ruled vast parts of black Africa and then was itself ruled for centuries by black Kushite kings. Later still the Egyptian Coptic church selected the archbishops of the Ethiopian Orthodox church and Egypt controlled Sudan for long periods.

Thus a case can be made for including Egyptians on historical grounds and geographically the case is stronger still, because Egypt is part of the African continent.

More methodological problems of selection have been caused in defining Africans. I have not limited my selection to pure Africans born and bred in Africa, but have also included those whose major lifetime contribution was in Africa, or those who lived and worked in Africa most of their lives and left their mark there.

This has allowed me to include such oustanding personalities as:

* Cleopatra who was born and bred in Egypt though she was of Hellenic descent.

* Jan Van Riebeeck who brought the first whites to South Africa, though he was a Dutchman and returned to Holland after a relatively brief sojourn in the Cape.

* Cecil Rhodes, who was an Englishman though he became Prime Minister of South Africa and made his fortune there.

* Mohammed Ali, (the Khedive of Egypt, not the boxer!), who is regarded as the founder of modern Egypt, though he was originally an Albanian.

I have also included many Afrikaner leaders who claimed that they were what their name implies, white Africans.

But I have not included many explorers, missionaries, colonial governors and others who may have made their names and reputations in Africa, but were essentially visitors doing a job on behalf of themselves or an external powers.

This has meant that I have left out many great men whose whole image is associated with Africa, yet are clearly not African – General Gordon, Mungo Park, Henry Stanley, David Livingstone, Albert Schweitzer and many others are not in these pages. They made great contributions but were not Africans in any sense of the word.

I have tried to achieve the widest possible basis for selection over the aeons of history, but there are still many gaps. There were many great civilisations like the Axumite civilisation in Ethiopia, or the Nok civilisation in Nigeria where almost nothing is known about the lives and personalities of their rulers.

Inevitably I have had to concentrate on those eras in history that are well documented, though I have tried to include other important personalities where information about them is fragmentary. Modern historians have come to the view that Queen Candace of Kush, probably never existed, though she is mentioned by the Romans and in the Bible. She was also a quintessential Kushite queen and she probably existed under another name. I have included her as a mysterious persona.

My choice will probably be criticised because most of my characters are kings and princes, rulers and adventurers, men of action and not men of letters. This is partly because written language did not exist in many parts of Africa. I have included a number of famous writers – Ibn Battuta, Ibn Khaldun, Leo Africanus – but real writing by Africans does not start much before the nineteenth century. Likewise though Africa's painters, craftsmen and potters have left their work for us to admire almost nothing is known of them as people.

And women are insufficiently represented because women rulers were remarkably scarce in Africa since the time of the pharaohs. Africa is yet to produce its first woman president.

My book is essentially journalistic, not based on profound academic research. I have tried simply to tell the stories of the men/women I consider to be Africa's greatest. And even more risky, at the beginning of each profile, I try and assess why they have achieved greatness. They were the makers of African history and deserve to be remembered as such.

My thanks go to Patrick Gilkes who helped me with his deep knowledge of Ethiopia, to Matthew Rake who slaved for months over the proofs and to Baffour Ankomah who again helped me with all aspects of production.

Alan Rake
July 1994

Maps

1. Pharaohs of Egypt and Kings of Kush

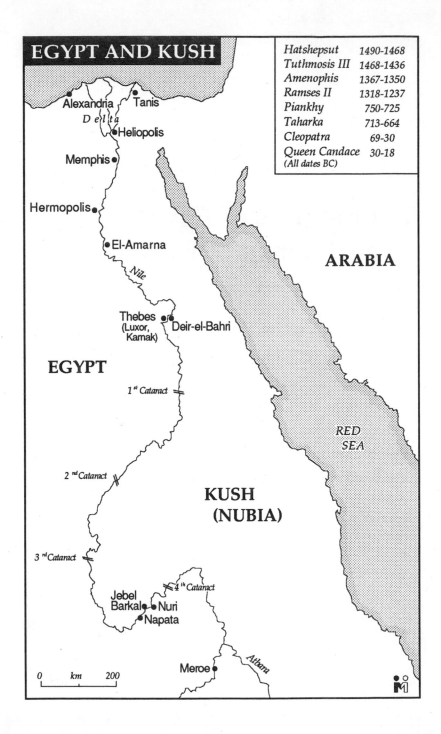

EGYPT AND KUSH

Hatshepsut	*1490-1468*
Tuthmosis III	*1468-1436*
Amenophis	*1367-1350*
Ramses II	*1318-1237*
Piankhy	*750-725*
Taharka	*713-664*
Cleopatra	*69-30*
Queen Candace	*30-18*
(All dates BC)	

Alexandria

Tanis

D e l t a

Heliopolis

Memphis

Hermopolis

El-Amarna

Nile

Thebes
(Luxor,
Karnak)

Deir-el-Bahri

EGYPT

1ˢᵗ *Cataract*

ARABIA

**RED
SEA**

2ⁿᵈ *Cataract*

**KUSH
(NUBIA)**

3ʳᵈ *Cataract*

4ᵗʰ *Cataract*

Jebel
Barkal

Nuri

Napata

Meroe

Atbara

0   km   200

Queen of Intrigue

HATSHEPSUT
Reigned.1490-1468 BC

Queen Hatshepsut is revered by feminist historians as a great ruler who overcame entrenched male prejudice, did a man's job and eschewing war, allowed the arts to flourish. All this is true. Because she had inherited the stable civilisation of the New Dynasty, there was no need to prove herself as a warrior, and as a patron of the arts she has had no equal. But she had to struggle and assert herself to succeed her father and husband with all her inborn political cunning and resourcefulness. So great was the enmity of her stepson, that when he eventually succeeded her he successfully managed to expunge her name from the pages of history, until the archaeologists, more than 3,000 years later, restored her to her rightful place as a pharaoh.

Makare Hatshepsut came to the throne of Egypt about 1490 B.C. at the time of the XVIIIth dynasty (the New Empire), one of the golden ages of Egypt's 5,000-year-old history.

She lived 1,500 years before the time of Cleopatra (q.v.), at least 3,500 years ago.

And yet there is a mystery that surrounds her. After her death her stepson obliterated her name on her monuments and her successors expunged her name from the lists of the pharaohs. It is only painstaking archaeological research of modern times that has reinstated her to her rightful place in history.

She was born the daughter of Tuthmosis I, who was not of an established royal line, yet her mother Ahmoi was a true Theban princess.

As was often the custom among the pharaohs, with their inbred and often incestuous relationships, she married her half brother Tuthmosis II. He was the son of her father by another wife of lesser importance.

Though the women of ancient Egypt played a major role in society and shared the status and social activities of their husbands, only two queens before Hatshepsut had ruled in their own right. Egyptian kings were prepared to give their wives a prominent supporting role, but power remained in their own hands.

Hatshepsut proved her administrative abilities to her own father who during his reign made her his aide. On his death the succession passed to his son Tuthmosis II, and Hatshepsut continued to exercise her administrative skills by supporting her husband.

Tuthmosis II's reign, which was not particularly distinguished, lasted 20 years. When he was away fighting in Nubia or other parts of the empire, Hatshepsut was able to carry out the administration of the kingdom and build up a strong team of officials loyal to her personally.

It was when Tuthmosis II died about 1490 that a real succession crisis exploded. It was caused by the peculiar, incestuous relationships in Egyptian royal families. Tuthmosis II had a son, Tuthmosis III (q.v.) by another wife Isis. Thus Hatshepsut was both Tuthmosis III's aunt and his stepmother.

HATSHEPSUT'S RELATIONSHIPS

Tuthmosis I -m- Ahmoi -m- A lesser princess

Hatshepsut -m- Tuthmosis II -m- Isis

Tuthmosis III

Tuthhmosis claimed the throne, but she pointed out that she was the daughter of a king by his first wife as well as being married to a king. She claimed that her father had always wanted her to succeed, especially as her young stepson was the son of a lesser queen. But, though he was still a minor, he felt that the succession should have passed to him.

Hatshepsut may first have ruled as a quasi-regent, but she wanted to be ruler in her own right despite the prejudice against her for being a woman and the entrenched conservatism of priests in the male dominated court.

She was crowned and took on the royal name Makare and set about establishing her legitimacy. She claimed that her accession had been blessed by the gods and was also in accordance with her father's wishes. She adopted male clothes and adopted all the royal rituals to show that she could do a man's job.

But it was also necessary to show the world that she was the rightful queen, so she embarked on an extraordinary building programme. She restored many earlier temples in Upper and Lower Egypt, while at Karnak she completed the temples started by her father and her husband.

Under the towering cliffs of Deir el-Bahri opposite Thebes, she built one of the most magnificent temples of the ancient world. Its three huge terraces and stylish columned porticoes are still a breathtaking site and yet much of the brilliant embellishment has long since been destroyed. The two obelisks gilded in gold and silver, with their glittering peaks to catch the rays of the sun, have long since gone.

Her architect and personal favourite (possibly her lover) Senenmut embellished the temple with statues and paintings which glorified her reign.

Hatshepsut was not a warrior queen; she cultivated the arts of peace. This patronage of the arts was not entirely due to her need for self-glorification, for she genuinely loved beautiful things.

Her forebears had left her a kingdom stretching from the Euphrates in the north to the land of Cush, below the fourth cataract (modern Sudan) to the south. Everywhere in this empire she encouraged trade. She brought cedar from Lebanon, turquoise from Sinai, metals and skins from the Libyan coast.

Her one great journey to foreign parts was to the land of Punt - today's Somalia. No Egyptian monarch before her had attempted the dangerous expedition in primitive boats, down the Red Sea and around the Horn of Africa.

Sailing at the best time of the year to avoid the monsoon and hugging the Red Sea coast, her five boats, whose design had not changed much since the days of King Sahure ten centuries earlier, eventually landed in the land of Punt where the people's houses were built on piles.

The bearded King of Punt and his plump wife arrived to greet them in great awe, asking, "Did ye come down upon the ways of heaven through the air, or did ye sail upon the waters, upon the sea of God's land?"

A huge banquet was then provided, before serious talk about trade began. Queen Hatshepsut had brought the natives of Punt trade goods, jewelry, necklaces, daggers and other glittering artefacts. In return she procured timber, ivory, perfumes, resin, pepper and wild animals.

The greatest trophy that she received was incense; some had been already purified, while 31 incense trees were dug up and their roots carefully wrapped in leaves so that they could be transplanted at the temple of Deir el-Bahri in Egypt. To this day their withered stumps can still be identified at the temple.

Hatshepsut died about 1468 BC after a 22-year reign. She had enjoyed a long life, as she was already an adult adviser to her father when he died in 1510 BC. She had outlived her husband's 20-year reign and then, during her own reign, had been locked in family antagonism with her stepson Tuthmosis III. She had been a great peacemaker and administrator, establishing a brilliant group of civil servants who had furthered her reputation as a patron of the arts.

The circumstances of her death are not known but immediately afterwards, Tuthmosis III, with controlled fury made a savage attack on all her monuments. Everywhere his masons expunged her name and her images. They smashed the sphinxes and tablets and buried their remains in an attempt to wipe his hated stepmother from the pages of history. For thousands of years he appeared to have succeeded. Then in 1906 an American archaeologist discovered her tomb and painfully reassembled the smashed fragments that told the true story of a great queen who had ruled in a man's world.

The Warrior King

TUTHMOSIS III
r.1468-1436 BC

Tuthmosis III is known as the warrior king, the "Egyptian Napoleon", who took the most glorious dynasty of an already golden age to its zenith. On his death he left an empire which stretched from the Euphrates in the north to the fourth cataract of the Nile and the land of Cush in the south. The Nile had become a stable and unthreatened centre of the world.

But he was far more than a great emperor and military genius. He was a man of culture; a poet, painter, and designer of pottery. He was a patron of the arts and builder. In the words of the great archaeologist James Breasted, "His character stands forth with more colour and individuality than that of any other king of early Egypt save Akenhaton... he reminds us of an Alexander or a Napoleon."

Tuthmosis III came to power in 1468 BC at a time when the glorious XVIIIth dynasty (the new empire) was almost at its zenith in terms of military conquest and artistic achievement.

Tuthmosis had been forced to wait for 22 years before he could claim what he considered was his rightful succession. For two decades he had fretted under the rule of his hated stepmother and aunt Hatshepsut (q.v.) She had seized the throne while he was still a minor, claiming that she came from a more direct royal line.

But Tuthmosis saw her as an ambitious and domineering woman who blocked his accession despite the fact that he was the son of her husband Tuthmosis II, who had died in 1490. His claim had been weakened because his beloved mother Isis was a lesser queen, indeed many say she was a foreign concubine in his father's harem.

Tuthmosis was a man of outstanding qualities. He was short, chubby faced, powerfully built and immensely strong. He had immense energy and drive. He had occupied his time while waiting for the succession with a brief period in the priesthood and then in the army.

Before he became King he had campaigned in Syria and as far as the Euphrates, in Asia Minor. He also had extraordinary artistic gifts, writing poetry, painting and designing pottery. Later in life he proved himself a brilliant administrator and military strategist.

When he finally came to power in 1468 he was so enraged at his mis-treatment by his stepmother and by the efforts she had made throughout her life to promote her affinity with the gods, that he ordered his masons to deface all her monuments. Everywhere her image and name were crudely erased from the many monuments that she had erected to her own glory. Even the graves and monuments of her close favourites were desecrated. Particular care was taken to erase the memory of the courtier and architect Senenmut, whom Tuthmosis accused of having an affair with his stepmother.

The pieces from the defaced monuments were buried deep in a quarry and Tuthmosis appeared to have erased his stepmother's name for all time. She never appeared on any future list of pharaohs. His revenge lasted until archaeologists of the 20th century resurrected her name.

Hatshepsut's reign had been artistically glorious, but she had avoided all military confrontation and when Tuthmosis finally came to power he found that revolts were brewing round the fringes of the great Egyptian empire.

Tuthmosis first directed his pacification campaigns to Syria, where his first major battle was with Syrian chariots and infantry at Megiddo. He chronicled the capture of that city on the walls of a temple at Karnak. In a series of five carefully planned campaigns he consolidated his conquests in Syria.

He developed a rhythm, campaigning part of the year and spending the rest of the time at home administering his capital at Thebes, honouring the gods and building great works of art.

After subduing the Syrians he turned on the Phoenician ports where he seized some Cretan ships sending them back to Egypt laden with booty and timber.

In the thirty-third year of his reign he crossed over the Euphrates where he defeated the King of the Mitanni and set up a tablet next to one erected by his grandfather Tuthmosis I. Marching westwards, he then received tribute from the Hittites and the King of Babylon. In all he fought 17 campaigns in Syria until the revolt was finally extinguished.

Between campaigns he returned home to rebuild and adorn his temples using the labour of his captives and the plunder of the conquered cities. He personally designed the beautiful sacred vessels of the sanctuary of Amun with his own hand. His obelisks at Karnak and Heliopolis had golden cowls which caught the fire of the sun and at night cast mysterious reflections of the moon.

Towards the end of his reign he turned south, extending the empire upstream past Nubia and the second cataract to the country of Cush and the fourth cataract at Napata. It was there at the sacred mountain of Jebel Barkal that a magnificent stele was found which recounted his exploits in Syria.

Tuthmosis had many wives and concubines. Three queens decorate the chamber of his tomb; his favourite was probably Meryetre who gave him the son Amenophis II, who was to succeed him.

Tuthmosis spent much time on Amenophis' education, training him to be a deadly archer and horseman. He had been brought up a warrior and wanted his son to have the same martial qualities. He taught him how to train horses and care for them.

Tuthmosis lived until he was 82. He had ruled personally for 32 years and would have been on the throne for much longer if his stepmother Hatshepsut had not seized power for 22 years. To avoid any succession problem after his death, he ruled jointly with his own son Amenophis, whom he "associated on the throne" in a kind of joint rule during the last years of his reign. He died in 1436 BC and was buried in the Valley of the Kings.

Heretic King

AMENOPHIS IV (AKENHATEN)
r.1367-1350 BC

Amenophis IV was by no means the greatest of the Egyptian Kings of the glorious New dynasty, but he was undoubtedly the most unusual. He was a mystic, a religious leader who was probably the first monotheist in human history, believing in the creative life-giving force of the sun and rejecting all other gods. He also presided over a creative flowering of naturalism in social life and art which was to survive long after his revolutionary religious message had been dismissed by his successors as a heresy.

He had no interest in military conquest, indeed he led no army outside the frontiers of Egypt during his reign, instead he was obsessed with his new religion to the exclusion of all else. But he went too far and too fast to carry his people with him and future generations were to refer to him as the heretic king.

A menophis IV was born the son of Amenophis III and the powerful, dark-skinned Queen Tiye. His exact birthdate has not yet been ascertained, but it is recorded that he came to the throne in 1350 when he was still a young man. He was crowned while his ailing father was still alive.

Controversy abounds around his name. Some Egyptologists say he was born ugly and deformed, others that he may have been mentally unstable, affected by the generations of heavy inbreeding among the Kings of the XVIIIth dynasty on the throne of Egypt.

There is some evidence that he may have been physically ugly because later in his reign he did allow his artists to depict him as potbellied, with a woman's hips and other non-masculine features.

Another important influence in his youth was that of powerful women who surrounded him. His mother, Queen Tiye, who remained at his elbow most of his life, was a strong personality with considerable influence over her husband and surely over her son.

The young Amenophis also married the legendary Queen Nefertiti, one of the greatest beauties of classical times, possibly the daughter of a Mittani king. Throughout his reign he accorded her status and power almost equal to his own.

He was crowned in the traditional capital of Egypt, Thebes, in about 1350 when he was still a young man, probably in his early 20s.

He was never interested in military conquest. During his 17-year reign he did not lead a single army out of Egypt. His father, the indolent, pleasure loving King Amenophis III had only led one expedition to Nubia. Both Kings were able to afford this luxury because of the great military achievements of their predecessors, particularly Tuthmosis III (q.v.) who had brought the Egyptian empire to its zenith. So solid was the kingdom that they had created that their successors could afford to ignore the minor quarrels and skirmishes on the northern and southern frontiers.

It was religion that was the real fascination for Amenophis IV. During his youth he had trained as the high priest of the sun god Aten at Heliopolis and he came to believe that Aten was more important than any of the 2,000 other Egyptian deities.

He particularly rejected the God Amun, the favourite of most of the priesthood. This tendency to promote Aten at the expense of Amun had been apparent in the last years of his father's reign, but he took it much further. No longer did he allow the sun god to be represented by Re-Harakhte, the human figure with the falcon's head. He replaced Re with a new sun god Aten, whose symbol was a disc representing the sun, with rays radiating outwards, ending in life-giving human hands.

After the fifth year of his reign he banned the worship of any other god but Aten. He changed his own name from Amenophis meaning "Amun is satisfied" to Akenhaten meaning "believer in Aten". He then set his masons to erase the name of Amun from the holy monuments of his predecessors.

Next, in his sixth year (about 1361 BC) he abandoned his capital at Thebes, where Egyptian kings had lived for centuries, and created an entirely new capital at El-Amarna, at a virgin site on the plain of Hermopolis. He used the wealth created by his martial predecessors and that confiscated from the priests of Amun and started to build a huge new city, with some of the largest and most magnificent temples ever created in the ancient world. He marked out a vast area where the new god Aten and his believers could reign supreme. He swore a personal oath never to move beyond these generous boundaries of Aten's domain.

Some historians have said that Akenhaten's motives were mainly political. That he wanted to break the power of the conservative priests who followed Amun, or that he wanted to create one god that would unify all the people of the world, not just in ancient Egypt, but these explanations are far too narrow.

It is difficult for modern man to understand just how revolutionary was Akenhaten's new religion. It was the first time any civilisation had recognised a single god, a monotheistic life-giving force. He saw Aten the sun god as the visible symbol of a life-giving force, of creation, nature, activity - a force which indeed prevailed over the whole world. His new god was a single god, but not a jealous god.

The archaeologist, James Breasted wrote, " He gave the first signal of the religion that the West upholds today."

But in contemporary Egypt his heresy was such that the traditional priesthood and establishment dismissed him as a fanatical cult leader of a new hedonistic religion, a man who, if not evil, was deranged and unbalanced. Someone who because he had been born physically ugly had turned against the traditional gods.

Akenhaten's new religion led him to revolutionary views about life and art. Under him social and artistic conventions were abandoned in the name of a new naturalism. Artists were encouraged to paint and sculpt what they saw and felt. This explains why Akenhaten did not mind when he was depicted as potbellied with hips like a woman.

He positively encouraged his artists to show scenes of intimate family life depicting his love for Queen Nefertiti and her children. In one picture he is shown fondling his daughter sitting on his knee, in another the Queen has her arm round his waist and appears to be kissing him. Like children of today, his daughters are shown playing in the most natural way. In another picture one of them appears to be playing with a horse. Akenhaten was depicted as an affectionate family man and may have been so, but he was also a man with strong sexual appetites. Much of his correspondence with the Mittani Kings, living to the north of his empire, concerns the supply of fresh concubines for his harem.

Meanwhile the political needs of his vast empire were neglected. The Syrian princes were still squabbling, while beyond them the Hittites were remorselessly advancing. Akenhaten ignored a flood of letters from his despairing subjects appealing for help against outside invaders. By the end of his reign Egypt had virtually lost control of Syria. He was storing up trouble for his successors.

Akenhaten died about 1350 BC leaving only daughters. His son-in-law Tutankhamen succeeded him and began to restore the old temples and gods. Akenhaten's religious revolution had gone too far, too fast for the majority of his people. And the priests were desperate to restore the old order and the privileges which went with it. Akenhaten's monuments to Aten were in their turn erased while the old gods were restored. The priests condemned him to wander the next world for all eternity.

By the time of Ramses II, Akenhaten's era had been dismissed as a heretical interlude and he was being described as "That criminal Akenhaten." But he had sown the seeds of a new religion.

A group of modern admirers tried to hold a ceremony at El-Amarna, the site of his capital, in 1993 to exorcise the curse that had been put on Akenhaten by the priests, but as they started to invoke the magic words, the heavens opened and a torrential storm broke. So great was the downpour that the exorcism had to be abandoned. Akenhaten's spirit remains condemned to ceaseless wandering.

The Great Bighead

RAMSES II
c.1318-1237 BC

Egyptologists have spent decades in sterile argument over
Ramses II, debating the question of whether he was a great
Pharaoh or just a great self-publicist. In fact he was both,
certainly a great ruler who brought peace and prosperity to his
nation during his 63-year rule. After years of trouble he achieved
lasting peace with the Hittites. He built, expanded and
embellished temples and monuments along the length of the Nile.
But he was also a bighead who never missed an opportunity to
perpetuate his name, by building colossi of himself and boasting
of his own exploits on the walls of his temples. He even "usurped"
the monuments of his predecessors by removing their names and
inserting his own. Everywhere in Egypt today, visitors will find
monuments to the glory of Ramses. That is just how he wanted
it.

Ramses II was born about 1318 BC when the Egyptian empire was in
a time of crisis. The pharaohs before him had ruled for short reigns
and had been obsessed with parochial and religious problems while the
Asiatic hordes were overunning the outlying parts of the empire in the
Near East.

His ageing grandfather Ramses I was a plain soldier, the vizier and
chief of the archers of King Horemheb, who died without successors. He
was plucked out of the ranks of the military by the dying King Horemheb,
to become pharaoh and found the new XIXth dynasty, but he ruled only
two years before he died.

Ramses II's father King Sethi inherited all the problems of the empire
and developed a reputation as a warrior king during his wars against
the Hittes in Syria and Palestine, but again he achieved little and ruled
for a relatively brief 11 years.

Ramses II was "associated on the throne" with King Sethi for the last
years of his reign as a co-ruler - this was frequently the way the pharaohs
and assured a smooth succession.

He must have learned his military craft at the feet of his father. Very little is known about his early life, but his father was determined that he should grow up a warrior, not a dreamer and religious mystic like his ancestor King Akenhaten (Amenophis IV) (q.v).

We know he was handsome, tall and strong. His mummified body was discovered along with those of dozens of other Pharaohs by the Abderrasul tomb robbers in 1871. Much later it was taken to the atomic research station at Saclay, France for treatment with gamma rays to arrest decomposition. It can still be seen in the Cairo museum. He must have been fit as well as powerfully built, because the story goes that King Sethi insisted that his son should go on a two mile run every day before breakfast.

Responsibility came early. He was only a youth of 18 when his father died and he inherited the throne about 1300 BC.

He had a flair for publicity and from the start was determined to register his name virtually as a God in the eyes and minds of his people. Immediately after his coronation he journeyed up the Nile to Abu Simbel, where he was later to build one of his famous temples, and later descended the Nile on the rising flood as if he was himself bringing the fertility of the river to his people. He paid his respects to the priests at Thebes and continued as far as his birthplace Tanis in the Nile Delta.

He was determined to restore the Egyptian empire to its former glory. Despite his father's military prowess there was still trouble from the Libyans to the west, the Nubians to the south and above all from the war-like Hittites who were pressing south from today's Turkey into Syria and Palestine, then the distant outposts of the Egyptian empire.

Ramses began a series of campaigns against the Hittites under their King Mutawallis, in Syria. His hour of glory came in the fifth year of his reign. He marched north at the head of an army of 20,000 men following the same route, across Sinai and through Palestine that had been followed by his ancestor Tuthmosis III (q.v.) before him.

His spies reported that his enemies, "filled the whole land covering the hills and the valleys like locusts..." And soon their story was confirmed by a group of deserters, who told him that King Mutawallis was so terrified at the thought of confrontation with the Pharaoh that his army had retreated north beyond the Kadesh plains.

The young and impetuous king, believed the story and decided to take advantage by seizing the unprotected town of Kadesh. He pushed ahead with his bodyguards, leaving the main divisions of the army struggling to keep up with him as they marched up the narrow Bekaa valley leading to the plain.

Mutawallis had set a trap. As Ramses prepared to storm Kadesh with his advance party he found himself surrounded by the entire 30,000 force of the Hittite army, with their deadly charioteers ready to cut the Egyptians to pieces on the exposed plains.

But Mutawallis, instead of pressing home his advantage, inexplicably stood and watched on the other side of the Orontes river while Ramses and his handful of chosen warriors fought the battle of their lives. It was a grim battle that raged for two days.

Ramses held on long enough for reinforcements to arrive and save him. Both sides suffered huge losses but he escaped alive and made a dignified withdrawal.

He was going to make sure that everyone else knew that he had been a hero. His priests adorned the temple walls with his version of the story, "His Majesty rose like his father Mont and took on the weapons of battle, and he girt himself with his corselet; he was like Baal in his hour ... Then His Majesty set forth at a gallop and entered the fray being alone by himself; none other with him. He fought alone against 2,500 chariots. He threw himself against them like a god of war. He killed all the princes of the Kings allied to the Hittites. He killed their generals. He destroyed their chariots and exterminated their infantry. He did so well that they cried out in fright, 'This is not the work of a mortal, it is the work of a God'."

That was the message he wanted to get across to his people, he was their God.

Ramses proclaimed this victory on monuments and temple walls up and down the Nile valley. In the words of the Egyptologist John Wilson, "There is no episode in Egyptian history that occupies so much wall space in Egyptian temples."

Ramses had indeed been courageous, but it was his gift for self-publicity that had turned a near defeat into a glorious victory. In fact neither side won at Kadesh. Ramses did not capture the city, nor press his campaign, he simply beat an organised retreat back to Thebes ready to resume his campaigns another day.

Like his glorious ancestor Tuthmosis III he campaigned in the dry season and spent the rest of the year at home. It was a dingdong war, with the Egyptians and the Hittites winning some and losing some until they had fought themselves to a standstill.

In 1275 BC, after nearly 20 years of intermittent fighting, a peace treaty was signed with the new King Khattusil. The pact recorded in Egyptian and Hittite was scrupulously followed and was never broken.

A few years later Khattusil gave one of his daughters in marriage to Ramses in a great colourful ceremony when the two monarchs ate and drank together like brothers, "for peace and brotherhood were between them." And Ramses was delighted with his new wife who was "fair of face like a goddess...she was beautiful in the heart of His Majesty and he loved her more than anything." A statue of them both is on display in the Cairo museum with the delicate Hittite Queen hardly reaching Ramses knee (signifying his regal status as a monarch rather than his height).

During his long rule spanning 63 years, Ramses had many other wives and claimed to have had more than 100 sons and 50 daughters.

With his northern frontier secure Ramses devoted his energies to a vast building programme. He decided to move the capital Thebes to his birthplace Tanis in the Nile Delta, leaving the old city as a religious centre.

He built temples to glorify his name the length of the Nile. At Abu Simbel, by the fourth cataract, he built the great statues which had to be moved in the 1960s during the construction of the Aswan dam. At Karnak he completed the Hypostyle Hall of the temple of Amun Re, with its huge pillars. He seized building material from Akehaten's (q.v.) crumbling city at El Amarna and used it to build more temples of his own. He enlarged and extended the temple at Tanis and erected there the colossus of himself with still more colossi at his mortuary temple at Thebes.

He even "usurped" the temples and monuments of other kings, often improving, extending or embellishing them but signing them with his own name rather than those of his predecessors.

He was an extraordinary self-publicist. A "bighead" in modern terms. Lord Clark described him as a megalomaniac. But in all his boasting his monuments usually celebrated some battle that was worthy of record as a real achievement.

He died about 1237 BC, after 63 years on the throne. It had been a long and glorious era in which the Nile was never threatened. He gave Egypt peace on its frontiers and time to build great works and allow the arts to flourish.

African King of Egypt

PIANKHY
r. c.750-725 BC

Piankhy is particularly relevant to this book because, unlike the pharaohs before him, who were often light-skinned Egyptians, he was a black African from Kush. He is often wrongly described as the first of the "Ethiopian" pharaohs. He was a great commander and organiser who proved himself militarily invincible, but he was also an extraordinarily pious man with total faith in the god Amun and a great love of religious ritual and ceremony. He had a strict code of chivalry and was generally merciful, never pursuing violence for its own sake. He was also curiously sentimental about animals, particularly horses, but his reign was almost totally devoid of artistic achievement.

Little is known about Piankhy's origins. He was the King of Napata, capital of Kush, near to the fourth cataract of the Nile. He is known as the "Ethiopian King", but really he was a dark-skinned African from Kush, a kingdom that was on the point of emerging as a major regional power. He was wrongly described as an "Ethiopian" because this was a generic name used by all ancient historians to describe Africans or men with dark skins. He lived on the upper reaches of the Nile, in today's Sudan certainly not in today's Ethiopian highlands.

He was probably a direct descendant of the last Egyptian governor of Nubia posted by the Pharaohs several centuries before to the southern fringe of their empire. While Egypt had declined into a kingdom of warring princes, invaded by emerging northern "barbarians" (the Libyans to the west and the Assyrians from the Middle East), the predecessors of Piankhy had built a stable kingdom extending over the whole of Kush where they had absorbed Egyptian influences in art, trade and religion.

For nearly 2,000 years before the Kush empire was born, Nubia had been dominated by Egypt and provided it with gold, valuable timber, ebony, ivory, construction materials, slaves and fighting men, but now, in the first half of the 7th century BC, it was Egypt that was in decline, while Nubia enjoyed stable and strong government.

Piankhy's objective was to establish dominance over the remains of the Pharaoh's civilisation in Middle Egypt. As he advanced down the Nile his main rival Prince Tefnakht, at the head of a coalition of princes, was pushing upstream into the same area from the Nile Delta. Tefnakht advanced south up the Nile as far as Hermopolis. He took that city and waited for Piankhy.

Piankhy, already a great general, showed he was a superb organiser too by mustering a transport fleet that stretched for miles on the river, ready to supply his troops who were marching downstream along the banks of the Nile.

He took a number of minor towns with ease, expertly besieging some and graciously receiving the tribute of others.

He was a devout man and a curiously chivalrous commander. His sense of fair play seemed even greater than that of the Knights of the Round Table in King Arthur's Britain.

He instructed his troops that they should warn the enemy in advance when they wanted to fight: "If the enemy says that the soldiers or horsemen of some other city are late, then wait until his army has arrived. Only fight when he tells you to fight. If his allies find themselves elsewhere, then wait for them."

Piankhy, a highly religious man, insisted that his troops purify themselves in the Nile and pray before battle. He seemed to have total trust in his god Amun, who he was sure, would give him victory. He felt he was the child of god and deserved no less.

During his youth he had worshipped Amun at his great temple at Djebel Barkal which had been built by the Egyptians centuries before as their southernmost shrine. It lay just across the Nile from his capital Napata and was now the religious centre of the growing Kushite kingdom.

When it came to the fight for Hermopolis, Tefnakht fled leaving the garrison to defend itself. Piankhy felt his adversary had behaved dishonourably and laid seige to the city. Eventually the half-starved garrison threw themselves on his mercy. Piankhy spared them, but was furious that they had allowed their noble horses almost to starve to death. As a true animal lover, he cried out, "As truly as I am alive and love Re, this is harder to my heart than all the harm you have done by your obstinacy."

News of Piankhy's mercifulness and military might, made city after city open their gates to him as he proceeded down the Nile. He arrived at Memphis in lower Egypt. The city was protected to the East by high waters of the Nile and elsewhere by high ramparts which the defenders were further reinforcing. Piankhy decided to attack from the river side. He grappled the enemy boats that were moored to the harbour walls and his men used their ropes to pull themselves into the city. This time, as the defenders resisted him, there was a massacre and he took an enormous haul of prisoners.

Piankhy then abandoned his invasion, deciding not to march further into the Delta which lay defenceless before him. It is not known why he did not press his attack to the shores of the Mediterranean. His army was strong enough and had thus far proved invincible. Maybe both he and his troops were tired and wanted to go home to Napata.

He returned to his capital, with a vast hoard of booty and inscribed a huge stela in the temple erected to honour Amun. It recorded all Piankhy's exploits in a naive, adulatory style. It was one of the most complete accounts of any Egyptian campaign and preserved his reputation. Otherwise he might have been forgotten because his reign was remarkably devoid of any other monuments recording his exploits, or indeed of any other artistic activity.

When he died about 725 BC he left his brother Sabacon to push the Ethiopian dominion to the Delta and as far north as Palestine and Syria. Sabacon founded the XXVth dynasty which ruled Egypt from Thebes until the Assyrians invaded about 664 BC. The Kushites then withdrew to the safety of Napata to found their own glorious civilisation.

Architect of Kush

TAHARKA
c.713-664 BC

Taharka was one of the great Kings of Kush who ruled Egypt. Like his father Piankhy (q.v.) he claimed two crowns, ruling over two lands - his comparatively new Kushite kingdom and the old world of Egypt. His family formed the XXVth dynasty.

He was an architect of his nation both literally and metaphorically. He left his monuments, temples and pyramids the length of the Nile valley. He also realised that if the Egypto-Kushite civilisation was to hold its own against the Assyrians and the other emerging powers of Asia Minor, he would need the latest technology. He encouraged the development of Africa's first iron smelting and manufacture that was later to make Meroe the "Birmingham of Africa," in the words of British archaeologist, Archibald Sayce.

Though he was a courageous general he was not particularly successful against the technically superior Assyrians but he is remembered for being the architect of the Kushite civilisation.

Taharka was one of the younger sons of the great Piankhy (q.v.), the great Kushite king who had conquered Egypt, made himself a pharaoh and founded the XXVth dynasty. He was a tough young man, tall and powerfully built, with a dark skin, flat nose and thick lips.
 He proved himself early in his career as the commander of the troops of King Shabataka, his elder brother (son of Piankhy), who established the Kushite administration firmly over the whole of Egypt. Shabataka transferred the capital of the kingdom of Kush from Napata, just below the fourth cataract of the Nile, to Thebes, the traditional capital of the Egyptian empire.
 At that time the once glorious Egyptian empire was in the middle of what the distinguished historian Dr A.J. Arkell describes as a "world war". The Kushites who now controlled the empire were threatened by the emerging power of the warlike Assyrians under King Sennacherib.

The young Taharka was sent by his brother to forge alliances with Hezekiah of Judea and King Luli of Tyre and Sidon in an attempt to arrest Assyrian aggression. Taharka is mentioned in the Book of Kings (2 Kings XIX, 9) as head of an "Ethiopian" army. But the Assyrians, under King Sennacherib, were so ruthless and committed to conquest that they swept these minor monarchs aside like dust. In the words of the Book of Kings, "Behold, thou has heard what the kings of Assyria have done to all lands, by destroying them utterly."

Under this external threat Taharka was forced to withdraw to Egypt, but his courage had been noted. As a mark of his leadership he was, "associated on the throne" with his brother - this association or joint-rule was common among the pharaohs.The Roman writer Eusebius says he may have murdered his brother but there is no evidence for this, though he certainly succeeded him.

About 688 BC he was crowned at Memphis, Pharaoh of the "two lands" (Kush and Egypt). In the year of his coronation there was a huge Nile flood which was taken as a good omen. The waters killed off the rodents and carried the valuable silt downstream from Nubia to Egypt where, according to Eusebius; "Every man had an abundance of everything, Egypt was in happy festival. For the inundation came as a cattle thief, it inundated the entire land the like of which was never found in the time of the ancestors." Taharka recorded this dramatic event in monuments erected in many places up and down the Nile.

Taharka ruled from Tanis in the Egyptian Delta so that he could keep an eye on the Assyrians. They were battle-hardened troops, well equipped with iron weapons and masters of chariot warfare while the Egyptians had scarcely learnt the techniques of iron smelting or the fashioning of iron.

Taharka rejoiced when the Assyrian King Sennacherib was murdered, but he was immediately succeded by the young and ambitious Ershaddon. About 686 Ershaddon, using camels for the first recorded time in Africa, sped across the Sinai peninsula and surged into the Delta. Taharka was taken by surprise because of the speed of the Assyrian *blitzkreig*. He fell back to Memphis which soon came under seige, falling to the invader. Taharka escaped, although many of his family including a son were captured.

Ershaddon took over in the Delta and erected a stele which depicted Taharka as a black captive in chains with a ring through his nose. This contemptuous insult steeled Taharka to strike back. After retiring to regroup, he marched south with a fresh army and retook Memphis and recovered control of the Delta in 669 BC.

Ershaddon died on his way to a fresh war, the following year but respite was short-lived; Assyria found another warrior-leader in Ashurbanipal. Like his predecessor he defeated Taharka, drove him back out of the Delta, sacked Memphis again and this time occupied Thebes in 666 BC.

Taharka then withdrew up the Nile, to his ancestral capital Napata, while Ashurbanipal forced the Delta princes to acknowledge his suzerainty. He was never persuaded to return and fight the Assyrians a third time.

Instead he stayed in Kush and worked on developing the art of iron smelting, for which his successors were ever thankful. Iron became the basis of the Kushite civilisation when the capital was moved to Meroe, further up the Nile, in the next century (see Candace). Meroe became the "Birmingham of Africa" as it manufactured weapons and artefacts to become Africa's premier power.

Taharka was far more than a super-General. In the true Pharaonic tradition, he was a great patron of the arts. Everywhere he built monuments and temples to the Egyptian gods who had been adopted by the Kushites as their own. He was famed for his works throughout the Nile valley.

He is most famous for restoring the temple of Amon Ra at Jebel Barkal near his capital Napata. Nearby he cut the colossal figures of himself in the cliff face of the rock at Jebel Barkal, earning himself the nickname of the "Nubian Ramses".

He built by far the largest pyramid of his dynasty at Nuri on the opposite bank of the Nile from Jebel Barkal.

One inscription at Kawa tells how he employed an architect and gangs of workmen to rebuild a temple at Memphis; "It was built of good white sandstone, excellent, hard, made with enduring work, its face being towards the west, the house being of gold, the columns of gold inlaid with silver. Its towers were built its doors erected, inscribed with the great name of His Majesty. Its trees were planted and lakes dug, together with its house of Natron filled with implements of silver, gold and bronze, whereof the number is not known...His whole city was made to glisten with trees of all kinds."

Taharka even sent the daughters of the Egyptian princes he had defeated to be the local equivalent of Vestal virgins in the temple.

Taharka died about 664 BC and was buried with other Kushite kings in the pyramid he had restored at Nuri. Many of his monuments on display in the National Museum in Khartoum are testimony to his greatness.

Queen of Seduction

CLEOPATRA
69-30 BC

Cleopatra was essentially of Greek blood, though her Ptolemaic family had lived in Egypt for centuries. She was born at a time the great Egyptian civilisation was being extinguished by Rome. As a young and helpless girl she fought back using the only weapons she had, her wits, charm and boundless beauty. Two great Roman rulers - Julius Caesar and Mark Antony - fell for her and she bore them four children, but never until her tragic end did she ever lose sight of her main ambition, the restoration of the former Egyptian kingdom and the succession of her son. No tragic heroine has brought more inspiration to countless generations of artists, playwrights and writers, than Cleopatra, Queen of Egypt.

Cleopatra VII was the descendant of the Ptolemies, the Greek Pharaohs of Egypt who had ruled for two and a half centuries since the dynasty was founded by Alexander the Great. There had been six Cleopatras before her, all wives of Ptolemies, women of energy and force of character, often dominant over their effete husbands.

She was the second daughter of Neos Dionysus Auletes, Ptolemy XII. Her mother Tryphania was the daughter of Ptolemy XI, Soter II. Though she later came to symbolise Egypt, she did not have a drop of Egyptian blood in her veins. She was Greek, a product of the great Mediterranean-wide Hellenistic civilisation.

She was royal to her fingertips - cultured, well schooled and could speak many of the languages of the Mediterranean fluently. Her beauty was to inspire artists down the ages. Few contemporary likenesses of her have been found except in Roman statues and yet her legendary beauty was such that it could not have been illusory. And throughout her life she repeatedly demonstrated her wit, charm, intelligence, sense of fun and seductive powers.

But she was born in troubled times. Egypt for all its wealth, art and natural resources had become a vassal state of Rome, then under Julius

Caesar. Her father Auletes had been recognised as the ruler of Egypt, but in return he had been forced to promise a huge tribute of 6,000 talents, which he had not been able to pay.

Her father died in 51 BC leaving her as a young girl of 18. Her brother became nominal king though he was only 11 years old. Three years later he died by drowning in a canal while resisting the Romans. Cleopatra, overwhelmed by the tragedy of the situation, the plotting of her enemies who supported her brother and her general lack of authority, took refuge with her sister in Syria.

Meanwhile the rival Roman General, Pompey who had been defeated by Caesar at Pharsala on 29 June 48 BC wanted to take refuge in Egypt. Cleopatra's enemies in Egypt murdered Pompey as he stepped off his ship in Pelusium and decided instead to back Julius Caesar who arrived in Alexandria in October to assert his authority and extract tribute.

Courageously, Cleopatra returned from Syria in this time of trouble and regained her palace. She had to avoid those who were conspiring against her and the Roman troops and yet she wanted to parley with Caesar.

It was then that she came up with the celebrated ruse of having herself wrapped in a carpet and delivered to Caesar as a present. When the rug was unwrapped a laughing, brown-skinned girl, 21 years old and naked to the waist leapt forth. The 54-year-old Caesar, " the bald-headed seducer of women", as his men called him, was entranced. The apparition that had landed on his floor, could speak perfect Latin. They spent the night together and out of their union a solid political alliance was born.

Caesar won the submission of the valuable Kingdom of Egypt without having to annexe it forcibly and Cleopatra regained her throne. Caesar was able to present his people with the image of a conquering general who had triumphed over a foreign queen. In 47 B.C. she was enthroned with him and recognised as ruler of her kingdom as co-regent with her still younger brother, who was only seven years old.

Soon Cleopatra bore Caesar a child, Cesarion and she began to plan the establishment of a Romano-Egyptian empire. She went and lived with Caesar in Rome, though he was already married to his wife Calpurnia.

On the Ides of March (15 March 44 BC) Caesar was assassinated.

Cleopatra always unpopular in Rome and fearing the revenge of Caesar's successors, fled back to Egypt. Even there a Roman army was in occupation and she had nowhere she could escape from the long arm of Rome. But Cleopatra was never one to give up easily.

In the summer of 41 BC she journeyed to Tarsus, in Cilicia (Turkey) at the behest of Mark Antony. She knew him already from her days in Rome. Indeed some historians say she had been his lover there, before the death of Caesar. She also wanted him to reassert his support for the claims of her son Cesarion against Octavian, Caesar's nephew.

Once again she summoned all the wiles of an accomplished seductress. At 25 she was at her most beautiful and she resolved to tempt him with her charms. She sailed up the river Cyndus in a gilded barge with purple sails, with the rowers dipping their oars in the waters to the sound of a flute. She rested on a couch, adorned like Venus, under a canopy spangled in gold, with the fairest maidens and boys dressed like cupids on either side of her. It was a show of colour, music, movement and the sweet smell of incense. In the words of William Shakespeare; "The air which but for vacancy had gone to gaze on Cleopatra too."

An excited Antony prepared to meet her, but after she had given him a glimpse of her figure, she ordered her oarsmen to turn back. He would have to wait to have her. Days more feasting followed until he was irrevocably hooked and she finally abandoned herself to him.

Antony was a handsome man with a cherubic face, curly hair and the figure of an athlete. He was still in his 40s, much younger than Caesar had been. She was prepared to give him her love in return for furthering her ambitions. Their dalliance at Tarsus resulted in her delivering him twins, a boy Alexander Helios and a girl, Cleopatra Selene.

Antony dallied with her in Alexandria for several months in the winter of 41 BC luxuriating in the hedonistic lifestyle of the Egyptian court, despite the news of defeats of his armies by the Parthians and growing problems in Rome.

Earlier Antony had agreed that Octavian should rule the western Mediterranean, while he should be master of the east, but Octavian was threatening to abrogate this arrangement.

Antony, ever a weak and indecisive man, bowed to the pressure, returned to Rome to negotiate and was finally persuaded to marry Octavian's sister, Octavia.

Cleopatra felt betrayed as Antony stayed in Italy for four years, trying to secure his position against Octavian. But all the time he pined for her and eventually he returned, divorced Octavia and resolved never to go back to Rome except as a conqueror.

Cleopatra then made Antony promise her marriage, the recognition of her eldest son Cesarion as the heir to the throne, and the reconstitution of the Egyptian kingdom.

She was soon expecting a fourth child by him. In 34 BC Antony's military fortunes seemed to be taking a turn for the better. He assembled a vast army with the help of his vassal kings and won victories over his old enemies the Parthians and the Armenians.

He celebrated his triumph that year in Alexandria with Cleopatra at his side. He publicly announced that the 13 year old Cesarion was co-regent of Egypt with his mother and promised land and kingdoms for his own younger children.

Now war with Rome was inevitable and the future of the world hung in the balance. Antony taking Cleopatra with him, advanced to Greece and overwintered his fleet at Patras. On 2 September 31 BC he was ready to do battle with the Romans.

Cleopatra who had supplied 200 of her own boats to Antony, watched the clash of the Titans. The battle swung one way and another, but from her vantage point it appeared that Antony was losing. Fearing the worst she set sail for home, to be followed by a number of her own ships.

Overcome with anguish at the departure of the woman he loved, Antony threw all reason to the winds, abandoned his fleet, betrayed his men and chased after her in a fast boat. This turned an indecisive battle into total defeat and everything was lost.

For Cleopatra and Antony the dream of conquering Rome was over. Their hopes lay in ruins. Cleopatra was so devastated at their joint humiliation that she turned her back on the weak man on whom she had pinned her hopes, and entered her mausoleum. Antony followed her, then stabbed himself mortally, to die in her arms.

Octavian pursued her to Alexandria, determined to take her back to Rome, where she could be humiliated and made to walk as a captive, in a public triumph. He burst into her room while she was still sleeping and enjoyed her desperate entreaties. She was an ageing 38 and ill with grief and guilt. He was a cold, calculating young man of 25 and this time there was no sexual chemistry; even Cleopatra could not make her magic work a third time.

Octavian did allow her to bury Antony, and she found time to set her son on his way to India with his tutor. But Octavian kept his trophy, the wild Egyptian queen, under close guard.

Nothing was left for her but to kill herself. She ordered a deadly asp to be packed into a basket of fruit. She placed the snake to her breast and died of its venom.

Octavian captured Cesarion later and had him put to death. Despite Cleopatra's lifelong struggle, the glory of Egypt had been finally crushed by Rome.

Queen Who Never Was

QUEEN CANDACE
r. c. 30 -18 BC

Queen Candace is a strange choice for this book. She probably never existed though references to her were made both by the Greek historian and geographer, Strabo and in the Bible, in the Acts of the Apostles. There were many female rulers of Kush. Ancient writers thought they were referring to the name of a specific female ruler of the great kingdom of Kush, when in fact they were using the word meaning "queen". Very little is known of the other kings and queens that ruled Meroe. Great confusion exists over their names and dates. Yet they ruled the extraordinary Kushite civilisation - the first civilisation in Black Africa which lasted for 1,000 years. I have chosen Queen Candace to represent Meroe at the peak of its glory.

Candace could have been a confusion, or she could have been Queen Amanirenas who ruled Kush from about 30-18 BC.
Very few of the names of the Kush kings and queens have been precisely recorded. This is partly because historians are still struggling to translate the Meroitic script and partly because their system of kingship was selective (their rulers were chosen by the elite class from any member of the royal family) and their rule was often brief in duration, because they changed their rulers so often.
As a result the rulers of Kush are not recorded clearly, certainly not with the precision of the Egyptian pharaohs. Very little is known about them individually after the time of King Piankhy (q.v.) and his successors who were finally driven out of Egypt by the Assyrians about 650 BC.
Yet the Kush kingdom was Black Africa's first civilisation. It lasted at least 1,000 years and developed a social and military organisation that was as great as Egypt's. At first it leant heavily on Egypt, but then it created its own flourishing arts with their distinctive "African" style. It added its own Meroitic language and became one of the world's leading exponents of the technique of iron smelting.
After being under the domination of the pharaohs for a millennium,

Piankhy and his father Kashata conquered Egypt and founded the XXVth dynasty. They ruled the Nile from their capital Napata rather than from Thebes, the traditional Egyptian capital. They wore the double crown symbolising their rule over Upper and Lower Egypt.

Piankhy's son Taharka lived briefly at Tanis, in the Egyptian delta, but he was driven out by the rising power in the Middle East; the Assyrians, who were masters of modern technology. They had made two huge advances over the Nile civilisations, the wheel and the use of iron. Modern iron weapons and horse drawn chariots drove all before them.

Queen Candace's ancestors abandoned Egypt and their pharaonic pretensions and withdrew to their remote capital of Napata. There they built up the Kingdom of Kush which stretched as far south as Sennar and Kosti, well above the sixth cataract of the Nile.

About 540 BC the capital was moved south from Napata to Meroe, just above the Atbara confluence with the Nile.

There were many reasons for the move - Egypt had been defeated by the Assyrians and was less important as a trading partner. The climate was becoming drier and the grazing land at Napata had become overcropped and eroded.

In contrast Meroe had lush grazing, large forests and plentiful iron ore. Food was abundant and the wood could be made into charcoal to smelt iron.

Iron smelting and metal working were pioneered elsewhere in the Middle East, but the Kushites took to the new techniques with such skill that they made them the basis for a renaissance of their civilisation.

Queen Candace would have been born during the First century BC as the Kush civilisation was reaching its peak. Iron smelting was so extensive that the British archaeologist Archibald Sayce who found piles of slag everywhere around Meroe, described Kush as the "Birmingham of Africa." Iron implements were almost mass-produced. Equipped with the iron hoe and the iron spear the Kushites were able to expand their empire far and wide in Sudanic Africa.

Queen Candace would have been a contemporary of the Hellenic Ptolemies of Egypt. Her envoys and traders would have been in constant touch with the predecessors of Queen Cleopatra (q.v.).

Meroe's gold had long since been exhausted, but her traders would still take ivory, slaves, skins, ostrich feathers, ebony, cotton and iron work north, bringing Egyptian and Hellenic artefacts, pottery, sculpture and cloths south.

Kush was much influenced by Egypt and the Mediterranean civilisations, but it developed art forms that were very much its own. Its jewellery, pottery, glass, metalware, tools and weapons were clearly "African". The artefacts of its craftsmen included metal knives, swords, even razors!

Queen Candace and her subjects still worshipped the god Amon at Jebel Barkal and she left monuments to her name in many places along the Nile. The statues of the Kushite kings were in Egyptian style, but they had African features, broad noses and thick lips. Their queens were fat and rounded compared with the sylph-like Nefertitis and Cleopatras of the north.

Strabo tells one very apposite story. The Romans had conquered Egypt as far as Aswan by 25 BC. One day Candace's men raided the Roman frontier post and carried off the bust of Emperor Augustus. The Roman governor Gaius Petronius was furious and launched a reprisal raid, in 23 BC.

The Kushites retreated in face of the well-disciplined Roman army which finally took their ancient capital, Napata and sacked it, burning the city and the religious temples at nearby Jebel Barkal.

Strabo says that Candace (probably Queen Amanirenas who ruled 30-18 BC) tried to negotiate with Petronius. He describes her as a woman with only one eye, of very masculine appearance. She promised Petronius that she would return all the statues of the Roman emperor that her people had stolen, but she never returned the famous bronze bust.

Nearly 2,000 years later Garstang, the archaeologist, was working at Meroe trying to find more about the rulers of Kush. In the course of his excavations he came across a bust lying buried in the foundations of a Meroe palace. It was the head of Augustus. It can be seen to this day in the British Museum in London!

The Romans made no more expeditions into Kush. The civilisation lasted long after Candace's death until about 350 AD.

As the Kushite civilisation declined and was overtaken by another great African civilisation at Axum, its people dispersed southwards and westwards taking with them their political, sociological, and technical skills. They probably exported the system of selective kingship to other parts of Africa; certainly they exported their metal working techniques. Queen Candace's children began to spread their knowledge of iron working and their culture in Black Africa.

2. Early Adventurers

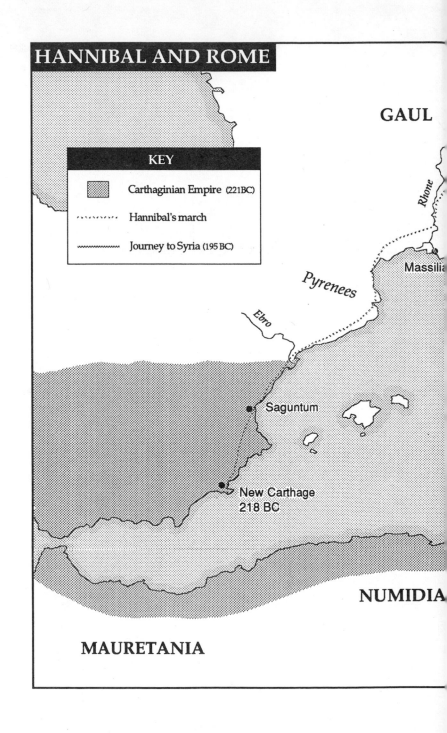

HANNIBAL AND ROME

GAUL

KEY

Carthaginian Empire (221BC)

Hannibal's march

Journey to Syria (195 BC)

Rhone

Pyrenees

Ebro

Massilia

Saguntum

New Carthage
218 BC

NUMIDIA

MAURETANIA

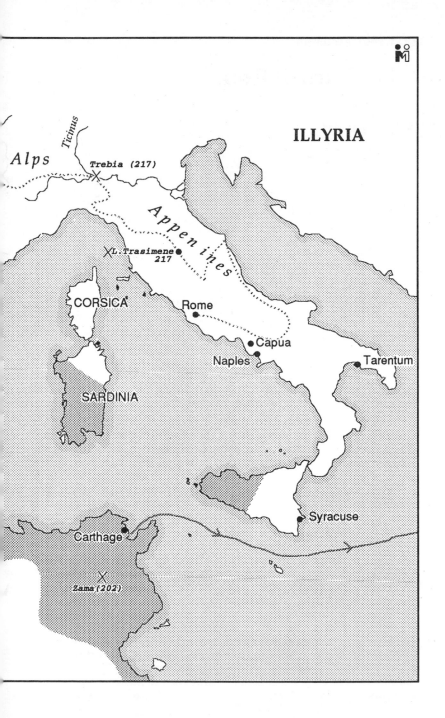

At the Gates of Rome

HANNIBAL
c.247-183 BC

No other leader born in Africa in ancient times was more important than Hannibal. His fame rests on his denial of Rome; his heroic resistance at a time the Romans were subjugating the whole Mediterranean world. He came within an ace of defeating Rome and his armies survived in Italy for 15 years, but eventually the forces ranged against him proved too powerful. One brilliant commander could not resist the expansion of an empire.

Hannibal is renowned for his great expedition and his prowess as a military commander, but he was much more. If he had not been born to be the adversary of Rome he might have been a great, liberal-minded politician, an enlightened leader who would have furthered the Hellenistic ideals of his time. Instead he was destined to tragedy as the Roman juggernaut carried all before it.

Hannibal was born about 247 BC. He was a younger son of Hamilcar Barca, the great Carthaginian leader who challenged Rome for supremacy in the western Mediterranean.

His father, a semitic Berber, from an aristocratic Carthaginian family, was the leading commander in the First Punic War when Carthage lost control of Sicily and Sardinia. Hannibal was born in Carthage while his father was still fighting a valiant campaign in Sicily, winning a succession of land battles before the Carthaginian fleet was totally defeated in a major engagement near the Aegetes islands.

The war finished in 240 BC. Almost immediately Hamilcar was confronted with a violent mutiny by his mercenaries. They were still waiting payment for their services on behalf of Carthage during the war. After three years of savage confrontation Hamilcar eventually put down the mutiny. He was given the task of retaking the Carthaginian colonies in Spain, with all their potential as a source of silver and tax revenue, which had been lost during the war.

Hannibal was scarcely ten years old when his father took him to Spain. He was intensely supersititious, with strong belief in the God Moloch and the significance of dreams, yet he had a Greek tutor and an Hellenistic cultural background. He took a broad Mediterranean view of contemporary politics, far removed from the political intrigues of Carthage, his native city. Indeed he was to spend most of the rest of his life living abroad.

He had his political and military training at the feet of his father, a colonial commander whose major obsession was to rebuild Carthaginian power and avenge the defeat by the Romans in the First Punic War. Before leaving Carthage his father took his young son to the Temple of Moloch and made him swear undying enmity to Rome.

Hannibal grew up an athlete, trained to run and box and to withstand the hardships of long campaigns in remote districts.

He learnt military strategy from his father as he gradually reduced southern Spain. One of his heroes was Alexander the Great, an even younger man at the outset of his career, whose exploits were still reverberating round the ancient world. His father died in 228 BC.

Hannibal was about 26, when he took over in 221 BC, as Carthaginian commander in Spain. No one contested his appointment. His charisma was well established and he was beloved of his troops. He had already developed a reputation as a dedicated and intelligent soldier.

Hannibal's personal confrontation with Rome started over Saguntum, a independent town on the east coast which both sides had formally agreed was within the Carthaginian sphere of influence. The pro-Roman party in Saguntum appealed to Rome for protection whereupon Hannibal laid siege to the city and after eight months captured it. The Romans made no effort to save Saguntum but sent Quintus Fabius to Carthage to protest and threaten war.

This episode gave Hannibal an insight into Roman strategy. If the strong militarist state was prepared to interfere in a remote area such as Spain, what would stop it attacking north Africa, and Carthage itself?

Hannibal felt his country was under threat, but we can only guess as to why he decided to respond with the extraordinarily ambitious scheme of taking the war to Rome itself; no Carthaginian literature survives to explain his motives.

He knew that he was up against the strongest military power in the world, which could put an army of 700,000 troops in the field plus 70,000 horsemen, drawn from Rome and its surrounding colonies.

Hannibal had to leave an army behind, under his brother Hasdrubal, to guard Spain and some reserves to guard north Africa. In contrast with Rome his invading army was no more than 30,000 infantry, 8,000 horsemen and 37 elephants.

The great expedition started in the spring of 218 BC. It passed through northern Spain and southern France without interruption, crossed the Rhone in August, and the Alps (possibly by the Little St Bernard pass) in October. Hannibal was welcomed by the Gauls, particularly those living to the south of the Alps who were in open confrontation with the newly emerging power of Rome.

The crossing was difficult, enduring snow to the south of the Alps and continual harassment by hostile mountain tribes. But his exhausted army, depleted also by disease, emerged onto the Po valley by December.

The Romans, startled by the audacity and speed of his expedition were unprepared and still trying to recall two armies that they had sent to Spain and North Africa. They managed to raise another scratch army which was assembled near the River Trebia.

But they did not bargain for Hannibal. The master tactician enticed them across the river Trebia, which was then in full flood and into an ambush on the other side. He surrounded the leading Roman troops and attacked those in the rear with a party hidden in the reed beds. The Romans were decimated and the Carthaginians had the run of the northern Italian plains for the winter.

In the spring of 217 Hannibal crossed the Apennines. It was there he developed opthalmia and lost the sight of one eye. Regardless of this handicap, he then struck south through Etruria, slipping past the Roman army that had been sent to seek him out. Near Lake Trasimene he set another trap for the pursuing Roman army. In the morning mist and fog it was surrounded and annihilated. Hannibal was now master of northern Italy and at the very gates of Rome.

Historians still ask why he did not press home his advantage and try to take Rome or at least lay siege to it. It was true he had no siege train, none of the heavy equipment needed to carry out a prolonged siege, but he could have bottled up the Romans and gradually reduced them while waiting for relief from Spain. Instead he recrossed the Appenines and moved south, losing his one chance of total victory.

He followed up his military successes with political alliances in the south. He persuaded Capua, the second greatest city in Italy, to throw off the yoke of Rome. Syracuse in Sicily also came over to his side.

He was to remain in Italy for 15 years never losing a battle on Italian soil, but the Romans found a new general in Quintus Fabius Maximus, a cautious aristocrat who used "Fabian" tactics to run a continual war of harassment against his dreaded foe. Hannibal was hounded like a bear at bay, never able to draw his enemy into direct confrontation.

As he waited for reinforcements from his brother Hasdrubal in Spain, the Romans found a brilliant new commander even younger than he - the 24-year-old Publius Cornelius Scipio (Africanus), who was to turn the tide of the war. In five years campaigning Scipio virtually drove the Carthaginians from their Spanish colonies which they had taken 30 years to conquer.

Hannibal meanwhile had been wasting his time in Italy, waiting for a relieving army, trying to sustain the morale of his troops and exhausting himself trying to protect his allies. The Romans besieged Capua in 212. Hannibal tried every strategem to draw them into battle and relieve the seige. He feinted with a diversionary attack on Rome itself. He came so close that one night he hurled a spear over the Colline gate, but Roman discipline held and Capua fell in 211. Two years later the city of Tarentum suffered the same fate.

His brother Hasdrubal eventually managed to slip away from Spain in 207 and follow Hannibal's route into Italy with a new army, but this time the Romans were ready and he was heavily defeated. Hasdrubal was killed on the field of battle. The first that Hannibal knew about his brother's death was when Hasdrubal's decapitated head was thrown over the ramparts into his camp.

Hannibal struggled on for four more years as Scipio Africanus went from success to success in north Africa, persuading the nomadic tribesmen from the desert to throw off the Carthaginian yoke and join him.

Hannibal with a heavy heart, abandoned his Roman mission in 203 and returned to defend his homeland, a country he had not seen since he was a child.

Hannibal and Scipio finally met at Zama, south of Carthage, in 202. This time the remnants of Hannibal's Italian armies assisted by local levies were no match for the well-trained Romans, who were bursting with confidence after their African victories. They also had the well-trained Numidian cavalry on their side.

Hannibal adopted his well-established tactics of trying to draw the Romans into a trap, but the hardened legionaries opened their ranks to allow Hannibal's elephants to pass through their own lines, then broke through the undisciplined Carthaginian troops. For the first time in his military career Hannibal suffered a crushing defeat.

Hannibal had to accept the opprobrium of his people. Their hero had let them down in their hour of need. Carthage was forced to sue for peace and pay a crushing indemnity.

But though he had lost prestige and popularity he survived to become an accomplished politician, not just a military genius. He was appointed chief magistrate where he had the unenviable task of collecting the tax to pay the Roman indemnity. He was powerful enough to introduce a system of direct democratic elections to the Council of State. But his enemies, particularly among the heavily taxed merchant oligarchy, were worried about his investigations of their own corruption and scandals and blamed him for the downfall of Carthage. They complained to Rome and persuaded the Romans to send a commission of inquiry to Carthage.

Though his old protagonist Scipio spoke out in his favour, Hannibal knew that he could not resist this conspiracy between his enemies in Carthage and the Romans. For seven years he had struggled to bring order and prosperity to his defeated country, now he faced persecution.

In 195 he went into exile to be honourably received in the court of King Antiochus III of Syria. Hannibal spent the next five years trying to persuade Antiochus to allow him to lead another expedition to Rome.

Antiochus never gave Hannibal his full trust, giving him an advisory post as counsellor rather than commander of his armies. When Antiochus and his army were heavily defeated at Magnesia in 190, the Romans demanded Hannibal's surrender. He was forced to flee again, this time seeking refuge in the court of King Prusias of Bithnya. Hannibal was given no peace there either; the Romans sent a mission demanding his surrender and King Prusias was powerless to resist.

For Hannibal there was no hiding place, it was a question of continuing to live a life on the run or surrender. Instead he chose to take poison from a ring that he always wore. He died far from home on the shores of the sea of Marmora. It was 183 BC, also the year of the death of his honourable rival Scipio Africanus; the ancient world lost two of its greatest military commanders.

Traveller of Islam

IBN BATTUTA
1304-c.1378

Ibn Battuta was arguably the greatest traveller in African history. Starting from Morocco, he travelled ceaselessly for 30 years covering countries as far away as China and central Asia. Of most interest to Africa was his journey into Western Sudan where he was one of the few writers to observe the great Empire of Mali at first hand. His religion was his passport, everywhere he travelled he depended on the hospitality and friendship of his Muslim co-religionists.

Ibn Battuta was born on 24 February 1304 in Tangier, a major town under the Moroccan Marinid dynasty. He came from a Berber family that had been settled in the city for generations. He was educated in law and theology. On 14 June 1325, just turned 21, he set off on the *hadj* to Mecca.

This journey was to give him a taste for travel that was to last the rest of his life. In all he was to make seven major voyages over the next 30 years, covering 75,000 miles that were to take him as far east as Peking in China, north as far as Bulgar in Asia and south to Kilwa on the East African coast.

He travelled by camel, horse, elephant (in India) and for thousands of miles by foot across the deserts of Africa, the steppes of Asia and the mountains of the world. He covered huge stretches of sea by boat, by dhow down the East African coast and by junk in Chinese seas.

He withstood hunger, fatigue and the hardships of the road, but given the enormity of his enterprise he had a remarkably smooth passage. Everywhere he depended on the hospitality and generosity of his Muslim co-religionists. Even in China he was surprised and delighted at the number of Muslims who entertained him.

In India he lingered at the invitation of the bloody tyrant Mahommed Tughlak who treated him well and made him a Malikite kadi (judge) in Delhi with an annual income of 12,000 silver dinars. He remained in the service of the dreaded ruler for eight years.

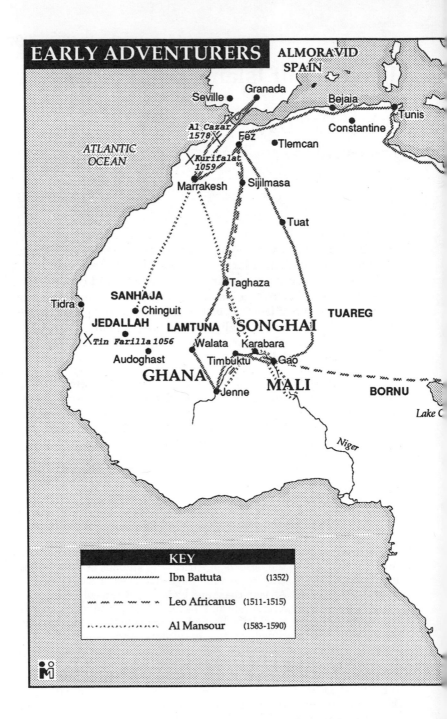

EARLY ADVENTURERS

ALMORAVID SPAIN

ATLANTIC OCEAN

Seville •
Granada •
Bejaia •
Tunis
Al Cazar 1578 ✕
Fez •
Constantine
Tlemcan •
Kurifalat 1059 ✕
Marrakesh •
Sijilmasa •
Tuat •

Taghaza •

Tidra •
SANHAJA
Chinguit •
TUAREG
JEDALLAH
LAMTUNA
SONGHAI
✕ Tin Farilla 1056
Walata •
Karabara •
Audoghast •
Timbuktu •
Gao •
BORNU
GHANA
Jenne •
MALI
Lake C
Niger

KEY	
.... Ibn Battuta	(1352)
~ ~ ~ ~ ~ ~ ^ Leo Africanus	(1511-1515)
·-·-·-·-·-·-·-· Al Mansour	(1583-1590)

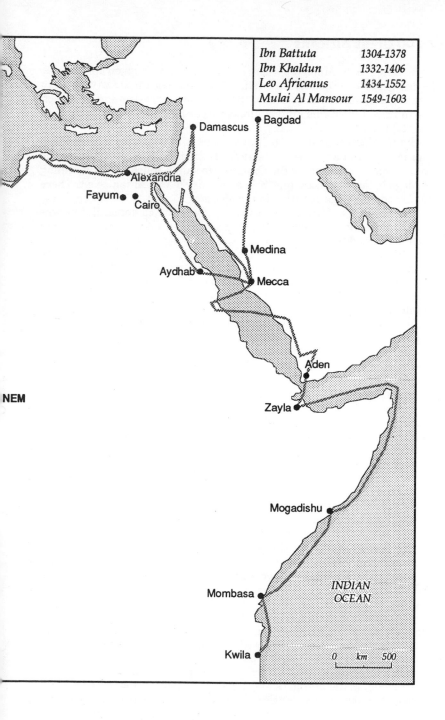

Ibn Battuta	1304-1378
Ibn Khaldun	1332-1406
Leo Africanus	1434-1552
Mulai Al Mansour	1549-1603

Damascus

Bagdad

Alexandria

Fayum   Cairo

Medina

Aydhab

Mecca

Aden

NEM

Zayla

Mogadishu

INDIAN
OCEAN

Mombasa

Kwila

0   km   500

He sailed to the Maldives where he confesses that, high on aphrodisiac foods such as Coco de Mer and fish, he took four legitimate wives, not to mention a number of concubines. "I passed the night sleeping with each one in turn. I lived this kind of life for a year and a half when I lived in the Maldives."

His third major journey in 1330-32 took him south from Mecca into southern Arabia and then by boat down the East African coast, to the Zenj, already colonised by the Omanis. He sailed south by dhow calling at Mogadishu, Mombasa and Kilwa on today's Tanzanian coast. There he turned north again, returning to Mecca.

After 24 years of travelling he eventually returned home. But he was still to make one more great journey. He followed the caravan trails and the established trade routes across the Sahara into the western Sudan between 1352-53. It was his last major journey, and of huge importance for Africa, because it gave him the chance to describe an unknown region. The great king Mansa Musa (q.v.) was dead, but one of his more successful descendants, King Sulaiman was on the throne of the Empire of Mali.

Ibn Battuta travelled by Sijilmasa, where all Moroccan caravans departed, and by Taghaza, where he found the houses built from blocks of salt hewn from its famous salt mines, and on to Walata, the northernmost city in Mali. In the last stage of his journey he was shown the way by a man who had acted as a guide for countless other caravans though he was almost blind.

Battuta was colour prejudiced. He writes that he was disgusted at finding negroes whom he had known only as slaves, being treated as masters in their own country. He reluctantly accepted the hospitality of a local Muslim official at dinner but was disparaging about the food that he served.

He travelled on to the Niger river which he mistakenly assumed was a tributary of the Nile, that first flowed west and then northwards into Sudan and Egypt. He found King Sulaiman in his court at Niani. He was scathing about the way the people prostrated themselves before the king after pouring dust on their heads.

But the hospitality of the Africans whom he met on his journeys, gradually won his heart and he eventually began to write of their great qualities: their kindness, love of justice and peaceableness. He was delighted to travel in an atmosphere of total security without fear of robbers or violence. He stayed in Niani for eight months. He visited Timbuktu but it could not have been a great centre of learning at that time, for he was little impressed. In 1353 the King of Morocco summoned him back to Fez. He travelled with a caravan of 600 women slaves via the mountains of Air, Tuat and back through Sijilmasa.

He dictated the story of his travels to Mohammed ibn Juzai, who as a professional writer and clerk may have embellished his story, at the very least ironing out inconsistencies. Juzai finished the work on 13 December 1355.

After his great work had been written and read aloud to the King of Fez (Marinid Morocco) little more was heard of Ibn Battuta, but he enjoyed a long retirement dying about 1378 at the age of 74.

Juzai wrote a concise testimonial; " This Shaikh is the traveller of our age and he who would call him the traveller of the whole body of Islam would not exceed the truth." He provides almost the only material for the historians and geographers on the first half of the 14th century. His writing spanned the known world and greatly stretched the knowledge of his time, particularly about Africa.

Historian of the Arabs

IBN KHALDUN
1332-1406

Ibn Khaldun's early ambition was to be a prominent courtier, a man of power serving one of the many Maghrebian sultans. For most of his life he struggled to achieve his ambition, but his clever cunning and love of political intrigue won him few lasting alliances and no prestigious postings. It was only when he began to put the experiences of a lifetime into his writing that he found his metier. He ended by becoming the greatest 14th century historian of the Arab and Berber people. The devious courtier turned scholar, found success where he least expected it.

Arab historians who began to study his written work soon recognised him as the greatest Muslim scholar of his day. He had done for the Arabs and Berbers of north Africa and Spain, what his contemporary Ibn Battuta (q.v.), had done for Islamic history in general and the Sudanic peoples of Africa, in particular.

Ibn Khaldun, or Abu Zeid Abder Rahman, was born on 27 May 1332 in Tunis. He came from a well-connected Arab family, originally from Hadramaut in Arabia, which moved to Spain at the time of the great Arab expansion of the 7th century. His forebears had fled from Spain to Africa at the time of the Almoravid invasion in the 11th century.

His grandfather had been the equivalent of the minister of finance in the court of the Sultan of Tunis. His father was a scholar who had passed his life in study and devotion, but died in the plague which ravaged the western Mediterranean in 1348.

After going to a Koranic school, he studied science, religion, law, philology and literature at Tunis university. He was inspired by his grandfather and throughout his life was determined to secure a major political position where he could quench his thirst for political intrigue.

North Africa was a patchwork of competing sultanates and kingdoms based on the major cities. Ibn Khaldun was ambitious and did not mind much which prince he served as long as he could further his career. His love of political intrigue meant that he was trusted by few and hated by many.

He first found work as a court secretary, with the Hafsid Kaid of Tunis, but this did not last long. He soon quarreled and found a new job with the Merinid Sultan of Fez, Abu Inan. Within a few years his intrigues incurred the anger of his new master, to such an extent that he was thrown in prison in 1356.

Released on the death of the sultan, he was sent as ambassador to Granada in 1363. Always seeking the "main chance", he trawled for another post and briefly served Peter III (the cruel), the King of Seville, before falling out with him too. Again he returned home to the Maghreb.

Ibn Khaldun's early life is a continual pattern of shifting allegiances and brief alliances, followed by disillusionment and quarrels as he tried to advance himself in the ever-changing pattern of Maghrebian dynasties.

He was devious and a charming flatterer, but always too clever to be liked or trusted. He rapidly gained advisory jobs, but never a major political post.

He became a travelling counsellor, ceaselessly journeying on missions for different monarchs. He served in Bejaia, Biskra, Fez, Tlemcen and Tunis between 1363 and 1374 before launching himself into the Sahara to forge alliances and recruit desert tribesmen as soldiers for the Sultan of Fez.

He spent four years in the Sahara and gained a great knowledge of the desert peoples. He spent some time in a *ribat* (a religious study centre) in the desert, where his ideas about writing a great history germinated for the first time. He was now 36 and he had come to realise that his life of interminable political intrigue had brought him no reward. He had made many enemies, yet secured no permanent advancement.

It was when he was staying with a desert tribe on the high plateau south east of Tlemcen in 1377, that he started his history of the Arab world. He stayed with the tribesmen for four years writing *Muqaddima*, the prologue of his *Universal History*.

In 1378 he returned to his home town Tunis, for the first time in 27 years, to further research and edit his great work which he finished in 1382.

He then set off to Cairo where he hoped to resume an administrative career in a more relaxed atmosphere. His reputation as a man of letters preceded him and he was welcomed by sultan Barkouk who made him the Malikite Grand Kadi. He saw his mission as a reformer and cleanser of corruption and soon made new enemies who complained to the sultan that he was unecessarily severe. While struggling to hold his post, he heard that his whole family who were sailing to join him had been drowned in a freak Mediterranean storm.

He consoled himself by doing a *hadj* to Mecca in 1387 and then retired to a small village of Fayum, where he continued with his study and research and further revision of his great work.

In 1399 he was recalled to Cairo to resume his duties as the Grand Kadi, but only 15 months later he was suddenly sacked as his opponents complained to the sultan of the harshness of his judgements. As the different factions manoeuvred for power, he was dismissed then reinstated no less than five times, as the sultan played off one kadi against another.

In 1400 he was sent to Damascus to parley with Tamerlane, the Mongol chieftain from Samarkand, who was besieging the city. With great courage, and heedless of his advancing years, Ibn Khaldun had himself lowered down the city walls by rope, before surrendering to the dreaded Mongol king. Tamerlane was fascinated at his effrontery and treated him with courtesy giving him a long interview and eventually a safe conduct back to Cairo.

Ibn Khaldun died on 16 March 1406, aged 64.

His *Muqaddima* was recognised as one of the greatest Arab-Muslim works of all time. His years of bitter practical experience had given him a deep and detailed insight into the sociology and history of his time.

His work was translated into Turkish shortly after his death and into French, English and German in the 19th century.

Chronicles of Gold

LEO AFRICANUS
1494-1552

Leo Africanus was an extraordinary man - a Moor, born in Spain who spent most of his early life travelling Africa, Egypt and Arabia. He was captured by corsairs and "given" to Pope Leo X, who encouraged him to write. He was a contemporary of the Songhai emperor Askia the Great and our knowledge of the great Songhai empire is due largely to him.

In just over a decade of intense travelling in his youth and early twenties, Leo had redrawn the map of Africa. He gave historians and geographers raw material which they worked and reworked for centuries. And in the process he created a legend of Timbuktu and the elusive golden trade that for centuries fascinated the world on the other side of the Sahara.

L eo Africanus's proper Moorish name was Al Hassan ibn Mahommed Al Wazzani. He also liked to be known as *Al Fasi,* or the *Man of Fez.*
   From his birth he wrapped his origins in ambiguity. "For mine own part," he wrote in his celebrated book the *Description of Africa,* "when I heare the Africans evil spoken of, I wile affirme my self to be one of Granada, and when I perceive the nation of Granada to be discommended, then I will professe my selfe to be an African."
   Despite this contrived confusion he was almost certainly born in Granada, Spain about 1494 to aristocratic and wealthy Moorish parents. His father was a landowner and his uncle had established the family taste for travel by being sent by the Moroccan Sa'adian sharifs of Fez as an envoy to Timbuktu.
   Leo was educated at Fez, then at the peak of its fame. He was a brilliant pupil with much pride in his education at the centre of learning for the Muslim world, hence his adoption of the name *Al Fasi,* or *Man of Fez.*
   He started earning a living as a lawyer at the Moristane Hospital for Aliens at Fez.
   But from the start his one desire was to travel. About 1510 while still

a teenager he travelled to Morocco, Tunis, Bejaia and Constantine. His knowledge of Islamic law brought him work as a clerk, notary and sometimes as a judge *kadi*. He was often employed by government officials or merchants. At other times he served the Sultan of Fez on diplomatic missions.

He was still only 17 in 1511, when he made his first great journey across the Sahara into Western Sudan. He followed the great trade routes used for centuries by the Sahara caravans, from Sijilmasa to the salt mines at Taghaza and on to Timbuktu, the centre of the great African empire of Songhai.

Leo describes the booming trade going north, "Fiftie men slaves and fiftie women slaves were brought out of the land of the negros, tenne eunuchs, twelve camels, one giraffa, sixteene civet cats, one pound of civet, a pound of amber and almost six hundred skins of a certaine beast called by them Elamt (gazelle)."

Leo was travelling at the time that Askia the Great (q.v.), the Songhai ruler and conqueror of Mali was bringing the Songhai empire to its zenith.

He was an inveterate traveller. He made a second journey to Timbuktu down the same caravan route in 1512 where he collected further material for the work that was to make him famous, the *Description of Africa*. He found the African people of the Sudan universally friendly and welcoming, in contrast to the aloof nomads of the desert.

It was his description of Timbuktu that turned the centre of learning into a legend whose fame echoed throughout the Christian and Islamic worlds. His description was complimentary yet he admits that most of the people, "lived in cottages built of chalk and covered in thatch." It was his fascination with gold and the wealth of Timbuktu that drew the avaricious curiosity of the world to the Sahara. "The rich king hath many plates and scepters of gold some whereof weigh 1,300 pounds and he keeps a magnificent and well furnished court... The coin of (Timbuktu) is gold without any stamp or superscription."

In successive journeys up to 1515, he travelled far further than the legendary Timbuktu. He visited Gao, the less glamorous capital of the Songhai empire, and Jenne on the Niger. He journeyed further eastwards along the Sahel, into Bornu and Kanem. He may even have visited Katsina, Kano, Zaria and the "lost city" of Zamfara.

Leo was clever enough to describe with conviction certain cities which he never visited personally. He made a classic howler by saying that the Niger river flowed from east to west towards its source. He also thought that Lake Chad probably joined up with the Nile after flowing under the Sahara, thus confusing generations of geographers and historians, but he did provide them with the meat of history that they chewed over for centuries.

In 1516-17 the wandering scholar travelled again to Constantinople and he made no less than three journeys to Egypt immediately after the

Turkish conquest.

As he was returning from Egypt about 1518 in an Arab galley, he was captured by Christian corsairs off Jerba. He was still only 24 but his rough, uneducated captors were impressed with his charisma and his knowledge of Spanish. He also carried a draft version of his *Description and History of Africa and the Notable Things therein contained.*

Instead of selling him into slavery the corsairs decided to present him to the pope as a gift. Leo X, a great patron of men of letters, was delighted at this human present. He took him into his court and granted him a pension. He even baptised him with his own name Leo after converting him to Christianity.

This quirk of history led to the wide dissemination of Leo's works. He first wrote his *Description of Africa* in Arabic, then followed with an Italian version *Descrizione dell'Affrica* which was published on 10 March 1526. This was published by Giovanni Ramusio in 1550. A new version in Latin followed. This book was finally translated into English, by John Pory, at the suggestion of Richard Hakluyt and published in London in 1600 under the title *A Geographical Historie of Africa.*

Leo meanwhile continued to live in Rome for some time longer, travelling less as he grew older. He returned to Africa some years before his death in Tunis in 1552, by which time he had renounced Christianity and returned to Islam, but the latter part of his life is obscure.

Moroccan Invader

MULAI AL-MANSUR
1549-1603

Al-Mansur the Moroccan ruler had a lifetime obssession; he wanted to plunder the gold of Africa. He is remembered mainly for the glamour of his African adventure - sending an army for the first time across the Sahara and conquering the Songhai, the greatest African empire of its age. But military success was only to lead to economic disappointment. By the time of his death less gold was coming out of Africa than if he had left the trade to follow its traditional channels.

Mulai Ahmad al-Mansur was born in Fez, the intellectual and religious centre of Morocco, in 1549. His father had founded the Saa'dian dynasty with its capital at Marrakesh. He claimed descent from the prophet Mohammed. His ancestors who had come from Arabia, established themselves in Morocco in the 14th century.

He had a highly disturbed childhood. When he was only five his father was driven out of Fez by a rival faction. In the chaos that followed, his father was killed and he took refuge in the south and then in Algiers. He was already 27 when he and his half brother Mulai 'Abd al-Malik returned and retook the throne. His brother was made sultan and he became his principal lieutenant.

Hardly had they time to install themselves when the deposed sultan returned from Portugal, where he had taken refuge, at the head of a polyglot force. The mercenary army included Portuguese, Germans, Italians, Spanish Andalusians, renegades and tribal Moroccan troops.

At the battle of Alcazar on 4 August 1578, the invaders were soundly beaten. The battle is sometimes known as the "battle of the three kings" because three kings died in the furious engagement - the Portuguese Don Sebastian, the former sultan of Morocco and 'Abd al-Malik, who had been seriously ill before the conflict started. He expired by the end of the day.

Al-Mansur, then 29, was nominated sultan on the battlefield, as the news of the Moorish victory spread throughout the Christian and Muslim worlds. After the battle he added the words Al-Mansur, meaning "the victorious" to his name.

Al-Mansur was a highly intelligent man, a poet and Muslim scholar. He taught himself to write in Arabic and even developed a numerical code so that his messages could not be intercepted.

Though there were tensions and feuds in his divided kingdom he soon asserted his authority using a judicious mixture of persuasion and force.

He decentralised government, keeping four of his sons occupied as *khalifas* (vice-sultans) in charge of important regions. He devised a new and successful tax system that kept the funds flowing into his exchequer throughout his 25-year reign. He built a powerful standing army of almost 20,000 men and used it only when force was needed to successfully crush local revolts. He imported arms from Protestant England, then under Queen Elizabeth I, who was only too keen to have an ally in the south against the rising power of Philip of Spain.

He found that sugar was an important source of foreign exchange and encouraged the local sugar industry to pay for European - particularly English - imports such as ships and maritime equipment. He loved luxury and built a huge palace near the Kasbah at Marrakesh, with marble and building materials imported from all over Europe.

But he is best remembered not for the 25 years of peace and stability that he brought his own country, but for what appeared to be a crazy scheme of African conquest.

Though he was threatened by Spain in the north and by the Ottoman empire that was creeping ever closer across north Africa from the east, he formed the bizarre idea of crossing the Sahara and defeating the powerful and wealthy Songhai empire. He thought this would give him control of all the trans-Sahara caravans especially the immensely lucrative salt and gold trade. He even thought he could secure the source of gold in the rainforests of West Africa.

His first objective was to wrest control of the salt mines in the Sahara desert that were still paying tribute to the Songhai emperors. The first expedition to Chinguit in 1583/4 was a disaster. Harried by the dreaded Tuareg, the blue men, all his men perished of thirst in the desert.

Not downhearted, he sent another expedition to seize control of the salt mines of Taghaza, in the centre of the Sahara. This time he found that the salt miners had fled their squalid camp on hearing of his approaching army. Ignoring this setback he sent a letter to the Songhai king, Askia Isaq, saying that in future he would collect the tribute on the salt. Isaq sent back a strongly worded reply, which he took to be an insult and an excuse for war.

Many of his advisers warned that it would be near impossible to take an army across the Sahara; no one had ever done it before. Though the Songhai had been warring amongst themselves, they were rich and powerful and could put a large army into the field.

Al-Mansur countered eloquently that a small, mobile force armed with the latest weapons could easily rout an African army - muskets and canons would terrorise primitive Africans armed with nothing but bows, arrows and spears.

Al-Mansur put together the finest fighting force he could muster; 4,000 men with 10,000 camels and 1,000 pack horses carrying powder, shot, mortars that fired stone balls and tents and water. As his commander he chose a blue-eyed Spanish eunuch named Judar, who had been captured as an infant in Spain and had grown up in the Moroccan court. Most of the expeditionary force originally came from Europe.

On 16 October 1590 the expedition set off on its 1,500 mile desert crossing. It followed the old gold and salt route through Taghaza reaching the Niger at Karabara in February 1591. There was insufficient water in the wells and oases for such a large army, and insufficient pasture for the beasts of burden. On the route they came across a monument saying that a rich merchant had once given 10,000 ducats for a cup of water, but this had been insufficient to save him from death by dehydration.

About half of the army perished. Only 1,000 weakened men were ready for their first engagement with the Songhai at Tondibi.

Even so Al-Mansur was proved right; the 100,000 Songhai bowmen and cavalry were no match for the frightening firepower of the invaders. Further easy victories followed, then came disappointment.

Judar found that the Songhai cities were squalid and impoverished. He said Askia's palace was so poor that even the master of the Marakesh donkeys would have refused to live there. Even the best families which should have had some money fled their homes and concealed their much vaunted gold wealth. Disease broke out in the Moroccan army and Judar was no nearer identifying the source of gold.

When Al-Mansur finally heard all this from Judar, he promptly dismissed him and appointed Mahmud Zarqun in his place. Zarqun adopted tough tactics in his efforts to tap the gold wealth. He sacked Timbuktu and sent a number of Muslim scholars and their wives and children, including the celebrated scholar Ahmad Baba, in chains back to Morocco.

But Zarqun had little more success than Judar. His firearms could not combat tropical disease, local lethargy and the tribalism of the Songhai. Soon he became involved in interminable local wars against the Borgu and the Tuareg.

Al-Mansur found that it was increasingly difficult to keep control of his lieutenants in Songhai. Shortly after his death the whole Sudanese empire was abandoned. Many of the Moroccan colonists became absorbed into the local community - some families still survived until the arrival of the French at the end of the 19th century.

Al-Mansur's dream of getting rich on African gold and trade come to nothing. The cost of sending troops and maintaining local administration at such a distance was probably more than the value of the gold recouped. Control of the trade alone would have been much more profitable and would have saved him the cost of his military ventures. By the time of his death the supply of gold from the western Sudan had practically dried up.

The Moroccan occupation did little for Western Sudan. The Songhai empire collapsed and the centre of the great African civilisation was about to enter its "time of troubles" marked by political instability, the displacement of people, a decline in wealth and deterioration in Muslim scholarship.

Al-Mansur is less well known for his rule in Morocco, but there he did bring 25 years peace and prosperity to a country that had suffered decades of turbulence. He also skilfully avoided the attentions of the two super powers - Spain and the Ottomans. He and Elizabeth I of England kept a long correspondence going, concerning their support for the pretender to the Portuguese throne and the Spanish.

Al Mansur died on 25 August 1603 - the same year as the English queen. Years of civil strife then started amongst his sons and the carefully constructed administrative, military and taxation system that he had nurtured collapsed like a pack of cards. It was the skill of his government at home, rather than the glamour of his African adventure that was his true achievement.

White Intruder

JAN VAN RIEBEECK
1618-1677

Jan Van Riebeeck, should perhaps not be in this book - he is neither a white African, nor even a settler. He only lived ten years in Africa before returning home to Holland, but by then his place in history was assured. The white man had established a toehold on the continent that was never relinquished.

A pattern of settlement was established for free white burghers, while other races were brought in to serve the needs of the new community. Indigenous Africans were forced to share their land and wealth with the new strangers. It was Jan Van Riebeeck's first settlers whose descendants remained, becoming Afrikaners with a language and culture of their own and the dominant force in southern Africa for over three centuries.

Johan (Jan) Athonizoon Van Riebeeck was born into a wealthy Dutch family in April 1618 in Culemborg, Holland. He trained as a surgeon and joined the Dutch East India Company, the most powerful mercantile organisation in the world, operating under a charter which gave it a monopoly over the lucrative trade with the Dutch East Indies.

He had sailed to the Far East in 1647 on the *Nieuw Haerlem* which was stranded in Table Bay after catching a southeaster. Eventually the ship was saved and returned home with Van Riebeeck, but leaving a party of 60 sailors guarding a valuable cargo of spices and sandalwood at the Cape. His report on the incident and his knowledge of the area gained during his stay, came to the attention of the 17-man council of the Dutch East India Company which was already on the point of establishing a permanent victualling post at the Cape.

They chose Van Riebeeck to establish a permanent station at the Cape. He was required to meet the needs of passing ships for fresh water, meat, vegetables and a safe haven to carry out repairs and remove barnacles from the wooden vessels.

On 24 December 1651 he set sail with his wife, an infant son and two nieces in two small boats, the *Drommedaris* and the *Goede Hoope*. After an uneventful voyage they anchored at Table Bay on 6 April 1652.

After setting up a temporary camp and securing fresh water supplies, he and the carpenters, masons and soldiers who had travelled with him started to build a temporary fort, while his gardeners planted vegetables.

Soon the chief preoccupation became the acquiring of sufficient livestock from the unwilling Hottentots, to supply the settlement and the passing ships with meat. Van Riebeeck insisted that the Hottentots should be well treated and no attempts should be made to take food from them, but they had little incentive to trade for beads and copper bangles and supplies were always slow in coming. It was not until contact was established later with the tribes of the interior that a regular supply of meat became available.

Van Riebeeck befriended a chief he called Harry, leader of the nearby Hottentots, who often dined at his table. He helped improve the supplies of livestock but things turned nasty when he murdered a company herdsman. Van Riebeeck's carefully cultivated relationship with the locals became most difficult. In the years that followed food supplies were heavily dependent on the on-off relationship with the wilful and unreliable Harry.

Van Riebeeck ruled through a Council of Policy elected from his followers. The more enterprising among them soon asked to be relieved from company employment to set up as free farmers on their own. They were still under considerable company control and had to sell all livestock and produce to the company at parsimonious prices fixed by the company. Many who won this freedom, felt that they were worse off than before.

Others wanted slaves to be imported to break in new land and build the infrastructure. Van Riebeeck at first aimed to establish a free society but food production continually lagged behind demand and soon he was asking company permission to bring in slaves to boost production. They duly came, in small numbers, from Madagascar, the East Indies and Angola.

By 1658 four years after his arrival Van Riebeeck had 91 paid officials, some of them professional soldiers, 50 freemen, 22 women and children, 10 convicts and 16 slaves - not 200, in all.

He was a man of considerable enterprise and his journal relates how he started sealing, whaling, fishing and growing vines and tobacco, in addition to the basic corn and vegetables. He also sent expeditions into the interior, not simply to barter cattle from friendly tribes, but to collect honey, wax, ostrich feathers, elephant tusks and hides and skins.

On the morning of 2 April 1662 two company ships sailed into Table Bay bearing Zacharias Wagenaer, a senior company official carrying a letter from the directors of the East India Company, the Lords Seventeen saying that Van Riebeeck was to go to Batavia in the Netherlands East Indies.

Van Riebeeck spent a month handing over the complex system that he had built up. In his ten years he had ultimately managed to improve relations with the Hottentots. His expeditions had opened new routes over the mountains to the west, where the Africans were often friendly and the supply of cattle more plentiful. He was in a position at last to supply all ships that passed with basic needs.

He had also established a community determined to make their home in Africa. Later they would be joined by refugee Hugenots and Germans, but Jan Van Riebeeck had already sowed the seeds of the Afrikaner race. For good or ill, the white man had come to stay in Africa.

Before he left with his wife and family, a son Abraham was born in the Cape settlement. He was to become almost as famous as his father, rising steadily in importance until he became Governor General of the Netherlands East Indies. This son of Africa died in Batavia in 1713. His father Jan had died earlier on 18 January 1677.

3. Golden Kings

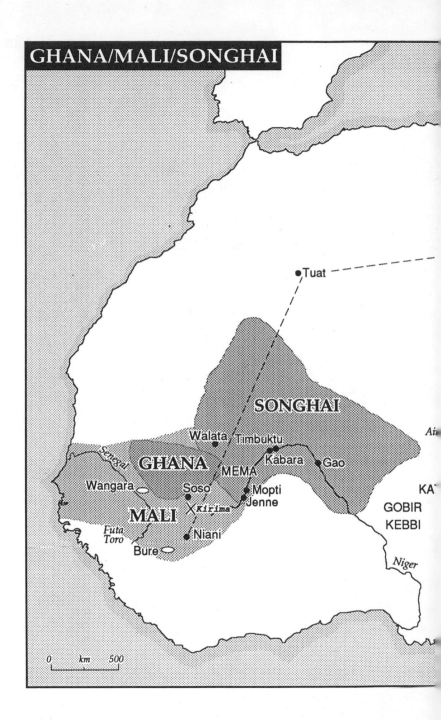

GHANA/MALI/SONGHAI

Tuat

SONGHAI

Walata Timbuktu

Senegal

GHANA

MEMA

Kabara Gao

Wangara

Soso

Mopti

Jenne

MALI

Kirima

Futa
Toro

Niani

Bure

Ai

KA

GOBIR

KEBBI

Niger

0   km   500

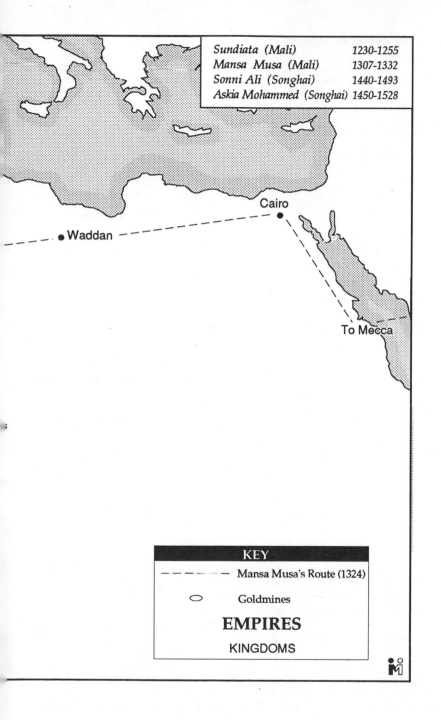

Sundiata (Mali)	1230-1255
Mansa Musa (Mali)	1307-1332
Sonni Ali (Songhai)	1440-1493
Askia Mohammed (Songhai)	1450-1528

Cairo

• Waddan

To Mecca

KEY

– – – – – – Mansa Musa's Route (1324)

◯   Goldmines

EMPIRES

KINGDOMS

Magical King

SUNDIATA
r.1230-1255

Sundiata was the founder of the great Mali empire. He is remembered to this day among his Malinke people with semi-mystical veneration as a magician-king. Offerings are still left to his memory along the banks of the Niger river. The Malinke rank him far more highly than his descendant Mansa Musa (q.v.), the golden king, who was lionised throughout Europe and Arabia by his contemporaries.

Sundiata was born weak and handicapped and was persecuted by his enemies, but he survived to defeat the Susu and profit by the final collapse of the great Ghana empire. He won a succession of victories and expanded the boundaries of the Mali empire almost to its maximum, an area far greater than that of Ghana, covering almost the whole of western Sudan. It controlled the sources of the gold trade which was to be the basis of its prosperity for almost two centuries.

Maghan Sundiata, sometimes known as Mari Jata, was born at the beginning of the 13th century. He was son of Mari Diata, a Malinke (Mandingo) chief of the Keita clan. His family had been Muslims for generations. They were converted to Islam from the tenth century.

But Sundiata liked to play religion to his own advantage. At a very early age he had been initiated into the Brotherhood of the Hunters, a secret society that exists to this very day. It was open to all Malinkes, regardless of class, caste or religion. Sundiata, like generations after him, heard the mystical incantation; "No longer do you have a mother or a father except Sanene and Kontron, the mother and father of all the hunters."

But Sundiata was no athletic huntsman. He was born a semi-cripple and his mother, Sogolon Conde, was scorned by the other wives of Mari Diata because her son was handicapped. This physical disability may have saved him from the wrath of the Susu king, Sumanguru, who after defeating the Malinkes, put most of Sundiata's brothers to death, but spared him.

Sundiata and his mother escaped and fled to the Soninke kingdom of Mema, one of the remaining fragments of the great Ghana empire, where the local king Tunkara took pity on them and allowed them to stay in his court. Tunkara felt sympathy because they were potential allies against Sumanguru who had caused the final downfall of Ghana empire. They were also nominally Muslims who were being persecuted by an animist king.

In Malinke country Sumanguru was carrying all before him. He was largely responsible for successive defeats of the Malinkes between 1220-1235.

Sundiata surprisingly outgrew his physical handicaps and became a warrior who found work in Tunkara's court. When Malinke envoys arrived asking Sundiata to take up the fight on behalf of his people, Tunkara thought so highly of him that he gave him some cavalry and helped him raise an army.

As he marched towards his homeland, the oppressed Malinke came out of hiding and flocked to his standard. Previously when they had fought as individual clan chieftains they had been systematically picked off by Sumanguru, now they were ready to unite under a new leader in a war of liberation. Sundiata was even joined by Sumanguru's own nephew who had revolted against his uncle, accusing him of interfering with his wife.

Sundiata also played the magical card. His people saw the developing war as one between two great magicians. Sundiata managed to win sufficient *griots* (witch doctors) to his side to be able to claim that he had the "key" to Sumanguru's greatest weakness. He told everyone that he had found out that he could be killed by any other means except "by iron". Sumanguru was so depressed that his secret had been discovered that this affected his confidence in the struggle ahead.

Sundiata also had many other things going for him. He was joined by the Bobo archers who specialised in sending flaming torches into the ranks of the enemy. He had brought a detachment of Mema cavalry from King Tunkara and for the first time the Malinke chiefs united and swore fealty to him.

This mixture of magic and diplomacy resulted in a major victory at the battle of Kirima in 1235, which was to prove the one event that launched the Mali empire.

Sundiata was totally triumphant and went on to sack the Susu capital Soso, and put his enemies to flight. The whole tribe moved south-west towards the coast away from the emerging empire of Mali.

Sundiata followed his victory by expanding the Mali boundaries in all directions until it stretched from Gao on the Niger, westwards as far as the Atlantic, southwards to the rain forests of West Africa, and north into the sands of the Sahara.

He also moved his capital from Kabara on the bend of the Niger, to

Niani (which gave Mali its name), much further upstream. Though it was situated in the extreme south of the new empire, it was a location that was easy to defend and very near to the forests and the source of gold at Bure which was to make Mali rich in future decades.

Sundiata also completely reorganised and modernised his system of government, his administration and the rules of succession. He made skilful alliances with the King of Ghana and the King of Mema who had helped him in his struggle. They were highly honoured and allowed to keep their title as kings but recognised his overall suzerainty, by becoming part of the Mali empire.

Most information on Sundiata comes either from Arab historians such as Ibn Khaldun (q.v.) or from the strong oral tradition of the Malinkes (there was, of course, no written language).

There is considerable confusion from both sources as to how or when Sundiata died. The date is generally agreed to be about 1255, but it is not known if he was accidentally killed by an arrow at a pageant or ceremony, or whether he was drowned in the Niger river where there is a place still known as *Sundiata- dun* (Sundiata's deep water). His people still make sacrifice to him along the river bank.

After his death the fratrilineal succession that he had set up led to a number of weak monarchs who lost much of the territory that he had gained. One of the last kings lost all credibility and the popularity of his people by testing his skill at archery by randomly shooting unsuspecting countrymen. But somehow the system that Sundiata had established held Mali together and it continued to prosper by controlling the sources of the gold trade in the rain forests.

Half a century after his death another great king emerged. His great nephew (the grandson of his brother Abu Bakr) called Mansa Musa (q.v.) gained the throne. His name was to reverberate down the corridors of history as the golden king. And the empire of Mali was set to last for two more centuries.

The Golden King

MANSA MUSA
r.1307-1332

Mansa Musa was the king who brought the great Sudanic, Mali empire to its zenith. He consolidated the position of Mali and brought it to the attention of the Arab world following his colourful hadj to Mecca in 1324. His reputation spread throughout the Mediaeval world as the golden king whose untold wealth was based on a never-ending supply of gold. This prompted the avaricious dreams of countless Arab and European explorers.

But Musa was far more than a symbol of mammon. He nurtured the source of his gold wealth and multiplied his riches by clever trade. He also consolidated the Mali empire and turned it into a great centre of scholarship and religious learning.

Mansa Kankan Musa was a Mandingo, born in the great empire of Mali built by his great-uncle King Sundiata (q.v.). Mali had risen out of the ashes of the Empire of Ghana, at a time when many other Sudanic peoples were competing for hegemony over Africa's rich goldfields.

Sundiata himself, was an exceptional man. His elder brothers had all been killed by the powerful Susu tribe, but he, being a sickly child had been spared. It was a mistake the Susu were made to regret because after a period of exile he returned to defeat the Susu and make his small Kangaba state into Mali, the strongest power in the Sudanic region.

At the time Mansa Musa came to the throne in 1307, Mali stretched over much of the same area that it does today, from the Senegal hinterland on the west, almost as far as Gao on the Niger river to the east. To the north its frontiers stretched into the Sahara and to the south into the tropical rain forests where the gold came from.

Mansa Musa is known throughout history as the king of gold. His wealth derived from Mali's position straddling the great Saharan caravan routes from the north into the heart of Africa. To the south of Mali lay the forests of Bure, and Wangara where the shy people of the rain forests panned gold, exchanging it for salt, dates, cloth and other merchandise brought by the merchants across the Sahara.

Musa never occupied the goldfields because he discovered that gold production almost ceased at times when the Wangara gold diggers felt threatened and was only resumed when they felt secure.

Musa also derived great wealth in exchanging the copper which had been discovered to the east of Mali and sold it at a profit in the north. Almost all the main caravan routes from Morocco, Tunisia and Egypt passed through Mali which lay along the southern rim of the Sahara.

The Malinke (Mandigoes) had been Islamicised several centuries earlier by the Almoravids based in the Senegal area. Musa himself was a pious man, devoted to Islamic studies, who had learnt the Koran by heart. He willingly attracted Islamic scholars from far afield and from the *jelada*, the intelligensia of the desert, who set up seats of learning in towns such as Timbuktu, and other parts of the Mali empire.

Musa built mosques and instituted a day of prayer on Fridays, but he also retained many of the pagan traditions of his people.

The Arab traveller, Ibn Battuta (q.v.) who is one of the prime sources on Mansa Musa, observed the complex social customs at the royal court. The king always ate alone. No one with shoes was admitted into his presence, nor were they allowed to sneeze in front of him. They were obliged to prostrate themselves full length before him after sprinkling ashes on their heads. When speaking in public Musa always spoke through an interpreter.

Much of his fame is derived from the *hadj* he made to the holy lands in 1324. This was well chronicled by Egyptian and other writers.

Musa set off for Egypt with a caravan of hundreds of camels and slaves. He travelled for more than a year through Walata and Tuat in the middle of the Sahara, then along the north African coast to Cairo. At least 500 slaves carried gold staves, others carried gold dust. Everywhere he dispensed his largesse and news of his caravan went before him.

His arrival in Cairo got off to a bad start. The Egyptian sultan Al-Malik an-Nisian insisted that he should prostrate himself and kiss the ground before him. At first Musa, realising that this would establish precedence, refused. But he later yielded and gave the sultan a gift of gold worth 50,000 dinars.

From that point the visit was a huge success. Cairo was stunned by the splendours of an exotic king. The sultan lent him a palace for three months stay in Egypt and escorted him on his way to Mecca, where he showered further gifts on the holy cities. He and his entourage were so generous that many Egyptian merchants officials and bankers exploited them. Before the visit was over he had spent all his money and was forced to borrow at usurious rates of interest.

The huge increase in the supply of gold on Egyptian markets was to wreak its own retribution. The gold price fell sharply and did not recover for several decades after Musa's departure.

Otherwise his expedition had been a huge success. For the first time a black king had revealed himself to the Arab world as a man of wealth, generosity and as a true Muslim. He had put Mali on the map, as Arab and European cartographers were soon to show.

Some who had loaned him money returned home with him where he repaid them all in full. He also attracted scholars who settled in Timbuktu. The poet and architect Abu Ishaq al-Sahili introduced the technique of baking bricks and built the great mosque at Timbuktu and a palace for Musa in the new material, which was impervious to the rain. Al-Sahili showed his love and respect for the city of learning by living in Timbuktu for the rest of his life, dying there in 1346.

Gao, the Songhai capital, on the extreme eastern frontier of Mali, had just been conquered by one of Musa's generals. Musa returned there on his way back from Cairo and took two of the Songhai ruler's sons to live with him virtually as hostages, to prevent any uprising.

This did ensure the quiescence of the Songhai until his death in 1332. After that the two sons escaped, reclaimed Gao and stirred up further trouble. Musa's successors were weak and soon fighting amongst themselves. The kingdom began to disintegrate. Twice his successors were deposed by royal rivals and twice by royal usurpers.

Musa's reputation was cast in gold and glorified in the glamour of his visit to Egypt. In the process he had broken the barrier of colour prejudice that had shut Africa off from the Arab world.

Songhai Strongman

SONNI ALI
c.1440-1493

Sonni Ali was the first great Songhai ruler who, in the golden age of Sudanic power, transformed a small competing kingdom into the greatest empire in the western Sudan. Energetic, ambitious and ruthless in pursuit of his political objectives, he never lost a campaign or single battle as a military commander. But he was not a cruel tyrant or barbaric infidel that early historians claimed him to be. He was a good administrator who built a strongly centralised system and a stable Songhai empire that was to last several centuries.

Realistic and not over ambitious, he turned a small Songhai kingdom into an empire which stretched from Walata in the West to beyond Kano in the east and his influence spread far along the caravan routes into the Sahara desert. His successor Askia Mohammad built on his foundations and refined the system he had established.

Sonni Ali Ber was born about 1440, though the exact date is not established and little is known about his early life. He came from a long line of Sunnis - the rulers of the Soninke people. His father Sunni Madawu, was the seventeenth Sunni and had a reputation of being a powerful magician. His mother came from Fara, where the people worshipped idols and carried out sacrifice. Though nominally Muslim, he was brought up in a semi-pagan environment.

In 1464 he inherited the Songhai kingdom from his father. It was the greatest and most powerful of all the western Sudanic kingdoms. It came into being as early as AD 900, but for centuries it had been under Moorish or Malian domination. Sonni Ali was to transform it from a kingdom into a sophisticated, well governed empire dominating the great bend in the Niger river and at its peak, stretching well beyond that. It controlled the great Sahara trade routes where gold and slaves were carried north by the camel caravans in exchange for cloth, salt, armaments and manufactures from Arabia and Europe.

Sonni Ali was described by the Timbuktu historian, As-Saidi as a master-tyrant, libertine, scoundrel and a barbarian. But As-Saidi was not impartial. As a Berber he despised Sonni Ali, who was a dark skinned negroid Songhai and he accused him of being uneducated and not being a true believer.

Sonni had been brought up in a semi-pagan family and was reluctant to surrender the African culture from which he derived much of his power. He was well versed in the traditional Songhai religion. His people thought he had inherited magical powers from his father and could transform himself into a vulture or make his soldiers invisible in battle. But he had received a rudimentary Islamic education. When he took power in 1464, he claimed to be a Muslim, observed Ramadan, and frequently prayed at the mosque. He did not follow the strict orthodoxies of Islam, indeed he tried to simplify the form of prayer to make worship easier and less demanding.

Some of Sonni Ali's behaviour during the conquests that were to build the great Songhai empire certainly appears to bear out As-Saidi's accusation of barbarity. Ali had a well organised army, cavalry that struck fear in all his opponents and even a fleet of 400 boats on the Niger river. He was a superb commander and easily captured Timbuktu, the city of learning, in January 1468. Most of its timorous scholars and religious leaders fled the city, but those who remained were not treated with the courtesy customarily accorded to men of learning. Sonni Ali put many of them to the sword, and sacked and burnt the city. "The godless tyrant slaughtered those people who remained," wrote As-Saidi, "and humiliated them."

Moreover Sonni Ali was cruel to the citizens of Timbuktu because he saw them as the allies of his greatest enemies the Tuareg, but later, he showed some remorse for the suffering inflicted on the *Ulama*, the religious leaders of the town. Later he allowed them to return and live under a *kadi* responsible to himself - an example of the mercy Sonni Ali was often to show his victims.

He then laid siege to the riverine city of Jenne with his formidable fleet. Jenne was well protected by its waterways but after a siege lasting many years, with famine and disease ravaging the armies of both sides, the town capitulated in 1473. The citizens of Jenne were not allies of the Tuareg and this time Sonni was as merciful, as he had been vengeful in Timbuktu.

He then marched into the desert and captured the trading city of Walata after a month's siege. To keep Walata in his empire he then embarked on the grandiose scheme of digging a canal for 200 miles to connect the city to the Niger river which was controlled by his powerful fleet. His engineers claimed the project was feasible and work began, but before it could be finished he had to abandon the project to fight the Mossi people who were raiding from the south.

He repulsed the Mossi and continued his campaigns against the

Fulani in the west and the Tuareg to the north. He took Mopti in 1477.

Sonni Ali was a resourceful military leader, administrator and organiser. He was never a mindless barbarian, though ruthless in pursuing his political ends. He built a strong centralised government under local rulers who were responsible to him. Between campaigns he had time to encourage agriculture and learning.

He died suddenly in November 1493, when his booty-laden horse fell into the Koni river and was swept over the falls. His son Sonni Baro saved his intestines and tried to preserve them in honey. Briefly Baro succeded his father, but within a year one of his father's commanders Mohammad Ture seized power and took the title Askia which means "usurper". He was to become the great Songhai emperor, Askia Mohammad I or Askia the Great (q.v.).

The Great Usurper

ASKIA THE GREAT
c.1450-1528

Askia Mohammad I, or Askia the Great, came to power as the new Songhai empire was rising from the ashes of the Mali empire in western Sudan. He developed trade, cultural and diplomatic contacts with Egypt and Arabia. He was the founder of a new dynasty that was to last a century while encouraging the spread of Muslim scholarship in Timbuktu and other centres of learning.

Askia built a prosperous empire and shaped its permanent boundaries. He also brought his kingdom to the attention of the outside world. He had little contact with the Portuguese who were venturing tentatively down the West African coast, but he particularly developed diplomatic and cultural links with Egypt and Arabia. Perhaps his greatest achievement was his respect and encouragement for Muslim scholarship. This was to survive in Timbuktu and other centres of learning long after the sun had set on the Songhai empire.

Askia Mohammad Toure usurped the throne from the son of his former ruler Sonni Ali Ber in 1493. He took the title Askia (meaning usurper) and founded a new dynasty, under that name, taking over from the Sonnis.

He was dark skinned and pure Soninke, unlike Sonni Ali who inherited much Berber blood from his ancestors. Though illiterate, Askia was a devout Muslim who came from the extreme west of the Songhai kingdom, probably the mountains of the Fouta Toro. He may have been distantly related to Sonni Ali on his mother's side; certainly he had served as one of his lieutenants. When Sonni suddenly died in a riding accident, Askia almost immediately seized power.

Sonni Ali had already established the shape of the Songhai empire. It stretched, like the empire of Mali before it, in a great band across the Sahel from the Fouta mountains in modern Senegal in the west, to Agades in the Air mountains, in the east. To the north it spread into the

Sahara where the caravan trails came in from north Africa and to the south it skirted the tropical rain forests.

Sonni Ali had been a tough warrior, a brutal but effective empire builder who had taken his kingdom by force largely from the declining Mali empire. He was known as the magician-king because he depended on his manipulation of occultism and the traditional superstitions of his people to maintain his power.

Askia was very different. He was a practising Muslim at a time when most of his people except for the intellectual elite were pagans. He was a civilised man, with great intellectual curiosity whose style was to persuade rather than force his rule on his people. He was given the full backing of the Muslim scholars of Timbuktu and the other Sudanic centres of learning such as Jenne on the Niger river and Walata.

He was an administrator and an organiser. He divided his kingdom into provinces and set up a complex bureaucracy, with local governors, tax collectors and other specialist civil servants responsible to a central government. He standardised weights and measures and put inspectors in charge of local markets.

He nurtured the Songhai economy and encouraged trade, sending gold, slaves, ivory and ebony north up the caravan trails across the Sahara, importing salt, cloth, iron, brassware, weapons and armour in exchange. His people bred horses and camels.

Much of the gold that made the reputation of the Mali king, Mansa Musa (q.v.), a century and a half before, continued to come from the gold workings in Bure and Ashanti. This still made Songhai rich. Unmarked gold coins were the highest value of currency equivalent to about 400 cowrie shells.

Like Mansa Musa he did the *hadj* (pilgrimage) to Mecca starting in October 1496 and returning in August 1498. His caravan had an escort of 500 cavalry and 1,000 infantry and his slaves carried 300,000 pieces of gold. He gave a third of this golden dowry to the holy cities that he visited. In Mecca alone he gave 10,000 gold pieces to the poor.

He befriended the caliph of Egypt and persuaded him to invest him as "caliph of the lands of Tukrur". This Egyptian blessing was much valued by Askia as he had usurped the Sonni throne and sought legitimacy for his new dynasty. He also consulted Egyptian scholars on practical and juridical matters.

On his return he developed the broadest cultural contacts with Egypt including the installation of a permanent Egyptian ambassador in his court.

His *hadj* prompted him to give even more support to Timbuktu as the cultural centre of the Songhai empire. It was a place of scholarship and of trade, arts, crafts, and commerce, yet the city of Gao which was the capital of the empire was even larger.

Militarily Askia tried to extend the boundaries of the Songhai empire left by Sonni Ali, but in practice he did little more than maintain and consolidate his frontiers. He finally wiped away the last vestiges of the

Mali empire which had been the dominant power in the western Sudan for three centuries.

About 1501, his armies marched west, almost as far as the Atlantic, conquering the minor kings and making them pay tribute to him rather than to the ruler of Mali. Next he tackled the autonomous Hausa states to the east. His armies reached Katsina, Kano, Zaria and Gobir which briefly became tributaries.

To the south he led a *jihad*-style campaign against the pagan Mossi. He won a number of victories and converted some of the people to Islam, but he did not secure permanent dominance of the region south of the Volta river. In the north he entered into an uneasy alliance with the Tuareg after an inconclusive campaign.

But Askia's attempt to extend the Songhai empire eastwards was to fail after initial success in Hausaland. The state of Kebbi to the east provided stiff resistance to him and survived the onslaught. After a decade Kebbi was able to bring the Hausa states into its own sphere of influence. Thus the first great attempt by the Songhai to link western and eastern Sudan, lasted only one decade.

Songhai lost its hold over the Hausa states in about 1515. This date marked the peak of Askia's power. He was ageing fast and gradually going blind. The struggle for succession between his 34 sons and other pretenders developed as he gradually lost control.

Askia lost his closest adviser in 1519 and struggled on until 1527 when his sons rose up in revolt against him. His brother Yahya, who tried to restore peace between the warring factions, was himself killed. On 15 August 1528, Askia then nearly 80 and worn out in the service of his country, abdicated. He lived less than a year in bitterness and disillusion.

After him his sons followed in a succession of short reigns as they fought amongst themselves in a series of fratricidal struggles.

Askia Mohammad I had consolidated the Songhai empire, which was to continue until the invasion of Mulai al-Mansur's (q.v.) Moroccans in 1591, which brought the dynasty to an end.

4. The Jihadists

Rabid Almoravid

IBN YACIN
c.1010-1059

Abdulla Ibn Yacin was a man of humble origins who started as a passionate Muslim reformer but ended as the spiritual leader of the huge Almoravid empire, that dominated the whole of western Sahara. It was a spiritual empire without a central base. It stretched across a thousand miles of the Sahara from Morocco in the north to the fringes of the empire of Ghana in the south. After his death the Almoravids, known to the Arabs as *al-Murabitun*, spread further into northern Morocco and through the whole of Muslim Spain.

Very little is known about the origins of Abdallah Ibn Yacin. He was a Djazula Berber from southern Morocco. His mother came from a village on the southern edge of the Sahara bordering Ghana.

This was significant, for throughout his life he travelled the thousand miles between southern Morocco and the empire of Ghana as he spread the Almoravid faith (a militant form of Islam) across this desert kingdom.

Some sources say that he acquired some of his Islamic learning in Muslim Spain, but the extent of his training is not certain.

He was "discovered" when furthering his studies at the Islamic study centre *Dar al-Murabitin*, run by Waggag Ibn Zallu near Sijilmasa.

When, in 1038, the ruler of the Sanhaja, Yahya Ibn Ibrahim returned full of zeal and ready to spread the faith, from a pilgrimage to Mecca, he asked Waggag who could help him. Waggag unhesitatingly recommended the brightest student in his *dar* (study centre), Ibn Yacin. Unlike many others he was zealous enough to forsake the home comforts of the community and take his fiery reformist message to the nomads of the Sahara.

Ibn Yacin was something of a fanatic, totally convinced of the need to take his teaching to the Sanhaja nomads who lived throughout the west central Sahara and to the cities on its urban fringes.

He first targeted the Jedalla people, a sub-group of the Sanhaja, living in the extreme west along the Atlantic coast. Starting about 1039, he set off into the desert preaching a message of Islamic asceticism and puritanical egalitarianism. When he was not accepted voluntarily he was quite prepared to use force.

His intolerant authoritarianism clashed with local beliefs and customs, and soon brought opposition. He was determined to make converts but he strictly banned his followers from using pillage, looting and rape when trying to convert recalcitrant people.

The extent of his discipline was demonstrated by one particular incident when he ordered the flogging of Yahya, his principal lieutenant. This man, who was not aware that he had done anything wrong and had no idea why he should be flogged, accepted the punishment prescribed by his leader without question.

Eventually, about 1053, a majority of the Jedalla rose in rebellion against Ibn Yacin and after defeating him at the battle of Tin Farilla, put him to flight. Trying to turn this to his advantage by imitating the *hidjra* of the prophet Mohammed, he withdrew to a *ribat* (religious hermitage) on an island somewhere on the Atlantic coast (probably one of the Tidra islands off present day Mauritania). He remained there for some time training a corps of followers in the new faith.

About 1055 he returned to Waggag at Sijilmasa and his old master encouraged him to resume his mission. It had become a *jihad*, against a powerful branch of the Sanhaja, the Lamtuna who dominated the central areas of the Sahara and the trade routes.

Ibn Yacin, now at the height of his powers, swept south at the head of an army of 30,000 men inspired by his fanatical fervour and belief. They were a well trained army, bound by his strict code of discipline, and in this second phase of his *jihad* Ibn Yacin met little resistance from the Lamtuna, who were quicky converted to his cause. In 1054 he reached Audoghast, a great trading town, on the fringes of the Ghana empire. Determined to assert his authority, he relaxed, for the first time, his rule against pillage and killing. Audoghast was brought to its knees in an orgy of destruction.

Ibn Yacin's reformist movement had by now become a militant force determined to spread the message throughout the Sanhaja. Most of them with the exception of the Jedalla, who had been cowed but not defeated, accepted the new faith and not only for religious reasons. They saw it as the key to restoring Sanhaja dominance of the lucrative trade routes and of the urban centres in southern Morocco and Africa.

Having secured Audoghast and the southern fringe of the new Almoravid spiritual empire, Ibn Yacin marched north once again to put down a rebellion in Sijilmasa. He then decided to take his *jihad* over the Atlas mountains and into *Maghrib-al-Aqsa* (Morocco). He sent his troops pouring through the mountain passes to seize control of the rest of the country.

It was in securing this final phase of his grand design that Ibn Yacin was himself killed, in mysterious circumstances during the battle of Kurifalat in 1059.

It is a tribute to Ibn Yacin that the Almoravid faith continued long after his death. The political and religious impetus that had given birth to the reformist movement persisted under its new leader Abu Bakr Ibn Umar. The Almoravids founded Marrakesh in 1072. The movement spread throughout the whole of Morocco by 1083 and by the end of the century to all parts of Muslim Spain.

The religious community founded on the island off the African coast became a semi-Islamic Moroccan kingdom, stretching from Spain in the north, over the desert sands to Ghana in the south.

Ibn Yacin had started a religious reform movement. His successors inherited a political empire.

The Great Almohads

MOHAMMED IBN TUMART
c.1080-1130
ABD AL MUMIN
c.1100-1163

Mohammed Ibn Tumart and Abd al Mumin are taken together as the two founders of the Almohad Caliphate. Each was dependent for his greatness on the other.

While Tumart was the spiritual leader who raised the banner of *jihad*, and declared himself the *Mahdi*, Abd al Mumin who succeeded him directly, was the warrior who established Almohad rule across the whole of the Maghreb.

They turned on the Almoravids for becoming lax in their interpretation of the faith and morally corrupt. Their purges of the Almoravids and the Christian infidels who lived in the Maghreb were violent and bloody. But after their conquests the Almohads too became great patrons of the arts and learning. The two pioneers brought peace and unity that was to last for a century.

Mohammed Ibn Tumart was born about 1080 in the Anti-Atlas, the southernmost chain of Atlas mountains. He was descended from nomadic peoples - the Masmuda Berbers.

In his early twenties he set off to study the Muslim religion in its original home in the Middle East, mainly in Baghdad.

There he began to have doubts about the way his religion was practised by the Almoravids in his home country, Morocco.

The Almoravids were also former nomads - Sanhaja Berbers. Fifty years earlier Ibn Yacin (q.v.) had raised the standard of religious reform and marched into Africa. They ranged the deserts on their camels and put the old ways and religions to the sword.

The great historian Ibn Khaldun (q.v.) once commented in a famous maxim, "the least civilised peoples make the greatest conquests." In the local context he was referring specifically to the Almoravids, particularly the veiled Lamtunas, who at the beginning of the 11th century took the blazing banner of reform across the Sahara and into Spain where Muslim kingdoms were already established.

But one generation after the Almoravids settled in their new empire they soon acquired a taste for the luxuries of city life and turned to art and culture rather than war. They lost the hard discipline of nomadic life and forgot their early asceticism.

This was the situation Ibn Tumart found as he returned, fired with religious zeal, from his studies in the East. On his journey home he stayed near Boujaia on the Mediterranean coast and met Abd al Mumin and other young men who agreed on the need to purge and reform their religion. They rejected the formal legalistic interpretations of the Koran by the jurists and wanted more freedom for individual interpretation.

In about 1120 Tumart arrived in Marrakesh and, while debating the finer points of religion and the spirituality of God, made a more immediate impact by criticising the declining morals of the Almoravids. He attacked the emir for wearing the wrong kind of veil and the emir's sister for going about unveiled in public. The emir was sardonically tolerant of the young firebrand, but when Tumart began to attack the fundamental beliefs of the legalistic jurists, blaming them for their failure to understand the teachings of the prophet, they drove him out of Marrakesh.

He took refuge with his Masmuda tribesmen in the High Atlas mountains and exploited the hatred of the mountain folk for the people in the cities who tried to rule them. For years he preached to his people until his leadership was recognised and he was able to raise the standard of a new *jihad*, justified by the need for religious and social change.

In 1125 he established his headquarters at Tinmel in the High Atlas south of Marrakesh. He proclaimed himself the *Mahdi* - one who had been sent to establish the true faith. He established strict discipline within his community and made spiritual exercises compulsory. He had an advisory consultative assembly, but purged it rigorously in 1128 keeping only his most fanatical disciples.

His followers became known as the Almohads *al-Muwahhidun*, those who believed in the unity of God. In 1128, in the great *jihadist* tradition, he attempted to lead his followers into battle. He tried to capture Marrakesh but he was repulsed and died shortly afterwards in about 1130.

But the cause was not lost. Abd al Mumin, his faithful disciple since the two men first met in Boujaia in 1120, took up the fight. He broadened the base for Almohad support because he came from the Kumya tribe, a sub-group of the Zanata. He was also a better and more ruthless soldier than Tumart.

Once in command he pushed north east along the Atlas mountains, thrusting aside all Almoravid attempts to stop him until he reached the

Rif mountains overlooking the Mediterranean. His enemies launched an army of Christian mercenaries against him in 1145 but he defeated them, captured the Almoravid emir, and took Marrakesh in about 1147.

Almohad hatred of the Almoravids was even greater than that of the infidel. Those citizens who would not come over to the new faith were put to the sword and their religious buildings and the emir's palace were "purified" by being totally destroyed. Later the Almohads forced the Christians who had been living peacefully in the Maghreb to convert to Islam under the pain of death.

Abd al Mumin arrogated to himself the title *Amir al Muminin,* Commander of the Faithful. He claimed he was placed third in rank to the Prophet Mohammed, coming immediately after the *Mahdi* Ibn Tumart, whom he succeeded. As ruler of Morocco he also called himself the caliph, a title that was to last almost to the present day.

The Almoravids were not entirely finished. Abd al Mumin met them and their new allies the Banu Hammad Arabs, in 1145 at Tlemcen and defeated them there. He then turned on the Banu Hammad and in 1151 took Algiers and their new town of Boujaia, followed by Setif. By 1160 he had reached Mahdiya on the Tunisian coast, wresting it from the Normans of Sicily.

It was the first time any ruler had captured and united the whole of the Maghreb. He placed the whole north western corner of Africa under the Almohad banner.

Abd al Mumin cemented his rule by playing off one Arab tribe against another and giving his allies lands on the Moroccan plains. He depended increasingly on them and it was they who took the *jihad* into Muslim Spain after his death about 1163.

Like other nomads before him, Abd al Mumin who came to power with the sword, found patronage of the arts also had its attractions. He built the Kutubia of Marrakesh and he made the early designs for the Giralda at Seville.

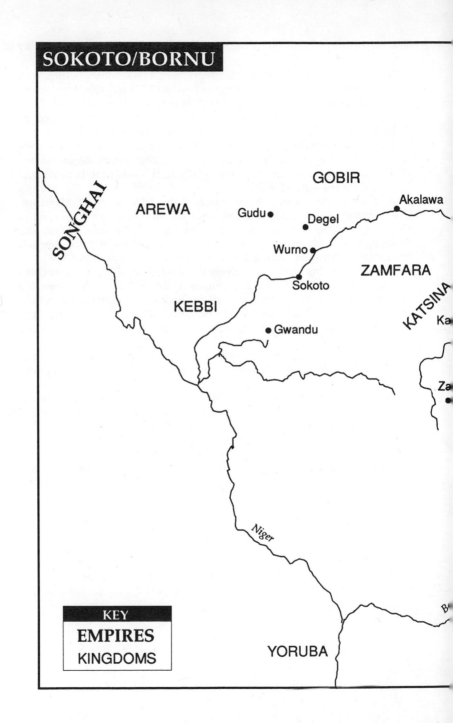

SOKOTO/BORNU

SONGHAI

AREWA

GOBIR

Gudu ●

Degel ●

Akalawa ●

Wurno ●

ZAMFARA

KEBBI

Sokoto ●

KATSINA

Ka

● Gwandu

Za

Niger

KEY
EMPIRES
KINGDOMS

YORUBA

B

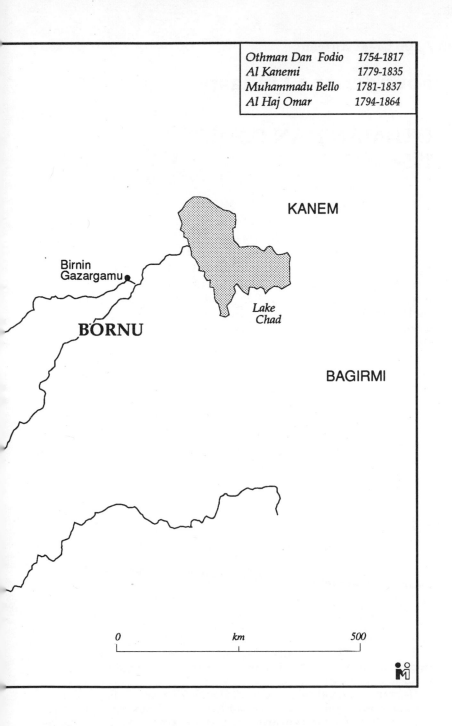

Othman Dan Fodio   1754-1817
Al Kanemi   1779-1835
Muhammadu Bello   1781-1837
Al Haj Omar   1794-1864

KANEM

Birnin
Gazargamu

BORNU

*Lake
Chad*

BAGIRMI

0   km   500

Founder of a Dynasty

OTHMAN DAN FODIO
1754-1817

Othman dan Fodio is revered by all northern Nigerian Muslims as the man who brought an Islamic revolution to their country. His *jihad* which was as much a social and political movement, as it was religious, changed the face of northern Nigeria and beyond. He left a spiritual message in which the scholar and the preacher were given as much respect as the warrior or traditional ruler. He became recognised as the spiritual head of all Muslims. This spiritual leadership was passed on to his successors who maintained it even after the British took over secular power in 1903.

He also founded the Sokoto caliphate which has ruled the north ever since, providing the leaders of Nigeria's first government at independence in 1960. The influence of his successors is still strong in modern Nigeria and the source of much friction between the north and south in Africa's most populous country

Othman dan Fodio was born at Marata, Gobir on the extreme north-west of Hausaland. His family, Torodobe Fulanis, had migrated there 14 generations before from the Fouta Jalon mountains in present day Guinea.

From the 15th century, the Fulani migrated into the Hausa kingdoms that had been established on the fringes of the Sahara. They seldom lived in the Hausa towns, but true to their nomadic origins, stayed in camps and hamlets in the dry plains outside the mud baked city walls. Many like Othman's family worked as students, scholars, clerks and advisers to the Hausa kings.

Othman was a determined but scholarly man, who received the traditional Islamic education in grammar, law, exegesis, theology, rhetoric and mysticism.

He grew up in troubled times, on the harsh fringes of the Sahara where life was slow, but discontent simmered below the surface. The Hausa kings had ruled for centuries but their kingdoms had become bureaucratic and corrupt. They taxed the people heavily, causing the collapse of industry and trade. Their system of justice had become cruel and arbitrary; but above all their Muslim faith had become worn and threadbare.

One of Othman's Islamic teachers was his uncle, another was Mallam Jibril of Agades who had himself led an abortive *jihad* against the Hausa kings. Othman's mystical asceticism thrived in the climate of discontent which was as much social and political as religious, though with his strict Islamic education, he saw it mainly in religious terms. He wanted society to turn back to the fundamentals of Islam, to the ideal society that existed at the time of the Prophet.

On completing his education in 1774, while still only 20, he carried his message of social and religious reform far and wide throughout the Hausa kingdoms, to the people of Gobir, Zamfara and Kebbi. His mixture of political and social rhetoric, directed against the unpopular Hausa kings drew huge crowds and enhanced his reputation.

He also had wide social appeal. He wrote poetry for the pastoral Fulani, he preached to the discontented peasantry and he wrote Arabic books for his fellow students. The system of Islamic justice that he preached appealed to the peasantry as a form of protection against their autocratic masters, while the Fulani nomads appreciated his condemnation of the taxes on their cattle. Not all his followers were true believers. Some were "Muslims in the morning and pagans by the evening." Others simply espoused his political cause.

By the time he was 30 his reputation had reached the ears of the comparatively liberal-minded King Nafata of Gobir who rather surprisingly made him tutor to his own children. For a time he gained considerable influence in the king's court, but he continued to live in a religious community at Degel well outside the city where he was free and able to preach his message in the surrounding towns.

But in 1802 Yunfa, who had once been his pupil, succeeded to the throne of Gobir and reacted against Othman's growing influence. Yunfa cracked down on his father's liberalising reforms and concessions to Islam. On one occasion he lost his temper and fired a pistol at Othman only for it to backfire and burn his own face. Relations between the two went from bad to worse when some of Yunfa's Muslim captives who were being transported past Degel were set free by Othman's religious community. Yunfa ordered Othman to leave and the community to be dissolved.

This and the persecution that followed led to a localised revolution which Othman was able to justify in terms of a religious *jihad*, or holy war, against unjust and corrupt kings. He claimed that Yunfa and the other Hausa kings had abandoned the true faith and become pagans so rebellion against them was justified by the Prophet.

His flight from Degel to Gudu on 21 February 1804 was called the *Hijra*, a festival which is still honoured in the Muslim calendar in Nigeria. The Fulanis draw parallels with the flight of the Prophet

Mohammed from Mecca to Medina in the seventh century. Othman unfurled his green flag of Islam and asked all his followers to emigrate. They acclaimed him their leader and the *jihad* started.

The 50-year-old preacher and scholar was not a natural warrior, but suddenly he found himself at the head of a great Jihad that within a few years was to sweep the Hausa kings from their thrones and during the next 30 years establish Fulani hegemony throughout northern Nigeria.

His followers were mostly foot soldiers armed with bows. Their few horsemen were little match for the heavy cavalry of the Hausa kings with their padded armour, but their faith was unflinching and the mass of the people were on their side. As the war progressed more nobles and professional soldiers joined the cause and showed the Hausa kings how alienated they had become from their subjects.

Early battles in 1804 were inconclusive but Othman became a rallying figure for Fulani all over the north. He took the title of Commander of the Faithful and the civilian title of Shehu. Every delegation which visited was blessed, given a flag and told to liberate themselves of the Hausa kings.

The Shehu left most of the fighting to his brother Abdullahi and his son Muhammadu Bello. In the short period between 1804-1808 the Fulani conquered most of Hausaland. Among the towns to fall were Zaria and Katsina; Yunfa's own capital at Alkalawa was among the last. He was killed defending it on 20 October 1808. This marked the end of the *jihad* in Hausaland.

This allowed the establishment of a Muslim government which took the form of the Sokoto caliphate. Othman made his home in Sokoto and put his son Bello there, in charge of the whole eastern sector. He appointed his brother Abdullahi in charge of the western sector with headquarters at Gwandu. He also appointed minor emirs, not on the basis of their clans or family connections, but on their ability and knowledge of Islamic law.

He retired to follow his scholarly pursuits in 1809, remaining a guide and interpreter of the new Islamic state and rule of law that he had created until his death at the age of 63 in April 1817.

Within a generation the Sokoto Caliphate had lost much of its Islamic idealism and become secularised. But Othman had founded an early version of an Islamic state which has dominated northern Nigeria to the present day. The current Sardaunas of Sokoto proudly trace their ancestry back to him and even to the prophet Mohammed himself.

During his lifetime the ascetic scholar had produced 37 children, yet he respected women and had fought hard for them to get the same Islamic education as their menfolk. His religious and social teaching lives on long after his death. No true Muslim has ever questioned the justice of his *jihad*.

Saviour of Bornu

AL-KANEMI
c.1779-1835

Al-Kanemi started life as a religious scholar and he is sometimes portrayed as a religious reformer, but his reforms were strictly within the territory he controlled. Indeed he was the person who stopped Othman dan Fodio's *jihad*, the religious revolution, from overwhelming Bornu.

Al-Kanemi's legacy lies in his military and political expertise which allowed him to take over and expand his kingdom, leaving his son to bring one great dynasty to an end and replace it with his own. The *Shehus* of Bornu rule to this day.

Sheikh Muhammad al-Amin Al-Kanemi, the founder of the Bornu dynasty, was born around 1779 to Sheikh Ninga, a Kanembu chief from Fezzan. His mother was an Arab. He received a comprehensive Islamic education and travelled extensively for further studies in far off places like Murzuk and Tripoli before doing his *hadj* to Mecca, while still a teenager. He stayed in Arabia to complete his education.

He returned home to find that the forces of Othman dan Fodio (q.v.) had unleashed their jihad, or holy war, that was sweeping through Hausaland, forcing one king after another from their thrones.

The Mai (king) Ahmad of Bornu was already under threat from his Fulani subjects who watched the powerful Hausa kings to the west collapsing before the new flag of Islam. By 1808 the Mai's position was desperate with his capital Birni Gazargamu in the hands of the Fulani insurgents.

Al-Kanemi had become a man of many parts. He was an Islamic scholar, a devout religious man, a political leader and a warrior chief.

The whole justification for the *jihads* against the Hausa kings was that they had become corrupted and lost their true religion, but Al-Kanemi could not see how this argument could be directed against the Mai of Bornu, who was a devout Muslim himself and ruled a country where the Islamic law prevailed.

He felt so strongly about this that he entered into a long correspondence with Othman dan Fodio and his son Bello complaining that the Fulani should not be directing their jihad at Bornu. The intellectual argument was protracted and inconclusive, so Al-Kanemi resorted to force of arms.

Though he was half Arab and half Kanembu, and not strictly from Bornu, he was wholehearted in his efforts to prevent the expansion of the jihad.

In 1809 he captured Birni Gazargamu, on behalf of the king, only for the Mai to lose it again to the Fulanis. He settled for a long drawn out campaign, but despairing of the Mai's abilities, Al-Kanemi forced him to abdicate in 1814.

This virtually gave Al-Kanemi the power to rule through a puppet ruler whom he had appointed. He was granted huge tracts of land along the southwestern side of Lake Chad. This was to provide him with wealth from tribute and taxation and land which he could distribute as patronage. He was able to build up a formidable army.

Many apocryphal stories surround Al-Kanemi's name. In one battle against the redoubtable Fulani commander Goni Mukhtar, popular tradition has it that several days before the battle Al-Kanemi engaged in special prayers and recitations. He also prepared a charm in the shape of a small calabash upon which he had written verses of the Koran. As he went into battle the calabash crashed to the ground and was broken into pieces. The same happened to the Fulani army and Mukhtar was killed.

On the death of the deposed Mai, Al-Kanemi became the virtual ruler of Bornu. Between 1815 and 1824 he re-established control over Kanem and Bagirmi. He then turned on the Fulani and forced them out of Bornu in the early 1820s and in 1826 actually pursued them into the centre of the Sokoto Caliphate, near Kano, before being repulsed.

When the British explorer, Hugh Clapperton, arrived in 1821 he found Al-Kanemi fully in charge of the sultanate of Bornu, " When the sultan gives audience to strangers, he sits in a kind of cage, made of bamboo, through the bars of which he looks on his visitors, who are not allowed to approach within 70 or 80 yards of his person."

Clapperton was highly impressed, "No one could have used greater endeavours to substitute laws of reason for practices of barbarity, and, though feared, he is loved and respected... Compared to all around him he is an angel, and has subdued more by his generosity, mildness and benevolent disposition, than by the force of his arms."

The last years of his life were spent consolidating his position. Until the end he shared power with the new Mai who ran a ceremonial court while Al-Kanemi retained the real power.

He died about 1835. Modern historians think it might have been a couple of years later, but the earlier date is firmly established in Bornu tradition.

Before his death he was able to hand over power to his son Umar who took on the title of *shehu*. In 1846 the Mai decided to get rid of the usurper and reassert his family control. He persuaded the Sultan of Wadai to fight Umar, but his plans misfired. Umar captured the Mai and wrought terrible revenge, killing him and his sons. His courtiers were hunted down and executed and the remnants of his army fled Bornu.

Thus ended the thousand-year-old Kanem-Bornu dynasty to be replaced by the Al-Kanemi *shehus*.

Architect of the Caliphate

MUHAMMADU BELLO
1781-1837

Muhammadu Bello was the son and the army commander of the great Fulani jihadist, Othman dan Fodio (q.v.). As his father grew old and concentrated on the philosophical and religious aspects of purifying Islam and converting the pagans, Muhammadu completed the conquest of the Hausa kings in Zamfara and Gobir. Later he tried unsuccessfully to subjugate Bornu.

But he was far more than a brilliant military commander. He was a high-brow bookworm, who loved learned works and wrote over 80 volumes himself covering theology, medicine, history and local government. He was a real founder-reformer who provided the intellectual and ideological basis for the *jihad* and the Fulani empire which followed.

Muhammadu was the son of the legendary Othman dan Fodio, the man who launched the great *jihad* (holy war) and founded the Sokoto Caliphate. He was born in 1781, one of 37 children of his revered father. He received a full Islamic education which made him a scholar for life.

He travelled with his father from the family home at Degel in 1804, on the great jihad which was to sweep the Hausa kings from their thrones. The movement which started as movement to purify the Muslim religion and punish the Hausa kings for departing from the true faith, soon became a political and social revolution, involving not just the Fulani scholars and nomads, but the Hausa peasantry and all those who had been heavily taxed and unjustly ruled.

As his father concentrated on the philosophical aspects of the *jihad*, he gradually became more involved as an army commander. Within a few years most of northern Nigeria apart from Bornu had fallen to the *jihad*. Bello fought in the campaign which pushed the King of Gobir from his throne in 1808.

In 1809 his father wanted to secure the administration of his new conquests and divided the new Fulani empire into two. He placed his son

Bello in charge of the western sector with its capital at Sokoto and his brother Abdullahi in charge of the eastern sector at Gwandu. Bello built his capital on a bluff above the Sokoto river where its steep slopes were well-defended from the north with its flanks protected by hills and valleys. His father lived with him in Sokoto until his death in 1817.

Bello succeeded him as Sarkin Musulmi, or Commander of the Faithful, he also became the first Sultan of Sokoto, the founder of the line that continues to the present day.

Though Othman expressed the wish that Muhammadu should succeed him, his brother Abdullahi thought that he would succeed his brother according to the Fulani custom of the time, but his subjects in Gwandu came out in rebellion against him. Muhammadu promptly rallied to his uncle's support and sent his own men to crush the revolt.

The two men met afterwards. Bello was on a great warhorse and Abdullahi on a mare. Bello, being the younger man made ready to dismount and salute his uncle, but Abdullahi indicated that he should stay mounted. He then bowed in the saddle and greeted Bello with his full title.

This healed the misunderstanding. The Sardauna of Sokoto in his autobiography, *My Life*, says that, "since then the two families have lived in perfect friendship and amity."

Abdullahi while owing allegiance to Bello continued to rule in Gwandu.

Both men had problems in defending their revolution and the boundaries of the new caliphate. Bello tried to extend the *jihad* into Bornu but there he was opposed by the redoutable Al-Kanemi (q.v.) who at first engaged him in a philosophical disputation on how he could justify aggression against Bornu which was already a reformed Muslim state. Bello who knew very little of the true situation in Bornu tried to justify himself by arguing that the King (Mai) of Bornu had been attacking his Fulani neighbours.

Arguments by letter continued for years but solved nothing. Bello found himself involved in a long campaign against Bornu and later against Zamfara and Gobir. Throughout his career he was involved in more than 40 wars and uprisings in defence of the caliphate.

In 1822 he built an alternative capital at Wurno and lived there rather than at Sokoto for the rest of his life. When the English explorer, Hugh Clapperton, arrived there in 1824 he was very impressed by the scholarly Bello who showed him his country and wanted to establish commercial relations with the British. This was just what the British government wanted to hear.

But on Clapperton's return to the coast two years later, to seek access for trade up the Niger, he found that Bello had changed and was actively hostile. In the years between he had been warned by the Arab merchants from Tripoli and Morocco that trade with British would be dangerous. They were not only economically untrustworthy but were seeking to put an end to the slave trade. Bello was also suspicious of the friendly relations between the British and his enemy the Shehu of Bornu.

But Bello was very thankful to Clapperton for bringing him an Arabic copy of Euclid from the King of England. He remarked that his family copy which had been procured in Mecca "was destroyed when part of his house was burnt down last year." Two days later Clapperton saw him sitting in an inner apartment studying the Euclid carefully.

Other travellers witnessed his love of high-brow books. He also wrote over 80 works himself covering a wide variety of topics including theology, local government, the diseases of the eye and the history of his region (western Sudan) and the history of the Fulani. But during his reign many valuable Hausa books and records were destroyed by his troops.

Though his reputation is based mostly on being the architect of the caliphate - a great administrator and just ruler - military problems continued until his death. He fought four wars with Kebbi before the king was finally killed in 1831. Other major disputes over succession occurred in Gobir and Katsina until 1835.

By the time of his death at Wurno in 1837 he had consolidated the Fulani empire that was to survive until the British arrived in 1903. Even under the British the family continued to exercise power until the present day.

Bello and his father before him were the real "founder-reformers" *Mujaddidun* who provided the intellectual and ideological basis for the *jihad* and the Fulani empire which followed. He was the true architect of the Sokoto Caliphate.

The Tukulor Jihadist

Al-HADJ OMAR
c.1794-1864

Al-Hadj Omar was a giant of his day. He rose from the humblest of origins to become the leader of the *Tijaniyya* brand of Islam throughout Sudanic Africa in the early 19th century. A man of huge energy, passion and charisma, he attracted a mass of faithful followers.

When he raised the banner of Islam in yet another *jihad,* he soon proved himself a great and ruthless military commander whose enemies crumbled before him as he extended his empire from his Fouta homeland across the Sahel as far as Timbuktu. Only France, nearing the peak of its colonial power was able to stand up to him.

It was his *Tijaniyya* fanaticism and the fact that he was building an almost wholly Tukulor empire that bore the seeds of his own destruction. When the early enthusiasm burnt out, his religious and tribal enemies regrouped and combined against him. By the time of his death in 1864 he had built a Tukulor empire stretching from the Senegal river to Timbuktu. His successors were to enjoy it for two more decades before the French pushed firmly into his empire.

Al-Hadj Omar bin Said Tall was born about 1794, at Halwar in Futa Toro country, on the bend of the Senegal river. His father came from a minor *Torodbe* (noble) family, a member of the clerical caste. He was a Tukulor, a tribe closely related to the Fulanis who were busy spreading the Islamic faith into northern Nigeria.

Omar received a strict Koranic education, not from the dominant *Qadriya* sect, but from the recently founded *Tijaniyya* brotherhood, founded by the Algerian al-Tijani.

The *Tijaniyyas* taught orthodox Islamic religion but were socially more democratic than the established *Qadriya* order they sought to replace.

Omar found himself in a religious minority but his long studies, his perfect knowledge of Arabic and his solid theological background won him great respect from his fellow Tukulors. He became a *Marabout* (religious teacher).

About 1826 he decided to make a pilgrimage to Mecca. In those days the *Hadj* was a leisurely affair and an occasion for prolonged visits along the way. He stopped at Sokoto, the capital of the Fulani empire, then under the control of Othman dan Fodio's (q.v.) son-in-law Muhammadu Bello (q.v.) for some time before continuing his journey to Mecca.

He stayed in Cairo and Syria from about 1827-32 during which time he visited Mecca, Medina and Jerusalem three times. There he met Muhammad al-Ghali, the chief representative of the *Tijaniyya* in Arabia, who made him the *Kalifa* (supreme commander) for the distant "land of the blacks".

On his way back he stopped again at Sokoto and this time stayed long enough (1833-37) to renew family links with the Fulanis by marrying one of Muhammadu Bello's daughters, Mariam. She bore him a son Ahmadou who was to succeed him as leader of the Tukulors.

When Bello died in 1837 Omar had to leave Sokoto. On his way he was imprisoned for a time by the Bambara king of Segu who had no love of the Muslims and their *jihads*.

He reached his home in the Futa Toro in 1840, but soon turned south to the Futa Jallon where a Muslim kingdom was already established. He was allowed to establish a *Zawiya* (religious community) at Dyegunko. There he taught from his book *Ar Rima* (The spear) which was to become the main mystical work of West African Islam. In it he produced a strict moral code with tight social regulations. He taught that there was nothing wrong in becoming rich and powerful providing one remained humble and submissive spiritually.

Omar's teaching and his reputation as an al-hadj won him a large following and considerable political influence. While he sought new converts he also enriched himself by trading in gold dust and receiving the contributions of the faithful. He used much of this money to purchase arms and gunpowder from traders in Gambia and Sierra Leone.

But his growing power and jihadist ambitions alarmed his hosts and in 1849 he was persuaded to leave Dyegunko and set up new headquarters at Dinguiray. From there he attacked a number of neighbouring animist kingdoms and in 1852 declared a *jihad* (holy war) against all animists in the western Sudan. He claimed he had a vision in which he was told by God to wage war against the unbelievers.

The *jihad* had long been established as a method of furthering religious aims. His Fulani relatives under Othman dan Fodio and his son Muhammadu Bello had launched one of the most famous *jihads* of all in the early decades of the 19th century. Omar had also been encouraged by Muhammad al-Ghali who had made him "commander of the faithful" in the land of the blacks, when he had done his *hadj* to Mecca. It was not only divinely inspired but regular practice to use war as a means of spreading the faith. Omar was also interested in purely materialist objectives. He wanted to spread the power of the Tukulor across the whole of West Africa and bring the minor kingdoms under his rule.

Already he had trained a huge army - numbering 40,000 men at its peak. His *talibes* (students of religion) formed the backbone of his cavalry. They were mounted on horses purchased from the Moors to the north. Others were professionals *(sofas)* or conscripts *(toubourrous)* plus converts and adventurers in search of booty.

His army was soon rampaging throughout the Futa Jallon, picking off the animist kingdoms one by one. Those who did not agree to immediate conversion were brutally massacred.

After conquering Tamla and Merieng he moved his capital to Tamba, the Tamla capital, in 1854 and went on to reduce the Mandingo Kingdom of Bafing. The Bambara kingdom of Kasso and Bundu followed shortly afterwards and in 1856 he took Nioro, the capital of the Kingdom of Kaarta.

He ran into the first real resistance when a local chief asked the French (already firmly established in lower Senegal) to help him defend his fort at Medine. Omar besieged the fort from April to July 1857 until the French governor Louis Faidherbe, after waiting for the river to rise high enough to take his transports, led a relief expedition to save the town. He commented later that Omar's men were like fanatics, "They march against our fire as if to martyrdom."

Omar lost many men in the unsucessful siege and from famine and disease, yet he was able to raise fresh followers. He marched deep down the Senegal river. In 1854 the French pushed him out of Podor, just a short distance from his birthplace in the Futa Toro.

The French were immovable and dangerous. Omar's ambitions lay mainly to the east but he had to safeguard his frontier to the west against French expansion, or rebellion by the African kingdoms they supported.

In August 1860 he concluded a treaty with the French in which it was agreed that they would remain in control of the whole left (west) bank of the Senegal river from their capital at Saint Louis to Bafoulabe, while he would control the right (east) bank. This farsighted treaty lasted long after Omar's death. His successors enjoyed its benefits until 1889.

After securing his western border he was able to march east towards the Niger, taking Niamina, then the Bambara Kingdom of Segou in 1862. Many of his men were armed with muskets or rifles which local blacksmiths kept in repair. Omar also had two field guns which he had captured earlier from a French boat stranded on the Senegal river.

In 1862 he had overwhelmed most of the Fula empire of Mesina, including its capital Hamdallahi. By 1863 he had arrived at the holy city of Timbuktu. But when he attempted to impose his rule over the Muslim Fulas of Mesina, he sparked a rebellion which spread quicky throughout his recently conquered empire. The *Qadriyas* took the opportunity to strike back at the hated, ever conquering *Tijanniyas*. The citizens of

Timbuktu allying themselves with relatives of the deposed Masina King, Ahmadou and the Tuareg, the blue men of the desert, drove Omar's men out of town, capturing his field guns.

Omar was besieged in Hamdallahi as his empire rose in revolt. He escaped from the starving city as it fell to his opponents and became a hunted man. Eventually his pursuers ran him down in the Bandiagara caves. There at the dead of night, early in February 1864, he met his death. Some reports say he was blockaded into a cave and asphyxiated or burnt to death. Others say his pursuers blew up the munitions his men were carrying and that he died in the explosion.

Strangely enough despite his death and the sudden rebellion that overwhelmed him, the Tukulor empire lasted until the French finally took over about 1889 during the scramble for Africa. At its height under Omar it stretched from the Senegal river in the west, to Timbuktu in the east and as far as the Futa Jallon in the south - to the present day northern borders of Sierra Leone.

Under the green banner of Islam he had created a Tukulor empire.

5. Great South Africans

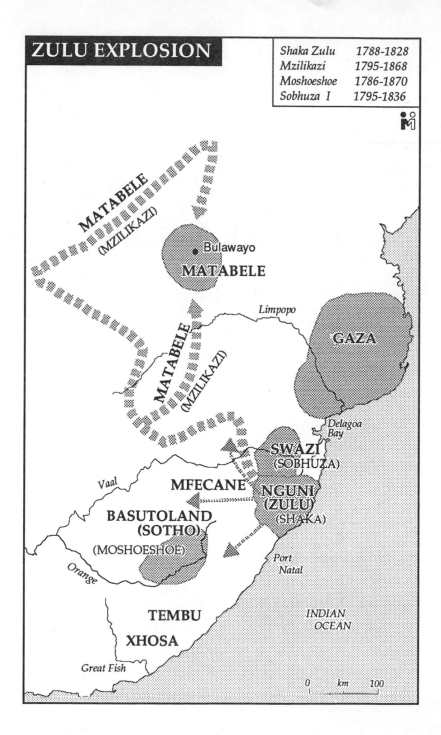

ZULU EXPLOSION

Shaka Zulu	*1788-1828*
Mzilikazi	*1795-1868*
Moshoeshoe	*1786-1870*
Sobhuza I	*1795-1836*

MATABELE
(MZILIKAZI)

Bulawayo

MATABELE

Limpopo

GAZA

MATABELE
(MZILIKAZI)

Delagoa Bay

Vaal

SWAZI
(SOBHUZA)

MFECANE NGUNI
(ZULU)
(SHAKA)

BASUTOLAND
(SOTHO)

(MOSHOESHOE)

Orange

Port Natal

TEMBU

XHOSA

Great Fish

INDIAN OCEAN

0   km   100

King of the Zulus

SHAKA ZULU
c.1788-1828

Shaka's name still reverbates today in legend and lore, in books, films and by word of mouth, as the man who transformed the tiny Zulu tribe into a fighting force of awesome reputation. Starting as a virtual nonentity from the most disadvantaged beginnings, he became the dreaded king who sent his enemies flying into the southern continent as he founded the Zulu empire.

His ruthless despotism and cruelty is often forgotten. He had all the attributes of the worst despots - capricious cruelty, total lack of respect for human life and the belief that might is always right. But he was also a great military leader. In a relatively short reign of a dozen years (he was scarcely 40 when he was murdered) he had transformed a small tribe into a nation, with a force and identity that would persist into the late 20th century. Of course this was at the expense of other peoples. He was more responsible than most for the *Difaquane*, the time of troubles and mass migrations that followed, but it was essentially the product of social and economic forces over which he had little control. At a time when only the fittest survived, Shaka showed the way.

Shaka was born about 1788 in a country trembling on the verge of crisis and upheaval. He was the son of Senzangakhona, chief of the small Zulu clan, and Nandi, a princess of the Lilangeni, but he was born out of wedlock. The casual relationship in which his father had seduced his mother, after watching her bathing, was tolerated in Zulu society, but the resultant offspring was not acknowledged. When Nandi noticed that she was missing her periods she thought it was caused by an intestinal beetle called *iShaka*, hence Shaka's name.

He was rejected by his father and spent most of his early years with his mother's people. His life was made a misery; everywhere he was the butt of jokes and social opprobrium about his illegitimacy.

The humiliation was such that Shaka and his mother moved in 1802, when he was a teenager, to find refuge amongst the Mtetwa people on the coast. There he found work as a herdboy. Later when he was about 22 years old, he joined the Mtetwa army.

Shaka's natural intelligence and fearlessness, sharpened by his unhappy childhood, made him throw everything into his military career. Soon he came to the attention of Dingiswayo, the chief of the Mtetwa, who became his protector and mentor, making him a commander in his army. Shaka watched how Dingiswayo was gradually extending his own influence over neighbouring tribes by negotiation, or failing that by force.

In 1816 Shaka's father Senzangakhona died, leaving a vacant throne and Dingiswayo encouraged Shaka to make a bid for it over the heads of a number of legitimate half brothers. Shaka seized power in the Zulu kingdom and single-mindedly set about imposing his own authority. In revenge for his adolescent humiliations, he demanded total obedience, meting out instant death to anyone who dared oppose him. Even his half brother Dingane, returning home with some idea of disputing the chieftainship, abandoned the plan and made his obeisance.

Shaka, using all the knowledge he had acquired from Dingiswayo, was ambitious, determined to build a powerful empire of his own. But the Zulus then were insignificant. He inherited an undisciplined army of about 500 men and set about expanding them into an effective fighting force.

Hi ambition was to create a powerful militarist state, with a standing army, welded together by a Spartan regime of discipline. He called up the whole male population and divided them into four regiments which had to compete for honours among themselves.

He did not allow any of his soldiers to marry before the age of 30. All the younger men, concentrated in regiments of their own age group (U Fasimba), had no master but their king and spent their whole time perfecting their military skills.

Shaka's love of meticulous planning and detail then turned to military equipment. He decided that modern armies had to be better equipped for close combat and introduced a dagger and a short-handled jabbing spear in place of the old-fashioned javelin. He made his troops discard their sandals and go barefooted so that they could run faster. No military stratagem was too detailed for his attention; he made clever use of spies and smoke signals, field craft and ambuscades.

He reorganised military tactics and battle formations. In attack his men would be arranged in a pattern resembling the head of a wild African bull. Two "horns" would probe the enemy from either side while the crack fighting force, drawn up in a block of elite troops, forming the "chest" would be waiting in the centre. This group would in turn be supported by another block of reserves.

Though growing fast in power and influence Shaka remained a loyal subordinate to Dingiswayo while he lived, indeed many of Shaka's apparently revolutionary military reforms had been learnt from his mentor. But in 1818 Dingiswayo was persuaded to visit his rival Chief

Zwide of the Ndwandwe, where he was made prisoner and put to death. Shaka was on his own, but he seized the opportunity to take over the Mtetwa tribe and fuse it with his own.

This expansion of Shaka's power came at a time when the whole of that part of southern Africa was in crisis. The peoples of the area, all members of the Northern Nguni, had been expanding fast over recent generations. Since the turn of the 19th century, they and their cattle were gradually exhausting deteriorating grazing lands.

The situation was aggravated by a climate that was exceptionally dry, with a succession of prolonged droughts leading to famine in the worst years. The competing Nguni tribes found expansion to the north and west was blocked by established tribes.

Shaka instinctively understood these geo-physical forces that would determine the shape of his region. When it came to a struggle for survival he was ready. His first task, after Dingiswayo's death, was to repulse an invasion of Zwide's Ndwandwe. Though the enemy were numerically superior, his new model army numbering some 40,000 triumphed, driving the Ndwandwe back across the Umfolozi river.

From 1820 Shaka was at the height of his powers. He sent his armies in every direction forcing neighbouring tribes to submit or flee. As his victories multiplied, his cruelty and despotism grew. As if he was taking revenge for all the humiliations of his childhood, he developed a reign of terror as a deliberate political weapon. After finally defeating the Ndwandwe, he exterminated many of the older people, forcing the youth to join his army and the young girls into servitude. His troops burnt homes and set crops alight adopting a deliberate scorched earth policy.

His cruelty and military prowess sent weaker tribes fleeing in what has come to be known as the *Mfecane or Difaqane*, the time of troubles, in which whole peoples were on the move looking for safety out of the range of the Zulus.

In 1821 Mzilikazi (q.v.) one of Shaka's former allies rebelled and fled northwards to find a new homeland for the Ndebele. After conquering several Sotho chiefdoms, he founded a new state between the Vaal and Limpopo rivers. Other peoples were sent fleeing from the expanding Zulu empire. By 1822 Shaka had extended his dominions southwards as far as the Tugela river and northwards to the Pongola. To the west the non-militarist Sotho were sent flying in every direction. Thousands died and thousands more were uprooted from their homes.

Meanwhile Shaka was becoming totally corrupted by his own cruelty and power. His people turned against him as he became more mentally unbalanced. European traders who were welcomed at his court, witnessed his killing fields, where the corpses of those who displeased him were devoured by vultures.

The trader Nathaniel Isaacs wrote, "He kept his subjects in awe with monstrous executions."

He himself never married for fear that his sons would murder him He even had some of the sons of his mistresses killed. He had two of the daughters of Sobhuza I (q.v.) who were sent to him as wives, murdered. Towards the end he insisted that his soldiers should not marry before the age of 40. When his mother Nandi died in 1827, such was his grief that he appeared to have become totally deranged. He created an atmosphere of near hysteria banning the sowing of corn, the drinking of milk and decreeing that all sexual intercourse should cease as a mark of respect to his beloved mother. Women found pregnant were put to death. Those who did not mourn sufficiently were arbitrarily executed.

He became so hated that his family hatched a plot to get rid of him by assassination. While his commanders were fighting a losing battle against Chief Shoshangane in the north, his two half brothers Dingane and Mhlangana, conspiring with a personal servant, ambushed him and speared him to death. It was 24 September 1828.

Shaka the monster was dead, to be succeeded by his brother Dingane.

He left others to consolidate his empire in the still more complicated environment which followed. As his assassins stabbed him to death in his cattle kraal he is reputed to have said, "You think that you will govern this country, but already I see the swallows arriving. You will not rule when I am dead. The whites are already here."

The Wandering Warlord

MZILIKAZI
c.1795-1868

Mzilikazi was a man of his age, a wanderer searching for a new home and security for his people. He was a product of the *Mfecane*, the time of troubles, in which the Zulus under King Shaka (q.v.) set a movement of mass migration rumbling across south eastern Africa.

Mzilikazi could have stayed in a subordinate role as one of Shaka's chiefs, but as if gripped by the wanderlust that was the spirit of his time, he chose to break away and find fresh pastures. After a lifetime of wandering, and winning new followers, he ended by founding a new nation, the Ndebele who have survived to the present day.

Mzilikazi was born about 1795. He was a Zulu, one of the many small Northern Nguni tribes living in what is now Natal. He was the son of Mashobane, the chief of the minor Khumalo clan. He was raised in the court of his maternal grandfather Zwide, the ruler of Ndwandwe, who was challenging Shaka for supremacy at the time the Zulus were poised to explode territorially, expand and build their empire.

In 1818 his father quarreled with Chief Zwide and was killed. Though Zwide sanctioned him as the new Khumalo chief, he felt insecure and sought the protection of Shaka who readily welcomed him. Shaka was glad to recruit a young leader bringing his whole clan over to his side. The two men became close friends and Shaka soon promoted him as commander of one of his regiments.

Shaka then installed him as a commander on the frontier of his expanding empire. In about 1821 Shaka sent him on a raid into Sotho country to retrieve stolen cattle. Mzilikazi was so successful in his mission that he decided to retain the captured animals and booty and strike out on his own.

To escape his master's vengeance, he speedily moved north at the head of a few hundred men. He wrought havoc among the smaller, less warlike Sotho tribes still suffering the consequences of the *Mfecane*, but his mission was not simply to destroy. He wanted to build his following and used the tactics he had already learnt from Shaka of absorbing the youngest and the fittest of the conquered peoples into his army. Gradually he built up his followers strength and numbers, as he led them through Swaziland and over the Drakensberg mountains. Some of Shaka's Zulus sent to pursue him were won over to his cause, other minor tribes sought his protection. Gradually his followers became known by their own name - Ndeble, in the Zulu language, or Matabele in Sotho. Mzilikazi welded them into a new nation with a character and way of life of their own.

By 1823 he had led them to a temporary resting place in Pedi country on the Oliphants river. When drought hit the region in 1825, he moved again settling and establishing a capital at Mhlahlandela, north of the present location of Pretoria. Trying always to keep out of range of the Zulus he moved again in 1826 to Mosega near the source of the Marico river. It was a fertile area and a good base for military operations and his armies were able to range far and wide over most of the Transvaal and beyond. He came into conflict with the Pedi, the Griqua and the Basutos and his old enemy where animosity was greatest, the Zulus, but he held his ground.

In 1829 Robert Moffat, a Scottish-born agent of the London Missionary Society was one of the first white men to visit him. He found the Ndebele protected by outposts formed by tree houses built 30 feet from the ground. Moffat climbed to greet them and was offered a bowl of locusts as refreshment. Mzilikazi was living most of the time in an ox wagon so he could range his territory. He gave Moffat a friendly welcome and showed he was a man of charm as well as authority. His rule was as absolute and despotic as Shaka's, though unlike his former master, he occasionally showed compassion and would pardon offenders. But towards Moffat he was nothing but friendly and in the years that followed the missionary returned many times to visit him.

Scottish traders also found their way to his camp and began to supply him with firearms. He needed these to beat off an attack in 1832 by Dingane, Shaka's treacherous brother and successor.

An even more serious challenge came from the white man. The Boer Voortrekkers had launched their Great Trek to find Mzilikazi encamped at the very centre of the veld grasslands that they wanted for their own.

The Voortrekkers made treaties with minor chiefs thus acknowledging their fear of the Ndebeles. Mzilikazi reacted by attacking isolated families. He then decided to attack the main Voortrekker force under Hendrik Potgieter at Vegkop in on 19 October 1832. The Boers formed a tight laager of 50 wagons with thorn bushes interwoven in the gaps. Mzilikazi sent in wave after wave of his men armed only with assegais. They were mown down in heaps.

Though Mzilikazi captured all the Boers' flocks and herds, they failed to take the laager.

Within a few months the Boers returned in force. In January 1837 they destroyed his capital at Mosega and put the whole population to flight recapturing much of the cattle lost and the town of Vegkop.

Another Voortrekker campaign was launched in October on Mzilikazi's last Transvaal stronghold at Kapain. The battle lasted nine days. Mzilikazi's troops were brave but desperately outgunned; his assegais were again no match for rifles. The Voortrekkers armed horsemen broke up the traditional Zulu-style military formation and sent Mzilikazi's men fleeing into the mountains.

Mzilikazi had lost half his army and knew there was no way that he could resist the white threat. He decided to move again, this time north, across the Limpopo. To increase his chances of success and put less pressure on food and water resources, he split his column into two. One group under his lieutenant Chief Gundwane went almost due north where it found a comparatively safe haven at Bulawayo, where the old Rowzi empire had already been defeated by other migratory tribes.

Mzilikazi led the other column north west into modern Botswana. He spent two years wandering and when he finally rejoined his people he found that they had installed his son as king in his place. He eliminated the dissident chiefs and reasserted his authority.

Out of range of the Voortrekkers and the Zulus he spent the rest of his lifetime establishing the new kingdom of Matabeleland in the area which has become Bulawayo, where he built his royal kraal. He encouraged his followers to mix with the local people and raided the whole area between the Zambezi and the Limpopo rivers. He replenished his cattle stocks by attacking the neighbouring Shona. He absorbed many of the younger Shona into the Ndebele tribe and gave a place of honour to their medicine men and doctors.

Robert Moffat found him in his new home in 1854 badly overweight and suffering from ailments in his joints (probably arthritis) which left him immobile. He accompanied Moffat on a wagon journey to the north, returning to trade ivory with white traders.

Two years later Moffat was back with two missionaries. They heralded the establishment of a London Missionary Society mission at Inyati. Mzilikazi saw the diplomatic value of missionary friendship but he never became a Christian himself.

He died of his aggravating ailments in September 1868 aged well over 70.

He was certainly a wandering warlord but much more besides. Though an implacable warrior his ultimate goal was always to absorb and unite the weaker peoples he encountered and to build a new nation.

He was highly adaptable to the dramatic changes of his time - the migrations, the growth of Zulu power, the coming of the white man. He was flexible and mobile.

In the last 14 years of his reign when he found a comparative sanctuary in Matabeleland, he became less aggressive. He developed a sophisticated, centralised administration. By the time of his death the wandering Zulu had built the Ndebele nation.

King of Diplomacy

MOSHOESHOE I
1786-1870

Moshoeshoe was a wise and clever king who created the Lesotho nation and ensured its survival over a long and troubled reign. His wisdom and adaptability ensured that his people survived and retained a measure of independence in the three-way struggle between the Africans, the Afrikaners and the British.

Though his people were always outnumbered by other warlike groups he devised one creative strategy after another to preserve his people's independence. He was even aware that by welcoming the white missionaries to live in his country his enemies would be dissuaded from further attacks. And he finally secured his people's survival by appealing to the British for outright annexation and protection against the predatory Boers.

Moshoeshoe, also known by the abbreviated name Moshesh, was the son of a very minor chief of a Sotho clanlet, the Bamakoteli, who lived in the Caledon valley. His name meant the "shaver" - a sobriquet he earned after a daring exploit in which he had "shaved off" the cattle of another tribe. His people lived a precarious existence mainly by cattle raiding. They ensured their survival by paying tribute to a more powerful Sotho tribe.

His youth was relatively uneventful. He told missionaries that his early life was privileged as a chief's son. It was carefree, confined to snaring, hunting and tending cattle, but as he was approaching maturity in the 1820s, he and his people were caught up in the violent upheaval that swept South Africa.

It was a time of severe drought and increasing pressure by population and cattle on limited grazing land. This had caused the warlike Zulu under their king, Shaka (q.v.), to seek more space, driving minor tribes from their lands, and sending them fleeing in all directions.

Known as the *Difacane*, or *Mfeacane* in the Sotho language this was no ordinary disturbance. Whole peoples were uprooted from their traditional lands, seeking new homes and turning on weaker neighbours.

Crops and cattle were seized. Land was laid waste. Starving hordes roamed the veldt, desperately seeking a new refuge. With no time to plant or sow, they had to live by pillaging others. Some even turned to cannibalism.

It was about 1815 when Moshesh established himself as chief of his own Bamakoteli clan. His fearless cattle raiding allowed his clan to wax and multiply, so that he was able to free his people from bondage and stop paying tribute to the former overlords.

Moshesh established a defensive position on a hill at Buthe Buthe to the east of the Caledon river. There he gathered his people and their cattle, establishing grain stores, and piles of boulders that could be used to repel attackers.

The repercussions of the *Mfecane* reached his people in 1822. Queen Manthatesi of the Tlokwa was approaching at the head of a huge horde of armed men. The Tlokwa made some desultory attacks on Buthe Buthe but were beaten off in a torrent of rolling boulders. Instead they resorted to seizing Moshesh's cattle and harvesting the crops planted by his people in outlying valleys.

But Moshesh knew that he could not survive for long in an outright military contest and instead used his innate cunning. He heard that the Tlokwa were in their turn, being pursued by a Zulu *impi*, so he sent messengers bearing gifts, telling the Zulus where the Tlokwa were and how they had gorged themselves at his expense. Soon the two predatory tribes were fighting between themselves ignoring Moshesh.

But clearly his small tribe could not survive major invasions of this kind for long. Moshesh sent his scouts deeper into the rolling mountains of Lesotho searching for a safer home. They came back with reports of a veritable sanctuary called Thaba Bosiu. It was a huge flat topped mountain surrounded by sheer cliffs that could be reached only by narrow passes.

In July 1824 Moshesh decided to lead all his people and their cattle in a major exodus to the promised land. For nine days and nights they travelled deeper and deeper into the Drakensburg mountains. He told the missionaries that some of the stragglers and older people had been attacked by cannibals along the route and carried off into the hills.

They reached Thaba Bosiu by night (hence its name - mountain of the night) and struggled up a steep pass to collapse exhausted on the top. The flat summit had about two square miles or pasture with plentiful spring water. The passes could be easily defended with mounds of heavy boulders and in the foothills were rich pastures where flocks could be tended in times of peace.

It proved impregnable resisting wave after wave of attacks by migrating peoples fleeing the *Mfecane*. He drove off Matiwane's Ngwane in 1826, the Koranna horsemen in 1830, and the Matabele in 1831 and later the mixed-race Griquas.

Meanwhile Moshesh in his wise, benevolent style, proved ever-welcoming to the refugees of the *Mfecane* who wanted to join him. He provided all peoples with food and shelter and incorporated them into his tribe. Soon they began to refer to themselves as Basotho - the people of Sotho.

Moshesh also worked hard diplomatically, making alliances with chiefs of equal status and paying tribute to distant rulers like Shaka, the king of the Zulus.

But enemies were plentiful. The Griquas had tried to gain Thaba Bosiu, armed with guns and attacking on horseback. The use of guns was spreading among the Kora bandits who refused Moshesh's diplomatic overtures.

Moshesh found no one willing to supply him with guns. It was then that his fertile mind came up with a new and revolutionary strategy. Against the advice of his father and other conservatives in his court he had already befriended two French missionaries from the Paris Evangelical Missionary Society - Thomas Arbousset and Eugene Casilis. He gave them a rousing welcome when they visited him in October 1833 in Thaba Bosiu.

Moshesh also saw how these representatives of the new white power could help protect his people. He welcomed them, became a Christian and for the rest of his long reign encouraged his new missionary friends and advisers to live in his midst. They were also to prove valuable allies as white encroachment, rather than the black, became his main preoccupation.

Hardly had the storm of the *Mfecane* blown itself out, when in 1834 the first ox wagons of the Afrikaners began to roll north in the Great Trek. Many of them settled in the vacant Sotho lands swept clean of people during the troubles.

By then Moshesh had formed a loose federation, based more on diplomacy than force, of the displaced peoples who clustered around the fringes of his domain. He was at the height of his powers, and beginning to acquire horses and firearms.

Britain under a far seeing governor Sir George Napier signed a treaty with Moshesh in 1843 recognising the state of Lesotho and its right to the lowlands to the west of the Caledon river as well as the area that forms present day Lesotho.

Moshesh was even prepared to grant some of the Voortrekkers some farms in the territory he controlled, but disputes over boundaries and grazing lands inevitably recurred.

In 1848 Britain's policy changed dramatically when a far less sympathetic new governor, Sir Harry Smith, recognised the Orange River Sovereignty leaving the land to the West of the Caledon river open to dispute. Mutual raids between the Basotho and the Afrikaners became more frequent. Moshesh found himself confronting both the Afrikaners and other Sotho tribes to the south of his kingdom.

His situation deteriorated further when the British administrator Major Henry Warden sided with the Sovereignty and sent a motley expedition of Voortrekkers and tribesmen to teach the troublesome king a lesson. Moshesh's mounted troops, fighting in their own mountains won a convincing victory at Viervoet in 1851.

Britain was too preoccupied with troubles in Xhosa land to send in a more powerful force but it continued to take the side of the Boers recognising first Transvaal in 1852 and then the Orange Free State.

Moshoeshoe knew that he could not resist the combined forces of the white man for ever, especially after the Orange Free State declared war on Basotho in 1858. Bit by bit he was forced to concede land and Voortrekker raids on his mountain strongholds became more frequent. The Sequiti war of 1865-66, (the war of the noise of the cannon) left him in desperate straits. He was approaching eighty and under severe pressure from the Afrikaners when he made another difficult decision.

He decided to appeal to the British for outright annexation. Many were opposed to such a move. The Afrikaners from Orange Free State saw themselves on the brink of outright victory. The Cape parliament did not want the cost of a new colony. Natal's governor cast covetous eyes on the unfortunate kingdom. But Moshesh had considerable sympathy in Britain itself and the missionaries who had lived with him since the 1840s were his loyal advocates.

Finally the governor Sir Philip Wodehouse came up with the plan of annexing Lesotho, not for the Cape government but for Britain itself. On 12 March 1868 Basutoland (Lesotho as it was then called) became a British colony.

Moshesh's creative diplomacy had saved his people but at a cost. In the treaty of Aliwal North of February 1869, Wodehouse was only able to regain part of the kingdom that had been taken by the Afrikaners; none of it to the west of the Caledon river. However the boundaries of Lesotho were established almost as they are today.

Moshesh had bought the security and independence of his people. It was about the best deal that he could do.

He died on his beloved Thaba Bosiu on 11 March 1870. He was over 84-years-old.

Last Dance of Freedom

CETSHWAYO
1832-1884

When Shaka Zulu (q.v.) lay dying at the hand of an assassin he warned his successors that they would find it impossible to govern, "I see the swallows arriving. The whites are already here." The consequences of this dire prophecy fell on his most renowned successor, his nephew Cetshwayo.

Throughout his long rule Cetshwayo was doomed to struggle between the twin grinding stones of British colonialism and Afrikaner expansion. These powerful forces would create a new South Africa and bring the disintegration of the Zulu nation. He was to lead his people on their last dance of freedom.

Cetshwayo was born in 1832. He was the nephew of both of the most famous Zulu leaders - Shaka and his brother Dingane, who succeeded him. His father Mpande was installed as king of the Zulus about 1840 and pursued peaceful and conciliatory policies towards the British authorities who ruled from Cape Town and towards the Afrikaner Voortrekkers who were beginning to encroach on Zulu lands north of Natal.

He proved himself as a young warrior with his father's Thulwana regiment and soon built his Usuthu clan followers into a troop personally loyal to him. Gradually he took more responsibility from his father, but found that his path was obstructed by another potential successor, his brother Mbuyazi.

A bloody war of succession followed in which thousands died. Finally matters were settled at the battle of Ndondakusuka in December 1856, where Mbuyazi was killed and his army defeated on the banks of the Tugela river.

The next year, with the succession clearly determined, the ageing Mpande retired leaving his son in effective control of the Zulu nation.

Cetshwayo was more suspicious of white intentions than his father had been. Shortly after his accession to power he was visited by Sir Theophilus Shepstone, the Secretary for Native Affairs in Natal, a vintage empire-builder full of ideas on how and why Britain should establish its rule in South Africa. Known to Cetshwayo as Somsetu, he was to play a crucial role in his future.

Cetshwayo wanted the support of the British against Afrikaner incursions into Zululand. Shepstone did not trust Cetshwayo entirely but recognised him as the most powerful figure in the Zulu hierarchy and recommended to his father that he should be crowned king as soon as possible.

This did not happen immediately, but Cetshwayo sought British protection against Voortrekker encroachment of the Blood river lands. Between 1861-76 no less than 18 requests were addressed to Shepstone to mediate in the frontier struggle.

Shepstone attended Cetshwayo's coronation on the death of his father in 1872 bringing an impressive retinue, a military band and two nine pounder guns. Cetshwayo made him vague promises to live at peace with his neighbours and to introduce human rights reforms at home.

But in 1877 Shepstone gave up his position as Secretary in Natal and was made administrator in the newly annexed state of Transvaal. This totally changed his perspective. He was now the defender of the Afrikaners and ready to turn on his former Zulu allies. He was worried that the new Afrikaner state might not be able to survive against the growing power of the Zulus.

Cetshwayo, irritated by the Afrikaner encroachments and the loss of Shepstone's support, had forgotten the promises he made at the time of his coronation. He had begun to reorganise a military state. He re-established the system pioneered by Shaka that had been set aside by his father. He insisted that his young men concentrate on becoming soldiers. He put them in peer groups and trained them as professional warriors. He refused to allow the younger men to marry until they had "washed their spears".

He even created a female regiment known as the InGcugce and offered them as brides to the soldiers of the veteran regiment - soldiers of over 40 years old. The young women did not take very kindly to this and refused to be married to these older men. Some fled, others were caught and put to death, their bodies being left where they had fallen.

Shepstone reprimanded Cetshwayo and reminded him of the promises made at the time of his coronation, but he countered with complaints about Afrikaner border incursions. In 1878 the problem had reached such proportions that a Natal Boundary Commission of Inquiry was established which surprisingly took the side of Cetshwayo, concluding that the Boers had no right to Zulu lands. Shepstone was dismayed as he now perceived the Zulus as the greatest threat to the peace and a burgeoning military power. He began to talk also of releasing the Zulus from the "pure military despotism of Cetshwayo". He wrote, "Zulu power is a perpetual menace to the peace of South Africa." It also stood in the way of Shepstone's greater ambitions of a federal state under British rule.

Shepstone convinced the newly arrived High Commissioner in Cape Town, Sir Bartle Frere, that until Cetshwayo's authority was broken there would be no peace. He sent a long memorandum to London to this effect and refused to give the Zulus the security recommended by the boundary commission.

Cetshwayo would have been quite happy to continue an alliance with Natal if that had guaranteed him against Boer incursions, but now Shepstone had betrayed him and the conclusions of the commission were ignored. Frere then provoked him still further by demanding that the Zulu military system be dismantled within 30 days and that his coronation pledges be honoured.

Angrily, Cetshwayo refused and prepared to resist the British onslaught; a gesture that was to mark the onset of the Zulu wars.

It came on 11 January 1879 when a force of about 7,000 British troops and about the same number of African levies under the command of Lord Chelmsford, invaded Zululand. One of the three columns was virtually wiped out at Isandhlawana when Cetshwayo attacked using the tactics established by Shaka. The British defending their camp, were trapped by a pincer movement of a two-pronged military formation - the Zulu "horns" and suffered very heavy casualties. Another British force at Rorke's Drift warded off a similar Zulu attack after killing thousands in a bloody engagement which is forever honoured in British military history.

Cetshwayo realising that he could not resist the superior British military technology for long, tried to reach a settlement and ordered his troops to stand off.

But the British were not to be appeased. Three months later Lord Chelmsford tried again. This time his new force was better supplied from ox wagons and armed with nine pounders and Gatling guns.

When the two sides met at the Zulu capital of Ulundi on 4 July 1879 Cetshwayo had no answer. His troops had inferior firearms and used tactics of mass assault that had not changed since Shaka's time. The Zulus fought bravely, surrounding the British square, but they were simply mown down by the Gatling guns and the nine pounders firing grape shot. When the Zulu attack was exhausted cavalry inside the square broke out and completed the rout.

For some time Cetshwayo hid in the mountains to the north. He was captured on 27 August 1879 and imprisoned in Cape Town.

Sir Garnet Wolseley who had taken over as High Commissioner in Cape Town, and Governor in Natal, and the Transvaal then imposed his own solution. The disputed lands were given to the Boers and the Zulu kingdom was broken up into 13 separate territories under different chiefs.

Cetshwayo was banished but soon found a champion in Bishop Colenso of Cape Town who wrote, "Having crushed the Zulu nation beneath his iron heel, Sir Garnet Wolseley passed on to find fresh fields...the usual subsequent collapse occurred, this time sooner than expected to reveal the black and dismal waste beneath." Zululand disintegrated into warring kingdoms, with far greater bloodshed and loss of life than in Cetshwayo's time. The chaos, insecurity and loss of life was reminiscent of the *Mfecane* (the time of trouble in Shaka's era). Liberal opinion in Britain was outraged and soon a campaign was mounted to reinstate Cetshwayo.

In the summer of 1882 he was invited to Britain for a month where he impressed everyone with his dignity. Dressed in a top hat, yet with bare feet, he was lionised by a sentimental public and given presents by Queen Victoria. He talked of himself as a "child" in the service of his "mother", the queen. While he was there the second Gladstone government decided to restore him.

He returned home on 10 January 1883, to be installed by his old sparring partner, Shepstone, but he was never offered his old kingdom back, much of his territory remained in the hands of rival chiefs who had been loyal to the British during the Zulu wars. In charge of his native Usuthu alone, he was but one of the competing rulers. His chief rival Zibhebhu retained all the kingdom and powers that he had gained in the interregnum and lost no time in mocking Cetshwayo and humiliating him.

Cetshwayo remarked, "I did not land in a dry place. I landed in mud... I came and found long standing friends and bitterly opposed enemies. There are no new friends since I came."

Within two months of his return, fighting resumed, this time between Cetshwayo and Zibhebhu. After a year of indeterminate conflict, in which more blood was spilt than the whole of the rest of his rule, he was again defeated and his capital at Ulundi destroyed. He was forced to throw himself on the mercy of his imperial masters, who gave him protection under a British commissioner in the Zulu reserve which they had established near to Natal.

It was an ignominious end. Shortly afterwards he died, at the age of about 52, reportedly after a heart attack. Certainly he was a broken man.

Shaka's bitter forecast had been fulfilled. The European swallows had come and wrested Cetshwayo's own independence and that of his people from him. Though courageous to the end, he had proved powerless to resist the new forces that had undermined him. He had seen his proud peoples set at each others throats. The killing continued while the white strangers brushed them aside and built a new nation.

Carved in Stone

PAUL KRUGER
1825-1904

Jan Smuts considered that Paul Kruger was the greatest of the Afrikaner leaders. His lifetime spanned the period from the earliest Voortrekkers to the Boer war. His whole career was spent in the struggle to preserve the independence of the Transvaal and of his Afrikaner volk. His policies led to two wars, defeat and disappointment, yet the stubborn patriot carved in stone, became the symbol of his peoples struggle and after his death he was mythologised.

To the Afrikaners Paul Kruger was a determined nationalist leader who spent a lifetime battling for the independence of the Transvaal against British pressure. To the British he was a narrow, stubborn, boorish leader, with a mind and face carved in stone. He was incapable of compromise and determined to have his own way whatever the cost. Brought up in the Voortrekker tradition, he plunged his people into two wars, but he remained a symbol of his peoples resistance. His death simply enhanced his reputation as the greatest of early nationalist leaders.

Stephanus Johannes Paulus Kruger, or Oom Paul (Uncle Paul) as he is known to his followers, was born on 10 October 1825. He was descended from a Huguenot family that was sent to the Cape by the Dutch East India Company in 1713.

His parents came from the narrowest and most bigoted of all the narrow sects in the Dutch reformed church - the doppers. He had little formal education and never read a book in his life except the Bible. He preferred the old testament to the new and thought hymn singing was a wicked levity. He was an ultra-fundamentalist who believed the earth was flat and that everyone was predestined to follow a precise course chosen by God.

When only ten years old, in 1836, he left with his parents on the Great Trek led by Andries Hendrik Potgeiter.

He was tough and hard. His life was a continual round of trekking, fighting and hunting. He claims to have witnessed the Afrikaner victory at Vegkop in 1836 over the great Matabele leader Mzilikazi (q.v.). Legend has it that he cut off the top of his thumb after it had begun to go gangrenous, then he stuffed his fist into the belly of a newly killed sheep, which stopped the infection spreading and saved his life.

Kruger's family settled north of the Vaal river. Though a farmer, he spent ever more time as a soldier. By the age of 20 he became a field cornet with more than 100 men under him. At 27 he took command in an expedition against the Bechuana chief, Sechele, in which David Livingstone's house was destroyed.

He was present at the Sand River Convention in 1852 when the Transvaal was first given its independence. He was close to the Pretorius family, particularly Martinus Pretorius who became president both of the Transvaal and the Orange Free State. It was this connection which led to his election as commandant general in 1863, a post that gave him command of all the Transvaal forces.

He became highly involved in internecine Afrikaner politics and the personality conflicts this involved. He backed Pretorius in trying to overthrow the government of the Orange Free State. Then he was involved in a long campaign against the more "liberal" Thomas Burgers. He did everything to undermine Burgers' authority even going as far as to incite the people to pay no taxes to the state that was already near bankrupt. His interference and machinations were partly responsible for Sir Arthur Shepstone's annexation of the Transvaal on 12 April 1877.

But Kruger was able to capitalise on this unpopular move. Throughout his career he was motivated by his mistrust and hatred of the British and by his desire to have and to hold the independence of the Transvaal.

He went on two delegations in 1877-78 to London, to present petitions and try to get the annexation of the Transvaal annulled. He did not achieve his objective but reinforced his reputation as a committed leader of his people.

Kruger was more personally involved in the first Boer war 1880- 81, than he was in the second. He took command of the Boer forces and became part of the triumvirate of presidents - along with Piet Joubert and Pretorius who assumed political control. After winning a succession of victories over the British, including the battle of Majuba, peace was achieved at the Convention of Pretoria in August 1881. Transvaal got self-government under British suzerainty and the *Vierkleur* flag, the symbol of Boer independence, was raised once more.

He became sole President on 9 May 1883 by defeating Joubert in the presidential elections.

Kruger had emerged as the undisputed leader of his people - he was to be re-elected as president for four more terms of office. His gnarled face, as if carved from stone, glowered balefully under a top hat when he attended the Volksraad (parliament) in Pretoria. He would sit on the *stoep* of his house when off duty, drinking coffee, smoking his pipe and spitting intermittently.

He ruled Transvaal virtually single-handed for the next 17 years. His overriding objective was to achieve full independence for the Transvaal and prevent federation in a British dominated South Africa. To ensure this he wanted a direct outlet to the sea for the landlocked state. For a long period after the war he negotiated with the British over Swaziland, which would provide access to Delagoa Bay.

He said that he would drop all Transvaal's claims north of the Limpopo if he could open a corridor through Swaziland. The British might have agreed, but only on condition that Transvaal joined the customs union. He felt this would compromise Transvaal's independence and refused.

Kruger's major conflict was with the mining interests which had discovered gold on the Witwatersrand in 1886, and the horde of foreign workers *uitlanders* who came to exploit the new riches. Kruger penalised the mining companies by granting concessions for essentials such as water and dynamite to his associates and by charging high tariffs on imports.

Meanwhile he taxed the miners heavily and even tried to conscript them into national service with the Boer commandos, while denying them the franchise. With regard to the *uitlanders* he once said, "This is my country; these are my laws. Those who do not like my laws can leave", and again, "I shall never give them anything; I shall never change my policy, and now let the storm burst."

After he was returned as President for a second five-year term in 1888, he tightened the franchise laws still further and continued to try to extend the frontiers of the Transvaal. He was proving to be a bad administrator and his government was becoming increasingly corrupt. Kruger said he saw no harm in distributing bribes to officials over a railway concession.

Kruger was even beginning to lose popularity with his own Afrikaner people. There is considerable evidence that the elections against Joubert in 1893 were heavily rigged. Joubert appealed to the Volksraad (parliament) but could make no headway as the majority of its members still supported Kruger.

Kruger's narrow obstinacy, his dark suspicion of the foreigner and his refusal to give an inch, were the basis for the plots that the British and Cecil Rhodes (q.v.) hatched. They planned to cause an uprising of the *uitlanders* as a pretext for intervention.

The ill-fated raid by Dr L. S. Jameson, at the instigation of Rhodes, in January 1896 was a product of this situation. But it was so badly planned and executed that Kruger, whose popularity was previously flagging even with his own people, emerged as the steadfast champion of his burghers against the machinations of the mining interests.

Kruger saw that the raid had dealt a terrible blow to his rival Rhodes and was cunning enough to treat Jameson courteously and actually hand him and his co-plotters over to the British for trial.

In 1898 Kruger was elected President for the fourth and last time. A conference was called in 1899 at Bloemfontein by the High

Commissioner to the Cape, Sir Alfred Milner, to try and resolve some of the problems in the Transvaal. Kruger did not yield an inch, claiming that every proposal threatened the independence of the Transvaal.

Further negotiations followed by letter but there was no resolution and Kruger finally sent an ultimatum which was to start the second Boer war over causes that had changed very little since the British provoked the Jameson raid four years earlier.

Kruger had been preparing for war since the raid. He had been to Germany to win friends and buy artillery. When the war started Kruger was too old, at 74, to go on commando himself. He had one early scrape when he was almost captured by the troops of Lord Roberts at Bloemfontein. He stayed in Pretoria with his government until the town was captured in June 1900 when he and his whole administration retired down the railway to Delagoa Bay.

From there he went into exile, at the end of 1900, to Europe. He received a warm reception, because the war had made Britain universally hated. He was mobbed in Marseilles and greeted with enthusiasm in Holland and Germany. But he was an old and broken man and Britain was grinding towards victory in the war he had left behind. After a period living on the Riviera he moved to Switzerland and died at Clarens, by the shore of Lake Geneva, on 9 July 1904. "I was born under the English flag," he said earlier, "but I have no wish to die under it."

His body was taken to the Transvaal and buried amid scenes of high emotion and grief. His people loved him enough to return him to office four times as President. Despite his narrow-minded negativism, and refusal to compromise he had proven a totally courageous patriot in defence of his countrymen and his beloved land.

Imperial Diamond

CECIL RHODES
1853-1902

Few men crammed more into a brief life than Cecil Rhodes. He was an adventurer, self-made millionaire, diamond magnate, gold financier but above all an old-style imperialist, who had a whole country - Rhodesia - named after him. He failed to achieve his greatest dreams, but he did transform the face of Southern Africa and bring it politically and economically into the 20th century.

Rhodes was in many ways the last of the great imperialists. He was a giant of the 19th century, confident enough, rich enough to try to force his dreams into reality. His death coincided with the beginnings of the decline of Britain's imperial power.

He had brought South Africa to the brink of union and prosperity based on mineral wealth. Rhodesia was to survive a stormy course for another 60 years, until the independence of Zimbabwe in 1980.

Cecil John Rhodes was born on 5 July 1853 at Bishops Stortford in Hertfordshire. He was the fifth son of the local vicar. The large family had been yeomen farmers for generations.

He was educated at Bishops Stortford grammar school, where he worked hard without doing particularly well. He left in 1869 when only 16 years old.

He might have gone straight to university, or into the church, but his health was bad. Since childhood he had been suffering from what was then diagnosed as tuberculosis. Recent research has put the blame on a hole in the heart. This condition was to dog his career and to play a part in his early death at the age of 49, but he compensated by his driving energy and fanatical determination to be successful.

Doctors advised him to abandon the idea of a home career and to join his eldest brother Herbert who was trying to grow cotton in Natal, South Africa.

He sailed to join him, arriving on 1 September 1870. Already his dilletante brother had abandoned his cotton fields and was caught in the great diamond rush that was to permanently change the face of South Africa. Cecil stayed on the farm picking cotton till July 1871, then set out to make his fortune.

He covered the 400 miles in an ox-wagon to Colesburg Kopje where his brother had three claims. Herbert grew tired of the unproductive diggings and went back to his farm, leaving Cecil in charge.

Rhodes was an awkward, uneasy youth with a high pitched voice, who drank a lot without being sociable. The few friends he made were close and worthwhile. He learnt the diamond business from the bottom, digging and sieving the stones and soon earning a fortune.

Colesburg Kopje, became a rough, tough diamond mining town called Kimberley. The claims Rhodes was working were part of the "big hole", the most productive diamond "pipe" the world had ever seen.

He made his money direct from the diggings, but his entrepreneurial nature soon realised that huge profits were to be made from ancillary services like the pumping equipment needed as the hole got ever deeper. He even brought an ice-making machine all the way up from the Cape by mule wagon. He sold ice cream and a slab of cake for a shilling, from a packing case on a corner of the diamond fields where temperatures soared to over 100 degrees in the baking South African sun.

By the time he was 19 he had made a small fortune, but instead of pressing on to even greater riches, he resolved to return and take a degree at Oxford. Before that, he travelled north for eight months through Bechuanaland and as far as the borders of the country that was to become Rhodesia, dreaming of discovering great new mineral riches to the north.

Rhodes never pursued money for its own sake, only as a means to his greater ambitions. For the next eight years he commuted regularly between Oriel College, Oxford and the ever productive big hole at Kimberley where he gradually accumulated more claims, expanded his business and became ever richer.

He later discovered that a doctor who had examined him on his return to Britain in 1873 had given him "only six months to live". Oblivious, he saw South Africa as the country of the future, the foundation of a great imperial dream that was opening to him.

He became a freemason in 1877 and a millionaire by 1880, at the age of 27, when he formed the De Beers Mining Company which owned 90 claims.

One major scandal rocked his financial career in 1876 when he was accused of offering a bribe to damage the water pumping equipment of a rival firm, so that his own machines would have to be accepted instead. Rhodes denied the claim and after a welter of accusations and counter accusations the matter was allowed to drop.

In 1881 he stood for Barkly West and won a seat to the Cape Legislative Assembly. He had not competed for Kimberley or an urban seat, but had chosen a rural seat with a Boer majority. Despite the antipathy of the Boers for the foreigners - the *uitlanders* - crowding into the mining towns, Rhodes showed his political skill by holding the votes of his Boer constituents for the rest of his life.

Through all this career-building, he still yearned for academic learning. Aged 28, in 1881, he returned to Oxford and finally took his BA. Even in the money-making squalor of Kimberley, he retained his love of books. Aristotle and Marcus Aurelius were his constant companions.

He was also a natural businessman. As his wealth increased he became a financier concerned to smooth out the massive fluctuations in the diamond market, by absorbing the smaller mines and controlling the supply of stones.

Rhodes never had a woman as a regular companion at any time in his life. When living in Kimberley, he had no mansion of his own, but lodged with other bachelors, known as the "twelve apostles" in a cottage opposite the Kimberley club. Some writers have tried to describe his character in terms of homosexuality, but there is little evidence for this. He was more likely to have been almost asexual, consumed instead by his grandiose ambitions and plans.

Later in life when dining with Queen Victoria, she asked him if it was true that he was a woman hater. He is said to have replied diplomatically, "How can I hate the sex to which your majesty belongs."

His membership of the Cape parliament gave him a platform to develop his political objectives. Rhodes saw South Africa as a federation of British and Boer states, each with considerable local autonomy, but under firm British control. This was how he reconciled his representation of a Boer constituency and his grander ambitions.

At the base of all his ideas was a passionate, near fanatical belief in the idea that the world should be ruled by the English-speaking race. When he was only 22 he left his fortune to the British Colonial Secretary for the "establishment of a secret society" whose aim should be, "the extension of British rule throughout the world."

He saw South Africa as the nucleus for British expansion into the rest of the continent. As the scramble for Africa reached its climax, he saw Britain ruling the whole continent from the Cape to Cairo, after thwarting the Portuguese challenge in Mozambique and the Belgians who were pushing into the Congo.

But first there was the immediate problem of keeping open the road to the north against the expansion of the Boer republics, particularly Transvaal under its rugged President Paul Kruger.

In August 1884 he was appointed resident deputy commissioner for Bechuanaland. Due to his own persistence Bechuanaland was eventually declared to be British territory and the protectorate was extended north up to the 22nd parallel in 1885.

Gold was discovered on the Witwatersrand in the middle of Transvaal in 1886, adding still further to South Africa's strategic importance and exacerbating Rhodes' problems with Kruger.

Another wave of *uitlanders* poured into the rand as Rhodes switched some of his financial interests from diamonds to gold. He launched the Goldfields of South Africa on 9 February 1887, retaining a huge interest in the company for himself. The ensuing boom in gold helped finance further amalgamation on the diamond fields.

His career now had four strands. Diamonds, gold, politics in Cape Town and his grand design for the north.

Rhodes' ambition was growing in a document entitled a "Confession of Faith" he wrote, "Africa is still lying ready for us, it is our duty to take it." "Expansion is everything, " he said later, "These stars you see overhead at night, these vast worlds which we can never reach! I would annex the planets if I could."

Behind the dreamer was the practical man. He saw the possibility of "another Witwatersrand" in the land between the Limpopo and the Zambezi (that would later be called Rhodesia). He set up the British South Africa Company (BSA) in July 1889 as his instrument.

Obstructing him was Lobengula (q.v.), the king of the Matabele whose rule was almost as absolute as that of his ancestor Mizilikazi (q.v.). He was being pressurised by adventurers from everywhere determined to extract concessions from him. First of these was Rhodes who sent a series of negotiators to Lobengula's kraal at Bulawayo. After years of indecision it was Rhodes' great friend Dr. L. S. Jameson who won the concession.

Meanwhile Rhodes had been securing a royal charter for his BSA company which gave him the powers of government as well as mineral exploitation in Zambezia.

In July 1890 the renowned pioneer column of 380 Europeans skirted Lobengula's kingdom and overcoming local resistance and a scourge of rinderpest, pitched camp at what was to become Salisbury, in September.

Meanwhile in Cape politics Rhodes skilfully reconciled the interests of his Boer constituents with his imperial ambitions. He was even known by the affectionate nickname "de jonge burgher", the young burgher, by the Afrikaners.

He lived at *Groote Schuur* (Big Barn) which he gave to the state on his death so that all future South African premiers could live there when attending parliament in the Cape.

He formed a close alliance with the liberal Boer, J. H. Hofmeyr, leader of the Afrikanerbond. On 17 July 1890, with the support of Hofmeyer, he became Prime Minister of Cape Colony.

His attitude towards black Africans, though personally friendly, was at the best paternalistic. He believed in the justification for white rule, echoed by white Rhodesians a century later, of, "equal rights for all civilised men below the Zambezi."

One of his first measures when he came to power was to pass the Master and Servant bill giving employers the right of corporal punishment of their employees. He also raised the franchise qualifications reducing the number of coloured and black voters in the Cape. In the Eastern Cape he disenfranchised the Africans and imposed a labour tax, which he referred to as a "gentle stimulus" to make them work.

His objective in South Africa was to achieve federation, but Paul Kruger's Boer republic of Transvaal stood in his way. It pursued reactionary policies in the interests of the burgers against the *uitlanders*. It penalised the mining interests by high tariff policies and the granting of monopolies for essential services. It irritated the miners themselves by making them liable for service in local commandos. The *uitlanders* were petitioning London to intervene.

This situation resulted in a number of schemes aimed to topple Kruger. One was actually dreamed up by the High Commissioner in Cape Town, Sir Henry Loch. It came to nothing. Rhodes then devised a similar plot which was to get the *uitlanders* to revolt and then intervene militarily on their behalf.

This was the background to the Jameson raid, organised by Rhodes' old friend Dr. L. S. Jameson. He had been briefed to intervene using forces from Zambezia under control of the British South Africa company, but was instructed not to act until an uprising was under way in Johannesburg.

The whole plot went horribly wrong. Jameson became impatient and set off on 27 December 1895 despite specific instructions to the contrary. The Boers had been monitoring the cable traffic and were fully aware of what was happening. The Johannesburg Reform Committee failed to organise an uprising. The column was tracked carefully and captured after a couple of minor engagements. Jameson and the conspirators in Johannesburg were all imprisoned.

Rhodes may have tried to stop the raid at the last minute, but he was undoubtedly behind the scheme. He took full responsibility for what had been done in his name. All he said of Jameson was, "He upset my apple cart" otherwise there was no blame or recrimination.

He resigned as Prime Minister on 7 January 1896 and refused to give evidence to the Cape committee of inquiry. His association with the raid left a bitter taste of disgrace.

He fought his corner at another inquiry in London and surprisingly retained his charter. He returned to Zambezia to find the Matabele in revolt against the seizure of their lands by the white settlers. Rather than suppress the revolt directly at the head of an army, Rhodes decided to negotiate. In a personal act of courage he camped almost alone for six weeks where he could have been seized and put to death, instead the Matabele decided he had come to listen to their grievances. They parleyed and peace was agreed after concessions by both sides.

He concentrated his last years on the country that was to become Rhodesia. He brought the railway to Bulawayo and planned the route to the southern end of Lake Tanganyika. He also concluded plans for a telegraphic land line to Egypt.

Twenty five years after his doctor had predicted his demise, at the onset of the Boer War, his health was seriously deteriorating. The war was fought over many of the issues that had prompted the Jameson raid, but this time Rhodes was a bit player, though he was caught up in the siege of Kimberley. He did not live to see the war end, nor the new South Africa that was created along lines he would have endorsed.

He became very ill and died at a little cottage by the sea at Muizenberg, in the Cape at 6am on 26 March 1902. His hectic life had been crammed into 49 years. His body was laid to rest in the Matopos hills, the ancient burial place of the Matabele kings, a place he had noted on earlier journeys.

His legacy lived on after him in the Rhodes scholarships that underpin the "club" of privileged English-speaking students who enjoy his beneficence to this very day. Rhodes House, Oxford is a testimony to what was best in the imperial ideal.

Despite some nationalist objections, his body still remains under its plaque, "To brave men", in the Matopos hills. His unfortunate friend Dr. Jameson is buried alongside him.

Yesterday's Afrikaner

JAMES HERTZOG
1866-1942

For two decades Hertzog fought to liberate his Afrikaner people from the legacy of British rule in South Africa. In the process he curtailed African rights and encouraged segregation. At the end of his career he felt that he had achieved his purpose only to find younger extremists determined to push his philosophy to its logical conclusions. In his twilight years he wanted to slow the process, but a new generation had overtaken him. The forces of Afrikaner nationalism and apartheid were in full flood.

James Barry Munnik Hertzog was the son of a German immigrant from Brunswick. He was born on 2 April 1866 in Soetendal, near Groenberg in Wellington, Cape Province. Like his great contemporary Jan Smuts (q.v.), he was educated at Kimberley and Stellenbosch graduating with a BA in 1889.

He continued legal studies in Amsterdam, Holland where he gained a law degree in 1892, returning to South Africa the same year. He went into private practice in Pretoria, before being made a judge in Orange Free State.

He made little political impact before the second Boer War, when he joined the Afrikaners as a legal adviser to the military commander. He introduced a much needed code of discipline for the Boer troops and was promoted to General. After the fall of Pretoria in June 1900, the Boers broke into smaller fighting detachments and he was given command of the Orange Free State. He led a Boer expedition into the Cape at the end of 1901. His small group reached Rhynsdorp, but it was forced to retreat.

The Boers sued for peace at the Vereeniging peace talks in May 1902. He negotiated alongside Smuts and signed the agreement on behalf of the Orange Free State.

While Smuts had resolved to accept defeat and concentrate on reconciliation, Hertzog kicked at the humiliation. The war had made him even more anti-British.

In 1906 he founded the *Orangia Unie* party, built on narrow lines of Afrikaner nationalism. His bitter hatred refused reconciliation. He concentrated on getting equality for the Dutch language and on agitating for changes in the flag and anthem, the symbols of the Afrikaner nation.

When South Africa achieved self-government in 1907, he was appointed Attorney General and Minister of Education. He enforced his controversial language policy, but the reaction among English speakers was such that after a commission of inquiry he was forced to allow parents to choose the language of instruction for their children.

He was an uncomfortable member of the cabinet of Louis Botha, reacting passionately on all nationalist issues and repeatedly heaping invective on Smuts, whom he considered to be nothing less than an imperialist stooge. But he remained in government, being given the portfolios of Native Affairs and Justice in 1912.

In that capacity he passed the first piece of anti-African apartheid legislation - the Natives Land Act of 1913, which segregated non-whites, leaving Africans in their reserves with only 7.9% of the land area in South Africa.

Meanwhile his campaign against the British continued. Typical of his tactless rhetoric was a speech in December 1912 when he erupted, "South Africa must be governed by pure Afrikaners ... The main object is to keep the Dutch and the British separated...I believe in imperialism only when it benefits South Africa. I am ready to stake my future on this doctrine."

Botha wanted to be rid of him, but he refused to resign his ministry. So Botha himself resigned and on being reappointed Prime Minister by the Governor-General, dropped Hertzog from the cabinet.

Hertzog walked out into the wilderness accompanied by only a handful of supporters. But he saw himself as the champion of the Afrikaner people and wrote a lengthy manifesto justifying his stance.

In 1914 he formed the National Party and went from *dorp* to *dorp* in the Afrikaner heartland, winning support. During the war he remained resolutely neutral refusing to support the British, but only giving moral support to the Afrikaner rebels.

In the March 1920 elections his party actually won 44 seats, three more than the South African Party, but Smuts forced him to stay in opposition by forming an alliance with the Unionists.

His turn was to come in 1924 when the Nationalists won 63 seats to the SAP's 53. Hertzog became Prime Minister with his majority bolstered by the 18 seats of the Labour party, which had lost confidence in the Smuts government during the labour troubles of the early 1920s.

Hertzog was at last in a position in which he could lend his full support to the Afrikaans language and culture movement. He was also determined to change the country's status from subordination to Britain to complete sovereign independence.

He attended the Imperial conference in London in 1926 and got Balfour to make his famous declaration in which Dominions were defined as "autonomous communities, in no way subordinate to one another...though united in common allegiance to the crown." During the rest of his term in office he was to consolidate this recognition of his country's full independence.

In 1926 he finally achieved a change in the South African union relegating the Union Jack to a small patch no larger than the two republican flags.

He saw segregation as the way to stop his people being swamped by blacks. Throughout his term of office the anti-black legislation flowed. In 1926 the Mines and Workers Amendment Act brought segregation to the work place by excluding Africans and Asians from skilled jobs in the mines.

He played on white fears in the "black peril" elections of 1929 when he won an overall majority.

In 1930 the Natives Urban Areas Amendment Act restricted the movement of Africans to the towns. In 1932 the Native Service Contract Act ordered that Africans return to their reserves or remain as tied labour on European farms.

But the economy was in difficulty as the world went into recession, the value of the currency plunged, and investors sent their capital abroad. His allies in the Labour party split into factions and Hertzog gradually lost his majority. When Smuts suggested a coalition with the South African Party, he seized the offer and the alliance swept the board in the 1933 elections. One year later the United Party was formed. He remained as Prime Minister with Smuts as his deputy.

He was then able to toughen his anti-black legislation still further. In 1936 the Natives Representation Act removed the coloured voters from the roll of electors and gave them three white MPs to represent their interests in parliament.

Meanwhile he improved the lot of white farmers guaranteeing prices for their produce and introducing a land bank. By introducing bilingualism he opened up the civil service to Afrikaners.

But even Hertzog's segregationist policies were not sufficiently extreme to satisfy the die-hard Afrikaners. In 1935 the Purified Nationalists under D. F. Malan went over to the opposition. They joined secret far right organisations such as the *Broederbond* and the *Ossewa Brandwag* which, as war threatened, were far more sympathetic to Hitler's fascists than the British.

Hertzog again, as in the first World War, wanted to remain neutral but Smuts, supported by liberal Afrikaners and British South Africans, was determined to bring South Africa into the war on the side of Britain. In September 1939 Smuts carried the day in parliament by 80 votes to 67. Hertzog's draft of a constitution for the new party was also heavily defeated at the Orange Free State Congress. His leadership had been emphatically rejected, so he resigned.

Broken and saddened at the rejection of all he had done for his people in his long years of office, he retired to live out his twilight years on his farm at Waterval near Pretoria. He was sometimes seen walking among his thorn trees, a lone and solitary figure. He died on 21 November 1942.

The Great Healer

JAN CHRISTIAN SMUTS
1870-1950

Smuts was arguably the greatest political figure that South Africa has produced. His brilliant career spanned over 50 years, and two world wars. He was an acknowledged statesman on the international stage, playing a major part in the creation of both the League of Nations and the United Nations. Perhaps his greatest contribution was in healing the strife between Briton and Afrikaner, though he never fully faced the inter-racial problems that were to engulf his country after his death.

Jan Christian Smuts was born on 24 May 1870 in a humble homestead farm at Ongegund, Bovenplats, in Cape Province. His father was a farmer and representative in the Cape House of Assembly. His mother of French Huguenot descent. The first Smuts to settle in the Cape had arrived with the Dutch East India Company in 1692.

Jan Christian was a brainy intellectual, taking to academic studies with enthusiasm and aptitude.

At first he was taught at home going on to Victoria College, Stellenbosch at the age of 12. His brain was clear and receptive. He had a photographic memory and could memorise books at the first time of reading. He passed his matriculation with distinction in 1887.

In 1891 he passed his degree, taking a double first in science and literature. He decided to take law at Christ's College, Cambridge, but had to sell family livestock and borrow from his tutor as his parents could not afford to send him abroad. Once there he won a scholarship, but had to borrow more to see himself through his course.

He avoided social life and studied with commitment, emerging with distinction when he took both parts of the law tripos simultaneously, in October 1894. He turned down the offer by Christ's College of a fellowship in law and was called to the bar in the Middle Temple.

In 1895 he sailed home and took up law in Cape Town, filling in time while waiting for briefs by writing political articles for the local press. The struggle between the Boers and the *uitlanders* (outsiders) for the diamond and gold wealth of the Transvaal had already started. The young Smuts felt the first stirrings of Afrikaner nationalist feelings.

He made his first major political speech at Kimberley Town Hall, warning that the principles of democracy as known in the West could not be exported to Africa: "You cannot apply to the barbarous and semi-barbarous natives the advanced political principles and practice of the foremost peoples of civilisation. Too often we make the mistake of looking upon democracy as a deduction from abstract principles instead of regarding it rather as the outcome of practical politics."

After Cecil Rhodes'(q.v.) foolhardy Jameson raid in 1896, when he tried to seize power in Transvaal, Smuts came to the conclusion that the, "British connection was harmful to South Africa's best interests."

The Jameson raid depressed Smuts so much that for two years he avoided politics and concentrated on his profession. He also married Sybella Krige, a childhood sweetheart, and moved from the sleepy Cape for good, settling in the growing frontier town, Johannesburg.

Meanwhile the Transvaal President, Paul Kruger (q.v.) had followed his career, describing him as, "one of the cleverest lawyers in South Africa." On 2 June 1897 he was offered the post of Attorney General, causing the *Star* newspaper to remark, "Though he may have all the precociousness of a Pitt, we still consider that twenty-eight is rather too young."

He was also legal adviser to the Transvaal Executive Council and inevitably became involved in the abortive negotiations with the British High Commissioner Alfred Milner who wanted the *uitlanders* to have full citizenship rights in the Transvaal.

Though he strove for peace, Smuts was far too junior to have anything but a marginal effect on the negotiations. At the outbreak of the Second Boer War in September 1899, he was fully committed to the Afrikaner cause. At first his role was administrative, running the government in Pretoria. One major organisational feat was the transfer of the cash from the national bank and local mint to safety in Middleburg. His home in Pretoria practically became the Boer headquarters until the fall of the town in July 1890.

Smuts made the change from administrator to full-time soldier effortlessly. The weedy lad soon became a battle hardened general, organising commando units in the Transvaal. The British had already gained the upper hand and were pouring reserves into the country. Smuts asked Kruger for permission to negotiate, but was instructed to fight on.

In June 1901 he was ordered to lead a Boer expedition into the Cape, where he could create a diversion and keep the maximum number of British troops occupied. His expedition, which finally arrived in O'okiep in South West Africa in May 1902, was described as a classic operation. Leading a band of a few hundred men he travelled over 2,000 miles, keeping 35,000 British troops busy for nine months until the war ended in April 1902. In the meantime he had escaped death by a hair's breadth when his horse was shot from under him in an ambush. Starving, he had nearly killed himself by eating a poisoned fruit. He and his men had all escaped barefooted from another ambush and he had ordered the execution of a spy.

By the time of the Vereeniging peace conference of 15 May 1902 the retiring academic had become a tough, 32-year-old veteran, who was to play a major part in the negotiations. Always a realist, he persuaded his own "bitter enders" to accept a settlement in which the Transvaal became a state within the British empire.

He later described rule by High Commissioner Milner, from 1902 - 5 as the "darkest period in Transvaal history." In a state of disillusion he returned to his law practice, this time in Pretoria.

In 1905, he and Louis Botha founded *Het Volk* the first national Afrikaner political party. Its objectives were to reconcile the Afrikaner people following the traumas of war, and to struggle for self-government.

In 1906 he travelled to London to convert the new Liberal government of Henry Campbell-Bannerman to the cause of self-government. He delivered a brilliant ten-minute speech which convinced the whole cabinet. In 1906 the Transvaal won Responsible Government, followed shortly after by the Orange River Colony.

He campaigned in the February 1907 elections for "a new and great nation, neither Boer nor British, but a nation that shall make South Africa into a big free country." *Het Volk* won an overall majority in the elections. Botha became Prime Minister in the Transvaal and Smuts the Colonial Secretary and Minister of Information. Smuts soon showed that he was the intellectual powerhouse in the new government, doing most of the cabinet work, even helping inexperienced ministers with their own portfolios.

At the height of his intellectual powers, he then began the campaign for union of the four South African colonies - Cape Province, Natal, Orange River Colony, and Transvaal. He insisted on union rather than federation at the National Convention of May 1908 where he drafted, argued, advocated and carried the unitary constitution. Later he described his work at the convention as his "greatest single work for his country."

The Union of South Africa, when it was established in 1910, was largely his achievement. He took three out of the nine portfolios in the new national government - mines, defence and the interior.

One of his first acts was to help merge all the Afrikaner parties including *Het Volk* into the South African Party.

Only J. B. M. Hertzog (q.v.), the nationalist firebrand, opposed his policies of conciliation, championing every Afrikaner cause. Hertzog was dropped from the cabinet and formed the National Party in 1914. Smuts meanwhile was engaged in a major confrontation with white mine and railway leaders over working conditions. After being forced into a humiliating agreement with the strikers, strikes recurred and this time Smuts showed a streak of ruthlessness, illegally deporting nine strike leaders before the courts could intervene.

He was also involved in passing the Immigration Act (1913) which stopped further Indian immigration and the Indian Relief Act which alleviated taxation and recognised the validity of Indian marriages.

Storm clouds were gathering over Europe and war was on the way. The Boer War was fresh in the memory of extreme Afrikaners, who saw their chance coming to settle old scores with Britain, but Smuts was resolutely pro-British and determined to convince his own people that their true interests lay in friendship.

Anti-war feeling was high in the Afrikaner community and many colleagues who had fought alongside Smuts in the Boer War were soon in open rebellion. Commandos were raised in Transvaal and the Free State, armouries were raided and a series of skirmishes ensued, lasting several months, but by early 1915 the rebellion was quelled.

This left Botha and Smuts free to pursue a campaign against the Germans in South West Africa. Again Smuts transformed himself smoothly from administrator to soldier and put down the Afrikaner rebellion.

In February 1916 he left to take command of operations in East Africa. He hesitated before leaving South Africa, which had become bitterly divided over the war, but he was glad to leave the political bickering behind and take on the hardships of a soldier. He hounded General Vorbeck Von Lettow the German commander, out of Tanzania, before being called to London to attend the imperial conference in March 1917. There he made a brilliant case of a Commonwealth of independent nations in preference to closer links with Britain.

His skill and clarity of thought led the British Prime Minister Lloyd George to offer him a place in his war cabinet. He was one of only seven members - a minister without portfolio, specialising in broad war strategy. At the same time he remained South Africa's Minister of Defence.

In London he worked from a suite of rooms overlooking the Thames. He was involved in successfully settling a number of strikes among the British police, munition workers and coal miners. He also played a major part in estabishing the Royal Air Force and even tried a secret mission to Austria to try get that country to break its ties with Germany.

After the war he did much of the practical and theoretical work in establishing the League of Nations. Most of his suggestions were warmly welcomed by Woodrow Wilson and formed the basis of the League's charter. He opposed demands for tough reparations from Germany. He worried about "the pot boiling over in a new war." He felt the peace treaty of 28 June 1919 was too punitive and only signed it under protest.

In August 1919 he returned to South Africa. In less than a month his great friend Louis Botha was dead and he took over as Prime Minister. The economy was exhausted and depressed and the South African Party came second to the Nationalists in the election of March 1920. Smuts was forced to form a minority government and then merge his party with the Unionists. He called a snap election early in 1921 and won a comfortable majority.

But Hertzog continued to press extreme nationalist causes, while the economy remained bitterly depressed bringing a wave of labour troubles. Black workers struck for better pay and were rigorously repressed. Nearly 300 squatters from the African "Israelite" sect were massacred at Bulhoek in 1921. Serious violence and shooting in a dangerous general strike threatened to plunge the country into anarchy, before Smuts declared martial law and forced the workers into submission. There were over 500 European and 150 African deaths. Two months later he sent in bombers to curb a Hottentot uprising.

This intensely unhappy era was brought to a sudden end when his party was annihilated in the elections of June 1924. Smuts lost his own seat, Pretoria West and only maintained his position in parliament when the member for Standerton stood down in his favour.

He was delighted to hand over the cares of office to Hertzog who found himself running into similiar economic difficulties in face of the world slump of the 1930s, which brought a collapse in commodity prices and financial impoverishment as he clung to the gold standard.

Hertzog was glad to accept Smuts' offer to form a coalition government in 1933. He retained the premiership but made Smuts his deputy and state attorney, the position he had occupied 35 years earlier. The public overwhelmingly endorsed the coalition in the elections of May by returning the United Party to power.

But tensions were rising in Europe and differences between the parties soon reasserted themselves. Hertzog and most of his cabinet wanted to maintain neutrality, Smuts thought that South Africa could not isolate itself from world conflict. Smuts, ever the pro-British internationalist brought South Africa into the war by a narrow majority of 80-67, in September 1939.

Hertzog resigned, Smuts became Prime Minister and threw all his incredible energies into winning the war. Finding that the former defence minister had neglected his portfolio, his first task was to build South Africa's armed forces almost from scratch. South African troops won the first allied victory of the war by defeating the Italians in a lightning campaign in Ethiopia. On a tour of inspection he was almost shot down by mistake by allied planes in northern Kenya.

He was made a Field Marshal in the British Army on 28 May 1941. As the allied fortunes improved so did his popularity, while the opposition suffered in the propaganda war over its support for Hitler. Smuts won the support of many Afrikaner farmers by guaranteeing their wool prices and sales to Britain throughout the war.

Smuts confirmed this situation with a victory in the 1943 elections by 105 seats for the United party to 43 for the opposition.

After the war he played a major part in the establishment of the United Nations, by drafting the UN Charter's Declaration of Human Rights. But he was not able to wrest control of South West Africa from the UN and he disappointed many by his ambivalent policies towards the Indians and Africans. In 1946 he introduced an act to give Indians the franchise, but he withdrew their previous right to own fixed property. This pleased no one. India later delivered a bitter attack at the United Nations and broke off trade relations.

As Smuts stature grew and he was acknowledged everywhere as a world statesman, he found it increasingly difficult to reconcile his international idealism and breadth of vision, with his internal policies when he was at best a paternalist, not ready or willing to face growing racial tensions.

He recognised that segregation was not working, but was under increasingly bitter attack from his nationalist opponents who wanted a full blown apartheid system.

Though in his late seventies, he continued to be in demand internationally, attending conferences and interminably making speeches in the capitals of the world. Cambridge made him chancellor of the university in January 1948.

But at home a tide of extreme nationalism was running. He was also demoralised by the deaths to his eldest son, and his most promising political colleague J. H. Hofmeyer. He went into the elections of May 1948 exhausted and insufficiently prepared.

But even he was shocked by the result. He had been routed in a nationalist landslide, by 80 seats to 65. He had lost every rural seat and took the defeat very badly. In the words of his son, the biographer, "It was worse than a personal slap in the face."

He felt like abandoning the leadership of his party, but was persuaded to remain. He had little time to enjoy his semi-retirement; on 11 September 1950, four months after his 80th birthday he died. The whole world paid tribute, none more evocative than that of Clement Attlee, the British Prime Minister: "A light has gone out in the world of free men."

The Gentle Crusader

ALBERT LUTULI
1898-1967

Lutuli came late to politics and when he finally assumed the leadership of the African National Congress he found himself confronted by the full force of Afrikaner nationalist repression. A morally upright man with sincere religious beliefs and a faith in non-violence, he made little political progress, but he did maintain the love and respect of his people and the unity and leadership of the ANC, for more than a decade, in its darkest hour during the 1950s.

Albert John Lutuli was born in 1898 near Bulawayo in Southern Rhodesia, where his father was a Congregationalist mission interpreter and the reigning chief of the Abasemakholweni, a sub-division of the Zulu tribe.

His family returned to South Africa when he was ten years old, and he entered Groutville mission school in Natal and later Adam's College, the American Mission secondary school, where he qualified as a teacher and stayed on to teach Zulu history and literature. He rejected a bursary to do further studies at Fort Hare University because he needed to earn money to support his family.

He continued teaching until 1936 when he was elected chief on the death of his uncle. He was hesitant to take on the chores of petty litigation, raising taxation and law enforcement, but finally his sense of duty persuaded him to give way to his people's wishes. He also immersed himself in his church as an organiser and a lay preacher.

For 17 years he remained in Groutville, though he managed to travel too - to India in 1938 as a delegate of the Christian Council of South Africa and in 1948 to the USA, to attend the North American Missionary Conference.

Gradually his conscience and his devoutly held Christian beliefs took him into politics. After serving a few years on various race relations committees, he joined the African National Congress in 1945. The year after he was appointed to the Natives Representative Council, which soon afterwards wound itself up as a protest against its political impotence.

But he had already developed the taste for politics, rising quickly through the ranks of the ANC until he became the president of the Natal provincial division, in 1951.

The tide of Afrikaner nationalism was in full flood and African political rights were being fast eroded. The ANC and the South African Indian Congress responded by launching the defiance campaign aimed at apartheid laws. This campaign accorded precisely with his views of passive resistance so he encouraged his people to resist specific measures without using violence.

In October 1952 the government summoned him to Pretoria and he was ordered either to resign from the ANC or from his chieftaincy.

He refused to do either, with the memorable words; "Who will deny that 30 years of my life have been spent knocking in vain, patiently, moderately and modestly at a closed and barred door? What have been the fruits of moderation? The past 30 years has seen the greatest number of laws restricting our rights and progress until today when we have almost no rights at all."

The government stripped him of his chieftaincy, but his stand was recognised by the ANC which elected him President General of the party in December 1952.

In November 1952 he was banished to his village for two years. In 1954, the moment his ban lapsed, he flew to Johannesburg to protest against the Western Areas Removal Scheme under which the Africans lost their remaining rights in the urban area and were forced to leave Sophiatown and move to a township outside town.

He was promptly served with another two-year ban.

In December 1956 he and 64 others were arrested on a charge of high treason but released without charge a year later.

In 1959 he did a speaking tour in the Western Cape where he addressed large crowds of all races, including many whites. Again he was banned, banished to his village and prevented from attending any gatherings, even church services, under the Suppression of Communism Act.

His restriction order was suspended so that he could give evidence on behalf of those, like Nelson Mandela, still caught up in the treason trial. On 26 March 1960, as political tension mounted, he publicly burned his pass. This gesture of defiance taken up by his followers brought the confrontation at Sharpeville in which 69 peaceful demonstrators were shot dead and hundreds of others wounded. Lutuli called for a national day of mourning.

He was himself detained on 30 March along with 2,000 others, under the state of emergency which followed.

He was awarded the Nobel peace prize in 1960 and after international pressure allowed to go to Oslo in Norway to receive it. The nationalist newspaper *Die Transvaler* declared that the award was an "inexplicable, pathological phenomenon" and other Afrikaner newspapers wholeheartedly condemned it. However he received the prize on 10 December, saying it was on behalf of the "sacrifices made by people of all races in South Africa, particularly the African people who have endured and suffered so much for so long."

Other international honours followed. In 1962 he was made Rector of the University of Glasgow, but not allowed to travel to attend the installation cenemony. He published his autobiography, *Let my people go*, in the same year.

But his active political career was stifled by the continuing banning order and a stroke which impaired his movement and vision. He was hit by a train as he tried to cross a railway and died on 21 July 1967.

Always a perfect gentleman, he believed like Gandhi that passive resistance could succeed without adopting violence in any form, but he made little progress. He rose to leadership at the time Afrikaner nationalism reached its peak, crushing all resistance in its path, with a raft of repressive legislation. He maintained a calm dignity and steadfast belief in his Christian principles, earning him the love and respect of his people. He preserved the leadership and unity of the ANC in its darkest hour.

Architect of Apartheid

HENDRIK VERWOERD
1901-1966

Verwoerd is always known as the architect of apartheid, not the originator, but the man who pushed it to its logical conclusions under the new name of separate development. As he took power the principles of apartheid were already well established. His job was to try and make them work.

A narrow-minded, fanatical, racist he gave apartheid an intellectual and ideological gloss. He was beloved of his own Afrikaner people, who truly believed that he could show them an alternative solution to the race problem and their fear of being swamped by the black majority. It was he who gave a moral justification to apartheid under the pretence that it was really separate development, allowing Africans to pursue their own culture in their own Homelands.

His fanaticism aroused the undying enmity of all fair-minded people and bred a sense of hysteria even among his own Afrikaners. This led to two assassination attempts. In the second he was stabbed to death in the parliamentary chamber on 6 September 1966.

Hendrik Frensch Verwoerd was born, not in South Africa, but in Amsterdam, Holland on 8 September 1901. He was the son of a building contractor, who wanted to be a missionary by spreading the message to Africa. He and his family emigrated to the Cape in 1903, where he opened a grocery shop.

He sent his son Hendrik to Wynberg High School in Cape Town. Later the Dutch Reformed Church sent him as a missionary to Rhodesia. Hendrik followed him as a teenager. He had to attend an English-speaking school where his school mates taunted him over his strong Dutch accent.

He returned to study theology, then psychology at Stellenbosch, where he needed to show that he was more Afrikaner than the Afrikaners.

"When it came to Afrikaner nationalism he was a fanatic," a fellow student recalled.

He deliberately turned down a scholarship to study in Oxford and instead continued his education in 1927, at German universities - Hamburg, Leipzig and Berlin - where he drew inspiration from the German National Socialist philosophers.

He returned to Stellenbosch from 1927-32 as a professor of applied psychology. There he championed poor-white causes, but protested against a government decision to give asylum to German Jewish refugees. He became a member of the Broederbond, the secret Afrikaner organisation which was later to provide the philosophical basis for apartheid.

In 1937 he jumped at the chance to become editor-in-chief of a new Afrikaans daily *Die Transvaler*, the mouthpiece of the National party for the Transvaal.

He edited the paper throughout the war revealing a pro-Nazi bias and anti-semitic views. When the leading English daily the *Star* accused him of having Nazi views he sued, but lost his case.

He stood in the elections of 1948 when the nationalists swept to power, but did not win his chosen constituency, Alberton. Prime Minister D. F. Malan wanted him in his team and appointed him to the Senate in 1950 and Minister of Native Affairs, where he was able to apply his developing apartheid philosophy direct on the African people.

Verwoerd is generally known as the architect of apartheid, but the system was already well-developed when he came to power. The writer Allister Sparks, in his book *Mind of South Africa*, writes, "It was Nico Diederichs who first laid the philosophical base for it, Geoff Cronje who first conceptualised it, Piet Meyer who was its key backroom strategist, and Verwoerd who finally implemented it in its most absolute form."

Verwoerd gave a philosophical cloak to the crude policy of *Wit baasskap*, white mastery advocated by Prime Minister Hans Strijdom. He called it separate development. At first this meant removing Africans from white areas and sending them back to reserves where they would be ruled by local chiefs.

He was responsible for the 1952 Native Law Amendment Act which limited black rights to live in white areas. In 1953 the Reservation of Separate Amenities Act made apartheid compulsory in all public places. In 1954 the Resettlement of Natives Act and the Native Urban Areas Amendment Act further limited African settlement and allowed mass removals from urban areas.

These social polices were matched by education acts which put all African education in the hands of the state rather than the missions and enforced segregation at universities.

In April 1958 he was elected to parliament for the Heidelberg constituency. When Strijdom died in September, he was elected leader of the National Party and Prime Minister.

Verwoerd assumed full power in the 1960s when most other black

Verwoerd assumed full power in the 1960s when most other black African countries were winning their independence, but with his obsessive, doctrinaire logic he was determined to see apartheid through to its logical conclusions. He saw this in a system of separate development in which Africans could be sent back to their own "Homelands" or Bantustans where they could develop in their own way; but as critics pointed out, only in small fragmented states in poor parts of the country. They were to be separate, but never equal.

Meanwhile African opposition to apartheid was rising. Protests against the pass laws resulted in Sharpeville on 21 March 1960 in which about 5,000 unarmed Africans who were peacefully demonstrating by burning their passbooks were massacred by the police. Sixty-seven died and a further 300 were injured.

An international outcry followed but Verwoerd, in a characteristic reaction, simply declared a state of emergency, banned the leading African nationalist parties and detained hundreds of opposition politicians of all races.

On 9 April 1960 he survived an assassination attempt when he was attending an agricultural show in Johannesburg. It was not politically motivated. He was shot in the head by a deranged white farmer. He made what his supporters considered to be a miraculous recovery.

He narrowly won a referendum making South Africa a republic in November 1960. He attended the Commonwealth Conference in March 1961 where he was forced to defend his apartheid policies and formally withdrew his application for renewed Commonwealth membership.

He returned home at the peak of his powers. Internationally isolated, with his back to the wall, he became even more determined to make his apartheid policies work. He claimed that God had, "determined that he should assume the leadership of South Africa." Speaking interminably in a nasal, high pitched voice he had immense charisma amongst his own people. They thought their survival depended on him.

He made further gains in the election of October 1961 as the white opposition crumbled and he was able to press ahead with his separate development policies. The Transkei was given self-government in December 1963 and other homelands were to follow shortly after his death.

But on a national level resistance continued. The remainder of his life saw a cycle of violence, followed by repression, the restriction of civil liberties, followed by more violence, despite the bannings, detentions and arrests. Informers and censorship turned South Africa into an effective police state.

In January 1965 the Bantu Laws Amendment Act went into effect stripping the blacks of most of their remaining privileges in white areas.

And the contradictions of apartheid soon became apparent. The Bantustans remained impoverished and ever-dependent on subsidy from South Africa. Their rulers became corrupt, inefficient, and authoritarian. Far from developing their own culture, they became even more dependent on the white state that had set them up. They never won international recognition and were treated as little more than glorified native reserves.

Meanwhile the white economy was booming and the need for African labour grew ever greater. The economic pressures to keep the pool of labour close to the towns was irresistible. And international pressures on South Africa were building with the first boycotts on armaments and the threats of further sanctions on trade.

Verwoerd was stabbed to death on 6 September 1966. A white parliamentary messenger attacked him as he was sitting in his seat in the chamber.

His policies had been shown to be inequitable and economically unworkable even before the dramatic assassination. Yet his sheer force of personality, his dogged pursuit of his flawed logic, had given his people hope that separate development offered an alternative to what was happening everywhere else in the world. More than two decades were to pass before the Afrikaners were to realise that his policies were unrealistic. He had led them down a blind alley.

Martyr to Apartheid

STEVE BIKO
1946-1977

Steve Biko has become a cult figure. His Black Consciousness movement motivated his people and inspired the student strikes in Soweto, in 1976. This later escalated into a popular uprising in the townships against apartheid. By then Biko was a marked man continually harassed, banned, arrested and detained by the security police. He died in September 1977 under police torture and became a martyr overnight. Since his death an avalanche of publicity has surrounded his name - books, films and articles have followed.

Biko's real achievement was that he made the South African blacks proud of their heritage and determined to take the struggle into their own hands. He insisted that blacks should do everything themselves, rejecting help from white liberals even if they were working to the same political ends. In this he clashed with the African National Congress and other non-racial political organisations who saw the struggle was that of all democrats against a ruthless dictatorship.

Despite the cult that has grown about his name, Biko only represented a phase in the liberation struggle. He involved and inspired the blacks, but contradictions remained. If he had survived, his relationship with the ANC would have been a difficult one. The movements such as the Azanian Peoples Organisation (AZAPO) which drew on his philosophy have become minor players in the mainstream of South African politics.

Stephen Biko was born on 18 December 1946 in King William's Town, in South Africa's Eastern Cape. He grew up, a large friendly bear of a man, in a huge, noisy family. Both his parents were politically active. He went to Brownlee Primary School for two years, going on to the

Charles Morgan Higher Primary School. He began his studies at the local Lovedale Institute, but it was closed over a student strike so Biko's parents sent him to the Marianhill Catholic Institute in Natal where he matriculated in 1965.

He then went to study medicine at the University of Natal medical school, but instead of studying for his exams he would stay up all night writing political pamphlets and pondering the predicament of his people.

Biko was a charismatic figure, tall, imposing and sure of himself. He rose rapidly in student politics to become an active regional secretary of the non-racial National Union of South African Students, but he was never happy with the organisation. He came to feel that as a white-led body it could not properly represent the aspirations of black students.

Gradually he began to formulate the philosophy of black consciousness. This started from the premise that black liberation had to start with the blacks themselves rather than relying on a white leadership, however liberal it might be. He saw the need to raise the political awareness of his own people. He urged them to take the political struggle against apartheid into their own hands.

This philosophy led him in December 1968 to form the all-black South African Students Organisation (SASO). It was officially inaugurated in July 1969 and he was elected its president. His objective was to crystallise the needs and aspirations of the non-white students and express their grievances.

Biko grew up at the time the American Black Power movement was reaching its peak; he applied its philosophy to the local struggle against apartheid. He coined the slogan, "Black man you are on your own."

Black consciousness expressed itself first through SASO. In 1970 Biko broke with NUSAS while curiously still recognising it as the major student organisation. He deliberately excluded all whites from SASO and other organisations even though they were often struggling for the same political objectives. This, in turn, led him into conflict with other African non-racial organisations such as the African National Congress.

He once said, "People tell us that it is a class struggle rather than a race one... We believe we know what the problem is and will stick by our findings."

He thought that the role of sympathetic whites should be to "fight for their own freedom and to educate their white brothers and serve as lubricating material."

In the early 1970s Biko expanded into other fields, organising black self-help schemes, black sports bodies and trust funds to provide help for political prisoners. In 1972 he established the Black People's Convention (BPC) as the political wing of the Black Consciousness Movement and the coordinating body for over 70 black organisations.

Black Consciousness came out of its narrow student base in the period 1972-75 and became a predominant influence among many educated blacks. Biko encouraged the setting up of black businesses whose profits could be ploughed back into community programmes. Eventually he shaped this into the philosophy of black communalism which aimed at a black, mixed-market economy, with some state control. He travelled South Africa lecturing and writing pamphlets and articles explaining his philosophy.

He was expelled from the University of Natal in August 1972 for "inadequate academic performance", without completing his medical studies. He then became a full-time organiser for black community programmes.

His radical activism naturally came to the attention of the South African authorities. He was regularly hassled and followed by the police until a banning order was imposed on him in March 1973. This restricted his movements to King William's Town and prevented him from speaking to more than one person at a time. Nor was he allowed to speak publicly or publish articles.

He spent his time organising local community projects while studying law by correspondence courses and was never afraid to break his ban, travelling to other parts of South Africa when politically necessary.

He was never free from police harassment and he was detained twice for brief periods after 1974 and then for 101 days. He was prosecuted for a series of petty offences including the breaking of his banning order. He generally won the cases brought against him in court, but was forced to rely on the BPC to provide the finance to fight the expensive cases.

The Black Consciousness movement inspired students to boycott their schools and white-imposed education in Soweto in June 1976. But the movement had failed to organise the hostel-based workers in the urban areas and this allowed the police to encourage the hostel dwellers to attack the striking students.

Further contradictions emerged at the SASO Congress in 1976 when attacks were made on the black middle class for thinking that it had a right to exploit black markets, by virtue of its colour. Calls were made by the BCM to look at the struggle not only in terms of colour but in terms of class.

On 19 August 1977 Biko was stopped at a police roadblock outside his restricted area. He was detained for the fourth time and accused of instigating riots in Port Elizabeth by distributing pamphlets. He was kept in chains and denied exercise.

After 22 hours of intensive interrogation and torture, he went into a coma on 7 September. The police found he was unable to eat or drink and rushed him, on 11 September, to Pretoria hospital. He was transported hundreds of miles, naked and in chains, lying on the floor of a police Land Rover.

On 12 September 1977 he died of a brain haemorrage. The Minister of Justice, Jimmy Kruger, said that he had been examined by three doctors including a specialist who could find nothing physically wrong with him. Kruger came out with the extraordinary explanation that he had died after a hunger strike.

A postmortem by four private pathologists, including the eminent independent pathologist, Dr Jonathan Gluckman, who was working on behalf of the Biko family, found that he had died of a brain haemorrage caused by head injuries sustained during detention. They also found that he had injuries to his ribs and more than a dozen abrasions and bruises. The officers who had interrogated him including the notorious Major Harold Snyman cynically defended their conduct in court.

Biko died a martyr. His death provoked a wave of outrage in South Africa and throughout the world. Even the diehard Afrikaner, *Transvaler* newspaper viewed his death "in a serious light". The *Financial Mail* wrote that Biko had been "a symbol, a hope and an inspiration" to his generation.

Indeed he had launched his fellow South Africans on the last phase of the liberation struggle.

6. Saints and Sinners

Father of the Church

SAINT AUGUSTINE
354-430

Saint Augustine, recognised as the greatest father of the Catholic church, was an African. He was born in Africa and spent most of his working life there. Yet he was very much a son of the Roman empire.

He lived in a time of trouble when the Roman empire was in full decline and the barbarians were baying at the gate. He wrote at a time when Christian thought and doctrine was still unclear, with a host of schismatic leaders competing with even more alien philosophies. Augustine tasted many religions before he finally came down in favour of the true Christian Church.

But at the end of his lifetime he had clarified his own beliefs and doctrines to such an extent that he not only dominated his contemporaries but passed on religious principles that were to last throughout the Middle Ages. Both the reformation and the counter reformation were to claim him and his teachings as their own.

Aurelius Augustine was born in 354 at Tagaste, a town in Numidia (now Souk Ahras in Algeria) which was part of Roman north Africa. Tagaste was about 45 miles south of the important Roman coastal town Hippo Regius (now Annaba). His father Patricius was a pagan, his mother Monica, a devout Christian and a sweet, tender lady.

It was a time of turmoil and change. The Roman Emperor Constantine had been finally converted to Christianity in 312, but the empire was still the battleground of a host of conflicting philosophies and faiths. Indeed the empire itself that had dominated the civilised world for more than three centuries was crumbling as the barbarian hordes pushed into Italy.

But Augustine had a secure family background. His father recognised his extraordinary intelligence and after a local education sent him to Madaura, then Carthage to study philosophy and Latin and Greek literature. But Augustine was still no Christian. He had even refused his mother's wish for him to be baptised. His reading was wide and varied, reflecting the intellectual ferment of his time.

He was also a dedicated lecher. While still a youth he seduced a young girl and had an illegitimate child whom he named Aedolatus (by God given). In his *Confessions* which he wrote much later he looks back on this period of his life, full of lust and sin, in the darkest terms.

But his father was determined to make him a rhetorician and spared no expense in financing his studies. At 19 he read Cicero's *Hortensius* which stimulated his thirst for knowledge, but as he sampled one philosophy after another he could find nothing to satisfy him.

Then he found Manichaeism. It was a mixture of Persian Zoroastrianism and Christian Gnosticism propounded by the prophet Mani from about 240. Under the Manichaean philosophy light and darkness are in continual conflict. The physical universe originates from darkness while the human soul is the product of light. Augustine saw his own struggle with the lusts of the flesh in these terms, but after joining the Manichaean sect and entertaining the philosophy for nine years he gradually became disillusioned. His belief was finally killed off after a disappointing discussion with a Manichaean bishop, Faustus.

He finished his studies and returned to Tagaste where he taught grammar and by the force of his personality made a great impression on his pupils. But still to the great anguish of his mother, he refused baptism and appeared lost to the Catholic Church.

In 383, at 29 years of age he returned to Carthage and then went to Rome for a year before finally getting a job as a teacher of rhetoric in Milan. It was an important post that could lead to high office. By then he had abandoned Manichaeism and took up Neo-Platonism instead. He began to believe in a single God and searched for truth outside the material world . He came under the influence of an established father of the Christian Church, Bishop Ambrose, who had already reconciled the Old Testament with Platonist spirituality.

But Augustine was still obsessed with sex and balked at the prospect of celibacy. Indeed in Milan he was still accompanied by his childhood common law wife and son, whom he loved dearly. He became betrothed to her though his intellect was leading him to the belief that the only true path to Christianity was celibacy.

It was then that he wrote that he had a vision. Torn between duty and desire he rushed into his garden and there he heard a child's voice crying, "Take up and read, take up and read". He opened up St Paul's Epistle to the Romans and read the passage, "Not in rioting and drunkeness, not in chambering and wantoness, not in strife and envying. But put ye on the Lord Jesus Christ and make not provision for the flesh to fulfil and the lusts thereof."

He wrote later, "Instantly as I finished the sentence, the light of confidence flooded into my heart and all the darkness and doubt vanished ... Thus has Thou converted me to Thee, so I no longer need to seek either wife or other hope of the world."

His conversion took place in the late summer of 386. Afterwards he devoted himself to an ascetic life of study. He was plagued with a chest complaint and withdrew to a country estate at Cassisiacum near Milan to recover. Then he finally presented himself for baptism along with his son Aedolatus. His mother arrived joyfully to witness her son's admission into the true church, but his happiness was not total. He sent his common law wife back home, something he never satisfactorily explained .

He began his philosophical polemics with an attack on Manichaeism. He wrote 13 books against the Manichees between 387 and 400. He argued specifically for free will against Manichee determinism in his book, *Free choice of the will.*

In 388 he returned home to Tagaste. He formed a small religious community and a monastic way of life that was to form the origins of the Augustinian order.

In 391 when visiting Hippo he attended a meeting where the people unexpectedly elected him their presbyter. Though he wanted to return to his monastery, he felt obliged to respect his followers' wishes. When the Bishop of Hippo died in 356, Augustine succeeded him and remained in that post until his own death in 430.

Apart from his ecclesiastical duties he continued to write learned philosophical works. He found most of the African churchmen of the time were Donatists. The Donatist schism had started at the beginning of the century. The Donatists claimed that many of the leaders of the Catholic Church were unholy and had betrayed the martyrs to the Romans before the time of Constantine's conversion. They then set up their own schismatic and fanatical church under Donatus.

Augustine attacked Donatism with every weapon he could muster. He used state power and coercion, quoting Luke, "Compel them to come in." He attacked Donatists personally, used popular propaganda and even composed doggerel verses and pop songs against them.

The Donatists argued that they had set up their own church because the Catholic Church had become unholy. Augustine said the Church was holy even if some of its members had transgressed. He drew the distinction between the Church and its members who were subject to the same human frailties as the Donatists themselves.

His next disputation was with the Pelagians, the followers of Pelagius a Scots or Irish monk who had established himself in Rome and built up a huge following. He did not believe in original sin passed down by Adam after his fall, but Augustine guilty of his own sinful past, was a vehement believer in original sin.

Augustine went further. He said that no matter how good, or kind, or dutiful or hardworking, an individual could not be saved without being given God's grace. Later he came to believe that even faith was a gift of God. And salvation was only given to those that God had chosen, his elect.

Augustine denied what to us seem the "enlightened" views of Pelagius - that every person is born innocent and is only tempted into sin by the conflict between duty and desire and that children who die in infancy are therefore blameless and saved even without baptism. Augustine persecuted Pelagians and wrote innumerable tomes to try to prove them wrong on these precise points. For 20 years, writing more than 15 books he campaigned against them. Augustine was responsible for having Pelagius excommunicated and his views declared heretical.

Augustine, in the tradition of St Paul, was obsessed with sex and chastity. Rebelling against his own inclinations with the fanaticism of the convert, he saw chastity as purity and sex as sinful. His preoccupation with this in all his writing coloured the whole mediaeval attitude to sex in the Catholic Church. The guilt he felt over sex still influences modern lay thinking.

Rome fell to barbarian invaders in 410. This prompted Augustine to write his longest work, *The City of God*, between 413 and 427. Many of his contemporaries blamed the catastrophe on the coming of the Christian religion and the forsaking of the old gods. Augustine pointed out that Christianity had nothing to do with worldly success or failure. The City of God offered inner peace and salvation of the soul, but no material reward. What was important was the growth of the heavenly city of the spirit and the vehicle for that growth was the Church. Temporal leaders however powerful were less important than the leaders of the Church.

In that book and his other great work, *The Trinity*, he covers all his theological thought. His philosophy has had a profound influence both on the Catholic Church and his great disciple St Thomas Aquinas and, at the opposite end of the religious spectrum, the Calvinist Church. The Catholic Church and the mediaeval popes claimed that Augustine justified the primacy of the Church over the state, while Calvin was delighted to embrace his doctrine of grace, salvation and predestination.

Augustine had much reason to immerse himself in theology and the spiritual world because in his seventy sixth year the Vandals had carved their way through the crumbling Roman empire and had arrived in Africa. In 430 they laid siege to Hippo Regius, his home town. He became ill and was unable to help his people. He died during the siege and was spared the sight of the barbarians as they plundered and burnt most of the city to the ground. Somehow his precious library containing most of his books was saved.

First Black Bishop

SAMUEL CROWTHER
c.1806-1891

Bishop Samuel Ajayi Crowther was the first African bishop in the Anglican church. He was honoured mainly for his great part in establishing missions in the hinterland of Nigeria, in malaria-ridden regions where the whites feared to go.

His extraordinary life started early in the 19th century when he and his family were captured and sold as slaves only to be rescued on the high seas by a British warship which took him to Freetown. The penniless young Yoruba was then virtually adopted by the missionaries of the Church Missionary Society who trained, nurtured and then heaped responsibility on him.

He was a genuinely saintly man, with an infinite capacity for hard work. He was the first man to write a Yoruba and later a Nupe grammar and dictionary and to translate the New Testament into Yoruba.

Later in his career he was subjected to criticism for being too lax in running his episcopate, but this was as much a reflection of white jealousies and the complexities of establishing missions in the virgin bush, as it was of his own performance. He is remembered as one of the greatest missionaries the continent has known.

Samuel Ajayi Crowther had an extraordinary early life. He was born about 1806 in Oshogun village near Abeokuta, in Yoruba country, western Nigeria. His family were farmers living the slow rhythms of African rural life, raising chickens and cultivating yams.

He was only a teenager when the violent Owu civil war broke out in Yorubaland. His village was attacked and his whole family captured. They were sold by an enemy chief to the flourishing slave markets on the coast where they were bought by Portuguese slave traders.

The slave trade had been declared illegal by the British parliament in

1807 and British ships were on the high seas looking for slaving vessels. But the trade was so lucrative that the traders still thought the potential financial gain was worth the risk.

The young Ajayi, who only later took the Christian name Samuel, was still a teenager when he and the rest of his family were shackled and herded aboard the *Esperanza Feliz* for the Americas. It was intercepted by the British warship *HM Myrmidon* which freed all its slaves, repatriating them to Freetown in Sierra Leone, where they arrived on 17 June 1822.

There was no easy way home for a penniless Yoruba family, hundreds of miles from their homeland, so for some time they were forced to stay in their new country.

Ajayi, a bright and friendly lad, was adopted by a schoolmaster at the Church Missionary Society (CMS) school and soon showed himself to be a brilliant student. Within six months he had learnt to read the New Testament in English.

He was converted to Christianity and was baptised on 11 December 1825 as Samuel Crowther. He took the surname Crowther from a distinguished contemporary CMS missionary.

He impressed his mentors so much that in 1826 they sent him to England, where he went to a CMS school in London - its first-ever African pupil. He returned home in 1827, to be enrolled by the CMS for further studies at its newly founded Fourah Bay Institution. Crowther distinguished himself and eventually became a teacher, being sent to various schools in the Freetown area.

In 1841 the Society for the Extinction of the Slave Trade and the Civilisation of Africa decided to launch the British-Niger expedition. It aimed to take Christianity to the Africans up the Niger river, whose estuary had been discovered barely a decade earlier. The expedition was launched by Prince Albert who was keen to establish a model farm which could be an example to local farmers. But there was almost total ignorance of the real conditions along the mosquito-ridden river. The European missionaries died like flies (42 out of 150 in two months) and Crowther noted in his journal, "I am reluctantly led to the opinion that Africa can be chiefly benefitted by her own children."

Back at the CMS mission the Rev. J. F. Schon was so impressed with Crowther's contribution to the expedition that he recommended him for ordination. He was sent to the CMS College, in Liverpool Street, Islington. After training he was ordained as a priest on 1 October 1843. While in England he found time to publish a *Vocabulary of the Yoruba Language* and began to translate the New Testament into Yoruba. Much later, in 1864, he published his *Grammar and Vocabulary of the Nupe Language*.

He returned to Africa as a missionary and was sent to Nigeria, briefly to Badagry and then to his home in Abeokuta where he was reunited with his sisters and his mother who had since found their way home. He baptised them using his own Yoruba version of the baptismal service. He also helped the Rev. Townsend establish a Christian mission there.

He returned to England in 1851 where he took up the anti-slavery cause with members of the royal family and the British Foreign Secretary Lord Palmerston. He read the Lord's prayer, in his own Yoruba translation, to Queen Victoria and she remarked how soft and melodious it sounded. One consequence of his socialising with the cream of British society was the dispatch of another Niger expedition in 1854. Crowther surveyed the possibilities of establishing a Niger mission and persuaded a number of chiefs to give up slavery and become Christians.

In 1859 he joined the explorer Dr. W. Baikie, who was working for the trader McGregor Laird, on another expedition. He established missions at Onitsha (which was to become the great crossing point between east and west over the river Niger) and at Gbebe.

Back in Britain he was made the Bishop of Western Equatorial Africa beyond the Queen's dominions, at an impressive ceremony in Canterbury Cathedral on 29 June 1864. His consecration as the first African Anglican bishop was made despite the indignant protests of Townsend, a white missionary who thought he should have been chosen instead. Crowther was given a diocese which covered the hinterland but excluded Lagos and Abeokuta which came under the Bishop of Lagos.

As bishop he spent the rest of his life looking after his community including the new missions established up the Niger river. Other missions were established at Bonny, Brass and New Calabar.

Crowther was a charismatic evangelist and he attracted thousands to Christianity, but the administration of an ever-expanding diocese was never easy. Many chiefs defended their animist beliefs to the extent of going to war. Traders were exploiting the locals and their unpopularity was passed on to the missions.

Local white missionaries were also jealous and resentful at being directed by a black man. There were racial overtones in their criticisms of many of Crowther's missions which were staffed entirely by Africans. They also complained that he did not force his new converts to give up all their animist practices and that his discipline was lax.

Towards the end of his episcopate, the CMS, reflecting the hardening racial attitudes of the times and doubts about Africanisation, sent out a white bishop to purge the organisation.

Crowther was mortally offended and distressed, because throughout his life he had been a truly saintly man with the highest ideals, and now after a lifetime of endeavour he was under attack.

The stress caused by the hostile inquisition must have hastened his death which came in Lagos, after a severe stroke on 31 December 1891. He had completed nearly 60 years of continuous missionary work.

Prophet of Nationalism

AFRICANUS HORTON
1835-1883

Africanus Horton was one of the most exceptional Africans of the mid-19th century. He was Africa's "Renaissance man" - a medical doctor, regular soldier, botanist, geologist, buisinessman, banker, gold miner, and a distinguished author, trained to read Latin and Greek and talk English with the upper class accent of an army officer. He retired as a medical doctor in the colonial army, with the rank of Lt.Colonel after 20 years of service.

And he was also a prophet of African nationalism. Many of his books had been devoted to persuading the British to put their trust in the newly emergent generation of African intellectuals. He wanted them to rise in the professions and colonial administration and lead their countries to independence. For a period in the mid-19th century it appeared that his dreams might be fulfilled, but then came a reaction as the scramble for Africa developed and whites were imported to do the top administrative jobs.

Horton's ideas were discarded, but after two world wars and almost half a century of colonialism events unfolded much as he had forecast. He was a prophet before his time.

James Africanus Beale Horton was born on 1 June 1835 at the pretty village of Gloucester, overlooking Freetown in Sierra Leone. His father was a Creole carpenter whose family had come originally from Iboland in eastern Nigeria.

He took the name Beale from a missionary who sent him to the recently opened Church Missionary Society Grammar School, where he learnt Latin, Greek, mathematics and religious studies. At the age of 17 he was sent to Fourah Bay College where he was destined for a career in the church.

But when the British Colonial Office suddenly decided to train some doctors to go into the army (on the assumption the blacks would be more resistant to tropical diseases than the whites), Horton was selected and sent for training at Kings College, London. He got an MRCS there before going on to Edinburgh University for his MD degree.

He became one of the first black medical doctors in West Africa and was inspired by his Latin studies to adopt the name Africanus. In 1859 he wrote a thesis, *The medical topography of the West Coast of Africa, with aspects of its botany.*

The same year he returned home and was immediately commissioned as a staff-assistant surgeon, equivalent to the rank of lieutenant. He stayed in the army for the next 20 years being regularly promoted until he retired with the rank of Lt. Colonel in 1880.

He was a small man, sociable, loquacious, impatient and impulsive. He was ever active, always busy with something. His training in England and in the army gave him the manners of an English gentleman, but he remained fiercely proud of his African identity.

Towards the end of 1859 he was sent to the Gold Coast (Ghana) and by 1862 he had published *The geological constitution of Ashanti, Gold Coast,* in which he suggested that there were gold-bearing rocks in the country long before it became black Africa's leading gold producer.

He took part in the disastrous campaign against the Asante (Ashanti) in 1863-64 when thousands of soldiers of the expeditionary force died of fever and malaria without firing a single shot. He was one of the few doctors left at the camp at Pra, tending hundreds of sick men, but he received scant thanks from the army.

After the disastrous Asante campaign a parliamentary commission recommended that Britain should gradually withdraw from its West African colonies (except Sierra Leone). It also recommended that black Africans should be encouraged and trained so that "little by little the administration of the colonies should be transferred to them".

The excitement created by the commission moved Horton from dilettante academic pursuits into politics proper. He wrote a number of articles for Ferdinand Fitzgerald, the radical editor of the *African Times.* Then, in 1865, on Fitzgerald's prompting, he produced *The political economy of British West Africa,* where he developed the theme that Africans were capable of governing themselves and that Britain should prepare their nations for self-government.

In 1867 he took a year's leave in Britain. There he wrote his deepest and best-known work *West African Countries and Peoples* published in 1868. Its sub-title was *In defence of the black race.* Horton was challenging the growing tide of Victorian naturalists and anthropologists who were trying to prove scientifically that blacks were racially inferior. The traveller Richard Burton was also popularising blatantly racist theories.

Horton countered, in his book, "In the history of the world, it would be impossible to find a people (blacks) who, with so few advantages, have achieved such results in fifty years."

He called for Britain to found a medical college in West Africa and take advantage of the blacks' willingness to learn. He pleaded that Britain should train his people so they could progressively run their own affairs. His views were praised in West Africa but largely disregarded in Britain. Not one leading British newspaper reviewed his works.

From 1868-71 Horton became an unofficial adviser to the Fanti Confederation in southern Ghana. Britain was reeling from the effects of the Asante campaign and was considering withdrawing from the coast. The Dutch actually did so, giving up their forts in 1871.

The Fanti and Ga thought they could take advantage and asked Horton to help them set up new self-governing republics. He also halted a violent attack of smallpox by forcibly vaccinating two old chiefs and compelling their people to follow suit. He was warmly congratulated and rewarded for his diligence by the Colonial Secretary! In an administration where senior ranks were almost entirely white, he was made the civil commandant of Sekondi fort.

His fortunes changed when he was blamed for a violent outbreak of warfare between two chiefs. Jealous white civil servants put the blame on him for mishandling the crisis.

The Asante attempt to regain the forts which the Dutch had abandoned on the coast provoked another Asante war in 1873. Sir Garnet Wolseley led the West Indian Regiment inland on a punitive expedition (see Prempeh I). Horton was ill with bronchitis at the beginning of the campaign and when he caught up with the expedition, he found that many of the soldiers were dying of disease as in the 1863/64 campaign. Horton once again tried to salvage the casualties of a colonial war, by assuming responsibility for most of the sick men, but he received no recognition for his painful work.

The Asante campaign was symptomatic of a change of thinking that was sweeping Africa. In the middle period of Horton's life, until the mid-1870's there had been a period of hope in which the colonial powers adopted non-racist attitudes, were keen to train Africans for responsible posts and were even considering withdrawing from West Africa. Hopes soared among the educated Africans particularly the Creoles of Sierra Leone who had produced a new crop of doctors, lawyers, teachers and administrators.

But gradually the climate changed. White civil servants wanted to guard their positions against the new wave of professionally trained Africans. Racism and the colour bar became institutionalised, while politically the European powers began to compete to occupy and hold the best parts of Africa.

Horton saw his Fanti and Ga friends lose their hopes of sovereignty and became disillusioned with politics. He was promoted to surgeon major, but saw little hope of further military advancement as he drew near to retiring age. He spent most of his time in Cape Coast where he developed a thriving private practice alongside his military duties.

He continued to write. In 1874 he published *Diseases of Tropical*

Climates and their Treatment. It was a thorough and practical work which soon went into a second edition despite his bizarre theory that malaria was caused by an excess of ozone. (It was two decades later that the blame was laid correctly on mosquitoes).

In 1875 he returned home and set himself up in a comfortable mansion which he called Horton Hall in Gloucester Street, Freetown. There he was the star of high society, entertaining lavishly.

He remained ceaselessly industrious, devoting his working hours to indentifying and taking out claims on potential gold-bearing areas. This he turned to good profit. Then, as there was no bank in Sierra Leone, he helped create one, the Commercial Bank of West Africa, which opened on 15 January 1883 in Freetown.

But his health was failing and he went to London for 14 months for treatment and recuperation in a healthier climate. He returned to Freetown and died shortly afterwards on 15 October 1883.

Few of his business activities survived long after his death. The bank was wound up and his gold claims came to nothing. His medical theories were overtaken. And politically all his ideas were reversed as the colonial powers tightened their grip, imported white administrators and blocked African advancement.

All Horton's dreams of the optimistic mid-19th century appeared to be reversed, but he was to be proved a prophet before his time.

After almost half a century of colonialism and two world wars, African nationalism began to surge. The colonial powers provided money for education and appointed educated Africans to top posts. The universities and particularly the medical schools, that he had asked for, were established. By 1957, his beloved Ghana was the first country to gain its independence in the new era.

The Smiling Slave Trader

TIPPU TIB
c.1830-1905

Tippu Tib came from mixed Arab African parentage and acquired the reputation as the most notorious slave and ivory trader in African history. At one stage he ruled a huge territory west of Lake Tanganyika and south of the Congo rain forest where his word was law and he built a huge personal fortune.

A tall, smiling, dark-skinned man of immense charm, he was also cunning and ruthless. His intelligence and drive was recognised by Henry Stanley and other European explorers, who used him in furthering their aims. Finally he was caught in the wave of European expansionism which marked the scramble for Africa. He was forced to abandon his kingdom to the newly-founded Congo Free State and retire to Zanzibar.

Tippu Tib's real name was Hamed bin Muhammed el Murjebi. He got the nickname Tippu Tib from the sound his guns made in the African bush, when his troops attacked. He was born in Zanzibar, son of an African-Arab father Muhammed bin Juma and an African mother from the Mrima people.

His grandfather had been an Omani merchant from Muscat, trading along the East African coast. Like the Sultan of Oman, who had moved his capital to Zanzibar in 1840, his grandfather also emigrated permanently to the island and set up clove plantations.

Tippu's father had been still more adventurous and determined to build a family fortune by sending out expeditions into the interior to trade in slaves and ivory. The Europeans had long since abolished the slave trade, but it continued to flourish in the African hinterland, Zanzibar and in all parts of Arabia.

Africans were also needed as porters for ivory which was readily available from the elephant herds wandering throughout East and Central Africa.

Tippu, a tall handsome lad with great charm and a slight nervous tick round his eyes, was only 16 when he went on his first expedition with his father into Tanzania, as it is called today. Two years later he was leading his own expeditions into the interior and acquiring a reputation as a bold and ruthless trader. Finding Tanzania stripped of ivory and its people wary of the slave traders, he built canoes out of local trees and crossed Lake Tanganyika.

West of the lake he was virtually unchallenged by other traders and gradually established a large area that he could dominate with his trained soldiers armed with muzzle-loading guns. He extended his rule over the local chiefs using a mixture of charm, guile, bargaining and force. Advancing into Tabwa territory in 1867, he overthrew Chief Nsama, despite his reputation for having cheated and killed other Arab traders. He captured a huge store of ivory from him which he sent back to the coast, in exchange for guns and equipment. Two years later he advanced into East Lunda territory and defeated Mwonga Nzemba.

Ever searching for untapped sources of ivory, he pushed north-west into lands where no Arabs had ever been. He tricked one ageing chief into thinking that he was the grandson of a long-lost sister and persuaded the old man to abdicate in his favour.

So effectively did he extend his power west of Lake Tanganyika that the other Arab traders at Kasongo and Nyangwe, on the Lulaba river recognised him in 1874 as their governor. Kasongo became the capital of a huge trading area which stretched northwards and westwards from Lake Tanganyika to the Congo rain forests. He and the vassals he appointed, ruled this huge area that he had carved out of the very heart of Africa. He had at least 15 members of his family helping him to control a territory which extended as far north as the Stanley Falls on the Congo river.

Until the whites came he was unchallenged. In 1876 the British explorer Henry Morton Stanley arrived at Tippu's headquarters and asked him for his help with his expedition down the Congo river.

Tippu received Stanley with his usual charm and courtesy and Stanley wrote later, "I soon came to the conclusion that this Arab was a remarkable man..." Stanley showed him his first repeating rifle and revolver which amazed him and made him very envious.

Stanley offered him 5,000 dollars if he would accompany him for 60 days march with 200 of his soldiers. Tippu kept his side of the bargain and ensured the success of the great expedition.

But by 1883 Stanley was back as the agent of King Leopold of Belgium. He established a post at Stanley Falls and told Tippu that he must restrict his activities to the area south of the new garrison.

By then the European scramble for Africa was at its most intense. In 1885 King Leopold was recognised as the personal ruler of the newly created Congo Free State. Tippu understood that he was under threat. He recaptured the inadequately garrisoned Stanley Falls in 1886 but was worried that he would not be able to hold it permanently.

In 1887 he met Stanley again, this time when he was visiting Zanzibar. Stanley conceived the brilliant compromise of confirming

Tippu as the governor of Stanley Falls on behalf of King Leopold, with a number of minor Arab traders under him.

The deal provoked criticism of all concerned. Stanley and Leopold were accused of empowering a notorious slave trader, while the other Arab traders accused Tippu of selling out to the Europeans.

As Tippu tried to curb slave trading and the Belgians mounted expeditions to take control in the area, there were frequent clashes between Tippu and those who opposed him. A second expedition by Stanley complained that it had not received the help from Tippu that had been promised.

By 1890 Tippu, then approaching 60 years old, had had enough of the insecure frontier life. In 1890 he retired to Zanzibar leaving a nephew in charge of Stanley Falls. In his absence the local Africans backed by the Belgians, rose against Arab rule and for 18 months fought a war of liberation, which broke Arab power and paved the way for even worse government by the representatives of King Leopold.

Tippu remained in Zanzibar, listening unhappily to the sad tales coming from the vast empire where he once ruled supreme. He died in 1905.

A Prophet Spurned

EDWARD BLYDEN
1832-1912

Edward Blyden lived a long and tempestuous life, quarrelling incessantly with his contemporaries in his adopted country, Liberia, but gradually building his reputation as an outstanding thinker and writer. He was an early pan-Africanist, determined to encourage black immigration from the New World "back to Africa." He failed to achieve much because in Liberia he was always viewed with suspicion by the mulattoe ruling class. Nor did he get his message across to the American blacks, though he did have some limited success in encouraging West Indian immigration. He wanted a West African University and political unification between neighbouring countries, but these ideals remained unrealised.

He rebelled against the classical mission education of which he was a shining exemplar, as professor of Greek and Latin and a pastor in the Presbyterian church. Over the years he came to the conclusion that Islam was closer to the African culture than Christianity. He made a speech in the assembly hall in Breadfruit Street, Lagos that lead to the establishment of the first schismatic African church.

Yet he was a curious personality, an Anglophile who enjoyed a number of ambassadorships to Britain. He carried on a long correspondence with Gladstone and Lord Henry Brougham. He was a champion of the native Africans against the immigrants, yet he always wanted more immigration. He was a prophet spurned in his own house yet famed in the world outside.

Edward Wilmot Blyden was born on 3 August 1832, in Charlotte-Amalie, the capital of St Thomas, one of the Virgin Islands in the West Indies. His parents were born on the island but came originally from Nigeria. His father was a tailor and his mother a teacher, who took a particular interest in his early education.

He was only ten years old when his extraordinary career began with his whole family moving to Venezuela. They stayed there for only two years but it was long enough for the young Edward to become fluent in Spanish. Later he extended his aptitude for languages to Latin, Greek, Hebrew and French.

His family were members of the Dutch Reformed Church and in 1849 Blyden decided to become a pastor. He went to the USA and tried to get into three different theological colleges but was rejected every time because he was black.

This discrimination against the young idealist who wanted to respond to the call of God, had a profound effect on him. He left the USA and resolved to start his life afresh in Liberia, the land of the emancipated slaves. He sailed from Baltimore in December 1850 arriving in Monrovia on 26 January 1851.

Almost immediately he succumbed to coast fever (probably aggravated malaria). When he recovered he continued his education at the Presbyterian school while working in his spare time as a clerk for a local merchant.

In 1854 he became teacher at the Alexander High School. He was an intelligent young man of boundless energy, full of creative ideas. He became a lay preacher in the best Liberian rhetorical tradition and joined the Liberian militia which was sent into the interior to pacify the indigenous Vai people.

This was his first contact with the African people of the hinterland and it had a profound effect on him. He responded much more readily to the native African with his unspoilt dignity and honour, than to the class and colour conscious society in the Monrovia enclave where he lived.

But he was successful in the narrow settler society too. In 1855 President Roberts appointed him the editor of the *Liberia Herald*. He held the post for a year while he worked on his first major political pamphlet, *A Voice from Bleeding Africa on Behalf of her Exiled Children*. Its aims were to boost the morale and restore the dignity and confidence of black Africans.

In his lifetime he wrote hundreds of articles and dozens of pamphlets that show him to have been one of the outstanding black intellectuals of his age. At the outset he was steeped in Christianity. He had received a mission education and was still a preacher and strong believer in God, but as time went on he came to the view that Islam with its universal pragmatism and simple message was more appropriate to black Africa than Christianity as taught from on high by the missionaries. He felt that the Islamic culture was more suited to the African personality.

In 1861, still not 30 years old, he was made a professor of Greek and Latin at the newly established Liberia College. His passionate interest in black education earned him the post of Commissioner of Education to Britain and the USA. He visited both countries where he studied modern education and tried to raise funds for the establishment of local schools and scholarships. He was offered two scholarships to Edinburgh University for his pupils but declined a full-time scholarship for himself in England.

Another of his objectives was to encourage the maximum black immigration from the US to Liberia. He offered free passage to black emigrants, but was largely ignored despite the outbreak of the American Civil War in 1861, which should have been an added incentive for blacks to emigrate.

He made a second trip to America in 1862 to peddle the attractions of a new life in a free country, but few American responded. Though Liberia was the land of the freed slaves, the Americans knew that the settlers were struggling to survive in a hostile environment. In the years between 1820-1865 only 15,000 new US immigrants arrived in the country. Blyden was forced to return to Liberia as the US civil war gathered momentum.

He was made President of Liberia College in 1862, a post he held until 1871.

In 1864 Blyden was appointed Secretary of State by the black President Stephen Benson. His colour was important as Blyden had become a champion of the blacks against the coloureds or mulattoes, as they were then called. Blyden who had been kept at arms-length by the ruling mulattoe families in Monrovia let this colour his whole attitude to race. He persuaded the American Colonisation Society to ask prospective immigrants to declare whether they were dark or light coloured in an attempt to keep further mulattoes out. Some mocked him when filling in their immigration forms, by declaring that they were "Ginger".

He held the position of Secretary of State for only two years in the face of the growing hostility from the backbiting ruling caste. But during that time he promoted the immigration of several hundred skilled blacks from Barbados, offering them each 25 acres of land. Among those who responded was one of Liberia's most illustrious future presidents, Arthur Barclay. But the immigration scheme collapsed and he was dropped as Secretary of State in 1866, having been accused of giving ground to Britain over a boundary dispute with Sierra Leone. He was also told that he could not hold a ministry at the same time as the Presidency of Liberia College. These flimsy excuses for his dismissal came after a long campaign by the mulattoes to remove him from power.

In May 1866 he went abroad to England, Gibraltar, Malta, Lebanon and Syria where he studied Arabic at the Syrian Protestant College. He returned home flushed with the idea that Arabic should be taught in Liberian schools to encourage future better relations with Muslim countries.

Edward Roye (q.v.), a like-minded soul, became President in 1869, and Blyden became a close adviser. Roye had ambitious plans for the advancement and development of the African peoples of the hinterland. Roye was an African-American and ran into the same class and race snobbery as Blyden. The families that had ruled Liberia unchallenged since its independence in 1847 and were mostly of the Republican party were determined to bring Roye and his True Whig Party down. The factions fought it out in the streets in October 1871. The thugs opposed to black advancement tried to set fire to Roye's house and Blyden was almost lynched in the confusion. Roye was finally forced out of office on 26 October and imprisoned pending impeachment, while Blyden was forced to flee to Sierra Leone. The most curious criticism directed against him was the accusation (by his opponents not by Roye) that he had committed adultery with Roye's wife.

Blyden took refuge in Sierra Leone where he was immediately given a job by the British colonial authorities. He became editor of the *Negro* newspaper and was sent on several missions to establish good relations with the people of the interior.

He returned to Liberia in 1873 where he found President J. J. Roberts doing another term of office (after the mysterious death of his friend Roye). The Republican Roberts thought sufficiently highly of him to offer him the post of Secretary of State, but Blyden did not want to get involved. Instead he went back to the USA where he was granted an honorary degree by Lincoln University, Pennsylvania.

He returned to become principal of the Alexander High School until he was appointed ambassador to Britain in 1877. Though the legislature tried to stop his appointment by denying him funds he went to England anyway. There he was granted honorary membership of the Athaneum club in recognition of his extensive written works.

He was recalled in 1878 and re-appointed President of Liberia College. He planned to transform the college into an institution that could attract blacks from all over the world. But when he was again offered a government post as Minister of the Interior in 1880, he accepted.

Here he had to tackle the border question with Sierra Leone once again and when he came up with the plan to cede part of the north-western corner of the country to the British, the Senate refused ratification. This unleashed another round of vilification and accusations that he was being soft because he had been granted refuge in Sierra Leone earlier. He was again forced out of office in 1882.

During this period his writing flourished and his reputation spread in the black world. He was made a fellow of the American Philological Association and received another honorary degree from Lincoln University. He returned to the USA to try to raise further funds for educational projects.

He returned to Liberia College in June 1883 to find that a new generation was ready to revive old quarrels. This time the new President supported the clique that opposed him and he was forced to resign.

He became Vice-President of the American Colonisation Society in 1884 and in 1895 stood for the presidency as the nominee for the Republican Party though it contained many mulattoes who considered him to be a racist. It was a tough campaign in which he did not get wholehearted support from his own party and he lost narrowly.

He moved to Sierra Leone and developed his ideas further on the relationship between Christianity and Islam. He came to the conclusion that Christianity had blocked African advancement and resigned his ministry in the Presbyterian church. In 1887 he published a major book entitled *Christianity, Islam and the Negro race*; it was widely acclaimed and he was made an honorary member of the American Society of Comparative Religion in 1889.

In 1891 he visited Nigeria and gave an address to a crowded audience in the assembly hall of Breadfruit Street, Lagos where he emphasised the incompatibility of the Christian Church and African society. This led to the formation of the United Native African Church, the first to break away from the mainstream churches. More schisms followed.

Blyden's energy was irrepressible. He returned home to be reappointed ambassador to Britain in 1892. There he struggled to win British support for Liberian independence against those who wanted to take it into the rapidly developing British Empire.

In 1896, always willing to take on a new challenge, he became Agent for Local Affairs in Lagos where he established a Muslim school teaching a secular English education. By 1900 previous quarrels were set aside and he was welcomed back to the Liberia College to assume his professorship of classics once again.

By 1905, mature and mellowing, he was appointed by the young President Barclay as ambassador extraordinary to London and Paris, where a major task was to negotiate a boundary with French West Africa. To preserve Liberia's independence he decided to offer Britain and France economic and political representation in Liberia, but again he went too far for the Liberian government who recalled him in 1905.

Blyden was always too opinionated and pushy to settle down in his chosen country and after this final disappointment he moved back to Sierra Leone to live there for the remainder of his life.

He died in Freetown on 7 February 1912. He was almost 80 years old. Despite his tempestuous relationship with his Liberian countrymen his international reputation had grown steadily. In the narrow Liberian context he had been frustrated, but the black world had honoured him as an outstanding thinker of his time.

CENTRAL AFRICA: 19th CENTURY

Sokoto

Lake Ch[...]

BORNU

0   km   1000

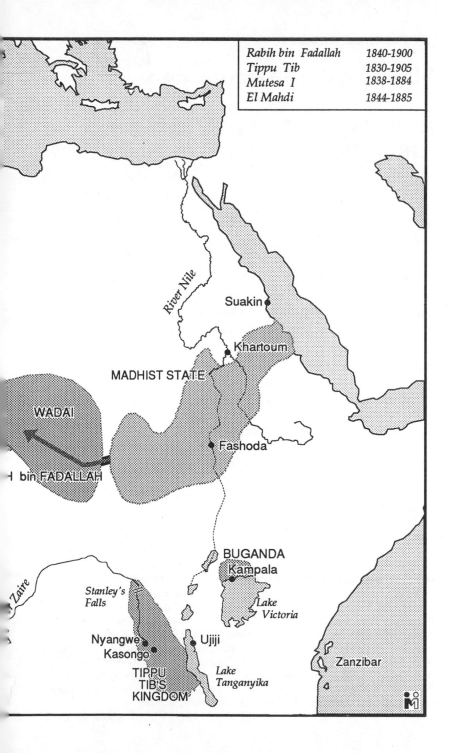

Rabih bin Fadallah	1840-1900
Tippu Tib	1830-1905
Mutesa I	1838-1884
El Mahdi	1844-1885

River Nile

Suakin

Khartoum

MADHIST STATE

WADAI

bin FADALLAH

Fashoda

BUGANDA

Kampala

Stanley's Falls

Lake Victoria

Nyangwe

Ujiji

Kasongo

Zanzibar

TIPPU TIB'S KINGDOM

Lake Tanganyika

River Zaire

Slave Trader Extraordinary

RABIH bin FADALLAH
c.1840-1900

Africa has had many extraordinary sons but few were more extraordinary than Rabih bin Fadallah, sometimes known as Rabah, or Rabah Zobeir.

He could be described as the first Chadian warlord, a slave trader, a notorious thug but he had the courage, drive and energy to take on the British and French at the height of imperial power at the end of the 19th century.

He challenged the British both in Sudan and in Nigeria and the French in Equatorial Africa. He also tangled with powerful African kingdoms like Wadai, Baguirmi and Bornu. The range of his activity was vast. He became the master of a huge territory at the very centre of the African continent.

Rabih bin Fadallah was born at Halfaya, north of Khartoum around 1840. He was half Arab, half Black and a slave. Maybe he was the illegitimate son of Zobeir Rahmat el-Mansur Pasha, who took him as his adopted son at an early age.

Zobeir was interesting enough in his own right. He is described as the "greatest slave trader who ever existed", certainly one of the most energetic and intelligent men in that reviled profession. He was known as the Tippu Tib (q.v.) of Sudan. His distinguished appearance and polished manners belied his cruel trade in humans and ivory.

Egypt under the Ottoman Khedives had declared its rule over the Sudan in 1841 and was still struggling to maintain control, while the British in their turn were trying to preserve their influence over Egypt, Sudan and the vital trade route through the Red Sea to the Indies.

Zobeir wanted to exploit the flourishing slave trade in the huge semi-desert wilderness of western Sudan. He had to compete with hundreds of other slave traders but there was little resistance from the Egyptian military garrisons which were hundreds of miles apart, conniving at the slaving that went on around them anyway.

Zobeir had under his command about 12,000 black slave soldiers, called *bazinqirs*, armed with modern rifles. He made himself the undisputed ruler of Bahr el Gazal province. In 1869 the Egyptians sent an expedition to restore control. Zobeir attacked, killed its commander and totally defeated the column. Later the Egyptians confirmed him as *de facto* ruler of the province and even made him a pasha. In 1873 with the backing of the Egyptians he attacked and conquered the ever wild and lawless province of Darfur to the north-west.

By this time Rabih, who was in his late twenties, had transferred from the Egyptian army to become a commander of Zobeir's *bazinqirs*, and was already well-versed in fighting in the desert and in making money out of slave trading.

Zobeir went to Cairo in the spring of 1876 to persuade the Khedive to give him a firman confirming him as Governor General of Darfur, but instead the duplicitous ruler forbade him to return and forced him to stay in Egypt.

His son Suleiman continued to rule in Darfur and Rabih remained an important commander of the *bazinqirs*. Suleiman's ambivalent relationship with the Egyptians persisted. He was confirmed as ruler of Darfur but, with the encouragement of his still exiled father, he wanted to extend his control to Bahr el Gazal.

This brought him in direct conflict for the first time with General Charles Gordon who had been installed by the Egyptians as Governor General of Khartoum. Gordon did not want a slave trader in control of one of Sudan's most important provinces. He sent the Italian Romolo Gessi to assert his authority. After a long campaign and a series of pitched battles Romolo finally ambushed Sulieman in 1879 and put him to death along with most of his leading commanders. But not Rabih who escaped.

In July 1879 he fled westwards taking with him 700 dispirited, demoralised *bazinqirs*, still smarting from their many defeats. The years under Zobeir and Suleiman had not been wasted. Rabih soon established his own chieftaincy in Kreich and Dar Banda south-west of the kingdom of Wadai, far into Equatorial Africa at the heart of the continent.

He resolved to set up his own personal empire where slave trading would make him rich. For the next 20 years he worked to make this ambition succeed.

One of the first places he conquered was Dar Kouti, currently within the Central African Republic, then a tributary state to the Wadai kingdom. There he began his empire building by appointing his own man Mohammad es-Senoussi, of rival lineage to the Wadai kings, as sultan of the region. Dar Kouti became an important caravan stop on the slave and ivory routes and for pilgrims on the way to Mecca.

His rivalry with the Wadai sultans continued in the 1880s as he gradually gained the allegiance of other tributary rulers in what is today the Sara region of Chad. His warrior force of footsoldiers and horsemen were always on the move, ranging far and wide through central Africa, seldom occupying any area on a permanent basis. His men did substantial trade with surrounding peoples but mostly lived off the land.

Rabih lived at the time when the Mahdi had suddenly materialised out of the sands of the Sudan waving the banner of Muslim irredentism. Rabih was asked to join the holy war, but his interests remained the conquest of central Africa financed by slave trading. Briefly he ordered his troops to wear the Mahdist *jibbeh* (cloth) - with square patches sewn on it as a symbol of poverty. He also sometimes declared that his conquests were in the name of the Mahdi, but his personal interests lay elsewhere.

Rabih was carving out his empire at the time the French too had major ambitions in the area. The scramble for Africa was at its zenith and France which had already subjugated a large part of West Africa was now determined to repeat the process in Equatorial Africa. At the time France even contemplated the possibility of thwarting the British in Sudan and the Nile basin.

An early French expedition in 1891 under the soldier/explorer Paul Crampel reached Dar Kouti, where it was annihilated by Mohammed Sanoussi on the banks of the Diangara river. Crampel was assassinated. This setback did not extinguish French ambitions. The conquest of Equatorial Africa remained an imperial objective.

Meanwhile, in 1892, Rabih decided to bypass the obdurate Wadai kingdom and attack the weaker Baguirmi state to the south-east which he defeated with ease. He then pushed into the Chari and Logone river regions repulsing another attack from Wadai.

Rabih used his Mahdist pretensions to secure an alliance with the Hayatu the Emir of Sokoto, who had earlier raised the Mahdist banner of revolt against the Caliph (Sultan) of Sokoto. Rabih married his daughter to Hayatu. Having secured his western flank he then challenged the Empire of Bornu. In a series of engagements he conquered the Shehu of Bornu, ruthlessly pillaging his capital Kukawa in 1893.

Rabih then let his army loose in Bornu, plundering, pillaging and massacring innocent civilians and creating a reign of terror that rebounded on him. The brutalities of his troops damaged the whole trading empire that he had painfully constructed and severed the valuable caravan routes through the very centre of Africa.

Then in his fifties he was probably at the peak of his powers, living in relative luxury in semi-permanent camps with tents of rich cloth among the wooden buildings.

His force of a few hundred men which came with him when he left Darfur in 1879 increased to 20,000, 5,000 of them armed with the new repeating rifles. These had been imported across the Sahara from Tripoli down the Fezzan caravan trails.

At one stage Rabih's old master, Zobeir, then living in Egypt under British occupation, tried to persuade Rabih to befriend the British as protection against the French. Rabih resolutely refused.

But he traded with Sir George Goldie's Royal Niger Company (RNC) that was pushing up the Benue river. The RNC was keen to trade anything except arms and gunpowder, so Rabih, who was always short of ammunition, managed to get supplies of these "banned" munitions from various Nigerian sub-chiefs. They in turn purchased them from the British, often from the RNC.

Rabih clashed with the British because he hoped to extend his sway over the Sultan of Sokoto who still blocked his route to Kano. But the RNC secured the Benue river first and drew the minor chiefs in the area under its umbrella. In 1897 the RNC planned to attack Rabih but the scheme never came to fruition.

A far more direct challenge came from the French, still determined to link the Atlantic to the Indian Ocean. Yet another expedition pushed north-eastwards towards Rabih's heartland in 1896-98. The historically famous Fashoda incident occurred when a small company under Commandant Marchand finally made it to Fashoda in Sudan. There he was forced to back down when faced with a far superior force under General Kitchener that had advanced from Egypt.

Rabih defeated another French force in 1899 and killed its leader, the naval Lieutenant Brettonet, on the Shari river. But the French persisted with a three-pronged attack on the man who thwarted their hope of progress towards the east. Three expeditions from the Congo, Senegal and Algeria all pushed towards Lake Chad. Rabih fought many inconclusive battles until his army of about 5,000 troops met the united forces of the three French expeditions at Kousseri on 22 April 1900.

In a fierce engagement the French commander Major Lamy was killed and so was Rabih himself. Rabih's reputation for slipping out of the tightest crisis was such that the Senegalese soldier who killed him, cut off his head and carried it to the French camp to show that he was dead.

The man who had terrorised the heart of Africa for more than two decades was finally dead.

Idolised by some as a hero of the anti-colonial struggle, he was dismissed by others as nothing but a brutal warlord and slave trader. Both interpretations are equally true. A former slave had risen to a position in which he defied the challenge of the two leading imperial powers at the height of their expansionism and had reduced several established African kingdoms to subservience.

After his death, his sons fought on against the French and for several years more carried on the slaving business in Equatorial Africa.

Even the warlords that have fought over Chad since independence in 1960, behave in the warrior tradition established by Rabih a century ago.

Prince of Harmony

JAMES KWEGYIR AGGREY
1875-1927

Unlike most other personalities in this book, James Aggrey was not a politician or ruler, but he was a great human being, living at a time when race relations was becoming a crucial issue throughout the world. His radical African critics accused him of not being prepared to fight and confront colonialism, but he worked in areas such as education where cooperation was necessary for African advancement. He was a prince of racial harmony, not a political nationalist.

Though he lived in the USA for the greater part of his life, his fame is mainly connected to the work he did for the Phelps-Stokes Foundation which wanted to reform education throughout Africa and for the part he played in the foundation of Achimota University, in his home country, the Gold Coast.

He was once described as "a perfect avalanche of personality, with extraordinary charisma, charm, and energy." A natural orator and preacher who never needed notes, he could have a hostile gathering eating out of the palm of his hands within a few moments. Always true to his character and his message of racial harmony, he won love and respect throughout the world.

James Emman Kwegyir Aggrey was born on Monday 18 October 1875, at Anamabu in the Gold Coast, into a royal Fanti family. His father Kodwo Kwegyir worked as the spokesman (linguist) for the Chief of Anamabu and was involved in many of the 19th century wars between the Ashanti and the Fanti. He also worked for the merchants whose trade was concentrated around Cape Coast, as a "gold taker" assessing the purity and value of gold dust which was used as common currency.

Aggrey was the fourth of eight children by his father's third wife. He was baptised at the age of eight and sent to the newly founded Cape Coast Methodist School where he fell under the influence of the Reverend

Dennis Kemp. The young Aggrey was to play a major part in converting his father and the whole family to Christianity. At the age of 15 Kemp put him in charge of a class of almost 40 boys at Dunkwa village school.

In 1892 he went back to the Cape Coast Methodist School as a teacher while continuously studying to improve his own education.

In 1896 he briefly followed in his father's footsteps becoming an interpreter attached to the Telegraph corps of the expeditionary force in the seventh Ashanti "war", where not a single shot was fired in anger and King Prempeh finally bowed to British rule.

On his return he learnt printing and became a compositor and sub-editor of the *Methodist Times*. He also helped in translating the Bible into Fanti while continuing with his teaching. In 1898 he had hardly been appointed headmaster of his old school when he was called to America.

He had been given a scholarship by the African Methodist Episcopal Zion church to be trained at Livingstone College, Salisbury, North Carolina. The aim was that he would return and open a mission in the Gold Coast, but he was to stay in America for the next 22 years.

He graduated from Livingstone in 1902 with a BA, coming head of his class. He won a gold medal for English composition and delivered a salutatory speech in Latin. Earlier he had delivered the first Greek oration ever heard at the college.

The Zion church wanted him to return to the Gold Coast for mission work but his reputation had grown so strongly in America that he was finally persuaded to stay on at Livingstone as registrar/professor, later becoming the financial secretary.

In November 1903 he was ordained as a minister in the Zion Episcopal Methodist Church. In his vacations he continued his own studies at Columbia University, New York and by 1905 he was invited to run his own classes. In the same year he married Rosebud Douglass an African-American who hailed from Portsmouth, Virginia.

In 1912 he was awarded an honorary doctorate of divinity at Hood Theological College, where he had been studying. In 1914 he returned to Columbia to do successive summer courses studying sociology and education where he matriculated in 1918.

By this time Aggrey's reputation was expanding fast. He was a brilliant lecturer and preacher - back in Livingstone he preached regularly at two churches which were under his charge. He was seriously considered for the presidency of Livingstone College but was finally turned down on the grounds of his nationality.

In 1920 he got the chance to return to his beloved Africa. He was invited by the Phelps-Stokes Trustees to join a commission of inquiry that was to investigate the educational system in Africa and suggest improvements. An earlier commission had examined Negro education in the US, but this was to be the first in Africa. It would be fully backed by missions, educational institutions and the British government.

Dr. Jesse Jones, who had headed the earlier Negro commission, insisted that Aggrey should be a member. Aggrey was the only black on the commission which was to profoundly change education in Africa. He had all the necessary attributes - immense enthusiasm for his continent, the knack of motivating people and the gift of spontaneous oratory.

He set sail from New York on 3 July 1920 first visiting Britain then going on to Sierra Leone, Liberia, the Gold Coast, Nigeria, Congo, Angola and South Africa.

He was immensely popular everywhere he went, preaching his message of racial harmony while looking hard at the practical needs of education in Africa which had previously been moulded entirely in the white colonial tradition. Though Aggrey had himself been brought up studying Greek and Latin, he soon saw that Africa also needed more teaching in vernacular languages and technical education particularly in agriculture, handicrafts and hygiene.

He also championed the cause of women's education. One of his oft repeated aphorisms was, "If you educate a man you educate an individual, if you educate a woman you educate a family."

In Angola he was shocked by the Portuguese system which used undernourished children as forced labour. In South Africa he persuaded the Native Welfare Societies to open their doors to African membership for the first time (previously the organisation of the societies was entirely in white hands).

He returned to the US to continue his studies but was soon recruited on another Phelps-Stokes commission to Eastern Africa. On 25 January 1924 he sailed from the US on the second commission this time visiting Ethiopia, Kenya, Tanganyika, Uganda, Northern and Southern Rhodesia, Nyasaland and again South Africa.

Everywhere he talked and preached, he drew huge crowds. In Uganda he delivered the sermon at the Anglican cathedral, Namirembe and a huge multitude saw him off on Lake Victoria.

He was so constructively persuasive that the British Governor of Tanganyika said that he would rather have Aggrey on his staff than a whole regiment of soldiers.

At South Africa's Stellenbosch University he addressed a meeting of Afrikaner students - at first the atmosphere was icy but soon he had them eating out of his hands as he preached his message of racial harmony. He was offered a professorship in sociology at Fort Hare University. This greatly tempted him before he decided to concentrate his efforts elsewhere.

He hastened to the Gold Coast to take part in the foundation of Achimota College, a great new educational institution that was to become the country's leading university. Aggrey was recruited as first member of the staff and assistant vice-principal - the rest of the staff was almost entirely white and mostly recruited in Britain. He would have become vice-principal if he had more administrative application and ability.

One of Aggrey's most frequently repeated maxims was that one could play a tune on the white keys of the piano, or on the black keys, but for perfect harmony both were needed. When he was asked to suggest a crest for Achimota he picked up this message and a shield was designed showing black and white piano keys.

The concept of Achimota had been under attack by African militants who complained that it should not have started as an institutution of general education but should have become a university straight away. They also resented the fact that Africans were under-represented.

Aggrey and the enlightened Gold Coast Governor, Sir Gordon Guggisberg, thought otherwise, but they were nevertheless relieved when thousands travelled from all over the country and the world outside for the opening ceremony.

Aggrey was exhausted after his exertions on behalf of Achimota and travelled to Britain and on to the USA to visit his family. He also wanted to complete a thesis on British relations with Africa, for presentation at Columbia University for his PhD.

He wrote the notes for the preface to the work, which was to become his first book, on the S.S. *Mauretania* on the way there.

He found a room in Harlem and began his studies when suddenly he fell seriously ill. He was rushed, too late, to Harlem hospital. He died of meningitis on 30 July 1927. A great life was still unfulfilled.

Chorus of Approval

SAMUEL COLERIDGE-TAYLOR
1875-1912

Samuel Coleridge-Taylor was an African composer who took the musical establishment of Victorian Britain by storm. While still in his early twenties the boy genius composed his greatest work *Hiawatha* in 1898, which packed concert halls throughout Britain. His light, cheerful music was entirely in the European musical idiom and fired the imagination of his packed audiences, who were astounded that a black man could be so brilliant. Some critics place him as the greatest composer since Elgar, others go further and say he was the greatest concert hall composer to emerge from Britain for 200 years.

He travelled frequently to the USA where he tried to reflect the suffering and dignity of his fellow blacks in his later works. He tried to evolve a distinctive black music in his *Twenty Four Negro Melodies* and his *Danse Negre*. By the time of his premature death at 37, he had written 82 major opuses many of which are still performed regularly by choirs and orchestras today.

Samuel Coleridge-Taylor was born on 15 August 1875, at 15 Theobalds Road, Clerkenwell, London. His father Daniel Hughes Taylor was a physician. He had taken his medical studies at the Royal College of Physicians and worked later with a British doctor in general practice in London, where he treated Britons of all social classes and income groups.

Early in his career Dr Taylor found that the small number of educated blacks in Britain were accepted, indeed they were in demand for their exotic novelty value, but towards the end of the Victorian era, as imperialism reached its peak, race prejudice became more common.

When he moved his family to Croydon and set up on his own as a doctor, he found the locals did not like being treated by a black. He became the frequent target of racial scorn and eventually decided he could take it no longer. He left for home in Sierra Leone, leaving his English wife and young child behind.

His mother who was not rich enough to give him a fancy education, sent him to the local school - St George's, Croydon. There, as the only black child in the school, he was teased mercilessly. His schoolmates called him "Coaley" for obvious reasons and he became the subject of many nasty pranks. One child tried to set fire to his hair, to see if African hair would burn.

Jacob Beckwith, the music teacher, found that he was so musically gifted and keen to learn that he encouraged him to sing in the choir and take up the violin. He had abundant talent and was soon playing the instrument with feeling and technical skill.

Beckwith gave him extra lessons free of charge, but could not help him financially to advance his career. His mother apprenticed him for some time to a piano tuner, hoping that this would provide an income while furthering his musical career.

Beckwith brought him to the attention of Herbert Waters, a wealthy and philanthrophically minded retired Colonel and local choirmaster, who immediately appreciated his talent. He offered to pay for his further musical education despite warnings from some friends that "negroid brains" could not develop beyond a certain stage.

Waters ignored this anthropological advice and set about persuading Charles Groves the director of the Royal College of Music to admit him. Even Groves felt that his race would prevent him reaching the musical heights, but eventually Waters persuaded him that the young man was worth a chance. Samuel was admitted in the Christmas term 1890, to learn piano and the violin. It was to be the start of a brilliant career.

He was placed under the tuition of Sir Charles Villiers Stanford who soon found that he had a most promising pupil. Under his careful guidance a natural talent was encouraged to flower.

In 1890, Samuel abandoned the violin and devoted himself to full time composition. He set himself the highest standards. Any composition that he considered to be less than the very best was torn up and burnt. His friends often remonstrated, but he insisted that only the best was worthy of his public and posterity.

One manuscript, the *Melody in F*, was actually snatched out of the flames by a friend. It later became one of his most popular works.

He developed such technical skill and fluency that he once boasted, "I could set a butcher's bill to music."

He won the coveted Lesley Alexander Prize for music for two years in succession, as his reputation grew in London society and the world of music. By 1897 he had learnt everything that Sir Charles Stanford could teach him and he left the Royal College of Music.

An early break came when Sir Edward Elgar the leading British composer of his time, found himself too busy to write a piece for one of the most important musical events on the Victorian calendar, the Three Choirs Festival, in 1898. He recommended that Coleridge-Taylor be invited instead.

Taylor realised that this was a rare opportunity and worked and reworked his composition which he called, *Ballade in A Minor*.

The festival was in Gloucester. Prior advertising stated that the conductor was an Anglo-African, but most of the cream of British and European musical society who gathered for the great event assumed that he would be a white African, who had been born somewhere on the dark continent.

Instead they saw a small, delicately built youth with a shock of crinkly hair, which he brushed upwards to create the right artistic image. There was a stunned silence. Many among his audience had never had any acquaintance with a Black and they had certainly never seen a Black conducting his own music.

They listened entranced as the work progressed. It was new, original and technically perfect. And by the time it was over Taylor sat down to wave after wave of applause. The distinguished musical audience realised that the black man who had suddenly appeared on the Gloucester podium, was not just a talented musician, but an outstanding composer. Newspapers all over Britain and the world carried the news of his triumph.

For a short time he became a violin teacher at the Royal College of Music but his success was making his life complicated. His mind was full of new and original ideas that he wanted to exploit while he was still young and creative.

His next great composition was arguably his best known. *Hiawatha's Wedding Feast* was first played at his alma mater, the Royal College of Music, on 11 November 1898. Later the venue was switched to the Albert Hall where thousands trying to get in, were turned away.

He became a celebrity with everyone demanding his favours. He received so many requests to compose, conduct, and appear personally that he had to be selective. He composed the *Death of Minnehaha* in 1899 and *Herod the God of War* and *Faust* shortly afterwards.

He was invited to conduct some of the leading orchestras in the country and became Professor of Composition at the Trinity College of Music and Professor of Theory and Harmony at the Crystal Palace School of Music and Art. In the words of the music critic Joseph Bennet, he was, "certainly the man of the hour."

In 1904 he became the regular conductor for the Handel Society and spent most of the rest of his life teaching and composing in Croydon.

He became a great friend of the African-American poet Paul Lawrence Dunbar who told him that he should use his prestige to become a champion of black rights. He was also highly influenced by W. E. B. Du Bois' book, *The Soul of Black Folks* which he later described as the greatest book he had ever read.

This led him to three successful tours of the United States in 1904, 1906 and 1910 at the invitation of the Black bourgeoisie, based mainly in Washington, DC. He became hugely popular among the cream of black society and met Booker T. Washington and was invited to dinner by President Theodore Roosevelt.

Although he was a composer entirely in the European classical idiom his lyrics began to tell of the trials and tribulations of the black race. In his *Twenty Four Negro Melodies* and the *Danse Negre* he attempted to do for negro music what other composers did for their own nations - to evolve a distinctive national style.

He also became politically involved, writing a series of letters to the English newspapers vigorously refuting the pseudo-scientific claims about black men's inferiority.

Though internationally famous he never became rich. He foolishly sold the copyright of *Hiawatha* to music publishers for only 15 guineas, and they only guiltily passed on occasional royalties to him when their consciences were pricked by his impoverished state.

His last famous work was *A Tale of Old Japan* which he finished in 1911. He was never strong physically and the unrelenting pressure of work and the damp English climate finally took its toll. Only 37 years old, he died suddenly of pneumonia on 1 September 1912, in Croydon where he had lived most of his life.

7. Early rulers

Founder of Modern Egypt

MOHAMMED ALI
1769-1848

Mohammed Ali is an odd choice for this book. He was an Albanian who fought most of his wars outside Africa in Syria, Turkey, and Crete. He ruled Egypt as the representative of the Ottoman empire. He could hardly have been less African.

And yet his lifetime's contribution was in Africa. He can fairly be described as the founder of modern Egypt.

Though illiterate, he was a Machiavellian politician with great *sang froid* and a capacity for cool calculation. He was described as courageous, cruel, astute, full of wiles and boundlessly ambitious. He won virtual independence from the Ottomans after warring with them throughout his life and used the opportunity to drag his country from Oriental feudalism into the modern era. He modernised and Westernised his administration and built a strong army and navy. He improved education and pioneered industrial innovation. He encouraged the development of the much coveted long-staple variety of cotton that was to make Egypt rich.

Though his military adventures brought little territorial gain (except in Sudan), by the end of his lifetime he had ensured that his successors were hereditary rulers in Egypt who were able to gradually free themselves from Ottoman control.

Mohammed Ali was born at Kavala a small seaport on the border of Thrace and Macedonia about 1769. His father was an Albanian farmer and he spent his early, undistinguished years as a petty official and trader in tobacco.

He joined the local *bashi bazouks* (volunteers) and rose to second in command of the regiment. His life took on a new dimension when the Albanian soldiers were sent to fight Napoleon in Egypt. He took part in the battle of Aboukir on 25 July 1799. His men were routed and he had to swim for his life only to be saved by the gig of the British admiral, Sir Sidney Smith.

Back in Egypt again in 1801, he was in command of his regiment. He distinguished himself in a cavalry charge at the battle of Ramanieh.

He found Egypt in chaos. The French had left on the downfall of Napoleon and there was a political vacuum. The challengers wanting to rule Egypt were the Mameluks, originally mercenaries from the fringes of Asia, who had been in Egypt long enough to hold power from time to time. They were in conflict with the Ottoman governors ruling under the authority of the Porte of Istanbul.

Mohammed Ali was an opportunist and at first, relatively unimportant, though he had his Albanian regiment behind him. He started by supporting the Mameluks and then switched his support to the Ottomans. He backed the side which had the funds to pay the wages of his Albanian regiment.

In 1805 he was on an expedition to Nubia (Sudan) when the sheikhs of Cairo invited him back to end decades of anarchy and the ceaseless quarrelling between the Mameluks and Ottomans. He quickly restored order and established tough military rule. Soon he was involved in far-reaching administrative and educational reforms that rapidly modernised his adopted country.

Istanbul was too weak to deny him as a series of revolutions shook the Ottoman empire. The British tried to intervene and restore a Mameluk but their expedition suffered heavy casualties.

Mohammed Ali marked his victory by displaying the heads of the slain British soldiers on stakes along a Cairene avenue.

He quickly set about consolidating his power by building a modern army and fleet. He recruited French officers and engineers to build him a navy.

By 1811 he was strong enough to remove the Mameluk threat by inviting them to a party, locking the gates and slaughtering up to 500 of them in cold blood. The remaining Mameluks then fled to neighbouring territories.

He was then the undisputed master of Egypt and began military campaigns in Arabia, Nubia, Syria and even targeted Greece.

He defeated the Al-Saud Wahabis in 1818 and took the holy cities of Mecca and Medina. He and his sons campaigned in Nubia (1820- 21) in Crete (1822) and in 1823 he laid the foundations of Khartoum. He was only stopped from further adventures in Greece by the crushing defeat of his navy by the Western powers at Navarino in October 1827.

His victories were won with a powerful army of veterans under the command of European officers. He raised money to pay for his militaristic ambitions by selling licences of trading and manufacturing monopolies.

His relationship with Mahmud II, the Ottoman sultan, was curious. Technically Mohammed Ali was his *vali* (governor) subject to annual reappointment, but in practice he had been ruling Egypt for himself since the Cairene sheikhs had called him to do so in 1805.

Mohammed Ali's territorial ambitions soon brought him in direct conflict with the Porte. His son Ibrahim swept all before him in Syria and pressed on to the Turkish border where, in 1833, he inflicted a crushing defeat on the forces which had been sent to stop him. Ibrahim pushed into Turkey and came within 150 miles of Istanbul.

Mahmud in desperation appealed to the European powers to save him. With backing from the Russians and the British he was able to stop Mohammed Ali's advance. He offered him Greater Syria in return for signing the Convention of Khutahiya in 1833.

But Mohammed refused to pay further tribute to his nominal master and Mahmud countered by reorganising his forces while stirring up the Syrians in revolt. Inevitably the war resumed.

The Ottoman armies crossed the Euphrates and invaded Syria in April 1839, then disaster struck. In June its forces were totally defeated by Ibrahim at Nezib. In July the ageing Mahmud died leaving a 16-year-old successor on the Ottoman throne. Meanwhile the Ottoman admiral deserted and surrendered his whole fleet to Mohammed Ali at Alexandria.

Mohammed Ali was now absolute master of the empire he had carved for himself and the Ottoman empire looked as if it was about to collapse. The European powers then felt obliged to intervene.

The combined British, Austrian and Russian fleets under Sir Charles Napier sailed to break the power of the Egyptian adventurer. In August 1840 the huge armada appeared off Beirut.

This was the signal for the Syrians, smarting under Mohammed Ali's harsh taxes to rise in revolt. Ibrahim found himself blockaded at sea and in the midst of a hostile revolt on land and decided to beat a retreat.

Sir Charles Napier soon arrived off Alexandria and there, using a mixture of persuasion and threats, forced Mohammed Ali to reaffirm Ottoman suzerainty and to agree to sending back the Ottoman fleet. In return he was offered the hereditary *pashalik* of Egypt. This was ratified later in the Treaty of London.

Mohammed Ali was now over 70 and ageing fast. His dreams of ruling the whole of the Near East up to the border of Turkey and Crete had been shattered, though he was confirmed to be the ruler of an African empire to the south in Nubia, Darfur, Kordofan and Sennar.

Like many other great generals after a lifetime of brilliant fighting, he found himself reduced at the end of his reign to the borders he had inherited at the outset. But there was a difference, now he and his successors were confirmed as hereditary rulers over a country whose strategic importance had become greater than that of Turkey.

Though historians necessarily dwell long on Mohammed Ali's military struggle, his greatest achievements were arguably at home. He is remembered as the founder of modern Egypt. His reforms touched every aspect of Egyptian life.

He improved and Westernised Egyptian education, importing Western teachers and sending students abroad. He founded a modern medical school, a translation institute to translate European authors into Arabic, and a government printing press.

He improved communications, significantly shortening the route between Alexandria and Cairo by digging a strategic canal. He encouraged the development of long staple cotton, which transformed the quality of the crop and made Egypt's exports the most coveted in the world.

His efforts in industrialisation were less successful. He was handicapped by a lack of trained manpower and good managers. His monopolies were inefficient and bureaucratic.

He was much criticised in the European press for his foolhardy financial schemes and for apeing the ways of the West in commerce and industry.

His efforts were often crude and overambitious but he introduced a culture of modernisation that was to last long after him. His successors were gradually to win total independence from the Ottomans. He was, in every sense, the founder of modern Egypt.

Founder of the Nation

SOBHUZA I
c.1795-1836

The Dlamini or Ngwane chiefdom existed centuries before Sobhuza I, but it was he who rescued his people from annihilation by the Zulus, took them north and settled them within the current geographical boundaries of Swaziland.

He was a consummate survivor during the time of explosive Zulu expansionism. Other minor tribes, under less strong leaders than he, were sent flying across southern Africa to avoid the sword, drought and pestilence.

Sobhuza was an autocrat and disciplinarian who modelled his army on his great contemporary Shaka Zulu (q.v.), but he was also a clever diplomat who used negotiation and diplomatic marriages whenever possible.

When he died in about 1836, handing over to his wife briefly before his son succeeded him, he had built and settled the nucleus of a small nation, which has lasted to the present day. The Swazis took their name after his son Mswati.

Sobhuza I was first known under the name Somhlolo. He was born about 1795 into the royal Dlamini family, who lived in the Delagoa Bay region of South Africa. His ancestors buried their dead in caves in the tree-covered hills north of the Pongola river. His father King Ndvungunye ruled these northern Nguni people (who later came to be known as Swazis) from about 1780 to 1815, when he was killed by a freak bolt of lightning.

Sobhuza succeeded his father in the same year, taking on the title Ngwane IV or Ngwenyama, meaning King of the Swazis.

Sobhuza was a direct contemporary of Shaka, the Zulu King and Mzilikazi, (q.v.) his lieutenant. He grew up at a time in which the northern Nguni tribes were fighting each other in a ferocious battle for supremacy.

Shaka was in the process of making the small Zulu group the most powerful of all the Nguni. His rigid discipline and military efficiency came at a time all groups were struggling to cope with population pressure and drought. As the Zulus broke out from their homeland on the coast south of the Pongola river, rival groups were defeated, absorbed or sent flying.

Sobhuza first felt the repercussions when he clashed with Zwide, chief of the Ndwandwes. Their dispute was over rich, maize growing lands. Sobhuza recognised that he could not defeat the strongest Zulu King of the time and retreated northwards, leaving his settlement and residence at Shiselweni to be sacked and burned. In 1817 he prudently made peace with Zwide and agreed to marry one of his daughters Thandile, who became mother of the son who succeeded him. (A year later Zwide was attacked and killed by the ever triumphant Shaka.)

Sobuza's policy was to avoid conflict with stronger tribes wherever possible. He paid tribute to Dingiswayo and when he realised that Shaka was the up-coming power, he sent two of his own daughters to him as wives, making no protest when they were murdered later by Shaka in a fit of rage.

But he realised that he could not endure against constant Zulu pressure, so he took his people north into the mountains of Swaziland where he built a new settlement about 1820 at Lobamba (called Old Lobamba nowadays) near the Mdimba mountains. He settled his people along the little Usutu river valley.

Like a small-scale Shaka he was a ruthless autocrat, insisting on rigid discipline as he rebuilt his army and armed it with iron weapons forged from the recently exploited iron ore mines. He defeated and absorbed minor tribes living in the mountains and hid his people in caves when Zulus came on punitive expeditions.

By the time of his death in 1836 or possibly a few years later, he had forged the nucleus of a small nation living in the Swazi mountains in the area that forms the heartland of Swaziland to this very day. In a very real sense he was the founder of a nation.

A Tortured Soul

TEWODROS II
1818-1868

Tewodros was the most eccentric and complex of all the great Ethiopian emperors. One historian, in the 19th century described him as "the most remarkable man Africa had known". But towards the end he was drunken, deranged, cruel, schizophrenic and raging against the misfortunes of his fate.

Yet he was the first to see clearly that unless Ethiopia united under one monarch, the days of the warring princes "Zemana Mesafent" would continue indefinitely and Ethiopia would surely fall to foreign conquerors. But his ambitions outstripped his capacity to deliver. He achieved little, though he did show his successors the way ahead.

Tewodros II was born Kassa Hailu near Metraha, on the north east bank of Lake Tana. He grew up in the family of Kenfu Hailu of Dambya, though his precise parentage and date of birth between 1818-20 remains in dispute.

The missionary Henry Stern claimed that he was the simple son of a humble merchant selling Koso flowers as a cure for tapeworm infections, though his mother may have been of royal blood. Tewodros never forgave Stern for recounting this story which was common gossip around the throne.

He was born in a turbulent world. Ethiopia had not emerged from *Zemana Mesafent* (the era of princes) - a neverending succession of kings, dejazmatches and rases, regional rulers who fought interminably to assert their authority in their mediaeval provinces. The princes had done much as they liked for nearly a century. The emperor reigned nominally but never ruled completely.

None of this worried the young Kassa as he started his education at Takla Haymanot convent in Chenker where in hiding he witnessed the soldiers of the local dejazmatch castrating a number of his schoolmates.

He continued his religious studies at the Malherbe Selassie convent also learning history, law and Arabic. A handsome man with dark,

Ethiopian features, he was intelligent, impetuous and courageous. He excelled in military training, soon getting a reputation as the best shot, the best runner and the best swordsman amongst his peers. His natural aggression and athleticism and the lack of a structured family vocation led to a strange choice of career. When his adopted father died in 1839, leaving him nothing, he decided to become a shifta or brigand. He went into the bush in his native Kwara province at the head of 300 troops and lived off the land.

It was not a continual life of pillage. He encouraged his men to plough, sow and reap. He was a strange mixture of romantic idealist and cruel warrior. In modern terms he could be described as a schizophrenic. When he robbed the rich he often distributed the booty to the poor like a latter-day Robin Hood.

He was a tortured soul. He abolished slavery but as he grew older he became more irascible. He often punished his enemies and even his own soldiers with terrible mutilations and amputations.

In the 1840s, his army of followers and his reputation grew rapidly. The empress Menen tried to buy him off by recognising his claim to Kwara, which he already controlled physically, and by offering her granddaughter Tawabach in marriage. But Kassa did not abandon his shifta life.

In October 1846 he twice defeated Menen's army near Lake Tana.

Dejazmatch Wandyerad who had boasted that he would bring back the "koso vendor's son" was put to flight, then the Empress Menen herself was captured and held in ignominious captivity.

In a series of battles that followed he showed he was an outstanding military leader and strategist. One by one he reduced the princes bringing the *Zemana Mesafent* to an end. The last to fall was Dejazmatch Webe at the battle of Darasge. Two days later, on 11 February 1855 he had himself crowned emperor Tewodros II in the very church that Webe had prepared for his own coronation. He even employed the services of Abuna Salama, the bishop that Webe had brought specially from Egypt, to perform the ceremony.

He took the name Tewodros from the apocryphal book *Fekkare Iyasus* which had forecast that an emperor of that name would rule firmly and wisely for 40 years after a long period of anarchy.

Emperor, yet still a bandit of no fixed abode, he then turned his attention south, to the even more powerful kingdoms of Wollo and Shoa thus altering the whole thrust of imperial expansion. In the middle of the rainy season he began the long, exhausting and brutal campaign in Wollo which terminated in his capture of Magdala on 12 September.

He encountered less resistance in Shoa except from Halya Malakot who died during the campaign. After another victory at the battle of Barakat, Tewodros seized Malakot's son, an unknown 11-year-old child called Menelik (q.v.) and made him a prisoner at Magdala. Little did he know that boy was to become Ethiopia's greatest emperor.

Around 1860 Tewodros had reached the peak of his territorial power, from that point onwards the decline set in. His huge ambitions were never to be fulfilled and he was to see the little that he had gained steadily slipping from his grasp.

On a personal level the despair started when his much loved first wife Tawabesh died and he was never happy with the 12-year-old Tirunesh who replaced her. Sexually unsatisfied, he turned to drink and other women and became increasingly violent.

He was ever a man of burning ambition, who wanted change and reform to be fast and far reaching, but everywhere he was frustrated by the ingrained traditions of his people.

To expand his control he tried to take power away from the princes and rulers and set up his own appointees as governors and civil servants in their place, but this initiative was everywhere frustrated. Often, it would have been easier if he had left the princes to pledge allegiance and pay tribute in the traditional way.

He tried to get the church to pay taxes, but met with stubborn refusal. He was reduced to confiscating church land and giving it to commoners who would pay tribute.

He was determined to centralise and modernise the army and introduced ferocious discipline. He devised a new structure of command where responsibility was clearly defined in new ranks - commander of a thousand men, commander of fifty, commander of ten. He tried to limit the huge retinues that followed all mediaeval armies into the field and introduced payment for his troops instead of allowing them to pillage.

But these reforms, like so many others, were too revolutionary and broke down in practice. Payment was irregular, pillage frequently occurred. On one occasion in a fit of rage he had the limbs of his own soldiers amputated for ignoring discipline and fighting among themselves.

Tewodros was also passionately fond of modern armaments. He searched for weapons from every external source. He said the time would come when spear shafts would be made into wagon spokes. He forced his captive missionaries to forge a huge Sebastapol howitzer. Hundreds of men dragged it hundreds of miles, then up the craggy peaks of Magdala. When it came to be used against the British, it was found to be defective.

In foreign relations Tewodros' main strategy was to make friends with the imperial powers against the "Turks" (Egyptians) who occupied the whole Eritrean coastland and Sudan. His continual search for new friends led to the arrival of foreign missionaries and legations.

He was also desperate to recruit craftsmen and technicians who would teach his people to make weapons and armaments. He offered them lucrative rewards while he pressurised the missionaries themselves to make arms for him.

In 1862 he wrote to Napoleon III, Queen Victoria and to Russia, Prussia and Austria asking each foreign power to help him break the stranglehold of the Turks. His letters were almost universally ignored. He took out his frustrations by clapping envoys and missionaries in irons and holding them prisoner.

In another letter in 1866 he even offered to exchange his prisoners in return for arms and munitions and the supply of expert arms manufacturers.

The British Foreign Office actually recruited some armourers and sent them to Massawa, but refused to allow them to travel to Ethiopia until the European hostages were released.

Meanwhile things were going wrong internally. One by one the rases and princes, needled by his reforms and determined to take advantage of his mounting difficulties, rose in revolt. His soldiers irked by the new discipline, the limits on looting and lack of regular, promised pay, began to desert in large numbers. By 1866 the army which had numbered 60,000 at its peak was now reduced to a rump of some 10,000.

Year by year he was driven back into his heartland. In 1867 he was forced to abandon his capital at Debra Tabor and move to his last stronghold, defended by mountains and steep cliffs at Magdala, while the princes regained their old, feudal autonomy. His closest friends deserted him and he became a folorn, tragic figure of Shakesperian proportions.

But in the end his final downfall was to come at the hands of the British, the very people whom he had tried to befriend throughout his tempestuous rule.

His letters had remained unanswered. Foreign envoys were slippery and evasive. Frustrated, he lost all trust and decided to hold the European hostages until Britain supplied him with the armourers which he required.

The British parliament sent a huge expeditionary force of 32,000 men under Sir Robert Napier which arrived on the Eritrean coast in October 1867. Their advance was soon assisted by Kasa Mercha of Tigre (the man who was to become Emperor Yohannes IV). It was symbolic of the state of the empire. The man who should have been a key ally instead provided all the provisions that the expeditionary force needed for its advance.

The British laid seige to Magdala in April 1868, wreaking havoc with their new, Snyder long-range rifles. Tewodoros found that his beloved Sepastapol howitzer did not work, while the rest of his artillery fell short of the British lines. He suffered hundreds of casualties.

Tewodoros was beside himself, enraged, desperate and most of the time drunk. He released hundreds of Ethiopian prisoners but receiving no positive response from Napier, threw them all over the edge of the cliff.

In tears, he then ordered the release of the European prisoners and sent a flock of cattle down the mountain with a plea for peace. He received no response. That night most of his men deserted. The next day on 13 April 1868, he told his last few companions to leave while they still had the chance.

As the British mounted a final assault, he drew a pistol given to him by Queen Victoria, and shot himself through the mouth. The British found his corpse still warm and a smile on his face.

The historian Clements Markham wrote in 1869, "Thus ended the career of the most remarkable man that Africa has known this century (19th century)." But what had he achieved?

His aims were so far ahead of his time, that his creative ideas outstripped any possibility of achievement. Militarily and territorially he left nothing to his successors.

Yohannes IV had to start all over again to reduce the princes of *Zemana Mesafent*. His administrative and military reforms pointed in the right direction but were only half accomplished. The problem of Moslem encirclement remained the main preoccupation of his great successors (like Menelik) and continue even to the present day.

But many of his ideas and innovations showed the way to the future. He was a prophet before his time.

Ambition Drowned

EDWARD JAMES ROYE
1815-1872

Edward Roye was one of the more unusual early Liberian presidents. A black from Ohio, USA, he was an entirely self-made man who enjoyed huge success in his private life. He emigrated to Liberia and became a wealthy shipowner, newspaper publisher and businessman. He rose fast in local politics to become Speaker of the House of Representatives, Chief Justice and eventually President.

But because he was black the highly prejudiced early settler community never fully accepted him. They conspired against him when he became President, resenting the fact that he placed the interests of the majority of Liberians against those of their narrow mulatto community.

He tried to extend his presidency but was impeached, and died a mysterious death trying to escape imprisonment. His progressive plans for Liberia died with him.

Edward James Roye was a black American. He was born on 3 February 1815 in Newark, Ohio in a wealthy, black land-owning family. He was sent to Newark High School and then to the University of Athens, Ohio for three years, graduating in 1835.

His ambition was to make a fortune. He started by becoming a teacher; saving every penny until he could take up sheep trading.

In 1837 he moved to Terre Haute and cashed in on a growing fashion by opening the city's first bath house. He joined the Freemasons and did all he could to build a successful American business, but everywhere he was hampered by colour prejudice. It was difficult for a black to make his way in early 19th century USA, so he set out for Liberia.

He sailed across the Atlantic and arrived virtually at the birth of a new nation on 7 June 1846, just a year before independence. The American Colonisation Society had sent out the first freed slaves to settle there in 1822. The early settlers, under attack from tropical disease and resentful natives, were still struggling to maintain a foothold in a hostile environment.

But it was a land of opportunity and Roye soon built a prosperous shipping business, sending the first Liberian registered ships to Europe and the USA. He joined the opposition True Whig Party and became a political figure, gradually working his way into the House of Representatives, where he became Speaker, and later joined the Senate. In 1864 he was appointed Chief Justice of the Supreme Court.

His wealth and social standing gave him the chance to compete in the presidential elections of 1855 and 1867, but he came from the wrong party. The Republicans had been in power since before independence. They were mainly mulattoes and imposed very tight franchise restrictions on blacks, whether they were African natives or recent immigrants from USA. Roye was black himself, and was barred from the local Masonic lodge (despite the fact that he had been a mason in the USA); he wanted reform. He actually resigned as Chief Justice on a matter of principle, when the Republicans tried to bring trumped-up treason charges against the True Whig leadership.

Roye remained convinced that he could develop the new country better than the presidents before him. Fighting on a development platform, he won the presidential election on his third attempt in May 1869.

Roye wanted to open up the hinterland, build railroads, establish plantations and develop Liberia's export trade. In a famous speech shortly after his inauguration he said, "I believe that the erection of a railroad will have a wonderful influence in the civilisation and elevation of the native tribes. The barriers of heathenism and superstition will disappear before the railroad as frost and snow dissolve before a summer's rain...The natives will become the best of customers to bring the camwood, palm oil, ivory, gold, cotton country cloths, peanuts, iron ore, hides, bullocks, sheep, goats and other things to Liberian markets on the seaboard and thus multiply indefinitely the exportable products of the country."

It was an idealistic dream. No railroad was built in Liberia until iron ore was identified as a commercial export in the 1960s.

There were many other economic problems too. Roye's old Liberian sailing ships could not compete with the new steamships of the USA and Europe and Liberia's small-scale exports were uncompetitive against the specialist producers such as Nigeria (palm oil) and Brazil (growing the very coffee that had originally been introduced by Liberia).

Roye had plans to bring elementary education to all children in the country and set up commissioners for education in each district to supervise this. He also wanted to stimulate progress in banking, agriculture and transport.

He hoped some of these projects would come about by foreign investment, but he was opposed by many of his own people who thought it would bring foreign domination, while foreigners were reluctant to put their money into a little-known African country.

Roye decided to raise a foreign loan and took the precaution of first clearing it with the legislature. In June 1870 he travelled to Britain to settle a border dispute with Sierra Leone and to negotiate a loan in the City of London. In August 1871 a loan of £100,000 was finally agreed, on extortionate terms, with an independent group of bankers who retained £30,000 as the first year's interest.

The whole loan, bearing a 7% rate of interest had to be repaid within 15 years. Immediately Roye ran into problems. The Republicans who still saw him as a black upstart, were bitterly critical saying he had been duped into an adverse deal. Nor was the money put to good use. Instead it was kept in the local treasury where it was illegally sequestered by corrupt civil servants. They were only too pleased to outwit the black parvenu who wanted to shake up their comfortable world.

Roye's dreams of rapid economic development came to nothing as opposition hardened against him. He wanted more time to put his development plans into effect and tried to extend his statutory two-year presidential term of office for a further two years.

As the economic depression worsened, his opponents accused him of being a dictator, bent on prolonging his rule indefinitely. In October 1871 riots broke out in Monrovia between his supporters and those of the opposition. One of his closest friends was the celebrated writer and President of Liberia College, E. W. Blyden (q.v.) who had been championing the black cause and advocating greater immigration into Liberia. Blyden was almost lynched in the riots and an attempt was made to set fire to Roye's house.

In a confused sequence of events that followed, Roye's own vice-president turned against him and finally succeeded in having him arrested on 26 October 1871 and imprisoned pending impeachment proceedings. A provisional government was then set up.

Roye was tried before the High Court of Impeachment and found guilty on 11 February 1872. But before sentence was passed he escaped from prison and made his way to the coast where he hoped to find refuge on a British boat.

The exact circumstances of his death are still disputed. He may have been shot while he waited on the beach, or the canoe taking him through the heavy African surf towards the British ship may have capsized, or he may have been shot while already in the canoe. Still other stories say that he fell out of the canoe but drowned trying to swim to the ship standing well out to sea.

Whatever the truth, it was the last of Roye and his progressive plans for the future of his country perished with him.

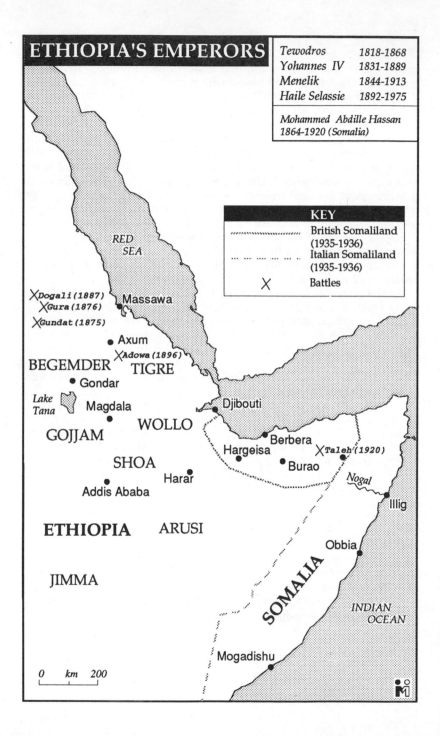

ETHIOPIA'S EMPERORS

Tewodros	*1818-1868*
Yohannes IV	*1831-1889*
Menelik	*1844-1913*
Haile Selassie	*1892-1975*

Mohammed Abdille Hassan
1864-1920 (Somalia)

KEY	
,,,,,,,,,,,,,,,,,,,,,,,,,,	British Somaliland (1935-1936)
... ...	Italian Somaliland (1935-1936)
✕	Battles

RED
SEA

✕*Dogali (1887)*
✕*Gura (1876)*

✕*Gundat (1875)*

● Massawa

● Axum

✕*Adowa (1896)*

BEGEMDER **TIGRE**

● Gondar

Lake Tana

Magdala ●

GOJJAM

WOLLO

● Djibouti

● Berbera

Hargeisa ● ✕*Taleh (1920)*

SHOA

Harar ●

● Burao

● Addis Ababa

Nogal

ETHIOPIA **ARUSI**

● Illig

Obbia ●

JIMMA

SOMALIA

INDIAN OCEAN

Mogadishu ●

0   km   200

Emperor of Unification

YOHANNES IV
1831-1889

Yohannes IV is the least well-known of the great 19th century Ethiopian emperors. Yet he carried the process of imperial unification much further than his predecessor Tewodros and it was his hard work which created the base for his famous successor Menelik, to make Ethiopia the greatest black power on the continent. To unify the empire he realised he had to delegate authority and win the loyalty even of princes he did not fully trust. He developed a culture of loyalty to the emperor. He was also a great commander; during his lifetime he did not surrender an inch of Ethiopian territory.

His original name, before his coronation as Yohannes IV, was Kassa Abba Bezbez, born in 1831 to Shum Temben Mirtcha. In imperial terms he was an odd man out. Unlike the emperors that preceded and followed him he was a Tigrean rather than an Amhara. His ancestors were from the most noble of the princely houses of Tigre.

He was born at a time the Ethiopian emperors were still fighting to assert their supremacy at home while trying to keep a host of imperial predators at bay. Egypt (part of the Ottoman empire), Britain, Italy and France all had aspirations in Ethiopia and the Mahdists were threatening in Sudan.

The emperor, Tewodros II, (q.v), was struggling to maintain the loyalty of the rases and princes in his unstable "empire" against the Egyptians, whom he described pejoratively as "Turks" and their British allies.

Kassa was 33 in 1864 when Tewodros recognised him officially as ruler of one of the main Tigrean regions. But a year later in November 1865, he was taken seriously ill and so thankful for his recovery that he briefly wanted to go into a monastery. He was dissuaded from this course and vowed instead never to acquire a personal fortune nor to take "vengeance" on his enemies.

He broke with Tewodros over the arrest of the Abuna Salama, the Coptic primate of the Ethiopian Orthodox church, and led Tigre in rebellion. Kassa allied himself with the British and when they decided to send a punitive expedition against Tewodros for killing British missionaries, he gave them free passage through Tigre.

When Tewodros died in his mountain fortress at Magdala on 13 April 1868, it was not Kassa, but Tekle Giorgis the King of Lasta, another pretender to the throne who became emperor.

Kassa was in no hurry to challenge the succession but he continued to subvert minor rulers during Giorgis' three-year rule. The final confrontation came on 11 July 1871 at the battle of Adowa, when Kassa threw 12,000 of his own men into battle against 60,000 under Giorgis. Kassa's troops were massively outnumbered, but they were better equipped and disciplined and had been well trained by an eccentric Scotsman called John Kirkham, who was long in Kassa's service.

Giorgis was wounded and captured. By tradition Kassa should have torn out his eyes and burnt him alive, but true to his earlier vow to show mercy to his opponents, he merely imprisoned him.

Kassa was crowned emperor as Yohannes (John) IV on 21 January 1872 at Axum, the ancient capital of Ethiopia. The feasting lasted three days with his men coming into the main hall in batches of 400 at a time to feast with the new Emperor.

It was the first coronation in Axum since the 17th century and the first time imperial power had switched to the Tigrean princes.

But now Yohannes had taken control he had a fight on his hands. In all parts of the empire there were princes in their own regions ready to take advantage, the most powerful being the young Menelik (q.v.), King of Shoa who felt he had a better claim to the imperial throne.

For three years from 1872-75 Yohannes concentrated on winning internal supremacy over the core regions of the Ethiopian highlands. Gradually he reduced the princes of Shoa, Gojjam and Yejju though he did not gain the submission of Menelik until 1878.

He was a devout man (his enemies would say a religious bigot) and he recognised the importance of the Ethiopian church in unifying his empire. He was especially proud when he persuaded the Patriarch of Alexandria, the head of the Coptic church to send him no less than four bishops to live permanently in Ethiopia.

External threats came first from Ismael Pasha who had been on the Egyptian throne since 1863. As the scramble for Africa developed, Ismael too wanted to establish a "great African empire" alongside the other imperial powers. His strategy was to surround and squeeze Ethiopia by pushing up the Nile and then pressing inland from the Red Sea coast.

Yohannes was militarily very successful against the Egyptians, winning the battles of Gundet in 1875 and Gura in 1876. Both sides took heavy losses but the coastlands were momentarily exposed to Yohannes. He was hesitant to press his advantage, as the Egyptians could simply summon reinforcements from Cairo. Instead he asked the British to intercede. In the convoluted negotiations that followed Yohannes agreed to return Egyptian prisoners but flatly refused to surrender an inch of territory.

He continued to expand his empire in the "softer" regions of Ethiopia to the south and west, while tussling with an ambitious Menelik, who often tested his resolve.

The Egyptians were suffering economic collapse at home while their garrisons in Sudan were being overrun by the Mahdist insurgents. Britain emerged as the dominant power in the region asking Yohannes for support. He wanted the return of his extreme northern territories of Bogos and free access to the sea through the port of Massawa.

General Charles Gordon was one of the emissaries sent to Yohannes during the infinitely complex negotiations, but he and Yohannes disliked each other from the start and nothing was gained by his intervention.

On 3 June 1884 the treaty of Adwa was finally signed and Yohannes sent his general Ras Alula to relieve a number of garrisons trapped in the Sudan. But in February 1885 the Italians occupied Massawa. They were supported by the British who hoped to enlist their help against the Mahdi. Yohannes recognised the Italian threat if they were to be permanently in Massawa ready to block the flow of arms into Ethiopia.

Britain tried to reassure Yohannes but he protested, despairing of all European promises. "I can do nothing with this. By the treaty all the country evacuated by the Egyptians was ceded to me at the instigation of England and now you ask me to give it all up."

In 1886 Yohannes was faced with a serious revolt in Wollo and an invasion by Mahdist forces which advanced far into Ethiopia burning a monastery and butchering all the monks in cold blood. In January 1887 his commanders counter-attacked and heavily defeated the Mahdist forces at Qallabat. In the same month Ras Alula wiped out an Italian column at Dogali, taking many prisoners.

This time Britain sent Sir Gerald Portal to intercede but again Yohannes refused to give up an inch of his territory. He summed up his position neatly in a letter that he asked Portal to take to Queen Victoria, "I am making war with the infidels (Mahdists). I do not want to fight the Christians (Italians)."

While he was trying to resolve his problems with the Italians the Mahdists attacked, totally defeated his troops at Sarweha and went on to sack Gondar. A second Mahdist invasion followed in 1888 while Yohannes tried to maintain the loyalty of Menelik and other plotting princes and worried about the smallpox and cattle plague that were ravaging parts of his empire.

On 9 March 1889 he personally led his army to lay seige to Qallabat. The battle of Mattama went well but Yohannes received three fatal wounds. He was carried from the battlefield to his tent, to die the next day 10 March. His head was cut off and carried in triumph into the Mahdist strongholds.

Yohannes was a moral and just man who had been totally dedicated to his task which he saw as achieving the unification of the Ethiopian empire. He delegated authority to his vassals and preferred submission rather than extermination of those who betrayed him, so the empire did not fall apart on his sudden death. Menelik survived and continuity was assured.

But Yohannes was overwhelmed by the complexities of external relations. Though he was insufficiently sophisticated or knowledgeable to triumph fully over the imperial machinations of Egypt, Britain and Italy, he left Menelik with a base on which to build an even greater empire.

A King Betrayed

LOBENGULA
c.1836-1894

Lobengula was seen by the Victorian imperialists as an uncivilised, warlike king who had slender claims to the throne. They claimed that he ruled despotically and tyrannised his Shona neighbours. In fact he had to be a strong ruler in order to survive and he did force the Shona to pay him tribute, but most of the antipathy against him was because he spent a lifetime passively resisting white encroachments.

He was caught between the rapacious demands of the white gold diggers and the scramble by the imperial powers to control central Africa. For nearly 30 years he resisted white penetration by persuasion and diplomacy, but he was at the mercy of unscrupulous men and economic greed. Frequently he was tricked into signing concessions that he did not fully understand. Nor could he cope with a Royal Charter Company that created a state within his state. From the first he was a man betrayed.

Khumalo Lobengula was born in the Western Transvaal, about 1836. He was the son of the great King Mzilikazi (q.v.) by the daughter of a Swazi chief, Fulata. Shortly after his birth, his father was to take his Ndebele people out of South Africa over the Limpopo river to Bulawayo where he was to create a new capital and his Ndebele kingdom in 1839.

Lobengula was a member of the Mahlokohloko *ibutho*, a unit of fighting men of the same age group.

When Mzilikazi died in 1868, another son Nkulumane was recognised as the heir to the throne but he had disappeared mysteriously several decades earlier. A special delegation was sent to Natal where he was thought he might be still living, but no trace of him was found. The chiefs then nominated Lobengula to succeed to the throne and he received the backing of most of the elders.

All this came as a surprise to local Europeans who knew Lobengula. Though he had no formal education, he liked to dress in European clothes and formed many European friends among the missionaries and adventurers who had penetrated his territory, but he appeared to have no ambitions for succession.

His enthronment caused considerable opposition in some sections of the tribe. His opponents disliked his mother's humble Swazi origins and many of them did not believe the Nkulumane was dead.

Even Lobengula himself was somewhat reluctant to become king while the uncertainty remained, but when other attempts to find Nkulumane failed, he was crowned king in the *Inxwala* ceremony of January 1870.

Almost immediately he was challenged by the pro-Nkulumane *ibutho*. Lobengula realised that he had to fight for survival and raised a force of over 5,000 men to challenge the rebels at Zwangendaba in June 1870. It was a bloody battle in which the rebel leader Mbigo and hundreds of his supporters were killed. Many others fled to the Transvaal where they continued to plot against him.

Lobengula was lenient with those who remained, but he was never totally accepted and further challenges against him recurred in the early years of his reign. At least one opponent pretended that he was the real Nkulumane. He tried to invade Matabeleland in January 1872, with the help of another half brother Mangwane. Lobengula repulsed the invasion and sent his opponents fleeing to Western Transvaal.

In 1878 a British delegation led by Robert Patterson, who had been sent to investigate reports of mistreatment of British travellers, said that he supported Nkulumane's claim to the throne. At first Lobengula took no action and allowed his mission to proceed but later Patterson and his whole party were killed. Lobengula denied that he had been responsible and claimed the party had died from drinking poisoned water.

Lobengula's relations with the whites were always difficult and complex. Adventurers of all kinds were pressing into Matabeleland hoping to make a fortune from mining concessions in gold and other valuable minerals. Somehow Lobengula had to protect his relatively newly created kingdom which stretched northwards from the Zambezi and eastwards to Mashonaland where he established partial control.

Competition among the imperial powers for the control of the region was intensifying. Transvaal wanted to push its borders northwards. Portugal, already established in Mozambique, and Germany in Tanzania, wanted to push westwards. The British were determined to seize the opportunity to fill the vacuum by raising the flag in central Africa which was rumoured to be so rich in mineral wealth.

To gain some protection against Transvaal expansionism, Lobengula gave his first mining concessions to the British explorer Thomas Baines in 1871 and to Sir John Swinburne in 1872. Neither of these concessions was exploited much and the threat from Paul Kruger, the President of the Transvaal, remained.

Lobengula, contrary to his reputation, was basically a man of peace who recognised the power of the white man and wanted diplomatic solutions to his probems. His first task was to achieve a settlement with the Transvaal government, so in 1887 he finally decided to sign a treaty with the Transvaal agent P. Grobler.

This move caused consternation in the British camp where Cecil John Rhodes (q.v.) was already dreaming of expanding northwards and fulfilling his great imperial African dream. Already a rich man from his South African diamonds and gold, he had the money to pursue his ambition, while the niggardly British government hesitated.

In 1888 he sent his representative, the missionary John Moffat, to negotiate with Lobengula. In October 1888 Lobengula was finally persuaded to grant the Rudd concession. He promised to grant the concessionaires, "exclusive charge of all metals and minerals contained in my kingdom" and gave them full power to, "do all things they may deem necessary to win and procure the same."

In return for this sweeping concession he was granted a retainer of £100 a month plus 1,000 rifles and 100,000 rounds of ammunition. It was the worst kind of colonial exploitation. Lobengula disputed the English text which he did not understand and claimed that he had agreed to a concession that was far more limited. Later, in 1889, he tried to repudiate the concession altogether and sent a delegation of senior chiefs to London, in 1889 to the Queen of England to protest.

Meanwhile Rhodes was in the process of getting a Royal Charter for the British South Africa Company (BSAC), which would give it powers to administer and set up a police force in the area of the Rudd concession.

Rhodes then responded to Lobengula by sending in the swashbuckling adventurer Dr. L. S. Jameson to negotiate. He was the man who was later to be responsible of the notorious Jameson raid which attempted to topple the Transvaal government in 1895.

Lobengula tried to negotiate a more limited agreement but was to find that he was up against the BSAC which had acquired new administrative and law enforcement powers under the charter.

By mid-1890 the BSAC launched its pioneer column to establish its claims and expand them into Mashonaland, where Lobengula still claimed he had a right to demand tribute.

Lobengula, who thought he would only be confronted by a handful of prospectors, became alarmed at the 200 armed police in the column, which totalled 380 men, and pleaded with them to stop, but they pushed on to build a new city called Salisbury in Mashonaland. This meant that Lobengula gradually lost control of the area as the whites moved in and extended protection to the Shona chiefs.

Lobengula still sought diplomatic means to prevent the growing encroachments on his kingdom. In November 1891 he signed the Lippert Concession with the Germans hoping they would counter-balance the BSAC. But shortly afterwards Lippert sold the concession to the BSAC which further consolidated its control.

By the early 1890s European settlers were flocking into Mashonaland while Lobengula tried desperately to preserve his right to exact tribute from the Shona chiefs. Jameson, who had become the BSAC administrator, drew up the boundaries between Mashonaland and Matabeleland. In June 1893 when Lobengula mounted a raid in the Masvingo area, Jameson, encouraged by the local settlers, used this as an excuse for war.

Throughout the Ndebele war which followed, Lobengula tried to negotiate a settlement, sending missions to Cape Town and London, but the British were determined to conquer the troublesome king. Jameson recruited hundreds of volunteers in South Africa promising them large tracts of land and gold claims. On 4 October 1893 a force of 1,200 men plunged into Matabeleland. Lobengula ran a defensive campaign and did not attack until he was forced to do so. His impis were cut down by Jameson's maxim guns at Shagani and in November at Imbembesi. Totally defeated, Lobengula ordered the burning of Bulawayo and fled northwards with a handful of loyal troops.

Even at the end Lobengula tried to sue for peace, but his messengers were killed before they could get through and he remained a hunted man. He died in mysterious circumstances, somewhere south of the Zambezi river, in January or February 1894. He certainly did not die at the hands of his triumphant enemies, but of some illness, possibly smallpox. His grave was discovered in 1943 in Kamativi.

Creator of a Nation

MUTESA I
1838-1884

Mutesa was the toast of Victorian England as the powerful ruler of Buganda the most advanced African kingdom in eastern Africa. Passing through the dangerous and empty Kenyan hinterland, the first white explorers found a king with a well organised court and social structure, thirsting to learn about the new world outside Africa. In 1862 John Speke showed him his first rifle. He was sufficiently feared and powerful to bid his page to go out and shoot a man, which the page did with alacrity.

But in his 28 years on the throne Mutesa proved himself far more than a capricious despot. He had done much for his kingdom. He had maintained its culture and integrity at a time imperial ambition was at its hungriest. He had gradually modernised and adapted, while playing off the foreign interests that were waiting to swallow him up. His country's population, size, and prosperity had grown immeasurably. A strong tribe had become a nation.

Mukabaya Mutesa was born about 1838 in Buganda, now part of modern day Uganda, on the northern shore of Lake Victoria. He was the eldest son of Kabaka (King) Suna who could trace his ancestry back at least 400 years and through eight named predecessors.

The succession of the eldest son was by no means automatic and Mutesa was only one of scores of sons who could have been chosen by the powerful officials of the court, but he was selected and his unfortunate brothers were banished to an island on Lake Victoria; in his father's day many sibling rivals had simply been burnt to death.

Mutesa came to power in a kingdom virtually cut off from the world. His father had banned all visits by slave traders and other Arabs who had tried to penetrate from the East African coast. Yet during his lifetime his remote kingdom was to become the centre of attraction for a plethora of white explorers including Speke, Grant, Charles Chaille-Long, Linant de Bellefonds and a host of Arab teachers and traders.

Mutesa was about 18 when King Suna died of smallpox. Tall for a

Muganda, with striking eyes, he had his hair cut short and piled in a ridge on his scalp, like an early Mohican. His neck and arms were decorated with bands of beads. He was intelligent, but nervous, high strung and lacking self-confidence.

When John Hanning Speke first arrived in the kingdom of Buganda on 19 February 1862, he said it had, "received not the slightest impulse, whether for good or evil, from European civilisation."

Yet it was a highly complex civilisation that had endured for centuries in a settled and organised way.

Speke found the Baganda had a court, centralised administration, a parliament (Lukiko) with a prime minister, specialist ministers, a treasurer looking after the royal treasury, even an admiral of the fleet of war canoes. Other officials had colourful functions such as the chief brewer and keeper of the drums. Chiefs were organised in a hierarchical structure. There was a judicial system and established social organisation. A highly organised system of spies and informers kept Mutesa informed about everything that was going on inside his kingdom and among his neighbours. Information came quickly from Arab sources on the coast.

The Baganda had built roads, bridges, boats and canoes yet they had no wheeled transport, written language, or written accounts. All men were clothed in dyed and patterned bark cloth, though many of the women went naked. Food was sophisticated with many meat and vegetable dishes washed down with beer and coffee. Both men and women smoked.

Yet the young Mutesa, still in his early twenties, asserted his authority with ruthless severity and sometimes wanton cruelty. When Speke first met him he affected a curious stiff-legged gait that was supposed to imitate a lion. No one could sit down in his presence or speak without permission. Etiquette was elaborate and the harshest of penalties fell on any transgressors.

When he spoke even the highest courtiers would fall to the ground repeatedly mouthing the adulatory refrain "n'yanzig". He would never look behind him when he wanted to sit, knowing that a page boy would be crouching in a kneeling posture to anticipate his needs.

When Speke arrived there was a curious cultural clash with neither man wanting to lose face. Speke was kept waiting for hours for an audience and then told he would not be allowed to sit down in the king's presence. Slighted, Speke "in hot ire," simply walked away from the palace until the panic-stricken courtiers implored him to return.

When he finally met Mutesa he was allowed to sit on his own chair in front of the throne, but neither proud man knew how to proceed. Speke knew no Kiganda and Mutesa no Swahili, and no courtier dared intervene. So they sat in silence.

Finally Mutesa asked, through an interpreter, whether Speke had seen the king?

"Yes," Speke replied, "For one full hour." Luckily Mutesa took this as a compliment.

It was at a later audience that the famous incident with the carbines took place. Speke had brought Mutesa some rifles among other presents. Mutesa had never before seen such weapons and was amazed at their magical powers.

First he asked Speke to kill some cows which he did, without too much difficulty, to great applause. Speke then showed him how to load a rifle. Mutesa gave it to a young page and told him to go into the outer court and shoot a man. He did this and returned with a look of glee on his face.

"And did you do it well?" Mutesa asked, " Oh yes capitally," said the urchin. Speke commented, "He spoke the truth, no doubt, because he dared not to have trifled with the king; but the affair created hardly any interest. I never heard and there appeared no curiosity to know, what individual human being the urchin had deprived of life."

Mutesa had to act tough and be tough. He was not a soldier by training but he had to put down a number of revolts by various pretenders and he had to guard his people against the ambitions of powerful neighbours such as the King of Bunyoro to the north west and Karagwe to the south.

He also realised that his hitherto isolated kingdom was exposed to Arab traders and slavers and to the white explorers who represented even greater power in the world beyond. Though Speke wanted his support in his quest to find the source of the Nile, it was over five months before he let Speke continue his travels on 7 July 1962.

Shortly afterwards Mutesa developed a progressive disease that was to restrict his mobility and confined him to his capital. He occupied his time with traders from Zanzibar who taught him Swahili and Arab script. He also developed an interest in religion and studied the Koran.

Buganda remained under threat. An attempt to support a pretender to the Bunyoro throne to the north failed largely because the Kabarega (King) of Bunyoro had been well supplied with arms from Khartoum. Later Samuel Baker pushing up the Nile from the south tried to annexe Bunyoro, but failed. Baker wrote to Mutesa in flattering terms, but was pushed out of the area by the Banyoro before a meeting could be arranged. Instead Mutesa formed an alliance with Sultan Seyyid Barghash, the most powerful figure on the East African coast. He sent the sultan a pile of ivory and asked for a Goan cook and a white wife in exchange. He got neither.

Meanwhile General Gordon on his first tour in Khartoum embarked on one of his more ambitious schemes which centred on the annexation of the African kingdoms in Uganda. In 1874 Gordon sent the American Charles Chaille-Long to Mutesa, and in 1875 the Belgian Linant de Bellefonds to negotiate. But Gordon was never sufficiently well organised nor supported by London to put his plans into practice. Mutesa was never directly threatened militarily.

The time had come for another distinguished explorer to leave his card. Henry Morton Stanley, still searching for the source of the Nile, arrived in Mutesa's court on 5 April 1875.

Mutesa, then in his late thirties, had changed immeasurably from the capricious, unconfident youth that had been discovered by Speke 13 years earlier. He had become a cunning monarch, acutely conscious of the threat to his kingdom from outside forces and the value and danger of foreign alliances.

Buganda's population had soared and his kingdom now stretched along the northern and part of the western sides of Lake Victoria. Trade with the Arabs had brought wealth. Western goods, cloths, beads and trinkets were plentiful. He had plenty of guns and ammunition and could summon an army of up to 150,000 men. He controlled the lake with his fleet of war canoes.

Despite his physical handicaps, and increasing pain, he had matured. Stanley found him, "Tall, clean faced, large eyed, nervous looking and thin."

His quest for the true religion seemed to have changed him too. His undefined animist beliefs had been replaced by an intense curiosity in Islam and Christianity. Indeed Stanley found that his interest was such that he would organise and listen intently to debates between Christian and Islamic scholars. Mutesa also cross questioned de Bellefonds and Stanley separately on the Christian religion and was surprised to find how much they concurred on important principles. Finally he sent a letter to *The Daily Telegraph* in London requesting that Christian missionaries be sent to the kingdom.

Stanley was bowled over and could never reconcile Speke's description of a cruel, capricious tyrant with this affable man always seeking to broaden his knowledge. Stanley endorsed his request for missionaries so that he could be converted to Christianity as an ally of Britain.

To the end of his life, Mutesa was probably never fully converted to either Islam or Christanity, but he was always prepared to listen. He also knew that Britain had become the most important foreign power in the region, though its policy was highly ambivalent.

Gordon, determined to pursue his own agenda and encouraged by the Egyptian Khedive, sent an Egyptian commander Nuer Aga to raise the Egyptian flag over Buganda. Aga actually succeeded in this presumptious scheme. Mutesa countered by raising his own flag and taking Aga's men prisoner. Gordon then had to send the German Schnitzer Emin (Emin Pasha), the Governor of Sudan's Equatoria province, to secure his release.

Mutesa received him graciously, discussed religion with him at great length and then sent him back to Gordon with his Egyptian soldiers. Mutesa had outsmarted all the foreign meddlers, which Gordon soon acknowledged by writing a letter recognising Buganda's independence.

By 1877 the first missionaries began to arrive in Buganda. There were Protestant Anglicans and Catholic French White Fathers. Mutesa enjoyed playing them off against each other and against the Muslim teachers who were already well established in his court.

Amongst the new style courtiers was a young, mission-trained

Zanzibari called Dallington who became Mutesa's clerk or scribe. He helped the king with Bible studies and also wrote haughty letters to foreign powers couched in a curious, imperious language.

Mutesa played along with the missionaries, hoping they would supply him with arms. He also wanted their friendship and influence while he remained uncertain of Britain's intentions. Finally Queen Victoria herself wrote him a letter saying that she only wanted the prosperity of Buganda while her government told the Khedive of Egypt that it would not countenance the annexation of Buganda.

This reassured Mutesa who was already becoming irritated with the missionaries attempts to reform him. They wanted him to adopt only one wife in place of the hundreds that he had at his beck and call. They also tried to curb his slave trading and his sudden unpredictable bouts of cruelty.

The Arabs who wanted his continued involvement in the slave trade, encouraged him to rebel against the missionaries attempts to reform him. But when Mutesa excluded them from his counsels they began to complain about his cruelties, excesses and total disregard for human life.

Alexander Mackay, of the Church Missionary Society, wrote, "Could this be the same man who had so impressed Stanley, who had been so affable when the missionaries first arrived?" He described him as a "monster and a murderous maniac."

Until the last, a darker side of Mutesa's nature ran parallel to the clever and scheming politician. He died in the autumn of 1884 in mysterious circumstances. He was not much more than 46 years old. Some say he was poisoned by one of his jealous wives, others that it was simply a progression of his earlier disease that could have been syphilis.

Even as he was on his death bed he was planning to send a delegation to France to counterbalance the influence of Britain. But as the French never replied to his diplomatic overtures he did send three officials to London, who returned much impressed by the great city over the seas.

After Mutesa, things fell apart. His successor, an 18-year-old lad called Mwanga, had all the vices of his forebear and few of his virtues. Things were to get much worse but Buganda was to survive as a kingdom well into the 20th century.

Father of Ethiopia

MENELIK II
1844-1913

Menelik is regarded as the most illustrious of all Ethiopia's emperors before Haile Selassie. He was a Shoan Amhara who claimed direct descent from King Solomon and the Queen of Sheba. He survived imprisonment by the emperor Tewodros II (q.v.) and the reign of the Tigrean emperor Yohannes IV (q.v.). When he finally gained power he was determined to unify and expand the empire. He moved the capital from the historic site of Gondar in the north to Addis Ababa.

He subjugated the southern peoples and tried to contain Italian political ambition by diplomacy. When this policy failed he defeated the Italians at Adowa in 1896, the greatest victory by an African army over an organised colonial army in history. He then set about consolidating the largest territory ever ruled by an Ethiopian emperor.

Menelik was born Sahle Mariam, heir to the throne of Shoa, at the very heart of Ethiopia. His father Haile Maualok was only one of the many kings and princes that owed theoretical allegiance to the Emperor of Ethiopia.

It was a mediaeval world entangled in hundreds of years of wars and battles, with powerful kings and nobles (rases) interminably fighting each other and holding fleeting supremacy in inaccessible kingdoms, in the Ethiopian highlands.

The emperors who claimed direct succession from King Solomon and the Queen of Sheba, were bent on unification. Their ally was the Christian Ethiopian orthodox church with its wealth and moral suasion. But the provincial warlords had schemed, plotted and fought to retain their independence for hundreds of years.

This was the world in which Menelik was born. He was a tough, robust child with innate intelligence and curiosity. He was given thorough education both academic and martial in his grandfather's palace.

He was still only eleven when Tewodros, the first emperor bent on

centralisation and modernisation, seized power and declared himself
emperor in 1855. Tewodros who came from Begemder in northern
Ethiopia decided almost immediately to bring Shoa under his control.
Menelik's father was killed in the first campaign and the young Sahle
was taken captive. Tewodros treated him honourably but kept him in his
remote mountain fortress at Magdala where he remained a hostage for
almost 10 years.

On 30 June 1865 Menelik, then 21 years old, escaped and reclaimed
his throne in Shoa. His people had been in a ferment of discontent while
the young prince had been away. Tewodros had sacked the capital
Ankober in 1859, but he had never brought it fully under his control.

Menelik was crowned king of Shoa and immediately adopted the twin
strategy of raising an army to defend his homeland while seeking further
contacts with the imperial powers who were rapidly developing a taste
for African adventure.

Dark skinned, with semitic features, he was a dominant giant of a
man with a tough, animal magnetism that gave him charisma.
Underneath his wide brimmed hats there was also a charming,
intelligent personality that elicited friendship as well as respect.

Tewodoros committed suicide in the depths of despair after defeat by
the British in 1868, before he had time to bring Menelik to heel. Menelik
considered his successors particularly Yohannes IV (q.v.), from Tigre in
the north, to be usurpers. Menelik's ancestors in the 18th and early 19th
century had been the emperors of Ethiopia. They, not Yohannes, claimed
to be the true descendants of Solomon and Sheba.

Meanwhile he had to fight to defend his kingdom, while fostering his
European connections. He was particularly interested in getting supplies
of the new repeating rifles and ammunition from the imperial powers.
But he was never strong enough to defeat Yohannes outright and was
finally forced to make peace in the Leche agreement of 20 March 1878.
In a formal ceremony of submission Menelik was forced to carry the
traditional stone of penitence and prostrate himself before the emperor
while ministrels sang songs chiding him for his ambition. There he
declared his loyalty to the emperor and agreed to pay tribute, in return
Yohannes did acknowledge him as negus (king) of Shoa, with the
following words;

"You are accordingly king and master of a land conquered by your
forebears. I shall respect your sovereignty if you will be faithful to the
agreements decided between us. Whoever strikes your kingdom, strikes
me and whoever makes war on you, makes it on me. You are accordingly
my eldest son."

Humiliated though he was, Menelik had learnt a lesson. His army
remained intact and he had to be patient. He had to adopt other
diplomatic ways of getting to the imperial throne.

Menelik with his ambitions to the north firmly closed, turned his
attentions south where he won easy military victories over weaker
opponents. He defeated the Oromo and Jimma and Arusi rulers between

1882-86. He then forced the Egyptians to withdraw from Harar in the south east. Menelik finally entered Harar in triumph on 6 January 1887.

While Menelik was pursuing his conquests to the south Yohannes was fighting almost continuously against the Egyptians and Mahdists in the north. Menelik was of little help to him, yet it was agreed under a treaty signed in 1882 that Menelik would be his successor. However relationships deteriorated badly in the period before Yohannes was fatally wounded on 9 March 1889 at the battle of Matamma against the Mahdists.

Shortly before he died Yohannes had named his nephew, Ras Mangasha as his successor, but Menelik was far more powerful and simply seized power and had himself consecrated as Negus Neghast (king of kings) on 3 November 1889.

Menelik took power at a time of crisis. The empire was near to collapse. The Mahdists were pushing into the highlands. The Italians had established themselves in Eritrea and were hungry to seize their share of the imperial cake, by invading Ethiopia proper. And a dire famine had gripped the land since 1882. Northern Ethiopia was suffering from starvation followed by epidemics of smallpox and cholera.

In the middle of all this Menelik, full of drive and vitality, had rapidly modernised his kingdom. He established a cabinet, a standing army and an organised tax system. He also established a permanent capital at Addis Ababa (new flower) in 1886, which was soon to rival and then surpass the earlier capitals of the Ethiopian empire in Axum and Gondar. Soon the nomadic warrior camps of his predecessors were replaced by a permanent city with his Gebbi palace, five churches, a large market and a first hospital and secondary school. He started a postal service and began work on the railway to Djibouti. He also did much to incorporate the south and west into a proper administrative framework.

Soon the nobility was building permanent homes on the surrounding hilltops alongside the foreign ambassadors, who wanted to establish relations with one of Africas few remaining independent states.

Long before the death of Yohannes, Menelik had maintained cordial relations with the Italians. They supplied him with firearms and the latest European technology. He was fascinated by inventions like electricity, the telegraph system and weapons of all kinds.

Less than two months after Yohannes death on 2 May 1889, Count Pietro Antonelli sealed their then flowering friendship with the treaty of Wechale. Menelik was recognised as emperor of Ethiopia, but in return the Italians were allowed to keep a considerable slice of the northern highlands which they had seized from Yohannes. In the Italian version of the treaty, another article bound Menelik to make all foreign contacts through the agency of Italy. This clause, not apparent in the Amharic version of the treaty, virtually made Ethiopia an Italian protectorate.

When Menelik got to understand this he realised that he had been double crossed. It became clear to him that the national interests of Ethiopia and the Italians were in serious conflict.

At first the Italians tried to persuade him to accept their version of the treaty. They failed and Menelik wrote a letter to King Umberto pointing out that "One independent power does not seek the aid of another to carry on its affairs, as your majesty understands very well."

He then wrote another letter, addressed to all European powers on 10 April 1891:

"I have no intention of being an indifferent looker-on if the distant powers have the idea of dividing up Africa, for Ethiopia has been for more than fourteen centuries an island of Christians in the middle of a sea of pagans..."

His plea fell on deaf ears in Britain but the French and the Russians were prepared to supply him with vast quantities of modern rifles, artillery and ammunition, which he imported through Djibouti.

In February 1893 Menelik abrogated the Wechale treaty, saying "Ethiopia has need of no one; she stretches out her hands unto God."

Early in January 1895 the Italians attacked Ras Mangasha - the Tigrean ruler who had challenged Menelik for the succession - and occupied most of Tigre. The Italian general Baratieri promised the Italian cabinet that he would bring Menelik back to Italy in a cage. He thought that Menelik, plagued with famine throughout his lands, would have no stomach for the fight.

Menelik mobilised his armies. Almost all the subordinate rulers rallied to his cause, even those he had recently defeated in war. He marched north at the head of a vast and remarkably united force. Even his wife, the empress Taitu rode at the centre of the huge, colourful mediaeval army of about 100,000 men.

In December the Italians received a serious shock when they suffered two minor defeats at Amba Alagi and Makalle.

Early in 1896 Baratieri withdrew to Adowa and waited. He knew Menelik's huge forces were running out of food in the famine stricken countryside. Their supply lines were far more overstretched than the Italians through Eritrea.

But Baratieri badly needed a victory to mollify Italian pride. His timing was bad. He finally provoked the battle when Menelik was on the point of making a tactical withdrawal. Then his advance columns became lost in the inacessible mountains to be picked off one after the other by overwhelming Ethiopian numbers.

The fighting raged for one whole day. At the end Menelik had won what is arguably the greatest victory by African troops over an organised colonial army in history. About 260 Italian officers and over 4,000 troops were killed with another 2,000 taken prisoner. The Italians had lost over 40 percent of their whole force, plus all its artillery and 11,000 rifles.

The Italians fled pell-mell into Eritrea. Menelik could have followed them if his supply lines had not been desperately overstretched. After two years of drought, his soldiers wanted to return home to plough and sow.

Soon his victory was formally recognised, not just by the Italians but by all European powers and his reputation soared throughout Africa and the world. It had been the first victory by an African over a European army since the time of Hannibal.

Italy recognised the total independence of Ethiopia, Britain and France signed successive treaties defining the extreme limits of the Ethiopian empire, with Somalia and the Sudan.

In return Menelik acknowledged the Italian occupation of Eritrea and released all his Italian prisoners.

He then set about consolidating the largest territory ever ruled by an Ethiopian emperor, covering boundaries similar to those of today, but his failure to demand access to the sea was to plague him and his successors into the future.

As he grew old and tired he continued to modernise his kingdom, putting more power into the hands of a cabinet formed in 1907, while suppressing minor uprisings in remote regions.

After a stroke, leaving him partly paralysed, he wrote a moving letter in May 1909, reminding his subjects of the troubles following the death of Tewdros and Yohannes and naming his grandson Lij Yasu as his successor. But as the boy was still a minor a quarrel developed over the regency, with Menelik's wife Taitu determined to rule herself. The struggle for succession continued long after he finally drew his last breath in December 1913.

Khama the Great

KHAMA III
1838-1923

Khama III, king of the most powerful tribe in Bechuanaland, the Bangwato, came to power at a time the scramble for Africa was reaching its climax. Worried about the Boer threat on his southern borders and his traditional rivals, the Matabele to the north, he decided to seek British protection. This served him well and preserved his people against the worst of imperialist adventurism.

He was also a committed Christian who forced his people to abandon their old gods and adopt the new religion and its ways. Ruling for over 50 years, he developed a reputation, both among his own people and internationally, as a model chief known as "Khama the Great."

Khama was the eldest of 16 sons of Chief Sekgoma I, the King of the Bangwato. His father was a narrow minded, traditionalist, but in 1857 Khama and his brother Kgamane fell under the influence of the Hermansburg Lutheran mission. Khama became a devout Christian and was baptised in 1860, despite the opposition of his father who felt that he had abandoned the customs of the people and had insulted his ancestors.

On 6 May 1862, at the age of 24, the young man with a tall (over six foot) athletic figure succeeded to the Ngwato chieftaincy. Three years later Sekgoma summoned all the young Ngwato to the traditional ceremony of *boquera* to reaffirm their traditional beliefs, but Khama refused to attend. This led to violent dissension within the tribe and eventually the ageing Sekgoma reclaimed the throne, with the backing of his brother Macheng who then tried to grab power for himself.

Khama temporarily took refuge in Serowe, but in January 1875 raised an army and defeated the army of his uncle and his father who was himself forced into exile.

Once he had secured his position as chief in the capital Shoshong, he introduced radical reforms to Christianise his people. He prohibited the trading and drinking of liquor and discouraged other traditional customs beloved of his father, such as initiation and rain-making ceremonies, and polygamy. Many of these practices, the *boquera and boyale* had died out entirely by the early 1870s.

He encouraged the London Missionary Society which had replaced the Hermansburg Lutherans, established Christianity as the official religion, and commanded his people to observe the sabbath. He fostered education and tried to strengthen the unity of his kingdom which comprised many other tribal groups as well as the Bangwato, who formed only a fifth of the total population.

Many political problems emerged as he sought to strengthen his chieftaincy. The Transvaal republic to the south was antagonistic and its settlers and adventurers were constantly pushing into his kingdom. Simultaneously the scramble for Africa was entering a crucial phase.

Khama weighed up the alternatives in discussions with one of his missionaries, who had since become a friend and adviser, John Mackenzie. In 1876 he decided to ask for British protection against the potential threat from the Transvaal Boers. Britain wanted to forestall the Germans, who had just seized South West Africa, but it was not until February 1885 that it formally declared a protectorate over Ngwato territory. Khama was delighted and even offered a large area of land for British settlement alongside the area allocated to his own people. His power and his people's way of life had not been affected but he had gained British protection.

In 1889 the British South Africa Company (BSAC) run by Cecil Rhodes (q.v.) was given a charter to prospect for minerals inside the British sphere of influence. This included Ngwato territory.

At first Khama was prepared to accept this new source of interference though he was becoming increasingly unpopular with some of his contemporaries for his acquiescence. Other tribes dubbed him the "white man's chief", but he was quite happy to volunteer a force of guides and construction labourers to assist Cecil Rhodes pioneer column against his old rival King Lobengula (q.v.) of the Matabele.

In 1893 he sent soldiers to fight alongside Rhodes men against Lobengula which allowed him to expand his borders northwards into Bakalanga territory.

But he soon began to realise the extent of the threat posed by the BSAC which wanted to prospect for minerals anywhere on his territory and take large areas of land into its own administration. He was worried that the British might hand over control of Bechuanaland to the company.

In 1895, he and other Bechuana chiefs went to Britain to appeal personally to Queen Victoria against the encroachments of the BSAC which, Khama claimed, contradicted the protection treaty of 1885.

The visit of the fashionably dressed Christian chief roused considerable public interest and sympathy among the British public. The Prime Minister Joseph Chamberlain promised that British protection would continue if the BSAC was granted a strip of land to the east so that it could build a railway connecting South Africa and Rhodesia. This was agreed.

In 1889 Khama moved his capital from Shoshong to Palapye and in 1902 to Serowe, where he had originally been exiled by his father. The boundaries of Bechuanaland were demarcated in 1899 and he ruled, some would say autocratically, over the largest reserve in the protectorate, which included many other groups besides his own Bangwato. He created a central administration and appointed district governors. He encouraged private enterprise and the raising of livestock using modern methods. He also launched a successful trading company.

Khama's domestic affairs were less happy than his foreign policy. He twice sent expeditions against subordinate tribes. That of 1922, the year before his death, against the Birwa people led to international protests.

In addition to the early conflict with his father he had an unfortunate family life. His first wife Elizabeta died in 1889 and his second wife Gasekete, the sister of Chief Bathoen, died two years later. He quarrelled with many other close relatives particularly his son Sekgoma II, who went into exile in 1898 taking 2,000 followers with him. He was not reconciled with his son until late in his life, in 1920.

He ruled, with one brief interruption at the beginning of his reign, for 51 years and died a legend. He was widely respected both inside his country and internationally as "Khama the Great." He died of pneumonia on 21 February 1923 at Serowe and was buried there.

Architect of a Nation

HAILE SELASSIE
1892-1975

Haile Selassie was born into a warring, disunited, mediaeval country which he dragged painfully into the twentieth century. A dominating personality despite his diminutive figure, he was a clever man of intense courage, ambition, energy and serious conviction. He began as a reformer and moderniser, who introduced more responsible government, and placed emphasis on education and development. But as he grew older he became unwilling or unable to finally tackle the forces of tradition in church and state to achieve real land reform, which was essential if his country was to achieve social equity and a modern agricultural system.

He was happier in foreign affairs where he gained an international reputation as a peacemaker and an architect of African unity, making his country the headquarters of the Organisation of African Unity. He ruled for 45 years. He became too old and too set in his ways to make the final changes that history required of him.

Tafari Makonnen was born at Ejarsa Gora in Harrar, on 23 July 1892. He was of the purest royal blood on both sides of his family. His father Ras Makonnen was the cousin and the most trusted and beloved of all the advisers to the great Emperor Menelik II (q.v.). He came from the same royal line as the Emperor, sharing a common ancestor Sahla Selassie who claimed to be directly descended through 255 monarchs to King Solomon and the Queen of Sheba.

Though diminutive in stature he was a clever scholar and gifted horseman and learnt French (his second language) from Jesuit missionaries at Harar, before doing further studies at the Menelik school in Addis Ababa and then at the Imperial court.

Menelik was so impressed at his prowess that he summoned him to Addis Ababa, appointing him at the age of 14, only a year after his father's death, as governor of Gara Muleta. He was given the official court title of *dejazmatch* - commander of the door. By 1910 he had proved himself a good enough administrator to be appointed to the difficult governorship, previously held by his father, of Harar.

On 30 July 1911 he married Waizero Menan, granddaughter of the powerful King Mikhail of Wollo. Menelik was undecided about the succession and may well have appointed Tafari, but before he died came down in favour of his grandson Lij Yasu.

Yasu was only 17, but Menelik blessed him, "Whosoever raises his hand against him shall be struck by my curse!... He shall be condemned to die a miserable death and no one shall know his grave." (These words passed into folk memory and were recalled at the time of the murder of Haile Selassie more than half a century later).

Lij Yasu ruled between 1913-16. He wanted to recognise Islam as a co-religion and sided with Germany against the other colonial powers -Britain, France and Italy. He antagonised them and they speeded his downfall, helping to depose him in a coup d'etat in 1916. Menelik's daughter Princess Zauditu then became queen, but Tafari was named as heir to the throne.

During Zauditu's 16-year reign Tafari was her close adviser, but not the regent as he later claimed. It was his drive and vision that set Ethiopia on the road to modernisation and development. This exposed him to conflict with traditional feudal forces. He and Queen Zauditu survived several plots and regional rebellions during the 1920s, as rivalry grew between them.

But he was not deflected from his desire for reform. In 1923 he won Ethiopia's admission into the League of Nations and in 1924 passed a decree for the abolition of slavery. He sent his students on scholarships abroad and travelled widely himself. In 1926 his army from Harar seized control in Addis Ababa and he virtually assumed control of the state.

On 2 November 1930, on the sudden and suspicious death of Zauditu, the 38-year-old Tafari was crowned Emperor Haile Selassie (*Power of the Trinity*), the King of Kings (*Negusa Negast*) and conquering lion of the Tribe of Judah.

His accession was greeted by another rebellion which he promptly repressed. This made him all the more determined to centralise power in his own hands and press ahead with reform.

In 1931 he introduced a two chamber parliament, with advisory powers only. He continued to expand the educational system and used every means to reduce the powers of the regional rulers. He taxed them to raise funds for the central exchequer, and appointed newly educated younger men to the governorships.

But he had made little progress when Italy, complaining of a spurious incident on the border of its colony Eritrea, invaded in October 1935. Mussolini was bent on restoring former Roman glories and avenging the defeat by Menelik at Adowa.

He took personal command, but it was like sending an army from the pages of ancient history against the Italian military juggernaut. In June 1936, with the Italians already in Addis Ababa, he went to the League of Nations in Geneva and made an impassioned appeal to the conscience of the world, but the big powers did nothing and he was forced to go into exile in Britain.

In January 1941 he recrossed the frontier with British troops under Colonel Orde Wingate and on 5 May, five years to the day after the Italian conquest, was restored to his capital Addis Ababa.

Ethiopia had lost over 700,000 men during the war and occupation but Haile Selassie preached reconciliation not revenge.

The 1940s was a period in which he had to reassert the independence of Ethiopia against restrictive British dominance. In 1942 he signed an Anglo-Ethiopian agreement, another followed in 1944 and by 1945 he had regained full sovereignty.

He recalled parliament, formed a new cabinet and set about the rapid expansion of education and communications. He also wanted a place for his country on the world stage. He sent Ethiopian troops to fight under the UN flag in Korea and signed a military assistance pact with the US.

At his silver jubilee in 1955 he brought in a new constitution in preparation for the first direct elections in 1957. But there was a property qualification for voters and the powers of parliament remained largely advisory. His prime objective was to establish a benevolent monarchy with power concentrated firmly in the centre.

He was an inveterate traveller and worked hard to give his country a leading role in Africa. In 1958 Addis Ababa was chosen as the headquarters for the Economic Commission for Africa. In 1960 he was host to the second conference of independent African states. In May 1963 he held the first conference of the African Heads of State at which the charter for the Organisation of African Unity was worked out. The following year the capital was formally adopted as the OAU headquarters.

While he was on his way to visit Brazil in December 1960, a section of the Imperial Guard revolted and attempted to put the Crown Prince on the throne, but the army and air force remained loyal. He returned home and entered Addis Ababa in triumph four days after the coup was declared.

During the coup the rebels shot many ministers and in the words of the US ambassador, "cleaned the rats out of the hen house". Some said that this needed doing because Haile Selassie never put his opponents to death on suspicion. But after the attempted coup he replaced his ministers with a younger generation which he had helped to educate and fashion. This put still more power into the hands of the monarchy. He allowed a new prime minister to choose his own cabinet but required that the list should be presented to him for approval.

Until this stage in his career he had been a reformer and moderniser, but as he assumed almost absolute power he lacked the desire and drive to make real progress towards democracy or curb the expanding wealth of the landowning classes and the steady dispossession of the peasants.

Meanwhile, in foreign affairs, his apparently successful incorporation of Eritrea into Ethiopia in 1962 (following federation in 1952) also went wrong. It gave birth to the Eritrean liberation struggle which was to continue as a running sore throughout his lifetime.

In his seventies he was becoming too old to change, though his foreign policy successes continued. He achieved an agreement with the Somali government in 1968. In the same year he organised the peace talks in August in Addis Ababa, which helped to end the Nigerian civil war and took a major part in bringing the Sudanese civil war to an end with a peace agreement in February 1972.

At home progress was more difficult. In February 1967 he introduced a tax reform bill (Proclamation 255) which was the key to modernisation of agriculture, giving minor concessions to the peasantry. But parliament refused to pass the bill. In 1968 three more bills to limit the powers of the landlords and the Ethiopian church were thrown out.

As the ageing Emperor's energies ran out, the privileged classes became more defensive, while the young students, whom he had nurtured clamoured for quicker change. A succession of student strikes ended in the repeated closure of Haile Selassie university and other schools.

The war in Eritrea was an increasing drain on the economy with half of the armed forces locked in a fruitless struggle. Then in 1973 came a severe famine, affecting tens of thousands. Haile Selassie's shame and refusal to acknowledge the severity of the catastrophe brought strikes, student demonstrations and finally gave the army the pretext to intervene.

It was a creeping coup. At first the soldiers merely sought better conditions for themselves, then gradually extended their demands to thorough reform of the whole feudal system.

At first he was retained as nominal Head of State, but finally the radicals prevailed and he was formally arrested and deposed on 12 September 1974.

On that fateful day he was summoned to one of his own rooms in the Imperial palace and a small group of officers formally read a proclamation to him accusing him of corruption and neglect.

An embarassing silence followed and then the old man, broken by the strain of seven months of revolution summoned up the courage of dignity of his forefathers and said, "We have served our people in war and peace. If we have to step down for the good of the people, we will not oppose this."

He was then held in his palace under house arrest, while his officials or associates were eliminated. The military government told of how he and his family had enriched themselves and sent money abroad to Swiss bank accounts, but he had kept most of his great wealth inside the country, often spending his own money on pet projects.

Scarcely able to understand how his glory, power and wealth had been wrenched from him, he became increasingly frail and ill. Forty five years of hard work and effort in modernising Ethiopia had been rewarded by disgrace at the hands of his people.

He died on 27 August 1975. The government said he had died of natural causes while under medical supervision, but some say he was suffocated and buried in the palace grounds without his family being allowed to retrieve his body. Ethiopia became a republic in 1975.

8. Heroes of the resistance

The Great Asantehene

OSEI BONSU
1779-1824

Osei Bonsu was arguably the greatest of the Asantehenes - the Asante kings. He ruled over a highly sophisticated civilisation and was the architect of Asante prosperity achieving many reforms in the fields of art, culture, diplomacy and systems of ruling tributary peoples. He totally defeated the Fante and became involved in a long haggle with the British, who refused to recognise Asante sovereignty over their rivals.

He was a clever and honourable man who recognised the power of the British and at every stage tried to negotiate a permanent settlement. He realised that the future of his peoples depended on their relationship with, what was then the world's greatest imperial power, but he could not overcome British suspicion and was repeatedly misunderstood by them. Eventually this led to war and the temporary defeat of the British.

At the time of his death he had extended the Asante empire to its greatest limits, virtually dominating the whole of what has become modern day Ghana.

Osei Bonsu (Tutu Kwame), is generally known by the name Osei Bonsu (Osei the whale). He was given this nickname because it was he who extended the Asante empire to the Atlantic coast. He bathed in the sea and was dubbed "the whale" the greatest creature of the ocean.

He was born in 1779 and in 1800 became the seventh Asantehene, a long line of Asante kings stretching back to the 16th century. He came to power in a palace coup backed by the senior army commanders who were dismayed that the former Asantehene, Osei Kwame, had taken on the Muslim religion. They were worried that the new religion would introduce alien egalitarian ideas and threaten the established order in Asante society.

The Asante civilisation had been established for centuries. Their heartland was the area that is today central Ghana, around the capital

Kumasi. They were a warlike people who had become extraordinarily wealthy by exploiting their gold deposits and the slave trade.

The glories of their civilisation bedazzled the first European explorers, who reported on the cultural richness of the kingdom. Arts and crafts were highly developed. Trained potters, weavers and goldsmiths made beautiful artefacts everywhere embellished in gold. Tailors made cloth using gold thread. Every year the ornaments of the Asantehenes were melted down and remade. Asante amulets were famed throughout the world.

Osei made a personal contribution by developing his capital Kumasi and by rebuilding the Aban – a stone-built palace of culture, with a great collection of arts and crafts.

The Asante grew rich on trade with the coastal peoples and the British, Dutch and Danes who had established forts along the coastline. When Britain abolished the slave trade in 1807, Osei Bonsu resisted the move strongly and argued his case at every opportunity, while his people continued to grow rich on trade in gold dust and kola nuts. He encouraged the formation of indigenous state-sponsored trading companies which challenged the foreign traders on the coast.

Osei inherited a complex bureaucratic, centralised state. All the power was concentrated in his hands and he made all the main appointments. He had a minister of finance with a whole department under him collecting taxes for a central treasury. There was a diplomatic corps staffed by professional *akyeame*, or "linguists", skilled in the process of negotiation.

Osei made various reforms: he insisted on making appointments on merit rather than based on family connections and he also devised a new way to control tributary tribes by appointing resident commissioners who raised taxes and acted as intelligence officers. He had a large standing army and could raise 80,000 men at short notice, 50,000 of them armed with muskets.

Since the 18th century, the traditional rivals of the Asante were the Fante, another group of tribes, who blocked all the trading routes to the coast. The Fante were also disliked because they were middlemen who could charge fraudulent prices and adulterate trade (mixing base metals with gold and diluting the rum).

Tensions between the two groups were mounting as Osei came to power. A prolonged conflict was then touched off in 1807 when two rebel chiefs from an outlying Asante province took refuge with the Fante. Osei raised a force to pursue them and in a series of battles defeated his neighbours. The two fugitive chiefs took refuge in the British fort at Anomabo on the coast. Osei laid seige and so great was his threat that the British commander surrendered one of the chiefs to him.

Osei was well pleased that the great colonial power had recognised his strength, but tensions persisted. Britain wanted to abolish the slave trade, while Osei Bonsu saw slavery as the traditional way to deal with prisoners taken in war. He told a British explorer that he could not afford to feed them and keep them as prisoners, "unless I kill or sell them, they will grow strong and kill my people."

Osei's other main complaint was that he could not get the British to recognise the Asante sovereignty over the Fante, even after he had totally conquered them.

A series of British diplomats arrived in Kumasi from 1816 onwards trying to negotiate a treaty with the Asante. Osei Bonsu greatly respected the British. He often told his visitors, "I want to be the greatest King in Africa, as the British King is the greatest in Europe." He was prepared to make many concessions to gain British friendship, but each time the British baulked at acknowledging his sovereignty over their traditional trading partners, the Fante.

In February 1819 Joseph Dupuis was briefly appointed British consul to Kumasi and he came very near to arranging a permanent treaty with a willing Osei, but their plans were ruined when a new goveror, Sir Charles McCarthy, arrived from Sierra Leone.

From the first McCarthy was antagonistic, referring to the Asante as "true barbarians" and saying that it was "useless to negotiate with them." Osei had been totally misunderstood. Soon he found McCarthy had formed a grand alliance of coastal chiefs and had stirred up the Fante in revolt.

Osei was finally driven into putting down a fresh outbreak of rebellion. Militarily he gained some quick successes. McCarthy countered by impetuously leading a force of 400 untrained men to "teach Osei a lesson." On 21 January 1824 he met Osei's 10,000 strong Asante army at Nsamanko. His troops were cut to pieces and he was himself killed.

Strangely enough, Osei died, probably of some undefined illness on the same day as his enemy Sir Charles McCarthy. He was only 45 years old. He had brought the Asante to the peak of their military power with most of the country under their control. Britain was to strike back and defeat them in a series of Asante wars in the 19th century, but the core of the great Asante civilisation was to persist to modern times.

Father of Algerian Resistance

ABD EL-KADER
1808-1883

Abd el-Kader was the first of the great heroes of Algerian resistance against the French. A highly educated and civilised man, he was not cut out to raise the banner of Islam in a religious and nationalist struggle, but for 15 years he resisted the new colonial power which was determined to secure the Algerian coast for France. Let down by his unreliable tribesmen and allies, he was finally ground into submission. For years he was held prisoner in France and finally released to live in Damascus, Syria. There his life's purpose underwent a total change. He showed that he was far more than a nationalist warrior or religious leader. He retired to become a scholar, writer and man of piety. He even turned down the opportunity presented to him by the French, to become the ruler of an independent Arab state in Syria. On another occasion he rescued the Christians of Damascus from death, showing his courage and religious tolerance. As a result he was decorated with the French Legion of Honour.

Abd el-Kader was born in 1808 at Guetna, near Mascara, in Algeria. His father Muhyi ad-Din, came from a noble family of sherifs and was celebrated throughout his country as a Marabout, or religious leader, of the Islamic Sufi order.

As a man of princely rank, Abd el-Kader received the best possible Islamic education in Oran, excelling in theology, philosophy and horsemanship. While still a youth he was taken by his father on the *Hadj* to Mecca and Medina. He and his father returned to Mascara shortly before the French occupied Algiers in July 1830.

At that time Algeria was in a state of dramatic change. A three-way struggle for power had developed. The Turks who had ruled for three centuries were fast losing their grip. The French were eager to take advantage and put an end to the officially sanctioned piracy by the Muslim corsairs, operating from Algerian ports and disrupting trade. France wanted to do this by taking control of the Algerian coast thus capturing the vast wealth accumulated by the local sultans.

The Algerians themselves had no wish to replace lax Turkish rule with a new Christian power. Abd el-Kader's father had been pushed into resistance of France by the tribesmen around Mascara. He had led a number of expeditions to try to recapture Oran from the French, but was not much of a military commander and was glad to hand over to his son who became the Emir of Mascara on 21 November 1832.

The young 24-year-old, burning with religious zeal and the outraged nationalism of his people, saw himself as the champion of Islam against the infidel invader and also against the corrupt and dissolute Turks, though their power was plummeting following the defeat of the Bey of Algiers and the capture of his capital in 1830.

By unfurling the banner of Islam in a religious and nationalist war, the young emir was able to rally most of the tribes of western Algeria.

For the next 15 years he was to carry his struggle against the French. At first he made little progress against a better armed enemy entrenched in the coastal towns, so he tried the tactic of negotiation.

He secured recognition from the French General Desmichels, for his rule over most of western Algeria, where he installed Beys of his own choice. But he soon found that the treaty did not give him the right to export grain or import armaments. This made him resume the war, winning a victory at Macta in 1835. The French struck back directly by capturing his capital Mascara.

They also sent out General Thomas Bugeaud whose first move was to sign another treaty with Abd el-Kader in May 1837. This confirmed Kader's rule in the whole of western Algeria, leaving France only in control of Oran and its environs. But Abd el-Kader was simply waiting for an opportunity to resume the war. He had a regular army of 8,000 infantry and 2,000 cavalry and could call up a further 50,000 Arab irregular horsemen whenever they were needed. He was well furnished with arms and ammunition that he stored in secret locations in the Tell mountains. He firmly and efficiently ruled the areas that he had conquered through *Khalifas* and traditional chiefs.

In November 1839 he felt he was strong enough to formally resume the war with France. General Bugeaud responded with a total change of policy. He decided to tackle the troublesome emir by pursuing a scorched earth policy, destroying cities, disrupting agriculture, burning crops and punishing all tribesmen sympathetic to Abd el-Kader. One by one he captured his arsenals and by the end of 1842 he claimed to have recaptured five-sixths of all of the emir's lands.

Abd el-Kader who was pushed into the far south, had lost his economic base, his armaments and most of his kingdom, but he continued to fight as a traditional Bedouin warrior, moving not only his army but his administration and his people and their flocks across the desert lands on the fringes of the Sahara.

This was no permanent solution, so he took refuge in Morocco in November 1843 and persuaded the Sultan of Morocco to support him in the holy war against the infidel. Bugeaud promptly turned his troops against Morocco and wrought terrible revenge on its sultan at the battle of Isly in August 1844.

Abd el-Kader refused to give up. At the head of a raggle-taggle group of exiles he crossed back into Algeria and was soon rallying the tribesmen in another holy war. With speed that baffled the French, he overran the country that had so recently been pacified and brought the tribesmen out in open rebellion. In September 1845 he surprised and annihilated a small French column in the Tagna valley. All the tribesmen flocked to his standard except the Kabyles, the renowned warrior tribe in the Djurjura mountains. This was the turning point; he was to go no further. Instead he retreated south and then to Morocco where the new sultan, fearing French reprisals, forced him to leave.

This time he found his route to the south blocked by the French. He was reduced to just a handful of troops and a group of defenceless half-starved civilians with nowhere to go, so he decided to give up.

On 23 December 1847 he made his submission to the new French commander, General Lamoriciere, who promised that he would be allowed to leave for Alexandria with his family. But the French government reneged on this agreement and he was held in France until 1852, first in Toulon, then Pau and finally at the Chateau of Amboise.

When Louis Napoleon Bonaparte (Napoleon III) came to power he finally granted him pardon on 16 October 1852, paying respect to his, "courage, character and resignation to unhappiness." Napoleon gave him a generous pension in return for a promise never again to disturb the peace of Algeria.

Abd el-Kader became a changed man in the years that followed. He recognised that France could not be dislodged in Algeria and steadfastly refused to give help or support to any other resistance group.

He went to live in Damascus, in Turkish-occupied Syria. In July 1860 when the Moslems took the city and started to kill the Christians there, he intervened and managed to save many thousands from death, saying he was only doing his duty, "On behalf of religion and humanity." The French recognised this act of heroism on behalf of his religious adversaries and decorated him with the grand cross of the Legion of Honour.

Another mark of his changed character came when he joined an Alexandrian order of Freemasons in June 1864. He justified this by saying that he had become "tolerant of all men no matter what religion they belonged to."

The French gained so much faith in him that in 1865 they proposed that he should become the ruler of an independent Arab state in Syria. But he refused, saying that after the failure of his great nationalist struggle in Algeria, he had vowed to devote the rest of his life to prayer and religious study, "for my remaining days on this earth."

In 1871 when the Algerians again rose in revolt he wrote to them counselling them not to disturb the peace.

He remained true to his new found philosophy, spending his remaining days in ascetic study and prayer, spurning physical pleasures and devoting his life to the glory of God. He seemed to have recognised that his attempt to liberate his country had failed in the face of insurmountable odds and there was nothing that he could do about it. He sought spiritual compensation as an alternative, almost as an atonement.

He spent much time writing theological and philosophical works and an unusual book about the Arab thoroughbred horse. He died at Damascus on 26 May 1883.

Jihadist of the Sudan

EL MAHDI
1848-1885

El Mahdi was not born great, but in his remarkably short life he achieved totally unexpected heights of greatness. He transformed himself from just another provincial Islamic teacher with a burning reform mission, to the creator of the Mahdist state in the Sudan, which he carved out at the height of European imperialism.

He set out as a burning religious reformer, and ended a great military leader and strategist. He started as an ascetic Islamic puritan and finished as a powerful despot indulging his latent sensuality.

His life was short but his followers, the Ansar, are still a powerful force in Sudan today. His descendants are honored as hereditary rulers. They look back on him as a national leader and golden symbol of nationalist resistance to oppressive colonialism - the rock on which the struggle for Sudan's independence was built.

Muhammad Ahmad ibn Sayyid Abdullah was born in 1848 at Dongola on the Nile in the extreme north of Sudan. His father was a Dunqulawi and both a *fiki* (religious teacher) and a boat-builder. His boats were not the steam-powered paddle boats then plying the Nile, but small fishing and ferrying craft.

His son showed little interest in boat-building and was sent to the Koranic school in Omdurman where he immersed himself in religious studies. His devoutness and asceticism, fired by the passionate idealism of youth, soon brought him in conflict with his religious instructors whom he considered too worldly.

In a blazing row he shouted down one teacher for transgressing the divine law. This immediately brought him a following among the other young students.

He moved to Aba island south of Khartoum, which has ever since been a centre for his Ansar followers. There he denounced a second holy man for allowing singing and dancing at his son's circumcision. His single-minded fanaticism was already becoming clear.

There were many contemporary descriptions of him, mainly by the distinguished prisoners whom he took as captives in later life. He was a strong and handsome man, dark skinned, with broad shoulders, a black beard and three tribal markings on his cheeks. He could be a charmer when he wanted. Contemporaries all speak of him as smiling with sparkling eyes.

Rudolf Carl Von Slatin, the captured Governor of Darfur wrote, "He smiled when he prescribed the most brutal tortures for some wretch who had blasphemed or taken a glass of liquor." All witnesses speak of his dominant personality and magnetic charisma.

In 1880 he travelled to El Obeid in Kordofan still bearing the strictly religious mission of restoring true Islam to the Sudan, but he was becoming ever more interested in politics too.

He found a fertile field of discontent. The Egyptian khedives (rulers acknowledged by the Turkish Ottoman emperors) were bleeding Sudan by heavy taxation which they imposed with harsh cruelty. Egyptian soldiers in all the key regions taxed the country dry and were indifferent to the slave traders illegally operating their vicious profession. The British hoped, by controlling the Egyptian khedives, to maintain indirect control of the vast country.

Everywhere Muhammad went he denounced the extortion of the tax gatherers. He wrote a pamphlet summoning true believers to purify their religion from the defilements of the "Turks" (an expression used to describe any northerners from the Ottoman empire) by driving them out of the country.

The Egyptians and their English advisers at first dismissed Muhammad Ahmad as yet another provincial *fakir* leading a rabble of fanatical followers. The English soldiers called them dervishes and dubbed him the "Mad Mullah". In August 1881 they sent a force of 200 men under Abou Saoud to bring the troublesome fanatic to Khartoum for punishment. But the party was ambushed by the primitively armed Mahdists and driven off.

This victory of spears and clubs over rifles brought a wave of religious exhilaration to Muhammad. The 33-year-old showed his new found confidence by declaring himself *El-Mahdi al Montasir*, "The expected guide". He called for a *jihad* to drive all the Turks from Sudan and for religious purification to bring the people back to the true faith.

The Mahdi's personal conviction, allied to the magnetism and charisma that touched all who knew him, soon attracted thousands to his black, yellow and green standard.

He defeated another force sent to arrest him, but he knew that he was not ready to resist repeated attacks. He wanted time to rally his supporters and organise. He embarked on a "long march" to the remote Nuba hills in Kordofan where he could rebuild his forces. His reputation expanded before him, spreading far and wide.

Another Egyptian expedition by Jebel Gedir, at the head of 7,000 troops was wiped out in June 1882, and by the end of the year the whole of Arab Sudan south of Khartoum was in rebellion.

In August 1882 the Mahdi laid siege to El Obeid, the capital of Kordofan. Meeting fierce resistance, he starved the garrison into surrender and allowed his tribesmen to butcher the survivors.

In September a still larger force under William Hicks, a former British officer in the Indian Army and the Governor General of the region, and Ala al-Din Siddiq Pasha mounted an expedition. The Mahdi let them penetrate into waterless scrub. He then persuaded the stragglers to defect before cutting the rest to pieces. Both Hicks and Ala Din perished.

The Mahdi's prestige soared. He was recognised throughout the Muslim world. Many countries sent envoys. In December Rudolf von Slatin, the Governor of Darfur, capitulated and became a prisoner of the Mahdi and his successors for the next 12 years. He adopted Islam so that his life would be spared.

The Mahdi, at the zenith of his powers as a military strategist, gradually turned his wild followers into trained troops. He imposed iron discipline on all his men introducing the harshest of punishments for drinking, smoking, adultery, lying, the clapping of hands, dancing and the company of strange women. These precepts, invoked in the name of Allah, were ferociously enforced. The most trivial offences drew flogging to death or the cutting off of hands and other limbs. He was the first Muslim leader in the Sudan to introduce his own currency with coins bearing his own name.

While the star of Mahdism rose in Sudan, the British government under Gladstone was only dimly aware of what was happening and hoped that the minor problems could be dealt with by the Egyptians. They even withdrew the eccentric hero General Charles Gordon from his governor-generalship of Khartoum in 1880 and allowed him to go home. But as more British soldiers were slain and as the Mahdi became increasingly bumptious and self congratulatory, imperial pride began to suffer.

A telegram from the Mahdi at this time summoned the Khedive of Egypt, the Queen of England, the Kaiser of Germany and the President of France to submit to the rule of Islamic righteousness.

In March 1884, Gordon was sent back to Khartoum with contradictory instructions to evacuate the Sudan and to hold fast. Gordon who had been away from Sudan for several years was convinced that he could defeat the Mahdi with a handful of British officers and their Egyptian troops.

The Mahdi did not allow him to equivocate for long. Already his General Uthman Digna, had cleared the Egyptians out of most of eastern Sudan except for the Red Sea ports. By October 1884 he was encamped outside Khartoum and tightening the noose round Gordon's neck.

The stage was set for a dramatic clash between the champion of Islam and nascent Sudanese nationalism and a hero of Victorian England.

Though never an establishment figure, Gordon was a dedicated Christian and believer in the imperial values of the time. As the world watched the two giant champions prepared for the showdown.

The Mahdi had 30,000 troops to lay siege to Khartoum. He knew his opponents were well armed and still supplied by steamers on the Nile so he decided to starve Gordon's men into surrender. Gradually the Mahdi cut off all forms of supply and communication.

Though he knew that a British relief expedition had arrived in Cairo and was getting ever nearer, he calculated that he still had time to starve Gordon out.

He was mightily encouraged when he captured the *Abbas* steamer which Gordon had dispatched downstream carrying all the strategic details of his situation in Khartoum, plus his diaries and even the cypher that the British were using to send messages. His troops also captured several Europeans, while Colonel Stewart, Gordon's deputy was killed.

"Now we have understood all," the Mahdi wrote to Gordon, inviting him yet again to surrender and receiving another refusal.

The Mahdi knew that the relief column under Wolseley was getting ever nearer. He sent his troops to confront an advance column and for the first time tasted defeat. His men were badly mauled at Abou Klea, sustaining heavy losses. But still he waited. Though he was frightened of the fearsome reputation of the British redcoats he hung on knowing that Gordon's garrison was getting weaker by the day, while the Nile waters were dropping to their lowest level.

On the night of 26 January 1885, his spies told him that the river mud had dried out to such an extent that troops could make a crossing. He decided to attack at about 3am. Within hours Khartoum was sacked by his ravishing hordes. Gordon was killed and his severed head was put on display in triumph.

The Mahdi's waiting game had paid off. Just. The relief column arrived three days later to find Khartoum shattered and smoking in Mahdist hands.

The British retreated ignominiously. The Mahdi's triumph was complete. But the totality of his victory brought a huge anti- climax. He had established an empire over almost the whole of Sudan and there was no further summit to climb.

Now was the time to taste the sweet fruits of victory. He became sleek and fat and established a huge harem. He personally selected the prettiest girls surviving from the sack of Khartoum. He put away his patched *jibbeh* (tunic) and began to wear silk shirts and pantaloons. His women rubbed his body with oils, manicured his nails and made up his face with antimony, painted round his eyes. He became so gross that a beefy black slave was employed especially to hoist him onto his horse every morning as he went to the mosque.

But he hardly had time to enjoy his new found life of luxury when he died on 22 June 1885. He had survived General Gordon by only five months. Some say he had been poisoned by an unwilling woman prisoner in his harem, others that he caught smallpox, but the most likely explanation is that he died of typhus in the insanitary conditions after the fall of Khartoum. His over indulged body was not resistant to disease.

So the man who had set out to purge Islam of its impurities, and had quarrelled with his teachers over their worldliness, died a debauched sensualist. He who had wanted to be a soldier of God, turned out to be a soldier of the sword, a consummate master of military strategy.

His Mahdist empire lived on after him under a chosen successor Abdallahi, the Khalifa, who was still more despotic, perpetrating his cruelty in the name of the Lord. The Mahdist state continued until his defeat by Horatio Kitchener at the Battle of Omdurman in 1899.

It had been a brief 14 years, but the Mahdi had raised the banner both of Islam and of freedom. He had formed Sudan's first Islamic state and was indeed the father of Sudanese nationalism. Whatever his moral defects, as the Mahdi he had asserted his headship of the community of true Muslims.

Merchant Prince

JAJA
1821-1891

Jaja was a slave who rose to become a Nigerian king, waxing rich and powerful on the lucrative palm oil trade. A man of exceptional ability, drive and ambition he overcame all social handicaps and founded the kingdom of Opobo, where he could establish his mercantilist domain. Ruthless when his commercial supremacy was challenged, he remained a great administrator and moderniser.

But a new challenge, in the late 19th century, came with the scramble for Africa as Britain decided to assert its political control and protect its own oil-traders. Jaja resisted cunningly for 18 years and built a prosperous nation before being forced into submission.

Jaja was born in 1821. He was an Ibo who came from the village of Amaigbo in the Orlu area, at the heart of Iboland, in Nigeria. While still a youngster he was kidnapped and taken into slavery by an Ijaw chief living in the coastal port of Bonny. His master found him "insubordinate and headstrong" and gave him to Madu, of the Annie Pepple House of Chiefs, one of the two main Houses vying for political and commercial supremacy in Bonny.

He started life in the lowest strata of Bonny society; not only was he a slave but an outsider. But his abilities soon became apparent and he was allowed to work his way up the commercial ladder, getting to know all those involved in the lucrative palm oil trade. He worked and saved, building a small business by buying a canoe and taking it up the creeks to trade.

He was already well established as the principal trader for the Annie Pepple House, when the head chief died, in 1863, leaving heavy debts and political turmoil caused by competition with the rival houses. None of the other chiefs was prepared to take on the responsibilities involved and, as was often the practice, they looked about for another candidate.

By then Jaja, in his early 40s and a man of proven abilities, was ready to accept a new challenge. He was offered the post as head of the House and jumped at the opportunity. Within two years he had paid off the Annie Pepple debts, but rivalry with other houses and jealousy from within had brought the chiefs of Bonny to a state of virtual civil war.

In 1869 he came up with an idea of exceptional originality. He decided to lead his followers away and found an entirely new state at Opobo, on another creek to the east where he could control all the traders of the hinterland and cut them off from Bonny. It was a masterstroke.

On 15 February 1870 he proclaimed Opobo independent. For the first time he had full scope to exercise his organisational ability and business acumen. He established plantations, built a port and established settlements where he could control the supply of palm oil to the European merchants.

He modernised selectively, retaining traditional social structures and native religion, while encouraging western secular (but not mission) education. He set up a school in Opobo run by a Sierra Leonean and an Afro-American.

In 1873 the British recognised him as King of Opobo in return for his promise to keep the peace with Bonny. He preserved the best relations with the hinterland tribes who were his main oil suppliers. Opobo became rich and mustered a formidable army. In 1875 he was strong enough to send a contingent to fight on the British side in the Ashanti war. Queen Victoria recognised his services by awarding him a sword of honour.

He was at the height of his powers. He encouraged the new European "supercargoes", steam ships of shallow draft, that could negotiate the creeks to trade in his kingdom and charged them "comey" or customs dues. He even developed some direct trade with Liverpool, cutting out the European middleman altogether.

In 1881 Jaja revealed his total ruthlessness in pursuit of his commercial goals, when a group of Kwa-Igbo tried to trade directly with European merchants. He sent troops in canoes, armed with breech loaded cannon and rifles. He plundered their villages and cruelly slaughtered men, women and children who were powerless to oppose him.

He was building trouble for himself. In the 1880s the scramble for Africa reached its peak and Britain was desperate to extend its protection to the whole of Nigeria before the French and Germans gained a foothold.

In 1884 Britain offered Jaja its "protection". He responded with characteristic cunning, delaying agreement by asking what a protectorate meant. He was told by the British Consul Hewett, " The Queen does not want to take your country or your markets, but at the same time she is anxious that no other nation should take them...she will leave your country still under your government, she has no wish to disturb your rule."

By 1885 Britain had proclaimed a protectorate over the whole oil rivers area and Jaja's interests soon clashed with British companies seeking to exploit the new opportunities. Britain insisted that Jaja should open up Opobo to free trade and forbade him to exact his comey. Jaja protested that this was in breach of the 1884 treaty and sent a delegation to London to protest.

As the quarrel escalated in 1887, the British Consul Harry Johnson decided to deal with his recalcitrant opponent by summoning him to a meeting on board the British gunboat, HMS *Goshawk*.

Jaja knew he was in danger and thought at first of taking a white hostage, but abandoned this plan after getting an assurance that he would be allowed to go free no matter what the outcome of the meeting. Johnson gave him his solemn promise, in writing, to this effect, but once on board the perfidious consul told him that unless he agreed to go to Accra, in the Gold Coast for trial, his capital Opobo would be bombarded.

Jaja did not want to leave his people to the mercy of the British guns so he had no alternative but to agree to trial in a foreign country. He was duly found guilty and banished to the West Indies on a pension of £800 per year.

But the people of Opobo were outraged at the treachery and deportation of their leader. Their protest was such that the Colonial Secretary set up a commission of inquiry under Claude MacDonald in 1891. He recommended that Jaja should be returned and reinstated. He set sail for home but died on the long voyage back on 7 July 1891. His body was buried in Opobo.

In 1893 Britain set up the Niger Coast Protectorate governed by a consul general responsible to the Foreign Office. The era of the kings and houses was at an end.

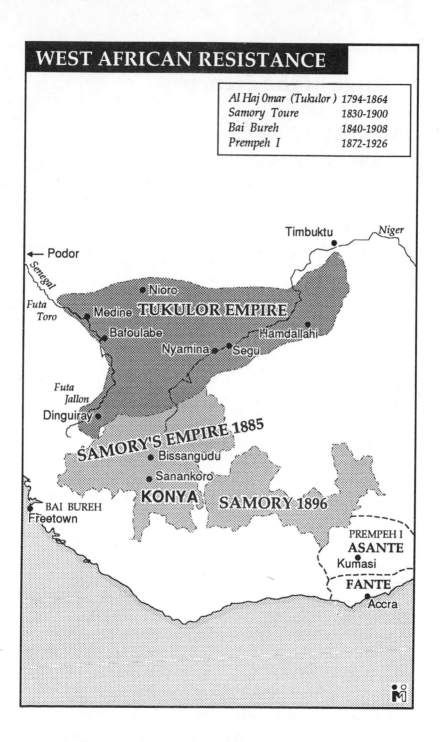

WEST AFRICAN RESISTANCE

Al Haj Omar (Tukulor)	1794-1864
Samory Toure	1830-1900
Bai Bureh	1840-1908
Prempeh I	1872-1926

Timbuktu

Niger

← Podor

Senegal

Futa
Toro

Nioro

Medine **TUKULOR EMPIRE**

Bafoulabe

Nyamina Segu

Hamdallahi

Futa
Jallon

Dinguiray

SAMORY'S EMPIRE 1885

Bissangudu

Sanankoro

KONYA

SAMORY 1896

BAI BUREH
Freetown

PREMPEH I
ASANTE
Kumasi

FANTE
Accra

Scourge of the French

SAMORY TOURÉ
(c.1830-1900)

The name of Samory Touré echoes through the ages as the
scourge of French colonialism. He was one of the greatest leaders
of African resistance at the end of the 19th century when
colonialism marked its most aggressive expansion. For 16 years
he harried and hassled a technically superior French army and
blocked the path of French expansion into the West African
hinterland.

Yet ironically, this role as a champion of African resistance was
thrust upon him. For most of his life he had no comprehension of
the French threat, his preoccupation was rebuilding the Malinke
empire and the founding of a new Islamic state. Indeed the rulers
and the peoples who followed him did turn to Islam as the force
which gave them unity and dignity under colonialism.

Samory Touré, arguably the most specialised military leader of his
generation, was descended from the Mandingo or Malinke, the
founders of the great Mali empire of the Middle Ages.
   He was born in the Konya region where his forebears, the Kamara
nobles, had lived since the 1700s. The family had practically abandoned
Islam and turned to animist religions. He followed his father into trade
in order to expand the family fortune. He travelled far and wide through
the rolling Savannah uplands of Guinea and as far as Sierra Leone on
the West African coast.
   Though he soon showed great aptitude for whatever he did, he was
never fulfilled as a trader. He was a difficult, remote personality who had
rejected his animist education, returning to the Islam of his forefathers.
   Guinea at that time was a mosaic of minor warring kingdoms fighting
for control of the rich territory on the edge of the mountains and forests.
The Malinke were disintegrating into warring kingdoms. The rising
power were the Sise, who, when they invaded Konya, captured Samory
and his mother. He persuaded his captors to let him join their army and
soon showed that he was a natural soldier.

Legend has it that he stayed in the Sise army for seven years, seven months and seven days, but it was probably a slightly shorter period which finished in 1858. When the Sise king died he did not hit it off with his successor Sere Brema and he quit his army.

But Samory remained a professional soldier and immediately found a job with a rival tribe, the Berete. Another quarrel with his latest masters caused him to return to lead his own Kamara people who by then were being squeezed by Sise imperial ambitions. The Muslim Sise were at the height of their expansion and the Kamara were a weak and declining power, but Samory had learnt a lot in his years of apprenticeship in the Sise army. In 1861 he swore a solemn oath at Dyala to defend his people.

He was a match for any of the Sise commanders. His army was small and weak, but entirely loyal to him and he had extraordinary tactical ability. He used the mountains and forests and his knowledge of the countryside to spring ambushes when the situation was right.

He established his capital at Sanakoro in 1862 and gradually expanded his authority over surrounding areas. He became reconciled with the Sise and helped them crush the Berete in 1864-65, but his old adversary Sere Brema, feeling Samory was becoming too ambitious, turned again to attack him.

Samory was forced once more into the southern rain forests of Kononkoro. There he established a new headquarters and started to train a new army loyal to him alone.

He waited until the Sise were enmeshed in a war with their northern neighbours the Wasulu, before emerging with his new force. In 1868 he took on the title of *Faama* signifying his ambition as a military leader. At the peak of power he had an army of over 30,000 men divided into infantry and cavalry units. He equipped them with primitive guns which his blacksmiths could repair themselves. Later he imported repeating rifles from Sierra Leone and his blacksmiths reached such a level of proficiency that they could make copies of the new guns.

Though he had become a Muslim, he was a total pragmatist. Throughout his career he found that military progress depended on playing off the Muslim kingdoms against those of the animists. He had no hesitation in switching when it furthered his military ambition.

His great era of expansion started in 1871. He thrust northwards destroying the kingdom of Nantenen-Famudu and then Toron. He emerged as the strongest military chief in the area, and vowed henceforth not to work for his Kamara "uncles" but on his own account.

By 1875 his empire was expanding fast. He crushed the Sankaran and conquered the entire Niger valley from his birthplace in Konya up to the Futa Djallon which was held by the Tukolor - the warring nomads of the Sahara. He destroyed the Sise empire and seized Kankan by 1881.

His army, replenished constantly from those he defeated, became the most powerful in the area. He established a new capital at Bisandugu and surrounded himself with Muslim advisers. Apart from the sheer glory of military conquest, he wanted to create a prosperous state built on trade. He devised a system in which his soldiers could be employed working on civil projects for at least half the year, when they were not actually engaged in fighting.

By the mid-1880s he had established the most powerful empire in the western Sudan stretching along the border between the Sudanese savannah and the West African rain forest, stretching from inside Sierra Leone in the west, to the Sassandra river in the Ivory Coast, in the east.

He had mastered the diverse tribal groups, animist or Muslim, which had opposed him. He was on the point of creating a stable state waxing rich on trade in slaves, and gold from the goldfields at Bure, when a new and totally unexpected threat loomed, that was to change the course of his life.

The French had arrived. The scramble for Africa had started. France in the grip of colonial ambition and determined to bottle up the British in Sierra Leone were pushing up the Niger and into western Sudan. They wanted to build a railway to Bamako in Mali. Smaller kingdoms crumbled before them, but Samory at the height of his powers, blocked their path.

His first brushes with the French came in 1882. They were inconclusive. He beat off the French forces of Borgnis Desbordes, while taking heavy losses. His brother received an even heavier mauling in 1883.

Samory recognised the danger of the French challenge, particularly so when they occupied his goldfields at Bure cutting him off from a prime source of wealth.

Always a calculating realist, he then turned to diplomacy. First he tried to persuade the British in Sierra Leone to take his kingdom under their protection. Meeting with total rejection, he signed a treaty with the French on 28 March 1886, in which he agreed to relinquish control of the left (east) bank of the Niger. In return he was left with the right bank and allowed to retain the valuable goldfields at Bure. The following year he agreed to place even his own area under French protection.

It was a measure of how desperate his situation had become. Nor were the French content to leave him in peace. They continued to conspire with his vassals, encouraging dissidence and rebellion in all parts of his empire.

Samory, already involved in a war in Sikasso on the extreme eastern border of his empire, was left greatly weakened. He made a treaty with the British in Sierra Leone in May 1890 which allowed him to resume supplies of modern weapons for the next three years. But the flames of rebellion, fanned by the French spread throughout the empire, while outright confrontation with a succession of French officers at the head of their *Tirailleurs Senegalais* was resumed from 1891.

Samory suffered a major defeat in January 1892 at the hands of France's new commander, Humbert. Though Samory and his men, fought like demons, clinging fiercely to every defensive position, they were heavily defeated. Samory lost his capital at Bissandugu, plus other strategic towns and his supply route to Sierra Leone.

Samory realised that he could never defeat the French and showed his flexibility by adopting a totally new strategy. In face of constant French pressure, he decided to abandon his homeland and the Niger, and to move his army, his people and their flocks hundreds of miles to the east. The grand exodus, towards what is now the north of the Ivory Coast, lasted most of 1894. Luckily for him, the French had other preoccupations with the Tuareg and Tukolor further down the Niger.

But by 1895 hostilities resumed, this time from the south, with the French in the Ivory Coast and the British in Ghana both concerned at the legendary commander who threatened their northern frontiers from his new base.

Squeezed between the competing imperial powers, far from his grassroots Malinke support, harried by local peoples, he found it difficult to recreate even a rudimentary system of government. He found himself surrounded on all sides by the new imperialists and their allies.

He made one last play to set the British and the French against each other by offering to secede Buna a town he pretended to control which was acually under British rule, but his bluff was called. In June 1898 he decided to head back to his heartland via his Toma allies in Liberia.

Rejected by the local people he took refuge in the Dan forests while a French column under Colonel Lartigue advanced through the rains against him.

Samory punished his opponents in one last glorious battle, but buoyed by this unexpected success he made the greatest tactical blunder of his career. He tried to take his exhausted army and its horde of camp followers through the mountains to Liberia.

He found his route blocked by Gouraud who in one swift action took him prisoner, in the rainswept mountain passes, on 29 September 1898.

The old man was given no mercy by the French who had hunted him for the last 14 years. They announced his deportation to Gabon. Despite a suicide attempt on the way, at St Louis in Senegal, he was indeed imprisoned on Ndjole island in the middle of the Ogooue river.

Within less than two years the ageing and exhausted man, taunted by failure and deprived of his proud freedom, died on 2 June 1900. Little physical trace remains. His very tomb has been swallowed up by the bush.

But his reputation as the scourge of French imperialism lives on. No man had fought harder or survived longer.

The Rebellious Chief

BUREH, Bai
c.1840-1908

Bai Bureh's reputation far outweighs his actual achievements, but he was one of the few heroes from the small country of Sierra Leone to make a stand against British imperialism. Most historians of West Africa acknowledge his role. His rebellion against the hut tax was an expression of the determination of the local chiefs to prevent Britain from expanding its rule from the colony of Freetown to the protectorate.

Bai Bureh wanted to defend traditional African society against encroachment and taxation by the new white imperialists. Though never able to hold out for long against technically superior forces, he proved a remarkably resourceful and determined champion of his people.

Originally called Kebalai, he was born in the Loko tribe around 1840, but this date is only approximate, based on calculations of his estimated age at the height of his rebellion in 1898.

His home was at the little village of Rokthenti on the Mabole river, a tributary of the Little Scarcies, just north of the present-day town at Makeni.

He served as a war chief of Bokari, the Loko ruler at Forekaria and took part in wars between the Temne (allied to the Loko) and the Susu in 1859.

In 1871 he was elected Chief of Kasse, assuming the title of Bai Bureh. There he received a stipend from the British and lived the life of a loyal stipendary chief. But the British control of the hinterland was sufficiently remote for him to become involved in a further war against the Susu (1874-75) and against another local chieftain, Kairimu (1889-92). His exploits in these wars gave him an almost mythical reputation for courage and independent mindedness.

Bai Bureh's martial exploits exasperated the British who wanted to extend their control from Freetown (the colony) to the protectorate (the hinterland extending over the rest of the country). Bai Bureh knew that this would mean the imposition of a district commissioner over him and considerable limitation of his own powers. A dispute developed and the British made several attempts to arrest him, but each time he beat off the expeditions of the frontier force.

Britain appointed a new governor Frederic Cardew in 1894. He was a single-minded authoritarian who announced the declaration of a protectorate and a total reorganisation of the administration in August 1896. Captain Wilfred Sharpe was appointed the new district commissioner of Bai Bureh's area, and was treated with contempt by him.

Seemingly unaware of the resentment that the new changes were having on the rural people, Governor Cardew then decided to impose a hut tax throughout the protectorate to pay for the expenses incurred by the new administration. The district commissioners were instructed to send out letters to the local chiefs to collect a tax of five shillings per year on each house, and ten shillings on larger dwellings, an appreciable sum in those days. Bai Bureh's men intercepted his letter and he was able to deny that he had ever received it. Bureh was determined to make a stand against an unpopular tax to pay for an administration that had been imposed upon his people.

The authorities could not accept insubordination from such a popular chief. Sharpe tried first to collect the tax from the local traders who refused to pay, saying that the chiefs had threatened to kill them if they did. He then decided to arrest Bai Bureh but his small West African Frontier force, composed mostly of West Indian soldiers, found itself surrounded by a much larger force of Bureh's men. Early banter and taunts on both sides suddenly flared into shooting.

This confrontation in February 1898 started the hut tax war. Bai Bureh took to the bush and used his military skills to organise a defensive campaign. He built stockades along the main routes out of palm logs buttressed with boulders and equipped his men to defend these positions with their trade guns - improved versions of the musket primed with gunpowder. Whenever the "Frontiers", equipped with modern rifles, attacked in force, Bureh's men would retire to another prepared position. Sometimes stockades were built on either side of the road so they could cover each other during an engagement with the troops.

In this way Bureh's men were able to harry the colonial forces for several months. The Frontiers retaliated with ferocity, destroying 97 towns and villages thought to be sympathetic to Bureh. But Bureh maintained a strict discipline over his supporters and earned a reputation for conducting an honorable war.

When Governor Cardew placed a price of £100 on his head, Bureh riposted by offering a reward of £500 on the Governor's head. Britain became so alarmed at the rising discontent, that it sent out a new regiment which eventually relieved the garrison at Karene.

In April the sporadic protests, that had become a general uprising against the unfair tax, then spread to the southern tribes who had no leader like Bai Bureh. The result was a ferocious war of intimidation and violence in which many Europeans and Creoles (descendants of the freed slaves) were murdered.

Bai Bureh realised the futility of continuing the struggle against the ever-increasing British reinforcements and finally surrendered on 16 November 1898. He emerged from the bush with raised hands urging the soldiers not to shoot as the war was over.

He was held prisoner first at Karene, then at Freetown when the military thought an attempt might be made by his supporters to rescue him. Governor Cardew wanted him tried for treason, but as he had lived and fought outside "Her majesty's dominions" in the protectorate, proceedings could not be brought against him. London recommended that he be released but locally his reputation was such that there was always the fear that he might escape and resume his resistance. He was kept in detention and on 30 July 1899 was deported to the Gold Coast. He was allowed to return home in 1905 to resume his chieftaincy for the few remaining years before his death in 1908.

Despite a special commission of inquiry by the British lawyer Sir David Chalmers, the hut tax was retained and the stand of Bai Bureh seemed to have achieved nothing. But Britain had learnt to deal less aggressively with its chiefs, who provided the basis for indirect rule in the protectorate until independence on 27 April 1961.

The 'Mad' Mullah

MOHAMMED ABDILLE HASSAN
1864-1920

Mohammed Abdille Hassan is scornfully remembered by the British as the mad mullah, the leader of the dancing dervishes, who stirred up factional and religious trouble among ungovernable tribesmen. But to every nationalist he remains a great military leader who fought three major world powers for more than 20 years. Indeed he was the last African to sustain a prolonged armed struggle against colonialism. He was not finally defeated until after the First World War in 1920.

He started life as a religious teacher, who adopted a strong puritanical faith and declared a *jihad* (holy war) in 1899. But his desire to purify Islam soon turned into a campaign against colonialism and an attempt to preserve national identity against colonial encroachment.

All he could do was stall the process, but the stone forts that he built still stand and the poems that he recited are still part of the rich Somali oral tradition.

Sayyid Mohammed Abdille Hassan was born in 1864, into the Habir Suleiman clan originating in the Ogaden. He also had strong links with other clans through marriage, particularly among the Dolbahante.

Little is known of his parents or his early life, but he was intelligent, single-minded and fired with religious zeal. It is said that he had learnt the Koran at the age of seven and as a teenager he was excited by the stories of the jihadist exploits of the Mahdi (q.v.) of the Sudan.

He went to Aden for Islamic studies and by the age of 20 he had become a religious teacher and a sheikh. He had been particularly influenced by Muhammed Salih who had broken with the *Qadiriya* sect, followed by most Somalis, and had set up his own *Salihiya* following, a new puritanical order that banned the consumption of the popular narcotic qat.

In 1894 he did his *hadj* to Mecca and travelled extensively among the holy cities, meeting other young zealots determined to bring radical reform to Islam. He also visited Mogadishu and some historians claim he went as far as the Mahdist stronghold in Kordofan in Sudan.

He was mature and well travelled when he returned to Somalia in 1895 to find it was firmly in the grip of the colonial powers. Britain had been consolidating its position in northern Somalia since 1884 and the Italians had been doing the same in the south of the country.

At the very time that he wanted to preach Islamic revivalism and purify the faith, he found that the educational and social system was under threat of a colonial administration and Christian missions. He noted that the missionaries were already pressing Christian names on his people and threatening the very foundations of the faith.

He settled in the northern port of Berbera where he started a Koranic school and soon clashed with the Roman Catholic mission. In 1897 he moved inland to Burao to be among his own Dolbahante people. There he became a mullah, a Muslim judge and theologian soon attracting over 5,000 followers. It was from Burao in August 1899 that he launched his *jihad*. It was both a religious and political movement, directed first at the majority of Somalis who followed the *Qadiriya* sect, but turning later into a holy war against colonialism.

He called his followers *darwish* to signify a brotherhood transcending clan-family affiliations. They became known to the British as dervishes. He built a 12,000 strong standing army which dominated the Haud (along the border with Ethiopia) and the Ogaden. He drew his arms from the Sultan of Obbia, who was from the Majerteen clan and by raiding caravans with a fast-moving camel corps.

His growing strength was seen as a threat to the British who sent Colonel E. J. E. Swayne to drive him out of Burao and across the Haud. He fought three pitched battles against Swayne but suffered heavy losses and was finally forced deep into Italian Somaliland.

But the British had still not broken the Mullah's power and they persuaded the Italians to allow them to mount another expedition, this time from the sea port at Obbia, which was under the Italian protectorate, in February 1903.

The Mullah gave Britain a bloody nose in two ferocious engagements before crossing north through the British lines and settling in the Nogal valley, leading to the port of Illig.

On 10 January 1904 another major battle took place at Jidballi. This time the Mullah lost over 1,000 men and was forced to flee into the extreme north east of the country (the very tip of the Horn of Africa).

Britain offered him safe passage to Mecca but he refused to desert his people. Instead he negotiated with the Italians and in March 1905 signed an agreement with them which allowed him and his followers to occupy the Nogal valley.

For several years he kept the peace with the colonial authorities, but trouble came from an unexpected quarter. Muhammad Salih, the leader of the Salihiya sect in Mecca, sent a letter accusing the Mullah of various transgressions. This caused a split among his followers and some left. He then launched those who had remained faithful to him to attack those Majerteen who had been spreading calumnies against him. His objective was to link up with sympathisers in the Ogaden and Haud.

Lord Asquith's Liberal government felt that further action against him would be costly and fruitless and issued orders to the British troops in March 1910, to abandon the interior altogether and withdraw to the coast.

The Mullah was at the peak of his power, dominating most of the north and parts of Majerteen Somaliland. But instead of being confronted with a colonial army he found himself involved in inter-clan warfare which wrought devastation over a huge area.

The holy war turned into a vicious fratricidal struggle. Yusuf Ali, the sultan of the Majerteens, was one of those who turned against him. Gripped with the passion of revenge, the Mullah killed one of his own wives, because she had the misfortune to be Yusuf Ali's daughter.

The Mullah found that the Italians, who had established formal rule over the Majerteens, were gradually cutting off his arms supplies, but he continued to have military success in the north. It was during this period that he built himself a succession of impressive, stone forts in the south east of the British protectorate. After wiping out a British punitive expedition in 1913, his dervishes pushed as far as the coast and actually fired on the coastal port of Berbera. This provoked Britain into mounting another punitive expedition in May 1914, which recaptured Burao, destroyed all his forts and drove his followers into the remote countryside, some finding refuge in caves in the mountains.

But his power was still not broken. He set his Arab masons, recruited in the Yemen, to build another massive fort at Taleh, near the Italian frontier. It had towers 60 feet high and walls 14 feet thick and was to be his headquarters for the rest of his life.

The Mullah had been harassed in the past not only by the British and the Italians but by the Ethiopians under the great Emperor Menelik (q.v.) who died in December 1913. The new Emperor, Lij Yasu had strong Muslim sympathies and certainly believed in a Muslim alliance against European imperial encroachment. Lij Yasu sent him arms and the Mullah hoped to benefit from this new alliance, only to find Yasu suddenly deposed in 1916 and the new Christian pro-European emperor Haile Selassie (q.v.) taking his place and renewing traditional hostilities.

The Ethiopian Governor of Harar wrote a letter to the Mullah: " Lij Yasu has gone and Ras Tafari (Haile Selassie), who is a friend of mine, rules in his place. He and I make arrangements in agreement and you know you cannot fight against us."

"My origin has apparently been forgotten," complained the Mullah, "I am the son of Ras Mikael and the cousin of Lij Yasu, the prince of Abyssinia." This was, of course not true, but it did show how much the Mullah valued the alliance with the Ethiopian Muslim leader.

Once again a window of opportunity closed on the Mullah as Britain emerged from the World War determined to finish him off.

This time there was no tinkering with easily ambushed land forces, or camel corps, but the new technology of aerial bombardment learnt during the war was used for one of the first times in colonial history.

DH9 aircraft were used in an attack on his camp at Medishe on 21 January 1920 supported by ground troops. The Mullah, knowing nothing of this type of warfare, put his faith in God. He gathered his people together around him under a white canopy, which actually gave the planes a clear target to aim at. The first bomb killed an uncle of the Mullah's and singed the Mullah's own clothing. He fled with his closest followers, though many others perished in the raid.

The British captured Taleh while the Mullah and a small band of followers weakened by disease and starvation retreated deep into the Ogaden desert. He died on the banks of the Shebelli river on 21 December 1920.

For 20 years he had resisted the world's leading colonial power. His armed struggle of resistance would have been commonplace in the 19th century, but he continued into the 20th century even after the First World War.

King of the Golden Stool

PREMPEH I
1872-1931

Prempeh I was a wise and tolerant ruler who might have been a great Asantehene (Asante king) if the British had allowed him to rule in peace. He was only 16 when he succeeded to the throne, which he held against rival contenders. He expanded and consolidated the Asante empire and forged new alliances, but it was his conflict with the rising might of Britain that was to dictate his fate and that of his people. Nearly a century of conflict with the world's leading imperial power was coming to a head. Prempeh tried with dignity to save his people's independence by diplomacy and persuasion, but he could not resist British imperialism determined to impose its rule by force using the latest military technology. He was destined to spend almost half his life in exile, only being allowed to return shortly before his death.

Prempeh, who became the Asantehene, King of the Asante, was born about 1872. He was the grandson of a former Asantehene Kwaku Dua I. His mother was the Asantehemaa, Yaa Akyaa. There had been three other Asantehenes since his birth and the succession was in dispute.

He claimed a clear succession down the female line, as was customary in Asante society, but he was only 16 and others disputed the claim, so he had to fight a civil war for succession to the golden stool, the symbol of monarchy. His party emerged triumphant and he was duly enstooled on 16 March 1888. He arranged for an officer of the Gold Coast government to witness and give his sanction to the ceremony.

He came to power at the nadir of Asante fortunes. His people had been soundly defeated by the British in 1874 when his capital Kumasi had been sacked and burnt, sending the people fleeing from the city. The British had then imposed a huge indemnity on the Asantehene as a punishment, demanding 50,000 ounces of gold. This had only been partly paid off by his predecessors. Afterwards a violent outbreak of smallpox had ravaged the kingdom.

But Prempeh, with the courage and optimism of youth, threw himself into the affairs of state. He crushed two immediate rebellions by the other factions who were still challenging his succession and sent his ambassadors to negotiate alliances with neighbouring tribes who were seeking to take advantage of the chaos in the Asante kingdom. When they refused to acknowledge allegiance to him he used force and imposed the customary annual tribute. In this way he regained most of the Asante empire to the north.

He also extended a hand of friendship to Samory Toure (q.v.) who was then at the height of his powers having conquered much of northern Gold Coast and part of the neighbouring Ivory Coast.

But Prempeh's main problem was his relationship with the British. His people had fought a succession of Asante wars with the British since the beginning of the 19th century and Britain, at the height of its imperial power, was impatient with the Asante's continuing resistance and its disruption of trade and political stability.

Britain continued to demand full repayment of the indemnity imposed in the previous war and was very concerned at Prempeh's efforts in forming an alliance with Samory Toure.

Prempeh's own priorities were to reassert his control over the tribes on the fringes of the British protectorate and to make every effort to keep his trade routes open to the sea. This inevitably led to conflict. Britain felt there would be no solution unless the Asante were crushed and brought under direct control.

In 1893 a mission was dispatched to Prempeh. It demanded not only that he should abide by the terms of the 1874 treaty, but insisted that he should accept a British protectorate and a permanent British resident in Kumasi. With calm dignity Prempeh refused to accept these conditions. He wrote, "Asante must remain independent as of old and at the same time remain friendly with all white men. I do not write this in a boastful spirit...The cause of the Asante is progressing and there is no reason for any Asante man to feel alarm at the prospects."

Prempeh refused to deal with the Governor of the Cape Coast direct and instead dispatched six ambassadors to London. There they waited patiently for six months but the Foreign Secretary refused to see them.

Britain insisted on getting agreement from Prempeh by a deadline of October 1895. When no response was forthcoming it decided to impose its will by force. It launched a punitive expedition under Colonel Francis Scott who mounted a major force which included the West Yorkshire regiment supported by West Indian and Nigerian Hausa troops, many armed with the latest Snider rifles and 12,000 porters.

Prempeh realised that his warriors, weakened by smallpox and armed only with muzzle loading guns would be annihilated. He sent a mission offering unconditional submission. But the British had already decided to teach the Asante a lesson by imposing a public humiliation on Prempeh. They did not stop until they reached Kumasi on 17 January

1896.

There Prempeh made a public submission to Sir W. Maxwell, the Governor of Cape Coast whom he had earlier refused to deal with. He and the queen mother were forced to come forward and publicly kiss the governor's booted feet. Prempeh had no alternative but to accept the British protectorate and promised that he would pay off the indemnity. But this was not enough, the British had already decided to arrest him and lay the Asante trouble permanently.

Prempeh and his mother, father and many other close relatives and paramount chiefs were taken to the coast and imprisoned on HMS *Racoon* which took them to Elimina castle, then on to lonely exile in Sierra Leone and finally to the Seychelles in the Indian Ocean.

Britain did not install another Asantehene and instead posted a permanent British resident in Kumasi directly responsible to the governor in Cape Coast. The Asante bitterly resented the humiliation of their king and the direct British rule that followed.

The newly appointed Governor, Sir Frederick Hodgson decided that Asante resistance would only be broken when the golden stool, the symbol of Asante power, was captured. It had been successfully hidden since Prempeh's arrest in 1896, but Hodgson decided to find it and sit on it himself as the Queen's representative. (Ironically it was so sacred to the Asante that not even the Asantehene himself would ever sit upon it, let alone a foreign usurper. The whereabouts of the stool was never found.)

Hodgson's final insult to Asante dignity sparked a further serious rebellion in 1900, which was crushed after prolonged conflict, with a further batch of Asante chiefs being sent into exile.

Prempeh, still exiled overseas, received sporadic reports of the sad events in his country, but he was powerless to intervene as the British finally annexed Asante in 1902.

His people never accepted his banishment and throughout the early years of the new century mounted a continual campaign to allow his return.

It was not until 1924 that he was allowed back as a private citizen with those of his family who had not died in exile. In 1926 the British recognised him as Kumasihene (King of Kumasi) but significantly, not Asantehene, which would have recognised his claim to the throne of the whole of Asante.

The Asante still considered him to be their king and even people well outside Kumasi recognised this by sending him secret tributes until the time he died in 1931. The British only relented in 1935 when his nephew Kwame Kyeretwie was installed as Nana Sir Osei Agyeman Prempeh II in 1935, the traditional ruler of the Asante confederacy.

9. Struggle against colonialism

The First Nationalist

HERBERT MACAULAY
1864-1946

Herbert Macaulay was the first Nigerian nationalist, yet he came from an impeccable middle-class background, where like his contemporaries, he wanted to conform and become a proper Victorian gentleman. Indeed, he first came to public notice when, dressed in an impeccable white suit and panama hat, he organised colourful celebrations for Queen Victoria's golden Jubilee in Lagos.

But he was irked by the petty racism of the colonials and soon began to campaign for native rights concerning taxation and land. After the World War, he turned to politics proper, founding the first African party, the Nigerian National Democratic Party and airing his views through his own newspaper.

He was charismatic, aggressive and argumentative, dominating local politics in the 1920s and 1930s, loyally taking up the allies cause in the second World War. He still had enough stamina in his old age to chair a modern nationalist party demanding rapid Africanisation and transition to independence. He died, aged 82, still stumping the country and making speeches in favour of more rapid political advancement.

Herbert Samuel Heelas Macaulay was born in Lagos on 14 November 1864. He was of impeccable pedigree. His grandfather was Bishop Samuel Crowther (q.v.), the most famous of all the freed slaves, who became Nigeria's first African bishop. After being repatriated to Sierra Leone he had eventually found his way back to his Nigerian homeland.

His father, the Reverend Thomas Macaulay, married Abigail Crowther the second daughter of Bishop Crowther in 1854. He was the founder and first principal of the Church Missionary Society Grammar School in Lagos and helped translate the Bible into Yoruba.

Herbert was a pupil at Lagos Grammar School until he was 14. His father died as he was completing his studies and he found a job in the public works department in Lagos.

In 1887 when only 23 he played a major part in organising the celebrations of Queen Victoria's golden Jubilee in Lagos. This came to the attention of the Governor of Lagos Colony, Sir Alfred Moloney who gave him the first scholarship awarded to a Nigerian to study land surveying and civil engineering in Plymouth, England.

In 1893 he returned home and joined the colonial service as a government surveyor at half the salary paid to Britons doing the same job. Macaulay was never one to bow humbly to the system. He was irritated by the petty racism that pervaded his professional and social life. By 1898 he broke away to set up his own private practice as a surveyor. He also developed an interest in politics.

At first his attentions were centred on local parish pump issues. In 1915 he took the side of the Eleko, the hereditary ruler of Lagos who refused to pay his water rates. Macaulay ran a passionate but unsucessful campaign in his favour.

The ownership of land was another dominant issue of the day. The colonial government wanted to take vacant land into its own control and hold and administer it "for the use and common benefit of the natives." A major dispute centred on the land held in nearby Apapa by Chief Amadu Oluwa which the colonial government wanted to take. Macaulay fought the case unsuccessfully through the local courts but refused to allow an injustice to be done. He travelled all the way to London to lodge an appeal before the Privy Council, in 1920, which ruled in his favour. The Lagos government was ordered to pay Chief Oluwa £22,500 for his land, plus costs.

Macaulay had forced a seemingly omnipotent colonial government to change its land policy. He returned home a hero. The government reacted in petty pique by deporting the Eleko of Lagos for the support that he had given to Chief Oluwa.

Macaulay responded by founding, in 1922, the Nigerian National Democratic Party. He also launched the *Lagos Daily News* the first daily newspaper in Nigeria, to propagate his views.

Macaulay's rivals said that his party was neither Nigerian, nor national, nor democratic. It was true he was largely concerned with issues involving the colony of Lagos. They were largely the concerns of the rapidly evolving black middle-class and yet he had a huge following among the ordinary people, the workers, the traders and the market women who saw him as a new style leader, highly sensitive to the broader public.

He was involved in many bitter disputes with his contemporaries, described by one as "wranglings, vain disputations and everlasting quarrels." He antagonised many by personal attacks in his newspaper.

Personally he was handicapped because he had earlier been found guilty and actually imprisoned for some undefined financial defalcation. He claims he had been politically framed by the authorities. The truth of the matter is difficult to ascertain but certainly his reputation was tarnished.

As a direct consequence he was not able to compete as a candidate in any of the legislative council elections in Lagos, where his NNDP party swept the board in 1923, 1928 and 1933.

In the early 1920s his opposition was so strident that the Governor refused to attend any parties to which he was invited, but after 1931 relations had improved so much that the Governor actually held press conferences with the NNDP on the same platform and regularly invited Macaulay as a guest to Government House. During the war he threw his whole weight into collecting money to save democracy, declaring, "Victory for democracy and the freedom of mankind depends on our contributions, our determination and our loyalty."

By then he was a mature 76 years old, remembered by Chief Anthony Enahoro as, "Always impeccably dressed in starched spotlessly white suit, black bow tie knotted painstakingly, white buck shoes and a white panama hat, he was the object of much adulation by the populace. One imagined he typified the term "Victorian gentleman."

By then young lions were disputing for political supremacy. The Nigerian Youth Movement wrested all three Lagos seats from the NNDP in 1938. Foremost of the new breed was Nnamdi Azikiwe, who founded a new nationwide political association, the National Council for Nigeria and the Cameroons (NCNC). It was as much a party of its time as Macaulay's NNDP had been in the 1920s. It embraced a Nigerian-wide following and stood for national issues such as Africanisation and a rapid transition towards independence.

Room was found for the old veteran when Macaulay was made chairman of the party on its formation in 1944, with Azikiwe as secretary general.

Macaulay at the age of 82 was stumping the country campaigning against the proposals of the Richards Constitution – which, though it contained the first elements of constitutional progress, had been imposed by the colonial Governor without consultation. The campaign was successful. Money was raised to send a delegation to London to contest the constitution, but the strain of constant travelling and speech making was too much for the old man. When he reached Kano on 7 May 1946 he was suddenly taken ill and died the same night. With him died the first generation of Nigerian nationalists.

An Unkind Death

BARTHELEMY BOGANDA
c.1910-1959

Barthelemy Boganda was a mission educated orphan, who turned himself into one of the greatest black leaders in Africa. He triumphed over the monopoly companies who had waxed fat on the forced labour of his people and over the white racist settlers, who tried to cling to the old order of exploitation. He became a member of the French National Assembly, and President of the territorial assembly for the whole Equatorial region. He won every election he contested, only to be killed in a mysterious air-crash before he could taste the fruits of independence. No one can tell for sure what sort of ruler he would have made, but he could scarcely have done worse than those who followed him. Equatorial Africa had lost its most talented son as he stood on the threshold of a new era.

Barthelemy Boganda always claimed that he was born on 4 April 1910, though the precise date is by no means certain as there was no registration of births at that time. He came from Bobangui in the Lobaye basin of what was then Oubangui-Shari (now the Central African Republic).

His early life reflected the sufferings of his people. Both his parents were killed by the guards of one of the big French owned rubber companies. As a frail 11-year-old, ravaged by smallpox and covered in sores, he was discovered by Catholic missionaries in 1921, at a local primary school. They soon found the weak and unhealthy foundling had a voracious appetite for knowledge and he soon became a brilliant pupil.

The missionaries baptised him on 24 December 1924 and raised funds for his education. They sent him first to the St Paul Mission in the capital Bangui where, each day, he did two hours of classes, learning Latin and French, before being ordered to work in the fields. He was sent for further education to the French Spiritain fathers in Congo-Brazzaville, to the Swiss Benedictines in Yaounde, Cameroon and to the Belgian Jesuits in Kisantu, in the Belgian Congo.

After 16 years of study he emerged to become on 17 March 1938 the first Oubangui priest to be ordained in his country.

During interludes at home he witnessed one of the most cruel colonial regimes anywhere in Africa. Power was almost entirely in the hands of the privately owned corporations extracting Africa's raw materials from their concession areas. In their plantations they were a law unto themselves forcing the peasants to produce under a regime of officially sanctioned forced labour and production quotas. Their own police enforced their tyranny with rhino hide whips. Boganda knew that his own parents had died as a result of this system.

So bad were the conditions that when a progressive governor, Felix Eboue tried to pass more power over to the traditional chiefs, in a society in where the people kept silent and avoided authority wherever possible, he could not find enough men able to take on the new responsibilities.

When France wanted to introduce local consultative assemblies in 1946, there were not sufficient qualified Africans to take up the offered seats. When forced labour was finally abolished in 1946 after the war, the local whites controlling the monopoly companies still maintained that there was no way of achieving economic progress without it.

That was the background that put Boganda into politics. With the encouragement of his bishop, he stood and was elected as the first member for Oubangui-Shari to the French National Assembly on 10 November 1946. Ironically, the diminutive priest was to start his campaign against colonialism, not at home but alongside the French deputies in Paris. He joined the *Mouvement Republicain Populaire* (MRP) because most of the local whites supported the *Rassemblement du Peuple Francais* (RPF), President De Gaulle's party.

In 1947 he wrote a letter to the French Minister for Overseas Territories stressing that he was not asking for anything new only the strict application of the law at home. He wanted action taken against the requisition of labour, arbitrary arrests, low wages, segregation, and the compulsory cultivation of cotton. He received no reply.

At home his frustrations were compounded because his African supporters were in a minority in a settler-dominated local assembly.

He had to turn to other methods of organisation. At first he tried to set up co-operative societies that could represent the direct interests of the peasants, but there were insufficient trained Africans to run them. They were weak, underfinanced and failed to break the monopoly control of the corporations.

Boganda next placed his hopes in the *Union Oubanguienne* which became a pressure group trying to influence the French parliament. Eventually he decided that France was not going to help him, he had to organise his people, at the grass roots. On 28 September 1949 he set up the *Mouvement d'Evolution Sociale de l'Afrique Noire* (MESAN). In the face of bitter settler hatred, but protected by his cloth and immunity from arrest as a member of the French assembly, he soon drew a mass following from his fellow countrymen.

In Paris in 1950, he married Michelle Jourdain, a French parliamentary secretary. This fired the racist emotions of the white settlers who were already boiling over at his political activities. The white backlash was ferocious and he was demonised as an upstart and a dangerous communist. Still he was determined to take his message to the people.

In January 1951, when on tour with his wife in Lobaye, tensions exploded between the peasants and the local settlers over the compulsory purchase of local produce. Boganda argued the peasants case, but in the ensuing fracas he and his wife were arrested. He was condemned to two months, and she to two weeks, imprisonment.

They were both reprieved on appeal. Boganda's name was on everybody's lips as the case achieved nationwide publicity.

This was the springboard which gave him a sweeping victory in the elections of June 1951 to the French Assembly. He gained more votes than all his four rivals put together, despite the resignation of some white elected MPs who refused to sit alongside an "enemy of France." In the territorial elections which followed in March 1952, MESAN gained a majority, despite white resistance and attempts at ballot rigging.

But settler resistance continued and the local assembly found it difficult to impose its will over the extractive companies. It was still obligatory to grow cotton, causing immense resentment among the peasants. Tensions over this and the alleged murder of a peasant by a European manager, exploded in May 1954 in Berberati. The new governor called in Boganda to try and calm the situation. He was doubtful, because it was not an area where he had much support, but he did intervene successfuly. He diverted a crisis that could have led to a general uprising. This did much to establish his reputation with the colonial authorities as a statesman who could be relied upon. And they accepted the argument that this incident, like many others, had been caused by white racist attitudes.

In January 1956 Boganda was again returned to the French National Assembly, this time with 84.7% of the votes. He followed his triumph on 18 November 1956 by being elected deputy mayor of Bangui despite opposition by well known white candidates. On 31 March 1957 Boganda's MESAN swept the polls in the territorial assembly.

His political supremacy was complete and he was able to exploit the situation as the French Assembly had passed the *Loi-cadre* in June 1956 which gave increased autonomy to the colonies.

Boganda still saw a future in which Oubangui, together with Chad, Gabon and the Congo (which formed French Equatorial Africa), would work through a common Grand Council and ultimately unite, before independence. He decided to concentrate his energies on the council, but its evolution was far from clear. The French governor remained its president with African ministers under him, both vying for control over a largely white administration.

Boganda, as chief minister, tried to work with the system and appointed his lieutenants as ministers, but soon came to the conclusion that the *Loi-cadre* did not provide a long-term solution. He wanted a new arrangement that would allow countries to choose their destinies either independently or, as he still preferred, within a greater federation. He even had the idea of forming a United States of Latin Africa which would include Angola and the Congo together with the Equatorial African states.

Meanwhile, accused by the colonial authorities of being unconstructive and neglecting economic development, he stumped the country telling the peasants that their future depended on increased agricultural production. "We cannot remain a race of beggars, the objects of European derision," he said.

When De Gaulle visited Oubangui in the summer of 1958 he presented Boganda with the same choice he had given all other African leaders, either a Yes vote for independence within a new French community, or a No vote for independence and isolation from France. In the referendum of September 1958, Boganda secured an overwhelming Yes vote, by 487,031 votes to 6,085. He wanted time to try and forge a union of all the Equatorial African nations because he felt that his country was too weak and underpopulated to go it alone.

But his hope to achieve a federation was premature. One by one the local assemblies of Congo, Gabon and Chad voted for independence for their individual countries within the community and on 1 December 1958, with his dream shattered, Boganda was forced to go the same way when he proclaimed a new state under the name of the Central African Republic.

The pre-independence elections were scheduled for 5 April 1959.

It was while he was campaigning, returning home on a regular flight when his plane crashed in Boda district on the left bank of the Lobaye. He was among the dead.

The grief of his people was overwhelming. The man who had come to represent all their nationalist aspirations had been snatched away as he stood at the gates of independence. He was their hero and the only leader capable of taking them smoothly into a new era. And black Africa had lost a great pan-Africanist.

The crash was wrapped in mystery. The official explanation was that flight had been "dislocated" while the plane was cruising at the correct altitude. A commission of inquiry was held, but its report was never published in the French official journal. Boganda had been snatched away at the dawn of independence. After him was to come political instability and cruel dictatorship.

Martyr to the Cause

PATRICE LUMUMBA
1925-1961

Patrice Lumumba died an unfulfilled hero, a martyr to the cause of African nationalism. A mercurial, brilliant, passionate man, with no experience of government, he had high ideals and stood steadfastly against tribal regionalism and in favour of national unity and pan-Africanism. But he was totally unable to cope with the deluge of pressures and events that afflicted the Congo when the Belgians thrust it, unprepared into independence. As the big powers outside, and his rivals within, scrambled to fill the political vacuum he found himself increasingly powerless. Tossed like a ship in a storm, he was not in control, events were controlling him. He was caught up in the tragedy of the Congo. The price was his own life as he achieved martyrdom to the African nationalist cause.

Patrice Lumumba was born on 2 July 1925, at the small village of Onalua in the Sankuru district in northern Kasai. His family was from the small Batetla tribe, a sub-division of the Bamongo who are spread across the centre of Zaire. Many Batetla had won prominent positions in the Belgian colonial administration.

His father, Francois Tolenga, sent him to local Catholic mission schools until the age of 14 when he rebelled and switched to a Methodist mission. After four years he was expelled for getting a girl pregnant and lacking application in his religious studies.

He carried his hatred of mission education for the rest of his life.

Aged 18, in 1943 he went to Kalima and worked briefly for *Symetain* a local tin-mining company. He soon got fed up with the small world of the mine and the lack of job prospects and travelled to Stanleyville (Kisangani) the capital of the Eastern Province, which was already attracting African nationalists from different tribal groups.

He worked as a tax-clerk and later in the postal administration, rising to assistant postmaster.

As the first stirrings of nationalism began throughout the Congo, he became President of the African Staff Association of Stanleyville, and other *évolué* proto-political organisations, barely tolerated by the Belgian colonial authorities. He also launched into a self-imposed programme of study and wrote many articles for the local press.

In 1954 he got his immatriculation card, which recognised him as an *évolué* and gave him certain privileges. He believed in western values and was not yet critical of Belgian colonialism, which made his rejection by whites in the Congo all the more traumatic for him. Behind his apparent ease and intellectual arrogance, Lumumba was always a sensitive soul tormented by many of the harsh realities of life.

In 1955 his prestige soared as he met and held a long conversation with the Belgian King Baudouin who was then visiting Kisangani. He also met the Belgian Minister for the Colonies. This confirmed him as the local leader of the African elite but it caused great irritation to the local administration and jealousy from rival leaders. From 1956 onwards he was under suspicion and continual surveillance by the colonial authorities.

But he was recognised in Belgium and invited for a visit in June 1956. As he stepped off the aircraft on his return to Kisangani on 6 July, he was immediately arrested and charged with embezzling 126,000 Belgian Francs (then worth $3,000) during the period he had worked for the post office. He claims that he had taken responsibility for theft by his staff, but the local authorities were determined to prosecute and he was duly tried and convicted to two year's imprisonment. This was reduced to one year when the Belgian Minister for the Colonies intervened.

To his followers this incident simply showed that the colonial authorities had been determined to get him. Ironically imprisonment gave him international publicity, crowned him as a martyr and made him more popular than ever. He wrote a book while in prison entitled, *Is the Congo, the land of the future, threatened?*. However events were already moving so fast that on his release his reflections were no longer relevant, nor worth publishing.

When he came out in June 1957 he decided that the centre of political activity would be Leopoldville (Kinshasa). He secured a job as a sales director of the big Bracongo brewery, a job that gave him direct contact with all the leaders of the elite. He had plenty of time for politics. He founded a host of embryo-political organisations such as the "think tank", the *Cercle Liberale* (CERS) and the *Federation des Batetla* from which he drew his tribal support.

These embryo organisations gave way to the *Mouvement National Congolais* (MNC) which he founded on 5 October 1958. It was a full blown anti-tribal, pan-African political party, and as Lumumba's creation lacked any economic policy. But unlike the tribally based ABAKO party of Joseph Kasavubu, it drew its support from across the Congo.

In August 1958 General De Gaulle arrived in Brazzaville, across the Congo river and offered the French Congo the choice of membership of the French community or full independence. Within two days Lumumba had drafted a memorandum demanding full independence for his country.

By December he was rubbing shoulders with Kwame Nkrumah and other militants at the All African People's Conference in Accra. On his return he told a mass rally that "Independence was not a gift to be given by Belgium, but a fundamental right of the Congolese people." Six days later, on 4 January 1959 there were serious riots, hundreds died, ABAKO was banned and Belgium was panicked into speeding up the independence process.

If Lumumba was to take advantage he had to have a mass organisation. He battled to absorb all the minor parties that stood for national unity, into the MNC, but was resisted by the tribalist organisations like ABAKO and CONAKAT led by Moise Tshombe in Katanga. He also faced dissension amongst his lieutenants, with Albert Kalonji breaking away to form his own faction MNC-Kalonji.

In October 1959 he addressed a meeting in his heartland, Stanleyville. Riots ensued, the police responded brutally and there were a number of deaths. Another wave of protest followed and he was arrested a second time on 1 November and sentenced to six month's imprisonment.

The Belgian government hoped to calm the ever rising nationalist feelings by pressing ahead with the independence process. A Round Table Conference was called in Brussels in January 1960. The Belgians soon realised they could not proceed without Lumumba - all his colleagues from the MNC would have boycotted otherwise.

Just two days after his sentence to six months penal servitude had been reconfirmed in Stanleyville, he was hurriedly released. The conference was almost in suspense until Lumumba arrived in Brussels with great fanfare on 26 January 1960.

Lumumba, a stringy, birdlike, charismatic figure duly made his mark as the only outstanding leader who wanted to preserve the Congo as a strong unitary state. The Round Table set the date for full independence only six months away, in June. The Belgian government, though still mistrustful, had reconciled itself to the fiery, passionate leader as their only hope to keep a united country.

In the general elections of May 1960 the MNC won 37 seats out of 137. Together with its allies it was by far the strongest single party. The regional parties like ABAKO and CONAKAT were shown to have nothing but tribal, regionally based, support.

On 23 June Lumumba became Prime Minister and was asked to form a government. He tried to draw his support from as wide a base as possible, even agreeing that Kasavubu, a man he despised and mistrusted, should become President, thus averting the possibility of secession by the Bakongo of Bas Zaire.

Lumumba, totally without governmental training or experience, found power thrust upon him, as tensions ran at fever pitch in a nation bursting with unfulfilled expectation. He wanted time to build stability and unity, but time he did not have. The major powers were rushing to fill the political vacuum, while vengeful rivals were conspiring for positions and power from within.

Independence arrived on 30 June with King Baudouin denying that Belgium had "scuttled the Congo", while lecturing the new government not to rush into hasty reforms. Lumumba, in a passionate, unforgiving speech, replied by dwelling on the miseries of 80 years of colonialism, saying that no Congolese would ever forget the independence struggle "paid in tears, fire and blood."

Soon things were spinning out of control. Five days after the independence celebrations the army mutinied, locked up its Belgian officers and mobs took to the streets. Belgium reacted by sending in troops to protect its nationals. Lumumba was shocked to see how little independence meant in reality and made an immediate appeal to the United Nations to protect his country against invasion.

Eleven days after independence, on 11 July Moise Tshombe, encouraged by Belgian mining interests, declared the secession of Katanga, cutting off the Congo from its principal source of revenue. Lumumba attempted to visit Katanga but was refused permission to enter by the Tshombe regime.

On 14 July Lumumba broke off diplomatic relations with Belgium and demanded that all Belgian troops be withdrawn within 12 hours. He threatened that he would ask the Soviet Union to intervene if he did not get UN support. Faced with this threat the UN security council decided unanimously that Belgium should withdraw and on 16 July began sending in UN troops.

But the UN proved itself singularly ineffective against the experienced Belgians. Lumumba threatened to use force though he could not even persuade his own senate to force all Belgian troops to leave.

Lumumba embarked on a tour of African capitals to enlist African support. The only practical assistance came from Ghana in the form of a token force.

As the world watched, conspired and quibbled over the Congo's fate, Kasavubu took advantage of Lumumba's declining power and credibility by dismissing him as Prime Minister on 5 September. Lumumba countered by dismissing Kasavubu as President. Parliament refused to accept either dismissal. Lumumba then called for the withdrawal of the UN forces for failing to carry out their mandate and again threatened to bring in the Soviets as an alternative. By this stage he had proved powerless to cope with the pressures and turmoil that had engulfed his nation.

This was the cue for military intervention.

Colonel Joseph Mobutu, his former Secretary of State, whom Lumumba had promoted to Chief of Staff of the army, seized power on 14 September and dismissed him from office.

The next day Lumumba was taken prisoner and beaten up by Mobutu's soldiers. Some troops mutinied but he did not seize the first opportunity to escape. Instead he asked for UN protection and was guarded by them for two months. He made various political pronouncements while under house arrest which were largely disregarded. The real power lay with Mobutu who was ruling the country with a reconciled Kasavubu, who by then had full US backing. Though the militant African countries protested over Lumumba's fate, most world powers were prepared to write him off as a loser.

He remained under house arrest until he escaped on 27 November and headed for Orientale province where his ally Antoine Gizenga was in control. So great was his belief in his own popularity that he actually gave himself up to Mobutu's troops on 1 December. But the detachment who captured him was led by a diehard enemy. Mobutu allowed his men to savagely beat up Lumumba, before throwing him into prison at Thysville to await trial.

On 17 January 1961 he was flown into Katanga, the stronghold of his enemy Moise Tshombe. His actual fate remains a mystery, but it appears that he was killed almost immediately he arrived in Lubumbashi. The Tshombe government said nothing until 10 February when he was reported to have escaped from his Lubumbashi prison. It then announced that he had fallen into the hands of hostile villagers who had killed him. No outside organisation had been able to visit him while he was in prison. It was widely assumed that he had been killed by the Katangese authorities themselves.

News of his death brought protestations throughout the world. Dag Hammarskjold, the Secretary General of the UN, was accused of failing to protect his safety. Mobutu was accused of delivering him into the hands of his enemies and Tshombe of organising his killing.

In a more stable society Lumumba may have been a great pan- African on the scale of Kwame Nkrumah, (q.v.). As it was he was a powerless individual caught in the remorseless machinery of Congolese and international politics.

Ruler of the Rif

ABD EL-KRIM
c.1882-1963

Abd el-Krim was a nationalist past his time. He fought one of the last wars against colonialism in the Rif mountains of Morocco in the 1920s. His sweeping military success against the Spanish took everyone by surprise and it was only when he decided to challenge France as well that the tide turned against him.

But for five years he was supreme in Spanish Morocco. He established the Rif republic, abolishing slavery and introducing constitutional government. Eventually his dreams were shattered by the crushing power of the joint Franco-Spanish forces. In 1926 he was sent into enforced exile.

Sidi Mohammed ben Abd el-Krim el-Khattabi, to give him his full name, was born about 1882 in the Rif mountains which fringe the coast of northern Morocco. His family came from Ajdir. His father was a man of letters who had the courtesy title of *kadi* (judge) though he never practised. He came from the warlike Beni Ouriagel tribe, a sub-group of the Zenetes Berbers.

He took orthodox, general studies at the ancient Karaouine University of Fez (1905-09). He emerged to find the French and the Spanish were both trying to expand their sphere of influence in Morocco. Spain had established a foothold in the enclave of Ceuta as early as 1580 and Melilla later. At the end of the 19th century Spain was trying to establish a legal claim to the northern littoral, including Abd el-Krim's home in the Rif. The Spanish were making arrangements with France to have their claim recognised to the northern littoral of Morocco; virtually to "sub-let" it from France.

Abd el-Krim's father did regular business with the Spaniards in Melilla and also with the German Mannesman brothers who wanted to prospect for mineral deposits in the area.

Abd el-Krim had no objections to working for the Spaniards and soon found a job as a teacher and, in 1915, as a *kadi* in the court for native affairs at Melilla. But the first World War was well underway and Abd el-Krim thought he could exploit the situation by befriending the Germans.

The French commander General Lyautey complained to the Spanish authorities about his German contacts. The Spanish promptly arrested him and held him for the greater part of 1916, though he made frequent attempts to escape. On one occasion he broke a leg when jumping out of a window. (He limped on a lame leg for the rest of his life). After 11 months in detention he was released.

His father died in 1920 and he found himself the clan chief, just as the Spanish decided to conquer the Rif. Abd el-Krim's natural instinct was to resist. During 1920-21 he toured the Rif and roused his warlike Berber mountain tribes to join him and fight the invader.

The Spanish General Sylvestre, at the head of a huge army, tried to push into the hostile mountains, while Abd el-Krim's men harried and ambushed the invaders. Neighbouring tribes flocked to his rebel banner and finally Abd el-Krim was able to challenge Sylvestre near Anoual on the coast.

He won a crushing victory. The Spanish were annihilated - 15,000 were killed or wounded, 750 were taken prisoner, and 20,000 rifles and 80 heavy guns were captured. The Spanish panicked and sent out another force under General Navarro who was also captured along with most of his artillery.

For the next five years Abd el-Krim fought a triumphant war of resistance, arousing the admiration of the Arab world. On 1 February 1922 he proclaimed himself the Emir of an independent Rif republic and imposed his authority using persuasion, trickery and force where necessary over the neighbouring tribes.

By 1924 he had extended his control over most of Spanish Morocco. He established constitutional government, abolished slavery and recruited a huge army by conscription.

He might have been able to hold Spanish Morocco for a considerable period had he not been carried away by the euphoria of victory. His army was triumphant, confident and impatient and had just received 16,000 rifles used in the World War smuggled out of Hamburg. He decided to challenge the French. At first General Lyautey's army was no larger than Sylvestre's, numbering some 60,000 men, but he doubled this figure by summoning new reinforcements in 1925.

During the winter of 1925-26 the French went on the offensive pursuing a hit and run guerrilla war in the Rif mountains. The French used spotter aircraft so that their heavy artillery could adjust its fire on the rebel encampments. For a time the war hung in the balance while an attempt was made to persuade Abd el- Kader, at a peace conference at Oujda, to stop fighting but he was not prepared to surrender the Rif's independence.

But he must have seen the tide was turning. In the spring of 1926 Spain sent yet another army under General Sanjurjo to fight alongside the French. This time Abd el-Kader's forces were outmanoeuvred and pushed back into their mountains. His men lost one skirmish after another, while his allies deserted and his enemies came out openly against him.

In his desperation he had the fantastic idea of taking refuge in Ghomara, whose people he had earlier brutally subjugated. Some Frenchmen in his entourage told him frankly that he was hated and risked almost certain death if he threw himself on the mercy of his old enemies.

There was nowhere else to go so he decided to save what he could by surrendering – not to the Spanish, still smarting from their huge losses in earlier campaigns, but to the French.

On 27 May 1926 he surrendered to Colonel Corap at Tamouren. Then he, together with his brother and some of the ministers of his ill-fated government, were sent to Marseille and eventually to exile in Reunion.

Abd el-Krim was grateful to France for not having delivered him into the hands of his Spanish enemies. He wrote many letters to France affirming his new-found loyalty and hoping to be set free.

During the Second World War he offered the services of his son to General De Gaulle.

After the war he was told he could return to France, though the French did not really want him. When his boat got to Egypt he and all his party were "allowed" to escape. He was welcomed by the Egyptian government which gave him political asylum, to the applause of many other exiled nationalists. Still only 64, he found useful work with the Arab League.

Morocco gained its independence in 1956 and the government of King Mohammed V tried everything to persuade him to return home where his reputation had soared in the popular imagination. He would have received a hero's welcome, but he refused as long as there were any foreign troops on Moroccan soil. In reality he did not trust the king, nor like the authoritarian rule that he was trying to impose on his country. King Mohammed paid him a visit in Cairo, in 1960, but still he refused to return.

He died of natural causes on 5 February 1963 at the age of 81.

The Danquah Tradition

JOSEPH DANQUAH
1895-1965

Danquah spent his whole political life under the shadow of Kwame Nkrumah and he never had the mass following of his great rival. He came from a royal family, drawing his support from the minority interests of the Asante (Ashanti) and the rich cocoa farmers. Not once did he manage to gain the upper hand over Nkrumah politically though he occupied the moral high ground. Despite his active record, he never had a real taste for the dirty world of politics. He was an intellectual, brilliant lawyer and distinguished author of a number of scholarly works on Akan religion, social customs, plays and poetry. Though he was interested in politics, he represented conservative interests at a time of revolutionary change. He is remembered as the founder of the conservative strain of Ghana politics, now known as the Danquah/Busia tradition.

Joseph Kwame Kyeretwi Boakye Danquah was born on 21 December 1895 at Bepong, Kwahu in the Eastern region of the Gold Coast. He was closely related to the Ofori-Atta family, one of the royal families of the southern state of Akyem-Abuakwa.

He was educated at the Basel Mission school of Kyebi and the Begoro grammar school, before becoming a law clerk. In 1915 he became secretary to his older brother Nana Sir Ofori Atta, the paramount chief of Akyem-Abuakwa.

In 1921 he went to London University to study law. He received his LL.B. in 1926, finally being called to the bar at the Inner Temple in 1927.

He returned home, set up a law practice and founded the *Times of West Africa* in 1931, which soon became one of the leading newspapers urging moderate constitutional reform. He became the chief promoter of the Gold Coast Youth Conference which brought together the educated leaders of the country to discuss national problems. It was at this time that he wrote most of his major works on Akan law, society and culture.

In 1934 he became secretary of the Gold Coast and Asante delegation that visited the British Colonial Office to demand unsuccessfully a majority in the Legislative Council of members not appointed by government.

He remained in London until 1936, doing research into the history of mediaeval Ghana. During his studies he came up with the idea that the Gold Coast should take on the name of Ghana.

He returned home to resume work as a barrister and in 1937 became Secretary General of the Youth Conference which demanded constitutional reform and self government.

In 1947 he was indirectly elected to the Legislative Council by the Joint Provincial Council of Chiefs. With a group of colleagues he then formed the United Gold Coast Convention in August 1947. Wanting a young and dynamic secretary general for the new party, he first approached Ako Adjei, who in turn suggested Kwame Nkrumah (q.v.), the rising star in London African circles.

Nkrumah responded favourably, returned home and soon galvanised the UGCC in a more radical direction. Serious riots broke out over cocoa prices in February 1948 and all UGCC leaders were detained including Danquah. He blamed Nkrumah and had him demoted from secretary general to treasurer. Nkrumah continued to press for more radical policies and a mass organisation, and clashed with Danquah, who was essentially a conservative and traditionalist. The split came in June 1949 when Nkrumah broke away and formed his own Convention People's Party (CPP).

Unlike Nkrumah, Danquah was prepared to sit on the colonial Coussey Commission set up to investigate the causes of the riots and to suggest constitutional changes, which were to form the basis of a new constitution in 1951.

In the general elections of 1951 Danquah won his own seat at Akyem Abuakwa but the UGCC won only 3 seats to the CPP's 34. It was clear that Danquah's moderation was out of touch with the rising aspirations of the people. Danquah became leader of the opposition but Nkrumah was appointed prime minister.

He was a founder member of the Ghana Congress Party which took over from the UGCC in 1952, but the party never really got off the ground. He switched support to the National Liberation Movement (NLM), a party with Asante as its base and federation as its principal aim, but he failed to regain his seat in the elections of 1954 or 1956.

When the NLM and other opposition parties formed the United Party in October 1957, he joined. When Ghana became independent on 6 March 1957 with Nkrumah asserting his authority, Danquah found himself in the forefront of the battle to prevent the erosion of human rights. Professionally he represented those detained and deported by the new government.

When Nkrumah decided Ghana should become a republic under a president in 1960, Danquah decided to challenge him in the presidential elections under the UP banner. He was heavily defeated securing only

124,623 votes to Nkrumah's 1,016,076.

Danquah's resistance to Nkrumah's increasingly oppressive laws and his defence of those arrested resulted in his own detention in 1961. He was held for 18 months under the Preventive Detention Act until freed in June 1962.

He was detained for a second time on 8 January 1964 and held for 13 months until he died in detention on 4 February 1965. The government announced that he had died of a heart attack but members of the opposition claimed that he had been tortured to death in an attempt to get him to confess his complicity in conspiracies against Nkrumah.

Danquah did not achieve much politically during his lifetime but he pioneered the conservative tendency in Ghana politics - the Danquah/Busia tradition - which persists to the present day.

A Light Extinguished

TOM MBOYA
1930-1969

Mboya was cut down in his prime, on 5 July 1969, by an assassin's bullet. This deprived Africa of its most logical, coherent and outstanding spokesman and Kenya of its most able and articulate minister. In Kenya politics, despite his immense ability, he was never an insider. At the time he died, any chance of his succession to Kenyatta was remote, but his rivals were so jealous and fearsome that he could manipulate the succession process that they organised his killing.

His critics spoke of him as arrogant, cold, cunning, too clever by half, but he was a constructive politician with a vision, not simply concentrated on power politics. He was a statesman, ever interested in wider issues - not a dreamer but a pragmatic achiever. In the words of a close friend, Dr Cherry Gertzel, "He symbolised a commitment to material development and a rejection of purely personal and predatory rule."

Thomas Joseph Mobya was born on 15 August 1930 on a sisal plantation in country farmed by whites that bordered on the Kikuyu tribal reserve. His father Leonard Ndiege was working over two hundred miles from his Luo homeland, as a headman on a white farm.

Two years later Thomas was baptised at Kilimanbogo Catholic Mission near the sisal plantation, where he received his first education. In 1942 he went on to St Mary's school, Yala. He was by no means a brilliant student, nor did he work particularly hard but he passed his African preliminary examination in November 1945 before going to the Holy Ghost College at Mang'u. There he passed his African Secondary School examination, but he had to give up his studies to find work to help his ageing father educate his younger brothers.

He trained to become a sanitary inspector at Kabete near Nairobi from 1948-50. He moved later to Jeanes School, an agricultural training college, where he began mature fast and get involved in student politics. His headmaster noted that he was, "an outstandingly able fellow."

He started work as a sanitary inspector with the Nairobi City Council in 1951. He soon became active in the African Staff Association, the council worker's trades union. This whetted his appetite for unionism. In 1952, when only 22 years of age, he founded the Kenya Local Government Worker's Union. He became its Secretary General in 1953-57 and took over the running of the whole Kenya Federation of Labour when most of its founder members were detained in 1953.

His career was flowering at a time Kenya was in crisis. The colonial government had reacted to the Mau Mau terrorism by detaining Kenyatta and all the other significant political leaders. The country was under a repressive state of emergency and political parties were banned. Mboya was too young to be involved in what was anyway mainly a Kikuyu movement, but he appreciated that a political vacuum had been created. The trade unions were the only legitimate means of political expression.

He came to public prominence for the first time when he mediated in the Mombasa Dock strike in 1955. This led to a Workers Travel Association scholarship to Ruskin College, Oxford to study industrial management, in 1955-56. He also visited the USA for the first time as the guest of the American Committe on Africa.

He returned to find the threat of Mau Mau removed and the colonial government willing to offer tentative political advancement. Eight seats were offered to elected African members under the Lyttelton constitution. Mboya had already founded the Nairobi People's Convention Party (PCP) on his return from Oxford and plunged himself into the political battle for the multi-tribal urban constituency of Nairobi.

Mboya narrowly defeated another Luo candidate and established himself as one of the first African leaders elected on a non- tribal basis.

He was in his element with a natural love and aptitude for the rough and tumble of politics. Though he had to fight for the leadership with his lifelong rival Oginga Odinga, his peers recognised his intellectual clarity and clear political vision. He bound them together in opposition to the Lyttleton constitution and won further advancement when eight more elected members were created.

At the same time his international contacts burgeoned. He became chairman of the regional committee of the International Confederation of Free Trade Unions (ICFTU) in 1958 and chaired the All African People's Conference in Ghana. He travelled frequently to the USA, getting an honorary doctorate in law at Howard University in 1959.

He took a leading part in the London Constitutional Conference in January 1960 which wrung many concessions from the British government including the right to organise nationwide political parties.

In 1961 he was a founder member of the Kenya African National Union (KANU) and became its Secretary General. Six of the African members, afraid of being dominated by the major tribes, broke away to form the rival Kenya African Democratic Union (KADU), but Mboya held true to KANU.

Though he was regarded with suspicion by many of his colleagues for his arrogance and authoritarianism, most recognised his huge political ability. He was also beloved by the ordinary people of Nairobi. In the elections of February 1961, the whole contest rotated round the question of whether he was loyal to the still detained Kenyatta or not. Though Oginga Odinga and other opponents tried to smear him, he won Nairobi East, a seat dominated by Kikuyu voters, with an overwhelming majority.

In March 1961 he flew to Kenyatta's desert prison at Lodwar and for the first time the two men had a long and deep conversation. Mboya recognised that Kenyatta, who was released in August, was the national leader. He needed Kenyatta's confidence and was prepared to be loyal to him.

Meanwhile Mobya pushed for an elected African majority as fast as possible. Kenyatta recognised his abilities and got him to prepare the African case at the Lancaster House Conference of February 1962 in London. There KADU, assisted by the British, forced through a regional constitution in the hope that it would protect the smaller tribes. Mboya got the conference to agree to a transfer of a million acres to the land hungry peasants.

Back in Kenya he was involved in organising a series of airlifts of Kenyan students to the USA, and on 20 January 1962 he married Pamela Odede.

On 10 April 1962 a number of African ministers were created in a new transitional government. Mboya became Minister of Labour under Kenyatta's premiership. It was a case of a poacher turned gamekeeper, as the labour leader divested himself of the leadership of the Kenya Federation of Labour. He soon demonstrated another facet to his talents, drawing up an industrial relations charter that was agreed by employers and unions and copied in other parts of the Commonwealth. He recognised the importance of foreign capital but wanted a socialist (planned) economy.

Mboya was always susceptible to attack by jealous rivals. He attracted so much international publicity that even Kenyatta began to show signs of jealousy attacking politicians who accepted imperialist money as "insects". But Mboya proved himself politically indispensable to the older leader who depended on him to do the hard work in translating policy into practice.

In May 1963 came the pre-independence elections. Mboya triumphed again, this time in Nairobi Central after a slightly closer contest. KANU emerged triumphant and Kenyatta appointed Oginga Odinga as his number two, as Minister of Home Affairs, while Mobya was given Justice and Constitutional Affairs, in a carefully balanced cabinet.

Early in 1963 he concentrated on finishing his book *Freedom and After* which one biographer described as a "catalogue of the aspirations of post colonial Africa."

On 12 December 1963 came independence, followed by a period of consolidation of power by KANU and the preparation for a republic. Here Mboya as Minister of Justice and Constitutional Affairs proved himself indispensable. He never intended to allow KADU to have its regional assemblies under the independence constitution and made their position so untenable that the party eventually collapsed with its members going over to KANU. He made threatening noises on press freedom but he vigorously upheld individual rights with a lengthy Bill of Rights.

Ironically KADU's defection to KANU strengthened the moderates and hence Mboya's position in the party. He became Minister of Economic Planning and Development in a general reshuffle at the end of 1964 where he could try to create a strategic plan for the economy. But he was far more than a technical minister. Kenyatta gave him broad scope as the chief government executive and spokesman on almost any issue.

Oginga Odinga, his main rival, was becoming heavily exposed. His connections with the Eastern bloc and sources of funding were being increasingly questioned. He had founded the Marxist Lumumba Institute and rumours abounded that he was building a secret army.

Meanwhile Mboya was at his peak. In April 1965 he published his paper on African socialism; far from being a traditional socialist document it backed foreign investment to boost growth, and advocated Africanisation not nationalisation.

With the wind blowing in his favour, Mboya's fertile mind dreamt up a clever way of dealing with Odinga. He called a full party delegates conference at Limuru and presented it with a new constitution, which would abolish Odinga's position as vice president. Odinga had no time to take counter measures. The new constitution was passed by 326-80.

Odinga resigned from KANU and formed the Kenya People's Union taking a large block of his followers with him, whereupon Mboya had the constitution amended so that each member would have to fight a by-election. Most were defeated and Odinga was in the wilderness.

Ironically the ostracism of Odinga made Mboya himself the main threat to the power brokers around Kenyatta. He had exposed himself as the main outsider and danger man.

As Kenyatta became increasingly frail and suffered from his first attack of thrombosis, the struggle for succession became the all-consuming issue. Kenyatta himself recognised Mboya's qualities, indeed he used him to sponsor any unpopular legislation, or to talk the government out of any crisis. But the inner circle of Kikuyus around Kenyatta saw Mboya as a threat, clever enough to manipulate the constitution or public opinion in his own favour in the succession stakes.

The more successful Mboya was in dealing with unpopular issues, the more his rivals feared him. They began to tinker with the constitution to prevent a sudden putsch and set about reducing Mboya's power base in the party and the unions.

In December 1967 a sentry guarding his house fired several shots at his car and he was persuaded by his friends to employ full-time bodyguards. Towards the end he was highly apprehensive that an assassination attempt was being planned.

On Saturday 5 July 1969, after a morning's work in his ministry, he went to Chhani's chemist shop in Government Road. As he left a gunman shot him dead.

The Luos erupted in an orgy of emotion. When Vice President Daniel Arap Moi tried to pay his respects his car was stoned and he was forced to turn back. Several months later Kenyatta was jeered when he visited Luo country.

A Kikuyu, Njenga Njeroge, was convicted of the murder and hanged, with the words on his lips, "Why do you pick me? Why not the big man?" The big man has never been exposed but it was almost certainly one of the inner Kikuyu circle, who saw Mboya as a predator seeking the presidency.

A New Pharaoh

GAMAL ABDUL NASSER
1918-1970

Gamal Abdul Nasser gave his people dignity and a belief in themselves after centuries of imperialist rule. He saw the British out of Egypt and finally extinguished their power in the Middle East, but he was less successful in achieving other great goals. Though he temporarily gained personal leadership in the region, Egypt was never strong enough to dominate the Middle East nor to prevent the interference of the great powers. He could never find a formula to accommodate the Palestinians or the Israelis. His quest for Arab unity floundered on the different national aspirations of the region and various attempts at a United Arab Republic were transitory.

At home he did achieve some social and economic success. He modernised his country, built the Aswan High Dam and improved agricultural productivity. He created a fairer society and transferred some land to the fellahin, but his centralised, nationalised, socialist economy was a recipe for failure and did not survive much beyond his lifetime.

Nasser was born in Bani Mur, Asyut, in northern Egypt on 15 January 1918. His father was an humble post office official, from a poor fellah family. Gamal spent his early impoverished childhood in Alexandria before his family moved to Cairo.

He had secondary schooling in Alexandria, then joined the military academy. He was a clever child, politically aware and insatiably reading politics and philosophy, particularly the works of nationalist writers. His reading convinced him that Egypt had reached a moment of destiny in which it could throw off the imperialist yoke.

He took part in the 1936 demonstrations against the complacent Farouk government. This delayed his entry into the military academy until he audaciously made a personal appeal to the minister responsible.

He graduated in 1938 and kept close contact with his fellow officers of the same year, who were later to form the nucleus of the free officers. He was promoted captain and became an instructor at the Military Academy in 1942. After a further course at Staff college, he fought in the 1948 war against Israel, after the UN had partitioned Palestine. There Nasser demonstrated his resourcefulness and courage in the Fajulla siege where his ill-supplied troops held out for five months until an armistice finally relieved them.

The war had done much to confirm his political leanings. He had shared the misery of ordinary soldiers, let down by a corrupt government that had kept them ill-supplied, often with defective weapons.

Popular discontent over the conduct of the war, and the continual interference by Britain in Egyptian affairs, led to demonstrations and martial law imposed by a nervous government. This situation led to the creation of the Free Officers Committee which vowed to eliminate British imperialism, feudalism and capitalism and to create a democratic, nationalist government.

Nasser was elected the President of the Free Officers executive in December 1950.

More violent incidents were met with panicky repression. The bloodless coup d'etat of 23 July 1952 was a pre-emptive move by the Free Officers who had been told that they were on the point of being arrested. The military and communications network were seized without violence and General Muhammad Neguib, as an avuncular figurehead, was made titular Head of State. King Farouk abdicated and a Regency Council was established with Free Officer representation.

Neguib became Prime Minister in September 1952, while Nasser remained Chairman of the Free Officer's Executive and later was made Deputy Prime Minister and Minister of the Interior in the Neguib government. He also became Secretary General of a new party, the Liberation Rally, which was to help him in his power struggle with Neguib.

Nasser outmanoeuvred the more conservative Neguib in the Revolutionary Command Council (RCC) and took over as Prime Minister and RCC Chairman in April 1954. Neguib lingered on as a powerless President.

After the coup in 1952 Nasser introduced serious land reform and redistribution. He had also built up a personal following in the Liberation Rally which was the forerunner of the National Socialist Union. When he took over from Neguib in 1954, he was in undisputed control of Egypt but major foreign policy issues demanded his attention. He hoped that the Sudanese would still opt for union with Egypt, though they had been promised independence within three years. He also had to get rid of the British.

An Anglo-Egyptian Evacuation Agreement, covering the withdrawal of British troops from the Canal Zone, was agreed in July 1954.

An assassination attempt in October 1954 gave him the pretext to clamp down on the Muslim Brotherhood and other extremist groups and impose more direct personal rule. Neguib, tainted by his past support for the Muslim brothers, was placed under house arrest. Nasser assumed full leadership of the revolution with his presidency confirmed in the referendum of June 1956.

Nasser turned his attention to international politics. He irritated the British by his adamant refusal to sign the anti-communist Baghdad pact in February 1955 and organised an alternative Arab defence agreement with Syria and Saudi Arabia in March. He played a major part in the non-aligned Bandung conference of April 1955, which was taken as a gesture of defiance to the West and an indication of his militant, leftist stance.

But further Israeli attacks on Gaza in February 1955 made rearmament imperative. He was still suspicious of the Soviets and their part in supporting communists in Egypt, but he found the West hostile and unresponsive to his pleas for more arms. By September he decided to turn to the Eastern bloc for supplies.

Relations with the West were progressively deteriorating. Though the last British troops left Egypt in March 1956, the British and Americans decided in July not to support the Aswan High Dam project. It was a huge blow to Nasser who saw the scheme as a symbol of what he could do for his people. He planned to dam the Nile, regulate the floodwaters and bring huge new areas of land under controlled irrigation. Its electricity would bring modernisation and industrialisation. Now he was being punished for being driven involuntarily into the arms of the communist bloc. Indeed he was forced to turn to the Soviets to finance the project that was so close to his heart.

Nasser's defiance of the West greatly increased his prestige in the Third World. Britain also saw him as a threat to its interests throughout the Middle East. This fuelled the personal antagonism between the patrician British Foreign Secretary, Anthony Eden, and the man he considered to be an upstart Arab who wanted to overturn the old order in the Middle East.

It was the loss of Western support, specifically over the Aswan dam, that caused Nasser to provoke the Suez crisis. He simply threw all caution to the winds and nationalised the Suez Canal Company on 26 July 1956 to the plaudits of his people. Britain and France then did a deal with the Israelis. Israel invaded and Britain and France ordered the two warring parties to draw back ten miles from the canal. When Nasser refused Britain and France bombed Egypt's air bases, destroying almost the entire Egyptian airforce.

Nasser lost the war but soon won the peace. The West thought his humiliated people might rise up against him, instead they gave him their full support and he became a hero throughout the Third World as the invading forces were forced to withdraw. He soon showed that the Egyptians could run the canal efficiently and Egypt remained in full control of the canal with its vast quantity of military stores.

Nasser was briefly the unchallenged leader of the Arab world with huge popular support among the Arab populace. For a few years Nasserism seemed to sweep all before it, but a reaction was almost inevitable.

Nasser's long-term goal was to achieve Arab unity. Early in 1958 he was approached by a group of Syrian politicians who argued that Egypt and Syria should form a unified state. On 1 February 1958 the United Arab Republic was officially declared, with Nasser elected its president by referendum on 21 February. But the form of union had not been thought out. The Syrians soon began to resent what turned out to be bureaucratic, socialist rule from Cairo. Syria formally withdrew from the union in September 1961.

Nasser's brief popularity with the masses created fear and jealously elsewhere in the Arab world. His socialist views alienated the more conservative regimes. This was exemplified in 1962 when he intervened in Yemen on the side of the Yemeni revolutionaries against the Saudi-backed royalists.

An attempt in March 1963 to form another union, this time a tripartite union of Iraq, Syria and Egypt was announced, but came to nothing. Nasser's efforts to back militant nationalists in Africa such as Patrice Lumumba (q.v.) in the Congo were also doomed to failure.

Nasser had been diagnosed as a diabetic and his health deteriorated seriously during the years he unsuccessfully pressed his Arab ambitions. Frequently he would go into fits of acute depression, but he had an iron will and unquenchable drive to achieve his goals. He ruled unchallenged through a legislature of elected members; all were from his Arab Socialist Union party willing to rubber stamp his policies. He assumed personal control of all the mechanisms of centralised government.

In the 1960s he introduced a series of measures to strengthen the revolution and set the country on the path of socialism. He launched a major nationalisation programme that increased the crippling bureaucracy and stifled enterprise and productivity.

By 1963 over 400 strategic companies were under state control including all banks and heavy industry. In May 1963 a National Charter was adopted which gave the masses a voice in the party at the grass roots, accorded equal rights to women and sanctioned family planning.

In 1966 he took further measures against the large landowners. His crowning glory at home in the 1960s was the completion of the first stage of the Aswan dam which was to bring great economic benefits and was seen as a symbol of Arab technological achievement.

Meanwhile in 1966 tensions between Israel and Syria were sucking Nasser into a third Arab-Egyptian war. Syria, fearing an attack by Israel, appealed to Nasser who felt morally obliged to enter into a defence agreement in November, which was later extended to Jordan. Nasser calculated that this time Israel had provoked the Arabs to such an extent that they could unite, drag in other allies and actually win a war.

In May 1967 he got the UN peacekeeping troops withdrawn from Sinai and shortly afterwards closed the straits of Tehran to Israeli shipping.

Israel retaliated with force, almost immediately wiping out Egypt's airfields, destroying the Egyptian army and striking as far as Sinai. It then turned against Jordan.

For Nasser the 1967 war, which only lasted six days, was a total disaster and humiliation, for which he accepted full responsibility. He declared publicly that he would resign and hand over power to his vice president. But though dismayed and traumatised, the Egyptian people still saw him as their leader and would not let him go. He saw that as the father of the nation he could not abandon his people in their hour of crisis.

But his health deteriorated further, leading to a minor heart attack and many visits to the Soviet Union for treatment.

He quickly rebuilt his army with full-scale Soviet assistance but began to adopt much more conciliatory, pragmatic policies, which lost him many of his traditional Arab allies. He accepted the UN resolution 242 in November 1967 which implied the recognition of Israel. This was followed by US Secretary of State William Rogers' peace plan in July 1970 which confirmed a permanent cease fire.

He ordered his troops to leave Yemen in December 1967, which allowed a partial reconciliation with Saudi Arabia and the Gulf states. His last act was to secure an agreement between King Hussein of Jordan and the PLO leader Yasser Arafat on 28 September 1970. He died the next day of a heart attack.

Man and Myth

KWAME NKRUMAH
1909-1972

Nkrumah was essentially the right man at the right time, in the right place, at the dawn of African independence. He was an idealist and a political visionary, in a tearing hurry to achieve the dramatic goals of pan-Africanism and the total defeat of colonialism in Africa. He sold his message with the flair of a born publicist, using the media and every psychological trick to get the widest attention. But as a flamboyant propagandist he raised expectations among his own people and Africans generally, that led to massive disappointment when he was not able to deliver.

Inside Ghana his slogan was "Seek ye first the political kingdom". He was quick to seize and hold power, but he was far too impatient and dogmatic for the hard slog of day-to-day government. His regime, born of naive idealism, sank into single party authoritarianism. He ruined the Ghana economy as his grandiose foreign policy initiatives collapsed one by one.

Nkrumah was charismatic, energetic, enthusiastic, but he tried to do too much, too quickly. His dream was shattered on the rocks of reality. By the end he was a disappointment even to himself.

But the myth remains. In the years since his death he has been rehabilitated. In the minds of the young and idealistic he stands for everything that Africa could have done, but failed to do. The man failed, the legend lives.

Francis Nwia Kofie Nkrumah was born at Nkroful in western Ghana, on an uncertain date, though he declared it to be 21 September 1909. His name, Kwame, indicates that he was born on Saturday - his mother's only child. His father was a goldsmith of the Nzima tribe, a sub-group of the Akan.

He was educated at Catholic mission schools before going to the teachers training college at Achimota. He graduated in 1930 and took up teaching in primary schools.

An uncle sent him for further education to Lincoln University in the USA, where he majored in economics and sociology. He became a lecturer in political science and obtained post-graduate degrees in education and philosophy from the University of Pennsylvania.

In June 1945 he went to London to attend the London School of Economics. There he plunged himself into the heady anti-colonial atmosphere of left-wing African and West Indian politics. He was one of the joint secretaries of the Fifth Pan African Conference at Manchester, alongside George Padmore, T R Makonnen, Jomo Kenyatta and Peter Abrahams.

His years abroad, he wrote later, "were years of sorrow and loneliness, poverty and hard work," but they helped him to formulate his "philosophy of life and politics."

Already the young Nkrumah had revealed his extraordinary charisma. He was energetic and driven by a burning ideological passion absorbed from his wide reading of such anti-colonial writers as Marcus Garvey. He founded and edited a new anti- colonial monthly called *The New African*.

J B Danquah (q.v.) and the other leaders of the United Gold Coast Convention, the leading political group of the time, urged him strongly to return to Ghana and become the General Secretary of the party.

On 14 November 1947 he sailed home and threw himself into the organisation of the UGCC, soon forging it into one of Africa's first mass political parties. One of his first skirmishes with government was when he took "positive action" and boycotted the stores of European and Syrian traders, leading to riots in which the colonial authorities shot dead 29 Africans and injured hundreds of others.

He was arrested on 12 March 1948 together with five other UGCC leaders. His fellows considered him to be the ringleader and blamed him for the repression that followed.

He was detained for eight weeks, then released to give evidence to the Watson commission which had been appointed to investigate the disturbances.

The inquiry aggravated the differences between himself and the other UGCC leaders and on 12 June 1949 he broke away to form his own Convention People's Party. It was a militant movement of a different breed, demanding "self-government now" and threatening more positive action. He also founded the *Evening News* to propagate his views. (It was to continue as a leading newspaper long after he was dead).

Disturbances broke out afresh in January 1950. A state of emergency was declared and he was again arrested and detained, this time in James Fort prison in Accra. This gave him a martyr's mantle as a "prison graduate" and his party swept the municipal seats in the February 1951 elections. Nkrumah himself, while still in prison, won almost all the votes in Accra Central.

The colonial authorities relented and realising they could not govern without him, released him after just under one year in prison, on 21 January 1951. The prison graduate became the overnight leader of government business in the legislative assembly, then in March 1952 he was promoted to Prime Minister.

Nkrumah's soaring popularity and that of the CPP was confirmed in the general elections of June 1954 and July 1956. The CPP achieved overwhelming majorities despite the opposition of the Asante cocoa growers organised in the National Liberation Movement. It wanted to delay independence but Nkrumah found an ally in the sympathetic governor, Sir Charles Arden Clarke, and on 6 March 1957 Ghana became the first African country to gain its independence.

Nkrumah wanted to achieve his socialist ideals in a hurry. His people had little training or experience, but he wanted to build a complex socialist society. He realised that not all his aspirations could be achieved immediately and warned in his first speeches that discipline was necessary and that he would not shirk from "emergency measures of a totalitarian kind."

Once in control he began rapidly to build up the power of the party and extend his own personal control - the Deportation Act and the Emergency Powers Act of 1957 were followed by the Preventive Detention Act of 1959. Municipal assemblies were abolished, the powers of the chiefs drastically curtailed.

By April 1960 a new republican constitution gave him wide-ranging personal powers as president elect and his well organised party machine assured his victory over Dr. J. B. Danquah in the presidential elections, when he took 90% of the votes.

On 1 July 1960 he became Ghana's first President and assumed full responsibility for the dismissal and appointment of all civil servants. The Presidential Affairs Act, the Emergency Powers Act and the Public Order Act of 1961 concentrated more power into his hands. Gradually he gained control of most branches of the executive, legislature and judiciary. He deliberately fostered the personality cult that grew up around his name.

Nkrumah wanted to remain in the vanguard in the struggle against colonialism, the "total liberation of the African continent" and the achievement of pan-African unity. He campaigned tirelessly against apartheid in South Africa and colonial rule in Rhodesia. He sent Ghanaian troops to boost the UN in the Congo in the hope of saving Patrice Lumumba (q.v.).

He called a conference of independent African states in Accra in April 1958 and, in December 1958, he hosted the first All-African People's Conference; both were designed to "help our brothers languishing under colonial rule."

He backed the rhetoric with cash, dealing out loans to fellow African countries. In May 1959 he announced the Ghana-Guinea union. Though it existed only on paper the "union" was extended to Mali on 24 December 1960.

At first Nkrumah was revered as the leader of pan-Africanism but as he pushed eagerly to achieve his ambitions the governments of other African countries became increasingly suspicious of his motives, methods and interference. The more conservative African states were particularly worried when he set up a Bureau of African Affairs which encouraged subversion against other African states considered to be too close to the colonialists.

Nkrumah specifically rejected progress towards pan-Africanism by stages and through existing regional organisations. Instead he wanted an all embracing union where he could use his charisma to emerge as the leader.

He became leader of the militant African states which met in January 1961 in Casablanca and adopted a charter of African unity. But the more he pressed and revealed his ambition, the greater the reaction against him. Ultimately it was the majority of conservative states that produced the Organisation of African Unity in Addis Ababa in May 1963. Its charter rejected all Nkrumah's pan-Africanist goals in favour of safeguarding the status quo, and enshrining the principle of non-interference in the affairs of independent states.

Ironically it may have been suspicion of Nkrumah that made many of his fellow heads of state opt for a negative and largely powerless organisation that would enshrine colonial boundaries for decades after independence.

In 1961 he made a famous "dawn broadcast" and inveighed against corruption in the government and party. (After his fall various commissions of inquiry revealed the extent of this corruption and implicated Nkrumah himself, though personal enrichment was never a prime objective of his.)

In September he sacked two of his chief lieutenants Komla Gbedemah and Kojo Botsio because of their "varied business connections." Four other ministers were forced to surrender surplus properties to the state.

He remained popular with the ordinary people, the unions, the party and the politicians who depended on his patronage, but opinion was turning against him among the middle class and wealthy farmers.

There were also men of violence who were dismayed at the pace of change that he was trying to force on the country. The first major attempt on his life came on 1 August 1962 when a bomb exploded near his car at Kulungugu killing four people and seriously injuring a further 56.

Nkrumah began to call himself "Osagyefo", meaning the redeemer and built a personality cult through the government-controlled mass media. He set up an executive closely paralleling the estabished civil service at his offices at Flagstaff house, which allowed him to short circuit the decision making processes of the state. He also brought the CPP party under his tight personal control, making frequent purges of its leadership.

Nkrumah's fear for his life became paranoia as a series of conspiracies were uncovered followed by trials that few considered to be genuine. Ex-Foreign Minister Ako Adjei, and ex- Information Minister Taawiah

Adamafio were acquitted of having anything to do with the bomb attempt in August 1962, so Nkrumah promptly dismissed the trial judge Chief Justice Sir Arku Korsah. Five hitherto unknown people were then condemned to death following a trial in which they were allowed no defence counsel, for another bomb attempt also in 1962.

In May 1963 Nkrumah gave himself increased powers to deal with matters of security. He assumed the right to detain people without charge, for up to 10 years. In December he adopted a bill giving himself the power to annul court decisions.

After sacking two prominent judges he forced the retrial of Ako Adjei and Adamafio for treason and this time secured death sentences. He then "magnanimously" commuted their sentences to 20 years imprisonment.

Joseph Danquah, the revered opposition leader, died in February 1965 after being held in detention for nearly 13 months. The government announced that he had a heart attack but Danquah's supporters alleged that he had been tortured to death.

Ghana was officially declared a one-party state on 21 February 1964. The CPP, under Nkrumah's total control, became the sole legal political organisation. He also assumed to right to dismiss any judge "at any time and for reasons that appear to him sufficient."

In June 1965 Nkrumah, the only candidate, was re-elected President for a second term. Elections were then called for parliament. The CPP drew up a list of candidates and all were elected unopposed. Party rule became authoritarian and corrupt.

Nkrumah who had come to power challenging the British colonialists on the grounds of the highest idealism by championing human rights had ended by suppressing the very liberties he stood for. The Ghanaian people were cowed and afraid to express their disillusion and resentment. Though no one could forecast a date, his time was running out.

Nkrumah's obsession with power and his consuming interest in foreign policy, in spreading his philosophy to Africa and the non-aligned world, in writing books and broadcasting, left him little time to worry about Ghana's economy. But his worries were growing.

When he came to power Ghana had £200m in foreign exchange reserves with a world cocoa price of over £400 per ton. But the collapse in the cocoa price and his own economic mismanagement plunged Ghana into debt. His socialist measures - state farms, state corporations, young pioneers and builders brigades were all a drain on state funds.

But he did give his people widespread free education. He also built roads, a new port at Tema and finished the Volta dam project, which generated electricity, though mainly to the advantage of the American Volta Aluminum Company which bought the power at a very low, long term prices. Much other money was wasted on prestige projects that were totally unproductive. The opening of the Volta dam in February 1966 was his last major triumph at home.

He fell from power on 24 February as he flew to Peking, en route to

Hanoi on a Vietnam peace mission. It was the army who finally summoned up the courage to oust him. Senior officers led by General Joseph Ankrah, who had been dismissed by Nkrumah in July 1965 as deputy chief of the defence staff, seized power with consummate ease and little bloodshed. The CPP collapsed like a pack of cards. Over 500 political prisoners were released and the Ghanaian people rejoiced uninhibitedly at the dictator's downfall.

As the new government systematically overturned everything that Nkrumah had built, he found himself cold shouldered by his embarassed Chinese hosts and by the Soviets when he flew to Moscow. He vowed that he would return home but instead went to Conakry, Guinea where Sekou Toure (q.v.) had proclaimed him joint head of state.

Nkrumah found that Sekou Toure's promises meant nothing politically but he remained in Guinea as a private citizen, plotting against the Ghanaian government and writing polemical books to support his cause.

Though the military government exposed two attempts to restore Nkrumah when they intercepted mysterious trawlers, full of communist arms in Ghanaian waters in 1967, Nkrumah remained put. He was also cleared of involvement in an attempted counter-coup in April.

The authorities put a price of $28,000 on his head and instituted a series of commissions of inquiry to expose his mis-doings. Little money was found in his bank accounts at home and though there were many allegations about the transfer of funds abroad, little was proved. His close associates were invariably found to be more corrupt than he.

Memories about Nkrumah's misdeeds faded rapidly as the military government failed to deliver. Early in 1972 after another military coup by Colonel Ignatius Acheampong, he was invited on 19 January to return to Ghana as a private citizen.

His life in Guinea had been sad and lonely. His friend Sekou Toure had given him no political power, indeed his special privileges were withdrawn after a few months and Nkrumah had to beg Toure for more freedom of movement. Towards the end he had been treated with suspicion and placed under surveillance. One by one the faithful who had accompanied him in exile abandoned him. Daily he was reminded of the failings of the authoritarian Guinean regime, far worse than his own had been in Ghana.

The sociable charmer became ever more lonely and embittered.

He was 62 when cancer was diagnosed. He flew to Bucharest in Romania for treatment and died in hospital, on 27 April 1972. Sekou Toure would not allow his body to return home for burial until he had been "rehabilitated" by the Acheampong regime, so he was buried in Conakry on 16 May.

The Acheampong government said that his "place in history had been assured as the principal architect of Ghana's independence, which hastened the pace of the liberation movement in Africa." The man who had given Ghana its hour of glory had gone.

Martyr to the Cause

AMILCAR CABRAL
1924-1973

Amilcar Cabral is remembered as a great hero, the man whose single-minded devotion to the nationalist cause, won independence for Guinea Bissau and hastened the collapse of the Fascist Portuguese government. Starting with a bunch of uneducated peasants, in a tiny unrecognised country, he forged a movement which within ten years was to bring down the Portuguese imperial empire.

Cabral was above all an African nationalist, but also a dyed-in-the-wool Marxist, full of boring jargon and abstract philosophy. But but behind the verbal smokescreen was a man who knew how to motivate and embolden the peasantry.

He died at the hands of the assassin's bullet, but the assassination came far too late to stop the victorious war of liberation. The movement he had established was strong enough to continue without him. Within a few months of his death his country had won its independence.

Amilcar Lopes Cabral was born on 12 September 1924 in Bafata in Guinea Bissau. His father was a *mestiço* Cape Verdian as were 80% of the population of the islands. There is a Portuguese adage, "God created the Portuguese and the Portuguese created the *mestiço*". The Portuguese had ruled Cape Verde since the 15th century and Cabral certainly had some Portuguese blood in his veins, but his mother was an African from Guinea Bissau, on the mainland.

Cabral's father sent him to the *Liceu Gil Eanes* on São Vicente for his secondary education. He was one of the very few to be chosen at that time for higher education at the *Instituto Superior de Agronomia* of Lisbon University where he trained as an agronomist and hydraulics engineer, graduating in 1950. There he made friends with other radical African students and married his Portuguese wife, Anna Maria.

He returned to Guinea Bissau, (jointly administered with the Cape

Verde Islands) to work for the Portuguese government. He was given the job of carrying out the first agricultural census in Portuguese Africa where he learnt about the conditions of the rural people who had lived for centuries under the harshest Portuguese oppression. At first he concerned himself with the technical aspects of his job, writing articles in academic journals on land utilisation and agricultural production.

But he was essentially a political animal and had already become a dedicated Marxist while a student in Portugal. On his return his eyes had been opened to the desperate poverty and backwardness of the rural areas. He began to dream of organising his people in a colonial struggle. He started by infiltrating entirely legal organisations such as sports clubs and setting up cells in the main towns.

On 19 September 1956 he and a handful of colleagues (including his brother, Luis Cabral, and Aristides Pereira who was to become the first President of an independent Cape Verde) met secretly in Bissau and formed the *Partido da Independência da Guinée Cabo Verde* (PAIGC) which was to become the spearhead of the liberation struggle. He also pioneered the liberation movement in Angola when he went there to work for a private sugar company. In December 1956 he was with Agostinho Neto (q.v.) and other Angolans when they formed the *Movimento Popular de Libertacão da Angola* (MPLA).

In Guinea Bissau, the PAIGC's policy of concentrating its revolutionary activity on the urban workers, received a rude shock in 1959, when the seamen who had been trained by the PAIGC went on strike for the first time in the colony's history, at Pidjiguiti docks. The strike was brutally repressed by the Portuguese who killed 50 dockers and injured hundreds more.

Cabral's lesson from the dock strike was to switch the struggle from the towns where the workers were easy targets, to the rural areas where the Portuguese were thin on the ground. Cabral also decided to train and motivate the peasants first, before embarking on the armed struggle.

Cabral was a Marxist theorist of the most boring kind. His strategies for starting the revolution have been tediously spelt out elsewhere, but his problem was real enough. How to motivate an uneducated peasantry cowed by centuries of colonialist exploitation.

He followed the Chinese or Vietnamese model and concentrated on the rural areas, but even there he found the ranks of the PAIGC were heavily infiltrated by the Portuguese secret police, PIDE. Many other party leaders were arrested.

He started a guerrilla training school in the bush. In 1962 isolated acts of sabotage began against government installations. Cabral went to New York and in June made a speech to the United Nations which revealed his political intentions.

The beginning of the armed offensive was marked by the attack on the army barracks at Tite, in the south of the country on 23 January 1963.

In 1964 the PAIGC called a congress at Cassaca in the forests of the south of the country where Cabral explained the philosophical basis for the movement and disciplined individualist commanders who had got out of line.

At first the Portuguese thought it impossible that such a backward hinterland could be producing a revolution. For a time they claimed that the guerrillas were simply bands of armed men who had come over the borders from Sekou Toure's (q.v.) revolutionary Guinea next door. But soon the real threat was recognised and Portugal put 5,000 men into their tiny colony, equipped with the most up-to-date weaponry. By the end of the war in 1973, the Portuguese had an army of 40,000 trying to hold down the rebels.

The rebels made steady progress starting on the Senegal and Guinea frontiers and steadily liberating more of the country.

Cabral established his headquarters in neighbouring Guinea and spent most of his time there when he was not visiting his forces in the bush.

He insisted that the liberated areas in the hands of the PAIGC should not be run simply as military fiefdoms but should have effective civilian administrations. Local committees ran their villages, their own militias, organised agriculture and basic production, and set up people's stores where peasants could barter rice for clothes. Cabral also advanced the status of women and abolished the practice of forced marriage that was extensively practised in rural areas.

Cabral travelled extensively winning the backing of the United Nations, the Organisation of African Unity and many Eastern bloc countries which helped him with arms. The Soviets supplied armoured vehicles and heavy artillery with a range of up to ten miles.

By the 1970s there were still only about 6,000 PAIGC troops facing over 30,000 Portuguese. Casualties on both sides ran into thousands. About two-thirds of the country had been liberated, some of it permanently because it was in areas inaccessible to the Portuguese.

The Portuguese held the capital and its outskirts as well as other major towns like Bafata and Bolama and fortified posts in small rural centres. The PAIGC had the run of most of the rest of the country though they were exposed to bombing and strafing by the Portuguese airforce and sudden raids by troops.

The PAIGC had formed armed local militias in each of the 30 administrative sectors under its control. Over the course of the war mechanised transport had been introduced but most movement was still by foot. The guerrillas' weaponry had improved greatly as the Eastern bloc stepped up its supplies.

Victory was well on the way when Amilcar Cabral was assassinated on 20 January 1973, outside his house in Conakry. After attending a diplomatic reception that night, his car was stopped. He was dragged from it at gunpoint, then shot dead. Sékou Touré announced a few days later that the PAIGC's naval commander, Inocentio Canida, had admitted responsibility for the killing and had been arrested.

Who was really behind the killing? Sékou Touré summarily tried and condemned five agents he had discovered in the ranks of the PAIGC living in Guinea and sent them back to Bissau where they were executed by firing squad. There has been no independent investigation since as Guinea was itself a closed society.

The Portuguese denied responsibility, but it is thought that they could have tricked Canida, as a leader of PAIGC dissidents into the murder, by promising him that if Cabral was removed, he would become the leader of an independent Guinea. Or the assassination could have been carried out by agents of PIDE direct, with Canida made the scapegoat.

Whatever the truth, Amilcar Cabral was dead. But his death did not alter the course of the war. The movement he had built appeared to gain fresh strength from the martyrdom of its leader.

Within nine months the PAIGC Congress, meeting at Madina do Boe on 24 September 1973, declared the independence of Guinea Bissau. This was recognised by the UN on 2 November and by the OAU on 27 November.

The liberation struggle which Cabral had launched just ten years before in the remote bush had achieved its goal. The war dragged on a little longer, but it had played its part in draining the strength of the Spinola regime which collapsed in April 1974. By 10 September Portugal formally recognised the independence of the new republic.

Yesterday's Revolutionary

MESSALI HADJ
1898-1974

Messali Hadj, heavily bearded and wearing a fez and dark rimmed glasses, was Algeria's first revolutionary. From a working class background he was an archetypal communist – tough, inflexible, authoritarian, refusing assimilation and demanding independence and democracy for his people. He was demonised by the French authorities in Algeria who imprisoned him repeatedly as he reorganised his political parties. In the 1930s and throughout the World War he was the outstanding nationalist leader, beloved of all militants.

But his views gradually moderated and he would have been prepared to fight the French on a constitutional basis if they had been sincere in their plans to introduce gradual democratisation. Instead they rigged the system to put yes-men into the new assembly.

While Messali was harassed and repeatedly arrested, a new generation led by men of real violence was emerging. The ageing patriarch found himself under permanent detention in France as Algeria exploded into war. They seized the leadership for themselves. He had become yesterday's revolutionary.

Messali Hadj ben Ahmed was born in 1898 in Tlemcen, Algeria. His father was a humble shoemaker who could not afford to give him more than a basic education.

He served for a brief period with the French army but never got further than southern France. After the war he went to Paris and got a job in the Renault car factory while continuing his education at the School of Oriental Languages at the Sorbonne. His interest in politics and the emancipation of his people led him to join the French Communist party. His fellow members helped him found the first Algerian nationalist newspaper, *El-Ouma*, printed in Paris in 1924.

He returned home with a French communist wife and they founded a new party *Etoile Nord Africaine* (ENA) in 1925. Essentially it was the first truly nationalist party in Algeria, aiming at the political and social emancipation of the Muslims, though it was immediately criticised by whites for being communist inspired. Messali certainly organised the party on communist lines based on cells, controlled by an authoritarian central committee.

Messali's absolute authority over his followers and his increasingly strident anti-colonialism worried the French authorities to such an extent that they banned the party and newspaper and imprisoned Messali in 1929.

He was soon released and in 1930 began active opposition organising marches and demonstrations in favour of total independence. He even appealed vainly to the League of Nations to set Algeria on the road to freedom. By then he had totally rejected the path of gradual evolution by assimiliation. Only one per cent of Muslims had become French citizens and they could be swamped by French *colons* in any elections. Furthermore the French abandoned the Blum-Viollet plan which would have granted full citizenship to an increasing number of Algerians.

Messali revived the ENA in France in 1934 and was rearrested. He was held in prison for a year while his party was again banned. He returned to Algeria in August 1936 and started a campaign against French assimiliationist policies.

He returned to Paris later that year determined to found a new party to catch the rising tide of nationalism. He formed the *Parti Populaire Algérien* (PPA) which stood for total independence and Arab unity and had no truck with assimiliation. He also broke his ties with the Communist party because of the failure of its French deputies to defend the ENA in its hour of need. Once again the party was broken up by the Algerian authorities who banned the new party and threw Messali in prison for the third time.

Messali realised that there was no hope in open confrontation with the French and went underground. The war which came in 1939 would have anyway put an end to overt political activity. The war gave the French government a ready excuse to arrest him yet again, for alleged subversive activities. This time he was condemned by the Vichy regime who looked upon him as a dangerous communist engaged in espionage. He was sentenced to 16 years hard labour. While he was in prison his clandestine PPA party grew fast in the hope that the end of the war would eventually bring liberation, but the nationalist initiative passed to his political rival Ferhat Abbas (q.v.). Hopes of all Muslims were raised high by the Allied landings in Algeria in 1942.

It was an explosive mix. Expectations were high, while conditions were tough. Harvests had failed and the war had dislocated transport; there was famine in some Muslim villages.

On 8 May 1945, VE day, demonstrations for total independence and against colonialism turned nasty, ending with bloody clashes between the Algerians and local settlers. At first the French took the brunt of the savagery. The response was equally violent with Arab villages bombarded by the French fleet and dive bombed from the air. About 30,000 Muslims died.

One of the main demands of the demonstrators had been the release of Messali. He was grudgingly released in 1946 and it looked as if French policies might change. The following year the government of the new Fourth Republic finally agreed to the establishment of an Algerian Assembly. It had two colleges of 60 members each, one representing the 1.5 million French settlers and the other the nine million Muslims. It had limited powers but promised constitutional change.

Messali decided to give the new system a try. He formed the *Mouvement pour le Triomphe des Libertés Démocratiques* (MTLD). He had already contested the elections of November 1946, where he won five of the 15 seats and the municipal elections of October 1947 in which he made sweeping gains.

But as the assembly elections of April 1948 approached, many of the younger militants in his party warned that France had no intention of surrendering real power. They had good cause.

The assembly elections of April 1948 were blatantly rigged by the French authorities and the settlers who dominated the civil service. The nationalist vote, also suffering from internal schisms, fell by half with the MTLD gaining only 9 seats out of the 60-seat college, and Ferhat Abbas' *Union Démocratique du Manifeste Algérien* UDMA 8 seats, in constrast with the pro- government candidates (the *Beni oui ouis*) who got 43.

The rigging was so blatant that the nationalists felt betrayed by France and abandoned all hope of constitutional advance.

Messali's moderation had been found wanting and he came under ferocious attack within his party while his followers melted away. His party went into decline with some members of the MTLD breaking away to join the violent, clandestine *Organisation Secrète* (OS) led by Ahmed Ben Bella, Hocine Ait Ahmed, Mohammed Boudiaf and others.

The OS began preparing for armed warfare under six district commanders by storing weapons throughout the country. It was exposed and broken up when the French unearthed activity in Bone early in 1950.

Messali did not benefit, his party continued to disintegrate as he struggled to preserve his authoritarian rule and preserve party structures. Tribalism also surfaced for the first time among the nationalists. Messali was an Arab and found himself opposed by his Secretary General Hocine Lahouel, a Kabyle.

Messali purged the party of some Kabyles and appeared to be winning, only to be arrested yet again in 1952 when leading a campaign in Orleansville. He was exiled to France and held in Les Sables-d'Olonne until 1962.

Two years after his arrest the MTLD disintegrated completely and a new breed of hard men took up the nationalist baton. The OS became the

Revolutionary Council for Unity and Action, determined to plan and carry out armed revolt against the French. Ben Bella its most prominent leader escaped to Cairo in 1952 where, fully supported by Gamal Abdul Nasser (q.v.), he planned insurrection.

Messali tried desperately to stay in the revolutionary swim. He formed a new party called the *Mouvement National Algerién* and appointed a commander in the hope of maintaining his following until a political settlement was reached. He even sent envoys to Ben Bella to see if there would be a basis for association. But Ben Bella wanted to keep the leadership firmly in his own hands, giving no share to a man he considered to be a discredited politician under permanent detention in France. Ben Bella showed his stance by having all Messali's representatives in Cairo put under arrest.

Messali's hands were tied and by the time he was released after the Evian agreement in 1962 his time had passed. He never dared return to Algeria and died in France on 3 June 1974.

Father of the Nation

JOMO KENYATTA
c.1898-1978

Throughout Kenyatta's early life the whites thought he was a dangerous, untrustworthy revolutionary, with extreme left wing sympathies. After he was convicted of "managing Mau Mau" in 1953, the Kenya Governor, Sir Patrick Renison described him as "a leader unto darkness and death."

But, ten years later, when he came to power in an independent Kenya in 1963, he turned out to be moderate, pragmatic, subtle and above all a symbol of national unity. He achieved the smoothest transfer of power from white to black rule and total racial reconciliation. His detached tolerance also contained the tribal situation in his own country, with his rallying cry *Harambee*, Let's pull together.

The atmosphere of stability he fostered allowed the creation of a comparatively free and prosperous state. His critics claim that he was too conservative and laissez-faire, his admirers look back on the rule of *Mzee*, the old man, as a golden age in Kenya's history. He was the father of the nation.

Kamau wa Muigai was born at Nagenda in Kiambu district near Nairobi possibly in 1898, or a few years earlier. His birth date is imprecise because he was deliberately ambivalent about it throughout his life. His parents were poor peasants and there was no system of birth registration.

He joined the Scottish Mission School at Thogoto, north of Nairobi, in November 1909 when the missionaries said he was a boy of less than 12 years of age.

The first whites had arrived in Kikuyuland in the 1890s and the railway reached Nairobi in 1898, but Kenyatta had not seen a single pink-skinned stranger in his childhood. After his father died, his step-father was prepared to let him join the mission and learn the alien culture of the whites. He started life on the troubled border between traditional Kikuyu culture and the new Christian civilisation. He was both initiated according to Kikuyu rites and later baptised as a Christian in August 1914.

He was an undistinguished pupil, either in scholarship or carpentry which he took as a trade. He left his school without the full blessing of the missionaries; he had been involved in too many scrapes and drank too much for them to trust him.

At the outbreak of the first World War, he moved to Masailand to avoid forced recruitment into the army. After the war he moved back into Kikuyuland and gained a reputation as a sharp dresser with a handsome, dominant face that was a great attraction for the ladies. It was at this time that he took on the name Kenyatta after the beaded belt, *Kinyata* in Kikuyu, that he always wore.

He married Grace Wahu, secured a well-paid job as a meter reader for the water department and got himself a motorbike which gave him great prestige in Kikuyuland.

Though loving the good life, Kenyatta began to take politics seriously when he joined the first African political organisation, the Kikuyu Central Association in 1924. Soon the timid, mission-educated youth was giving evidence to the Hilton Young Commission which was considering how to establish some form of "native representation."

In May 1928 he established a newspaper *Muiguithania* (The Reconciler), which timidly raised the question of African land rights for the first time.

The KCA wanted to send a representative to England to plead their case on land and gain permission to open schools in Kikuyuland independent of the colonial government. Kenyatta was determined to go and so few were the suitable candidates, that the KCA was delighted to send him. He sailed for Britain on 17 February 1929.

He did win the right for his people to open independent schools in the teeth of mission opposition, but he was in no hurry to return home. He had lots of KCA money and liked the good life and the freedoms of London's cosmopolitan environment.

He returned home briefly from September 1930 to May 1931 but hated being caught between an unsympathetic colonial government and suspicious political rivals, particularly the recently released KCA leader Harry Thuku.

Back in Britain his job was to present evidence to a joint parliamentary select committee on the Kikuyu land question, but he was consistently snubbed and not even allowed to present evidence in person. His political effectiveness diminished fast, but he remained in Britain enjoying the tea parties and the admiration of his leftist admirers.

In 1930 he was recruited by George Padmore, then a communist agent, to attend a meeting of the International Trade Union Committee of Communist Workers. This was followed by a visit to Moscow. Later during a prolonged stay, from 1932-33 he was trained at Comintern

International Institute. Kenyatta never became a communist, but he was certainly influenced by the Marxist dialectic as his writings showed. His articles in the left wing press about the stolen land of the Kikuyu had a hard edge, full of Marxist jargon.

But he did not enjoy living in Russia and he returned to London disillusioned with Stalin's purges. From 1933-36 he worked as an assistant in phonetics at the School of African and Oriental Studies.

In 1936 he took a post-graduate diploma in anthropology at the London School of Economics under Professor Malinowski. He crowned his course with the publication of his book *Facing Mount Kenya* which was widely acknowledged as an excellent work showing the adverse impact of white civilisation on the traditional culture of the Kikuyus.

The book jacket showed him in full regalia, the representative of tribal tradition. He even changed his name from Johnstone (given to him by the missionaries) to Jomo, which sounded more authentically African.

During this period he associated with many Africans from other countries who campaigned on behalf of Ethiopia, against international rearmament and finally against the war. He mixed these wider causes with the struggle over land rights in Kenya.

When war broke out the KCA leaders in Kenya were arrested and he had no funds to get home.

He was stranded in Britain and to avoid the raids on London or possible call up, he took evasive action (as he had done in Kenya in the first World War) by hiding himself at Storrington in rural Sussex. There he met and married Edna Clarke, a children's governess, while working as a farm labourer and winning a reputation as a raconteur at the local pub. Edna bore him a son Peter Magana on 11 August 1943.

As the war came to an end imperial values were increasingly questioned. Kenyatta became involved with many other famous pan-African leaders, such as Kwame Nkrumah (q.v) and George Padmore, in setting up the Fifth Pan Africanist Congress in Manchester in October 1945, which became a rallying forum in the campaign for African independence. Kenyatta presented a pamphlet *Kenya - A land in conflict* which warned of the dangers of revolution if the settlers did not give way.

In September 1946, after 15 years in exile, he returned home to the enthusiastic plaudits of his people. Though he was delighted to reclaim his 32-acre farm near his birthplace at Gatundu and to show his solidarity with one of the senior Kikuyu chiefs, Koinange, he knew that his main task was to become a non-tribal national leader.

He became vice principal at the Independent Teacher's College, Githunguri, which was to become a seminal institution in the nationalist struggle.

In June 1947 he became the President of a new, wider nationalist organisation the Kenya African Union (KAU). He soon united the Kikuyu behind him, drawing crowds of 30,000 or more to listen to his clever oratory. As tension rose between the nationalists and the settlers, the whites actually demanded his deportation.

The Kenya settlers wanted white rule and increased Rhodesia- style settlement. They saw Kenyatta as morally unprincipled, politically dangerous, untrustworthy and possibly a communist.

They pointed to his speeches in which, they claimed, he often said one thing in English and another in Kikuyu.

Meanwhile the new militants were demanding African advancement. In June 1951 the moderate leadership of the KAU was swept away and replaced by tougher, younger men demanding independence within three years and threatening violence if no progress was made. In order to secure unity for the cause and to regain their lost lands, the Kikuyu resorted to traditional oathing ceremonies and later to Mau Mau which involved the murder of loyalists and collaborators.

Kenyatta was caught in the dilemma of all nationalists. He was not in favour of violence or oathing, but he had to support his people's cause by every other means or lose his leadership.

Kenyatta tried to make responsible speeches though he was constantly accused by the whites of double-speak.

In August 1952 he called a mass meeting specifically to denounce Mau Mau. In front of the cameras and recording machines he said clearly, "Mau Mau has spoiled the country. Let Mau Mau perish for ever." Nothing could have been clearer.

The militants warned him that his denunciation had been too strong and that his life was in danger. They then embarked on the killing of still more loyalists, including the venerable Chief Waruhiu.

As the murders continued and law and order collapsed, the new Governor, Sir Evelyn Baring declared a state of emergency on 20 October 1952. Two days later Kenyatta and five other leaders of the KAU were detained and charged on 18 November with "managing Mau Mau."

The trial was a gigantic political frame-up, before a prejudiced judge, in which Kenyatta was already cast as the villain of the piece. The evidence against him was weak. The main prosecution witness, Rawson Macharia, admitted later that he had been bribed to perjure himself.

In April 1953 Kenyatta was convicted and sentenced to seven years imprisonment. Meanwhile Mau Mau violence continued with increasing ferocity. Far more murders and brutalities took place while he was confined to his desert prison at Lokitaung in the remote north, than before his arrest. Kenyatta must have known a lot about Mau Mau, but he certainly did not organise it.

In Lokitaung he was camp cook while his colleagues did hard labour. Divisions started between him and the younger militants, representing a rift that ran through Kikuyu society between those who wanted to continue the violent struggle and those who wanted to forget the past. Once he was attacked with a knife and almost killed.

On 14 April 1959 he completed his prison sentence but was immediately restricted, this time in improved conditions at Lodwar, 90 miles to the south. He was allowed more freedom and family visits.

The whites still considered that Kenyatta had been responsible for

Mau Mau. The new Governor Sir Patrick Renison described him as "the leader unto darkness and death." While he had been under arrest Kenya had made political progress and a new breed of political leaders insisted that they would take no part in any independent government without Kenyatta. "Uhuru na Kenyatta" became the slogan. The new Kenya African National Union (KANU) was formed in March 1960 with the presidency left vacant for him. In the February elections the Africans won a majority in the Legislative Council.

In April 1961 he was taken to a better prison at Maralal where hordes of visitors, politicians of all races, reporters and interviewers were able to report on his true beliefs and lack of vindictiveness.

The government, seeking to make amends, built him a new house at Gatundu and on 14 August 1961 he was finally released. He had been under arrest for nearly nine years.

Within a month, on 28 October 1961, he had accepted the presidency of KANU. In January 1962 he was returned unopposed for Fort Hall constituency and took his place in the Legislative council. He was briefly appointed Minister for Constitutional Affairs and took part in the Lancaster House conference leading to Kenya's independence in 1963.

On 28 May 1963 he became the first Prime Minister of an independent Kenya. He soon showed his priority was to build a united nation where all races could pull together under his slogan "Harambee". One of his first acts was to convince a group of die-hard settlers at Nakuru that they had nothing to fear.

On 12 December 1964 Kenya became a republic with himself as President.

He worked to establish himself as a statesman and national figure above all tribal politics. He was helped by the personality cult that developed around him.

He was a strong believer in a one-party state. The opposition was allowed to wither away and be absorbed into KANU, though Kenya theoretically remained a multi-party state until the time of his death.

He achieved some national unity at first with the appointment of Oginga Odinga, the Luo leader, as Vice President. But Kenyatta soon fell out with the more radical leader. Odinga was forced out of power and briefly detained while his party was proscribed.

The next major crisis came with the assassination in July 1969 of Tom Mboya (q.v.), the brilliant young Luo politician who had been one of Kenyatta's most loyal lieutenants. His unexplained killing unleashed another wave of Luo feeling against Kenyatta. He travelled into Luo country to pay his respects, but the crowds were hostile, his car was stoned and he ended having a public row with Oginga Odinga.

Though Kenyatta tried always to achieve tribal balance in his cabinet, the Kikuyu establishment monopolised most political and economic power. Corruption began to flourish among the leading families, including Kenyatta's own.

Josiah Kariuki, who championed the cause of the ordinary man, was murdered in 1975 when he was at his most critical. Kenyatta set up a commission of inquiry, but no one was punished. Obviously ageing and seeking a quiet life, Kenyatta calmed the troubled waters, though he was not prepared to risk upsetting the established order by pressing too hard.

As Kenyatta moved into his late seventies, the problems of ageing crowded in on him. He suffered a mild stroke in 1976, followed by other heart problems that restricted his travel and made him live at lower altitudes on the Kenya coast for long periods. He began to delegate authority more and more to his younger lieutenants, as they jockeyed for succession.

But the style of his government was well established. His government was moderate, pro-Western, entrepreneurial. He believed in strong, single party government, but tolerated a relatively free press and was not overly repressive. There were few political prisoners and *Mzee*, the father figure, was genuinely loved by people of all races and tribes.

He died on 22 August 1978 at Mombasa from a heart attack. His body was taken the next day to Nairobi to lie in State House. A queue stretching several miles filed past his body to pay their respects. He was buried in Nairobi on 31 August.

Reluctant Leader

ANTONIO NETO
1922-1979

Antonio Neto was a quiet, private person driven by his idealism into politics but never cut out to be a great leader. He did become the unquestioned head of his party and the first President of Angola, but he inherited a nation that was already tearing itself apart as foreign powers fought their ideological battles over the country. He was a studious intellectual, who preferred writing poetry to politics and had to struggle for the mastery of his party and later his country.

His ambitious rivals and foreign interests must take a share of the blame, but he failed in his greatest challenge. He missed the opportunity to emerge as the national leader and father figure in the run-up to independence, or afterwards when he came to power. The agony of Angola continued throughout his lifetime, though it must be said his successors were no more capable of finding a solution than he was.

Antonio Agostinho Neto was born on 17 September 1922 in Icolo-e-Bengo near Catete, just east of the capital Luanda. His father was a Methodist pastor of *mestiço*, or mixed-race, descent. He went to the Liceu Salvador Correia high school in Luanda. From 1944-47 he worked in the Portuguese colonial health services while earning extra money as a personal secretary to a Methodist church leader.

It was at this time, in his early twenties, that he gave expression to nationalist idealism. He had to do this by working through cultural associations, as all political organisations were rigorously suppressed by the colonial authorities.

In 1947 he went to Portugal to study medicine at the University of Coimbra and Lisbon. There he became active in the Portuguese youth movement and was imprisoned for the first time in 1952, for taking part in demonstrations. He was imprisoned again for publishing a book of nationalist poetry which was considered subversive. He was detained and sent down from his medical studies from February 1955 to June 1957. On his release he helped found the Anti-Colonial Movement (MAC) in Lisbon which embraced nationalists from all Portugal's overseas colonies.

He was one of the founder members of the *Movimento Popular de Libertação de Angola (MPLA)*, which was founded in 1956 by intellectuals who had been studying abroad.

He finally qualified as a doctor in 1958 and returned to Angola with a Portuguese wife whom he had married as a student in Portugal. He rejected a job in the colonial health services which only treated the wealthier members of society in the main towns and instead set up a private practice in Luanda where he could treat those really in need.

He returned to find that the Portuguese political police *Pide* were cracking down on all political activity, particularly targeting members of the MPLA. On 8 June 1960 he was arrested in his consulting rooms. People of his village mounted a protest and were punished by having their village burnt down by Portuguese troops. About 30 of his people were killed and 200 wounded in the incident. Neto meanwhile was deported, in chains, to the Cape Verde islands in September 1960 and transferred in 1961 to Aljube prison in Lisbon.

An international outcry prompted his release in March 1962, though he continued to be held under house arrest. Secretly he organised his escape and arrived in Leopoldville (Kinshasa) where the MPLA had its headquarters. At the time the MPLA was riven by rivalries between exiled leaders and factionalism within Angola. In 1956 Viriato da Cruz had led some dissidents out of the movement to join the *Frente Nacional De Libertação de Angola* (FLNA) and had gained early recognition by the Organisation of African Unity (OAU) at the expense of the MPLA.

But when the MPLA held its first national conference in Leopoldville, in December 1962, Neto emerged almost unchallenged as President. His task was to organise a war of liberation in Angola while travelling the world – particularly to the Soviet Union, the eastern bloc and African countries – to solicit moral and financial support.

When the MPLA fell out with the Congolese authorities in November 1963, Neto transferred the headquarters to neighbouring Congo-Brazzaville. A military front in Cabinda was opened in the same year. By 1965 the MPLA had proved to be the best organised nationalist movement both diplomatically and militarily. This was recognised by the OAU which granted the movement official recognition and support from its liberation committee.

But military progress was slow and the MPLA was still faced with factionalism. Daniel Chipenda withdrew his forces from Eastern Angola in 1973 and threw in his lot with the FLNA and Neto was unable to make real military progress until the military coup in Portugal which overthrew the government of Marcelino Caetano on 24 April 1974.

The struggle for leadership continued with the active revolt in May 1974 in which the Andrade brothers, former leaders of the MPLA, defected and took a small group with them. But Neto despite his studious, retiring nature still held the loyalty of the core of the party by his dedication and personal example.

Though he was obliged to draw his support from the Eastern bloc and believed in an egalitarian, non-tribal society, his Marxism was more rhetorical than real. Basically he was a left-wing nationalist trying to run a mass movement and a war of liberation.

In August 1974 he supervised the reorganisation of his guerilla army into the Popular Armed Forces for the Liberation of Angola (FAPLA). In the same month the new Portuguese government recognised Angola's right to self-determination.

In January 1975 the Alvor agreement was signed between the representatives of all the major guerrilla movements including the MPLA, FLNA and the *Uniao Nacional para a Independencia Total de Angola* (UNITA). It set up a transitional government and agreed a date for independence.

Neto returned permanently to Luanda on 4 February 1975 to the cheers of a huge welcoming crowd, but within a month the liberation movements began fighting between themselves for supremacy. Fear that Neto would emerge as leader of the country and the burning ambition of the other leaders prompted the internecine guerrilla war first with FLNA and, after July, with UNITA.

On 11 November 1975 independence was proclaimed and Neto became the first President as the Portuguese settlers fled and Angola disintegrated into a bloody civil war.

The MPLA was the most successful militarily, holding 12 out of Angola's 16 provinces but the conflict deteriorated further as the United States and the Eastern bloc took up ideologically based positions. South Africa invaded in December 1975 and the Soviets replied by sending massive military support and sponsoring Cuban military and assistance personnel.

The Angolans, together with their new allies, forced the South Africans to withdraw and asserted their military superiority, while settling down to a protracted guerrilla war with UNITA.

Neto established total dominance of his own party and carried out a major reshuffle in his government in December 1978 when he dismissed the prime minister and three deputy prime ministers.

But despite his political dominance over the greater part of the country he had missed his chance to overcome the jealousy of the other guerrilla leaders. Internal rivalries hardened further when foreign interests and ideologies became involved. As the years succeeded the divisions became entrenched and, though it was not his fault alone, he had missed his chance for national reconciliation. He could never emerge as the leader of a united nation. Suddenly he developed cancer and died while being treated in a Soviet hospital on 10 September 1979, leaving the problems of his war-torn country to his sucessors.

Father of Democracy

SERETSE KHAMA
1921-1980

Of all his achievements Sir Seretse Khama will be remembered for establishing a tolerant, democratic system in Bechuanaland (Botswana) that long survived him to become the envy of many other African nations. He also built a successful and growing economy based on its agricultural and mineral wealth.

His tolerant, democratic attitude survived his early persecution by the British who, reflecting the racism of the times, took exception to his marrying a white wife and banished him for six years. He remained a non-racist no matter what the provocation and soon showed himself to be a conservative pragmatist with whom the British could do business.

He emerged as a chosen son – the first Prime Minister and President in his country. With hostile white-ruled states on either side, he negotiated a delicate path for his country that gave it a measure of independence and took it along the road to prosperity. Internally he was virtually unchallenged. The vast majority of his people regarded him as the father of a democratic nation.

Seretse Khama was born into the Khama royal family on 1 July 1921. It was a glorious, but not an entirely happy background. His grandfather was Khama III (q.v.), the great king who had dominated the Bangwato in the 19th century. His father, Sekgoma II had been in continual conflict with his grandfather and had suffered exile for 17 years. Sekgoma died in 1925 after ruling for only two years.

Seretse was the unchallenged heir to the throne but, as he was only four years of age, his uncle Tshekedi became regent. He was educated locally then at Tiger Kloof in Natal and at Lovedale and the University of Fort Hare in the Eastern Cape of South Africa. While he was still studying at the University of Witwatersrand in 1944, his Bangwato people first asked him to return and assume the chieftaincy, but he was still only 23 and pleaded more time for further studies.

He went to Balliol College, Oxford to read law, being called to the bar in the Middle Temple in 1948. While in England he met and courted a young white girl, the daughter of a retired army officer, Ruth Williams. He married her on 28 September 1948 in the teeth of strong opposition from uncle Tshekedi, who was still acting as regent in Bechuanaland. He was also opposed by the chiefs who thought he would continue his defiance, take to modern ways and abandon African customs if he was enthroned.

He returned home in 1949 to put his case. At a historic *Kgotla* (meeting) in June, he told the assembled chiefs and headmen that they would have to take him as he was - married to a white girl. With great skill he won them round. They accepted that he was their rightful ruler and finally gave him their approval. This was later confirmed at a public rally in Serowe on 13 July 1949.

But this local support did not convince Britain. The curiously dated racist attitudes of the time, could not accept a mixed marriage, particularly in southern Africa. The Secretary of State for the Commonwealth of the Labour government, Patrick Gordon Walker, summoned him to London and offered him £1,100 a year tax free if he would renounce the chieftaincy and live in Britain. He was even offered a post in the Jamaican civil service. He refused all blandishments, so a judicial commission of inquiry was set up to investigate whether he was fit to rule. The inquiry never published its findings. Meanwhile the South African government protested to Britain at the dangers of a mixed race marriage to the political stability of the region. The British government, in what Winston Churchill described as a "very disreputable transaction," then refused to let him go home.

The sensational case hit world headlines and turned the young couple into international celebrities as the British government banished them to exile in Britain on 5 February 1950. Tshekedi then did the unexpected. He rallied to his nephew, abandoned the chieftaincy and went into voluntary local exile in the small town of Kwaneng.

This left a vacancy in the chieftaincy despite Britain's attempt to plug the gap with an appointee. The Bangwato never accepted this situation. Almost six years later Britain was finally persuaded to allow Seretse, Ruth and family to return home as private citizens on 10 October 1956.

In the years that followed Seretse worked in the local administration and tribal council. By the 1960s when, in the famous words of the British Prime Minister, Harold Macmillan, the "Winds of Change" were sweeping Africa to independence, Seretse found a new way forward. Though cautious and conservative by nature, he saw that he could build himself a new future as a modern politician.

When Britain set up Bechuanaland's first legislative council in December 1960, Seretse was elected as one of the five Africans for the Northern Protectorate. Now fully reconciled with the British, he was appointed as one of the two Africans to the governing Executive Council in 1961 and was decorated with the title, Officer of the Order of the

British Empire (OBE).

In January 1962 his friends – including Quett Masire, who was to take over as President of Botswana from him in 1980 – pushed him into helping form the moderate Bechuanaland Democratic Party (BDP).

This was the vehicle that swept him to success in the first democratic elections of 1965 when the BDP won 28 out of the 31 parliamentary seats. He was then able to form the first majority African government.

He played a leading part in the constitutional talks which followed in London, setting up a democratic, republican constitution. On 30 September 1966 the country became independent, changing its name from Bechuanaland to Botswana. Seretse was knighted and became the country's first President.

In his 15-year rule he followed conservative, pragmatic policies dictated by his position as the leader of a small landlocked country at the mercy of white-ruled neighbouring states. His priority was to maintain national independence at the heart of a troubled continent.

Though he was sympathetic towards African liberation movements, he could not encourage them to the extent of inviting retaliation against Botswana. Despite his caution there were more than 60 violations of national frontiers by his opponents during his years in office. Nearly 80% of Botswana's trade went through South Africa. The railways on which the economy depended, even in Botswana itself, were managed by the Rhodesians. Botswana was also a member of the Southern African Customs Union which brought it an essential share of customs revenue on all trade passing through South African ports.

When he was able he did assert independence of action, such as in 1970 when he gave Botswana its own currency and, in 1979, when he took his country into the Southern African Development Co-ordination Conference (SADCC).

As he said to the Lusaka summit meeting of non-aligned states in 1970, "If we appear reluctant to play an active and prominent part in the struggle for majority rule in southern Africa, it is not because we are unconcerned about the plight of our oppressed brothers...we want to see majority rule established throughout southern Africa and we are determined to contribute towards that noble goal. But there is a limit beyond which we cannot go without endangering our independence."

Internally he preserved a tolerant, democratic nation with a free press and an official opposition. He had neither the need nor the desire to introduce a one-party state. In the elections of 1969 and again in 1974, the BDP won overwhelming majorities and his Presidency was renewed, because the opposition parties failed to present any effective alternative.

Economically he started with two years of drought and a serious lack of finance, but gradually he built a viable economy, encouraging mining particularly in cupro-nickel and diamonds, while preserving the livestock industry.

As the country got wealthier he tried to control mine wages to avoid disparity growing between the miners and agricultural workers, but he had a tough battle against the mine unions, who wanted the same wages as the South African miners.

He was still only 59 when he began to develop stomach cancer. He went for treatment in London, returning home when doctors said he was incurably ill and they could do no more to save him. He died on 13 July 1980. All other events including the crucial independence of neighbouring Zimbabwe were overshadowed by the news of the death of a much-loved father to his people.

Descent into Tyranny

SÉKOU TOURÉ
c.1922-1984

Sékou Touré was born at a crucial time in Africa's history. He led his country's struggle for independence and then chose to reject France and try to go it alone. He was the prime exponent of a Marxist philosophy, the single party state, and the cult of personality. A man of immense charisma, energy and dedication, he was launched to the plaudits of the developing world. But his high ambitions were doomed to failure. He regressed into repressive tyranny. Internationally he was famous, his problem was at home.

A hmed Sékou Touré gave his date of birth as 9 January 1922, but he could have been born a few years earlier, as the actual date was never registered. His father Alpha was a small trader, later a butcher in Faranah in middle-Guinea, near to the source of the Niger.

His mother was the great, great granddaughter of the legendary leader Almamy Samory (q.v.). Legend had it that one of his descendants would "drive the French into the sea."

This enhanced his reputation, but in his youth his half brothers by a former marriage frequently reminded him that his mother was pregnant when she married Alpha. This meant that Sékou was treated as illegitimate, something which had a profound psychological effect; it brought him closer to his mother and hardened him to outside criticism.

He started his education at the local Koranic school and then the regional school at Kissidougou, before gaining admission to the prestigious Ecole Georges Poiret in the capital Conakry. Ahmed was a hard worker and voracious reader but rebellious, tough and opinionated. He learnt his politics in the classroom, organising his classmates to resist the "tyranny of the teachers." He was only 18 when he was expelled from school for leading a strike.

He did a variety of menial jobs before joining the post office in 1944.

By 1945 he was one of the founder members of the Post Office Worker's Union (PTT). He travelled in France and the Eastern bloc and returned

306 / 100 Great Africans

to form the Federation of Guinean Workers Unions, affiliating it to the French Communist *Confederation Generale des Travailleurs*, (CGT).

In 1946 he switched work to the Guinea treasury department and promptly organised the treasury workers. Sacked from the Treasury because of his political activities he went into full-time unionism, organising a series of strikes against the French colonial authorities.

By 1948 he was secretary general of the co-ordinating committee of the CGT for the whole of French West Africa and in 1952 he became the secretary general of the *Parti Democratique de Guinée*, (PDG) affiliated to the West African *Rassemblement Democratique Africain*, (RDA).

In 1953 he was elected to the territorial assembly and then, after the January elections of 1956, became a deputy to the French Assembly on the PDG-RDA ticket. In Paris he worked on the Commission for Labour and Social Security. Even more important he threw himself into the debates on the *Loi cadre*, which was to totally change French policy towards its colonies giving them more local autonomy while maintaining their links with the French Community.

Throughout this debate Sékou followed the RDA-PDG which wanted West African states to federate before independence. Sékou was already a member of the Grand Council for West Africa from May 1957.

Meanwhile his successes accumulated at home. He became Mayor of Conakry in the municipal elections of 1955. In March 1957 the PDG swept to power in the first national elections organised under the *Loi cadre* and he became Vice President of the new government council. In these elections the PDG had already developed intimidatory tactics to terrorise opponents. Thugs armed with iron bars attacked opposition parties with Sékou's full encouragement.

When De Gaulle decided to hold a referendum throughout France's colonies giving the people a choice of autonomy in the French Community or total independence, Sékou still held out for regional federation first. He also wanted to show Africa and the world that he was the only leader with the courage to stand up to the colonial master. As negotiations proceeded France made several concessions to ensure a "Yes" vote amongst RDA member states, but Sékou was bitterly resentful of what he considered to be De Gaulle's haughty patronage. Despite attempts by friends on all sides to avoid the clash, it was personal pique that finally decided the issue.

In September 1958 Sékou made the famous pronouncement, "We prefer poverty in liberty to riches in slavery," and got his people to deliver a resounding "No" vote to De Gaulle.

On 2 October 1958 Guinea took its independence with Sékou Touré as President, the absolute master of his tiny country. France broke diplomatic relations, withdrew all its assistance personnel, cut all financial aid, and even removed the office typewriters.

All the other Francophone countries voted "Yes" and Sékou Touré was expelled from the RDA. He was on his own. But in the heady atmosphere of the time, he was a hero both at home and throughout the colonial world as the one man who had dared say "No" to De Gaulle.

His attitude soon made him one of the leaders, alongside Kwame Nkrumah of Ghana of the militant, revolutionary states. In November 1958 the Ghana-Guinea union was formed, joined in 1960 by Mali. Though these "unions" never became realities they were supposed to be the basis for a union of West African states, even a union of the whole of Africa. Kwame Nkrumah was welcomed as a hero in Guinea after the coup which deposed him in February 1966. Sekou made him honorary joint President of Guinea.

In January 1961 after a conference at Casablanca, all the revolutionary states formed a bloc supporting militant causes and laying foundations for an African union, causing the more moderate states to react with their own agenda for an Organisation of African Unity.

At home Sékou Touré was determined to become the unchallenged master. In his very first speech after independence he asked all citizens to spy on each other. A decree suppressed the liberty of information. Private newspapers and personal radios were banned. All citizens had to declare the extent of their wealth.

Abandoned by France, and helped only by grudging aid from the Eastern bloc, Sékou launched a socialist economy. Foreign capital vanished and the economy collapsed.

Sékou, in interminable speeches on the *Voice of the Revolution* blamed everyone except himself. In April 1960 he "discovered" his first coup plot, which allowed him to summarily execute without trial a first round of political opponents.

A succession of plots followed during the 1960s in which he eliminated suspected opponents, teachers and students (November 1961), shopkeepers (1963), high officials and army officers (October 1965). As he became increasingly paranoid his accusations grew wilder, blaming neighbouring states particularly the Cote d'Ivoire and Senegal and the colonial powers for fomenting dissent.

By the end of the 1960s his dictatorship was at its peak. Over 500,000 Guineans had been driven into exile and the erstwhile hero had lost the confidence of his own people and his students abroad.

In February 1968 he carried out a purge of his top army officers. The trigger was the Labe incident when some private soldiers mutinied after being refused a glass of water by a party militant. When Sékou was informed he ordered their immediate arrest. They tried to hi-jack the plane taking them back to the capital but it ran out of fuel. The soldiers were summarily executed and a general purge of the army followed in which many top officers were killed.

In 1969 a young student maddened with hatred, broke through a security cordon and attacked and punched Sékou with his bare hands.

The first real coup attempt came on 21 November 1970 when the Portuguese government provided the boats for 200 Guinean exiles in an attempt to take Conakry. The plot almost succeeded. When his own army officers arrived to ask for the keys to the armouries, Sékou took them for rebels and cried out, " Kill me but don't deliver me to the people. Don't humiliate me." Those soldiers finally repulsed the invaders, but, because they had exposed the President, they were executed in the wave of repression that followed the coup attempt. Sékou even hanged the Minister of Education and demanded the return of many political refugees from neighbouring territories, to face instant death.

In the 1970s passions cooled and there were no more witch hunts until the Peul plot of 1976. This entrapped Diallo Telli, a distinguished diplomat and former Secretary General of the OAU. He was thrown into the notorious camp Boiro where over 10,000 had already died, tortured and eventually starved to death on 1 March 1977.

Meanwhile Sékou was trying to improve relations with his African neighbours, inviting many of them on state visits to Guinea. He tried to improve his international image as his people struggled with economic penury at home.

It was in June 1977 that Sékou's whole career was changed by a curious series of events unparalleled elsewhere in colonial Africa. A spontaneous revolt by market women against harassment by the dreaded economic police began in Nzerekore and soon spread to all parts of the country. Officials, ministers and the President himself tried to pacify them, but the revolt spread to all parts of the country ending in a shouting match at Sékou's palace. He promised the women he would abolish the economic police and allow them freer trade. Though he reneged later, the market women had seriously frightened him and from 1977 he adopted a softer approach to all internal issues.

Externally too, he decided to come out of isolation. He had not travelled out of Guinea for 13 years and there was scarcely a country that had escaped his vicious attacks on the *Voix de la Revolution*, now everything was to change.

In March 1978 he attended a summit in Monrovia with the Presidents of the countries he had described as the "valets of imperialism" - Houphouet Boigny and Leopold Senghor. On 20 December 1978 he welcomed President Giscard D'Estaing as part of his *Grand ouverture* to France and the West. He also made a number of *hadj* to Mecca to win Arab friends and persuade them to disgorge part of their oil wealth.

In August 1979 he visited President Carter in the US, who wanted to detach him from his Soviet alliance. On 23 September 1982 came the final triumph when he paid his first visit to France since independence and was given full honours, despite the determined opposition of the left and human rights protesters.

But at home many enemies remained. There were three more attempts on his life in February 1981 when a bomb exploded in Conakry airport and again in May. He was attending a show at the People's palace when one bomb exploded some way off while another rolled past his feet failing to go off.

At the party conference in 1983 he no longer proclaimed the revolution but stressed development and the new opening to the West.

In 1984 he turned his attention to the main inter-African issues as part of a determined campaign to host and thus become chairman of the annual meeting of the OAU. In March he invited trade unionists from all over Africa to a meeting at his palace. There he told them that he had started his career as a trade unionist and he would remain one for the rest of his life.

Then suddenly he felt ill. He retired to rest but was violently sick. The doctors diagnosed heart failure.

He was flown overnight to Cleveland, Ohio where he was rushed into emergency surgery. He died on the operating table, on 26 March 1984 at 21.23 GMT.

His Prime Minister Lansana Beavogui took power in Conakry and his body was flown back for a state funeral. But hardly had the distinguished foreign visitors taken their planes home than the army, determined not to let rule by the Toure family continue, seized power. The people spontaneously poured onto the streets rejoicing.

Sékou Touré was a tyrant who had failed to achieve even the goals he had set for himself. His attempt to build a socialist economy had failed and brought his people to penury. After years of playing off the major donors against each other, he had gained little. He ended dependent on the major international mining companies whose values he had castigated throughout his lifetime. His human rights record was appalling.

He played the great international stage, but his problem was at home.

Gentle Revolutionary

FERHAT ABBAS
1899-1985

Throughout his life Ferhat Abbas was a generous, open-hearted man of principle and peace. When his colleagues turned to hideous violence in pressing the nationalist cause, he was on the side of peaceful negotiation rather than force. He was always the diplomatic face of the nationalist struggle as he put the case of the *Front de Liberation Nationale* (FLN) throughout the world.

His integrity was revealed when Algeria finally won its freedom and imposed an authoritarian, single-party system. Abbas continued to campaign for the democratic freedoms that he believed in. His reward was imprisonment by the two governments that followed independence and rejection by the FLN which he had served loyally. He lived to a ripe old age to write his book *L'independence confisquee*. Only recently was his full contribution to his country and the nationalist cause finally recognised.

Ferhat Abbas was born on 24 October 1899 in Taher, Constantine the son of a local administrator and *kaid* (judge). His background was securely middle class in contrast to his lifetime contemporary and rival Messali Hadj (q.v.), who was the son of a shoemaker.

Abbas went to a lycee at Philipeville (now Skikda) on the coast and then did three years in the French army medical service an experience that was to have a profound influence on him. Though he was a Muslim he thought of himself as French entitled to the same rights as any Frenchman living in the French provinces. He believed in assimilation, the process of taking French citizenship, and that Algeria was part of France.

After leaving the army in 1923, he went to the University of Algiers to study chemistry where he founded and became president of the Algerian Muslim Students Union.

On graduating he settled to an orthodox and respectable middle-class career. He returned to his home town Constantine (now Setif) established a pharmacy and became a member of the local municipal council and eventually a financial deputy in the Algiers assembly. In April 1938 he formed the *Union Populaire Algerienne* and in 1939 founded a weekly newspaper *L'Entente*. During the war he stopped all political activity, "to dedicate our efforts to the service of the nation."

Though he was over 40 years old he enlisted, only to suffer the shock of the almost immediate defeat of his adopted motherland. He was demobilised in August 1940 and dispirited, returned to his pharmacy.

Within a few months (April 1941) his spirits had recovered sufficiently to petition Marshal Petain, the leader of the Vichy government for equal rights and the correction of social inequalities in Algeria. He asked for a peasant's fund to be set up to assist small landowners.

Petain had other, more pressing problems and after much delay sent a vague reply, promising nothing. One year later Abbas wrote again asking for a conference to discuss constitutional change. Again he was spurned. The American landings in Algeria in 1942 brought fresh hope of change.

On 10 February 1943 Abbas produced the Algerian People's Manifesto which demanded an Algerian nation linked to France and total equality and liberty for all races and the effective participation of Algerian Muslims in government. He backed the manifesto with a new political party, *Amis du Manifeste et de la Liberte*(AML).

De Gaulle made some concessions in December 1943 when he extended French citizenship to thousands more Muslims and promised their advancement in local government.

But as peace approached expectations of the nationalists all over north Africa, were rising much faster than France's willingness to bring change. Young Algerians returning from the war were impatient and drawn to the more revolutionary polices of Messali Hadj's *Parti Populaire Algerien* (PPA) than to Abbas's AML.

Nationalist fever exploded, at the celebrations of VE day on 8 May 1945, in an orgy of inter-racial violence in which an estimated 35,000 were killed. Repression followed and Ferhat Abbas who had not been involved in anyway was arrested and not freed until 1946.

As more youth flocked to the banner of the PPA, Abbas tried to keep his distance. As soon as he was freed from prison he formed the *Union Democratique du Manifeste Algerien* (UDMA) which still hoped for an independent Algeria federated to France, with pro-Western policies and alliance with other nationalist movements such as Habib Bourguiba's *Neo Destour*. In the elections of June 1946 to the Second French Constituent Assembly, UDMA secured 71% of the votes polled and 11 of the 13 seats reserved for Algeria. Abbas was returned both to the Algerian and French assemblies where he continued to press for autonomy, but within a French federation.

But the French colonial authorities backed by the *colons* (settlers) were so worried at the emerging power of the Muslims that they deliberately and heavily rigged all elections from 1947 onwards. The nationalist parties were decimated in the elections of April 1948 as the *Beni-oui-ouis* (yes-men) were returned in force.

Abbas felt bitterly betrayed. Throughout his life he had placed his faith in the French who were now using fraudulent electoral practices to suppress the will of the majority.

In October 1954 he wrote in his new newspaper *Republique Algerienne*, "Our people are tired of indignantly pleading without success before a tribunal that is ruled by racialism." He said his silence had been interpreted as acquiescence, "In reality fury is at its height, and the silence is of contempt and rebellion."

The rebellion broke out in November 1954. A new generation pledged to violence had taken over, targetting key installations all over the country. Everyone was taken by surprise. Even Abbas was shocked. He wrote in *Republique Algerienne* "We continue to be persuaded that violence will settle nothing." Even Messali Hadj was of this view.

Abbas tried desperately to persuade the French of the need for dramatic reform, but the *colons* were pressing for even tighter control and France remained weak and indecisive.

Abbas may have joined the *Front de Liberation Nationale* in May 1955, though he did not declare his formal adhesion until 26 April 1956 after he had flown to Cairo to join the FLN at its exile headquarters. Years of patient persuasion had failed. The moderate became a revolutionary. He told reporters: "I have knocked on all the doors...I cannot continue to stand bail for a situation of which I entirely disapprove...I am joining [the FLN] because there is no other way."

He became a member of the National Revolutionary Committee of Algeria (CNRA) in August 1956 and a member of the Committee of Co-ordination and Execution (CCE) in August 1957. He based himself in Switzerland and later Tunis organising FLN publicity and travelling the world with the nationalist message.

The kidnapping of Ben Bella and the other FLN leaders, their internment in France and the indecision of weak French governments turned the conflict more desperate and bloody.

Abbas's nature was to put a break on the men of violence and to try to negotiate a peaceful settlement that would bring independence. In August 1958 he was chosen as President of the Provisional Government of the Republic of Algeria (GPRA). His faction in the FLN recognised that violence had not worked and that a negotiated settlement was possible.

De Gaulle had come to power on 1 June 1958. He was gradually abandoning his integrationist policies and coming to the view that there would be no solution unless Algeria was given its independence. On 16 September 1959 he made his historic offer of "self determination." Though the *colons* reacted with fury negotiations stuttered forwards.

Publicly Abbas reasserted the FLN's determination to fight to the bitter end while privately he pursued every opportunity to negotiate. He still had huge support at home. On 11 December 1960 Muslim crowds demonstrated waving flags and shouting "Abbas to power." De Gaulle called a referendum to approve self determination. Negotiations continued fitfully until they broke down in July over the FLN's refusal to grant any special status to French citizens.

This temporary failure in the negotiation process was an excuse for Abbas's enemies in the revolutionary faction of the FLN to drop him from the presidency in favour of Youssouf Ben Khedda on 27 August 1961. A final peace agreement followed a few months later at Evian on 18 March 1962.

Abbas still had a huge following particularly among middle-class Algerians at home. When the FLN took power in July 1962 he was elected President of the National Assembly.

Always true to his democratic principles he soon clashed with Prime Minister Ben Bella who wanted to establish a one-party state.

He resigned shortly after Ben Bella became President and Commander-in-Chief taking all power into his own hands as head of the single party, FLN. Shortly afterwards in July 1964 he was accused of planning a coup and detained for the better part of a year. He was also expelled from the FLN.

He might have rejoined the government when the military coup of Houari Boumedienne brought Ben Bella's excesses to an end in June 1965, but he was not prepared to exchange one authoritarian regime for another.

He continued to campaign for a more democratic form of government At the venerable age of 77, in 1976, he was arrested again for publishing pamphlets calling for democracy. He was placed under house arrest for three years until the ban on him was lifted in 1979.

He lived in Kouba in the hills near Algiers working on his book *L'independence confisquee* which he published in 1984. The same year he was awarded the *Medaille de Resistance* by President Chadli. At last he had been recognised for the decent and dignified part he had played in the emancipation of his people.

He died in December 1985 and was buried among the martyrs in the El Alia cemetery next to Abd el-Kader (q.v.) and other great nationalists.

Killed in his Prime

SAMORA MACHEL
1933-1986

Samora Machel was brought up in the flame of avenging idealism and embraced Marxist-Leninism as the way of lifting his people from poverty and despair. But he was no ideologue, when he discovered that Marxism was not delivering economic success, he was brave enough to admit he was wrong and changed course.

The problems of Mozambique - lack of capital and skills, external intervention, guerrilla war and drought - remained overwhelming. Pressure by Mozambique's powerful neighbour South Africa forced him to try to achieve peace through the Nkomati accord. It was a mistake.

Machel was heavily criticised and failed to secure peace but once again he had showed the courage to try a new course. He was still struggling to bring peace and economic revival to his country when he was killed in the fatal air-crash of October 1986. He was not a martyr to the cause but a victim of circumstance.

Samora Machel was born on 29 September 1933, the third son of a peasant farmer, Moises. His birthplace was Xilembene, in the Chokwe district of Gaza province in the south of Mozambique.

He learnt his politics early at the foot of a great tree where old veterans told stories of the resistance struggle by the Gaza chief Ngungunhane at the end of the 19th century. Machel's family was so poor that several members were driven to South Africa to find work in the mines.

Early on he came under the influence of a Methodist pastor Abel Tchambale but the politically conscious Methodists were viewed with suspicion by the colonial authorities, so the Catholics controlled all education. The young Samora had no choice but to complete his primary schooling at Catholic mission schools.

He claimed that the Catholic missionaries, aware of his political leanings, refused to let him continue beyond the fourth grade unless he was baptised a Catholic. Desperate to continue his studies, he agreed to these terms and passed the exam.

He was then told he could only continue if he did religious studies at a seminary. He politely refused and trained to be a nurse later working at Xai-Xai and Lourenco Marques hospitals, where he earned a salary far lower than the whites who had been trained alongside him.

As he worked he educated himself privately and read widely, absorbing the excitement of Africa's dash for freedom in the early 1960s. Eduardo Mondlane the first nationalist leader, who had completed his education in the US, visited Mozambique in 1961. Samora met him and joined the *Frente de Libertacao de Mocambique* (FRELIMO) as soon as it was founded on 25 June 1962.

But membership was not enough and in 1963 he went into exile to Tanzania and then to Algeria with the first group of guerrillas for training.

He returned to Tanzania and set up the first FRELIMO training camp at Kongwa in southern Tanzania. He was an ideal instructor, tireless, sociable, energetic and already a convinced Marxist, yet trying to work out a philosophy that would suit Mozambique's own peasants. Within the party he was a pragmatist rather than an ideologue.

When the colonial struggle started on 25 September 1964, he was able to put 250 trained men into battle and attacked several colonial posts in northern Mozambique.

In 1965 he was made commander in Niassa province and opened a new front in the east. He trained his men to sleep rough and never spend two nights in the same place. He was a charmer, a good listener and openly friendly. This helped his promotion. He was made commander of the main rear base and of the centre for political and military training at Nachingwea in Tanzania.

In October 1966, on the assassination of Filipe Magaia, he assumed overall command of the FRELIMO forces and became Secretary of Defence which gave him a place on the central committee. He found the party in a state of crisis with much conflict among the leadership of the three parties that had merged to form FRELIMO, but by concentrating on the task at hand he avoided the political in-fighting. Parts of the country were liberated and he shifted the base camps, health posts and his people into the liberated areas.

When the FRELIMO leader, Eduardo Mondlane, was assassinated by a letter bomb in February 1969, a bitter power struggle broke out among his possible successors. Samora was trusted and popular and emerged as one of the three-man Presidential council which ruled as a triumvirate. After further ructions the council was dissolved and in May 1970 he was elected interim President of the party.

The war went well under his drive and educational flair and he pressed hard to move centre of the struggle away from the comfortable offices in Dar-es-Salaam and into the rapidly expanding liberated areas where the medical and education sections could work alongside the troops, near to the people. When the Portuguese regime of Marcello

Caetano suddenly collapsed in the coup of 25 April 1974, he led the negotiations with the new government which brought independence on 25 June 1975. The central committee elected him President. His first wife, Josina, had died during the war. In September he married again this time to his education minister, Graca.

On assuming office he was faced with almost insurmountable problems, the legacy of hundreds of years of colonial rule and all the tensions of southern Africa. The Portuguese had left en masse leaving an economic vacuum. The economy had to be rebuilt virtually from scratch.

As President of a single-party, Marxist state he opted for a full-blown socialist solution with public ownership of all land and buildings and the state running most economic enterprises. State farms were to provide the food for the people.

Grupos dinamizadores were set up the countryside to take over from the Portuguese administration and run the local economy. Just a month after independence, law, medicine, education were all nationalised. There were to be no private lawyers or doctors, so vast sums were needed to fund schools, education and health services, which expanded fast.

But Machel, ever short of finance and skilled personnel and with the productive sector strangled by inexperienced bureaucrats, soon found that the Marxist system was not delivering.

Other problems assailed him. He had always supported international boycotts of Rhodesia during the regime of Ian Smith's white government. In revenge the Rhodesians and exiled Portuguese set up the Mozambique Resistance Movement, known as MNR or Renamo. Its guerrilla campaign which started in 1976, shortly after independence, was to ruin the Mozambique economy, gradually draining the resources of one of Africa's poorest nations.

Machel also incurred the military wrath of South Africa because of his idealistic support of the African National Congress which had established bases in Mozambique. South Africa responded by mounting armed raids and bombing.

In 1977 FRELIMO held its third congress and agreed to transform itself into a "Marxist-Leninist Vanguard Party". But this was empty rhetoric, realities dictated a move in the opposite direction. The Soviet Union, Mozambique's principal backer, proved to be an unreliable ally, while nationalised firms and state farms run by party bureaucrats did not produce enough even to feed the people.

And in the early 1980's the country was hit by a severe drought.

Machel realised the economy was in tatters and his natural pragmatism reasserted itself over his fading ideological aspirations.

His change of heart at the end of 1980 was to alter the course of the whole economy. He launched a campaign against "inefficiency, bureaucracy and corruption," attacking the failure of wholesale nationalisation and "ultra leftist policies of excessive state involvement." He introduced a measure of private enterprise in smaller firms. He also began courting the West rather than the Soviet Union for economic and military assistance.

The MNR stepped up its attacks, and South Africa its harassment which eventually led Machel to sign an unpopular and humiliating non-aggression pact – the Nkomati accord on 16 March 1964. In practice it meant that Mozambique had to withdraw its support from the ANC, while South Africa agreed not to continue arming and supporting the MNR. Machel kept his part of the bargain, but South Africa did not and its covert support for the MNR continued.

Machel was heavily criticised elsewhere in Africa and by party ideologues at home, but his pragmatic stance was applauded in the West that began to provide serious economic assistance.

Machel soon found that his trust in the South Africans was misplaced as the guerrilla war intensified and South Africa, alleging infiltration, broke the pact by crossing the Mozambique frontier to plant land mines. Machel felt betrayed and joined the international chorus for economic sanctions against South Africa.

As relations deteriorated, Machel flew to a meeting in October 1986 with other Front Line state leaders in Zambia. On his way home, on the night of 19 October, the Tupolev plane piloted by a Soviet aircrew, crashed and he was killed. Controversy still rages as to the cause of the crash which occurred in bad weather on the South African side of the border, in the Libombo mountains, when the plane should have been landing at Maputo airport.

An international investigation absolved South Africa of responsibility, but doubts remain. One theory is that the South Africans may have confused the plane's pilots by putting out deceptive radio signals from its beacon at Nelspruit. A more likely explanation is that the plane, already off course, ran into high ground near the airport due to navigational error.

Whatever the truth, Mozambique had lost a popular leader, a man who had never been afraid to admit past mistakes and try new policies to save his country.

Frustrated by the System

OBAFEMI AWOLOWO
1909-1987

Chief Obafemi Awolowo was arguably the ablest politician his great country has ever produced. Ambitious, logical, incisive, clear-headed, even his most committed political opponents, give testimony to his ability and stature, though criticising his intellectual arrogance and unforgiving nature. For the whole of his political career he struggled to become the leader of Nigeria, but his dreams of the presidency were dashed by Nigeria's tribally based politics. He came from the large Yoruba tribe, but it was never populous enough to win dominance at a federal level.

Awo was Prime Minister in his own Western region, leader of the national opposition, number two in General Gowon's military government, and he held a plethora of important ministries, but never the top spot.

Awo called himself a "socialist" but in reality he was little more than a welfare statist. His own fortune was built on capitalism and achieved by flair, dedication and hard work. But in politics he was a progressive. He believed all people had a right to an equal start. In this lay one of his greatest contributions to his people. He will ever be remembered as a pioneer of free education and expanded medical services. Though he was passionately involved in politics and was always a tough street fighter, he had very clear goals in mind. He was never corrupt and wanted government to bring clear advantage to the ordinary Nigerian.

Obafemi Awolowo was born at Ikenne in Ijebu-Remo in Ogun state on 6 March 1909. He was born into a comparatively well off middle class family. His mother was a pagan, his father was a prosperous farmer and timber merchant. At Ikenne he saw the first Europeans being carried in hammocks by African bearers.

His father died young of smallpox and left his mother and her brood practically destitute. This forced the tough, self-reliant, ambitious child to snatch an education wherever he could find it. A succession of relatives let him down. He spent years grubbing for money to educate himself, going to a variety of schools of different religious denominations, including the Wesley College, Ibadan where he was also briefly a teacher.

Though he was never a brilliant pupil, he could have become a teacher but as he wrote later in one of his many books, *Awo*, his priorities were to become a politician, journalist and lawyer. But first he had to find the money. He tried every conceivable occupation that could be contemplated by an upwardly mobile Yoruba youth. He taught himself shorthand-typing and went on to public letter writing, teaching, clerking, money lending, free-lancing for local newspapers, the transport business and the buying and selling of cocoa. He briefly joined the *Daily Times* as a newspaper reporter.

His venture into commodity broking for his company, the Progressive Economic Corporation, brought him temporary riches before bankrupting him in the slump of 1938. He lost everything – his house, car even his clothes were seized and he was left with a mountain of debt which he took five years to pay off.

But even during this disaster his resilient spirit kept him active in political and union affairs. In 1936 he helped organise a successful strike on behalf of the Nigerian Motor Transporters and in 1940 another, which failed, by the Nigerian Producers' Association. In June 1940 he became Secretary of the Ibadan branch of the Nigerian Youth Movement, the only nationwide political party in the country.

He managed to pay off his debts, gained a Bachelor of Commerce degree in 1944 by correspondence courses and then began to beg, borrow, scrimp and save to raise enough money to send himself to Britain to study law. He set himself a series of five-year plans to achieve his ambitions.

He was already 35, when he left for Britain, in August 1944. There he condensed his studies to such an extent that he was called to the bar of the Inner Temple in November 1946. He returned home and set up a lucrative practice which earned him an average of £4,300 a year over the period 1947-51. He also plunged into politics, first as Secretary General of the traditional Yoruba cultural organisation the *Egbe Omo Oduduwa*.

In 1949 he founded the *Nigerian Tribune* newspaper. This was to become the mouthpiece of the Action Group, the political party he launched in March 1951. He became its first president and held the post until 1966 when the new military government banned all political parties.

In the elections of 1951 he was returned to the Western House of Assembly as the member for Ijebu-Remo. On 6 February 1952 he took charge of the Western region, as leader of government business and Minister for Local Government and later Minister of Finance. In 1954 he became first Prime Minister of the Western Region.

During the 1950s his main ambition was to help negotiate Nigeria's transition to independence, while he thoroughly reorganised government in the Western Region, setting a standard for other regions to follow.

He used his extraordinary authority and organisational ability to totally reform the West. He made the traditional chiefs surrender power to new locally elected authorities. He cut spending, increased taxation and introduced a series of five-year plans to set up an embryo welfare state that was the model for all other parts of Nigeria. Though the West started behind the East, his was the first government to introduce free primary education and free medical treatment for children. He pioneered cheap housing, agricultural improvements and extensive road building and paid for his programmes with strict financial management.

Simultaneously he participated in all the convoluted constitutional negotiations of the 1950s which were to bring self government and then the promise of independence in 1960. In the pre-independence elections of 1959, he gave up the Western premiership to campaign on a national level. But though the Action Group swept Yorubaland it failed to make much headway in other parts of the country. The Northern Peoples Congress won 148 seats in the Federal parliament, the National Council of Nigeria and the Cameroons, 89 and the Action Group only 75.

Awo tried to persuade Dr Nnamdi Azikiwe (q.v.) to unite with him against the north but failed. He was doomed, as leader of the opposition to be squeezed between the two majority parties.

Though Awo was a redoubtable opposition leader, his party was demoralised in defeat and his opponents were resolved to take advantage. Their instrument was Chief S. L. Akintola, Awolowo's deputy and premier of the regional government. Soon the strains between the two men led to a major split in the party, finally leading to riots inside the Western assembly. This was the signal for the Federal government to intervene on behalf of "their man", Chief Akintola. A state of emergency was declared and corruption inquiries were initiated against Western region institutions and Awolowo supporters. State funds were shown to have been diverted to the Action Group.

The northern-dominated Federal government then turned on Awolowo himself. In 1962 he and 30 others were charged with plotting to overthrow the government by force. It was blatant political vindictiveness but in the heated atmosphere of the time resulted in his being found guilty and sentenced to ten years imprisonment.

He served three years of his sentence, spending most of his time writing his book, *Thoughts on the Nigerian Constitution.*

Meanwhile things were going from bad to worse in his Western region. The local elections of October 1965 were blatantly rigged and Akintola won again. This resulted in three months of demonstrations and violence throughout the West.

Awolowo meanwhile was spending three years in prison. He was released by the government of Lt.Col.Yakubu Gowon in August 1966, after the military coups, which had been provoked by the national unrest.

The new young leader told Awo, "We need you for the wealth of your experience." He was appointed Federal Commissioner for Finance and

Vice Chairman of the Federal Executive Council. Thus Awo, the avowed parliamentary democrat with socialist leanings, who had been frustrated by the pitiless politics of the post independence years, suddenly found himself as the leading politician in a military government.

As Nigeria slid into civil war, he struggled through the National Reconciliation Committee to avert the crisis. He led a delegation into Biafra to persuade Colonel Odumegwu Ojukwu not to declare secession. His efforts failed and he concentrated on efficiently managing the war economy as Minister of Finance.

He resigned in 1971 because he was disappointed that there would be no quick return to civilian government after the war. He continued in private law practice.

The next military ruler, General Murtala Muhammed, wanted him as one of the 50-member constitutional drafting committee, but he declined to serve.

It was only when the ban on political activity was finally lifted in September 1978 that he returned to politics founding the Unity Party of Nigeria. The UPN contested the elections in April 1979 and Awo, showing all his old flair, held the first party convention and published the first manifesto. He campaigned on a "socialist" platform promising much of the welfare statist programme, including free education, that he had pioneered in the Western region in the 1950s. But his party failed to gain any seats outside the Yoruba areas and in the presidential election he failed narrowly, polling 4.9 million votes against the northern candidate Shehu Shagari's 5.6m.

He ran again unsuccessfully in the 1983 elections when he hoped that a new progressive southern based alliance, the Progressive Parties Alliance, would wrest power from the National Party of Nigeria. In the 1983 presidential he got only 7.9m votes to Shagari's 12m. Both times he claimed that the elections had been rigged and that he had been cheated. In 1983, at least, his accusation was probably true. It was the main rationale for the fourth military coup which followed within months in December.

Awolowo was 72 after his second presidential defeat and he began to withdraw from front-line politics. He concentrated instead on his lucrative and expanding law practice and his many business interests. Over his lifetime he had built up many companies in estate management, industrial promotions, financial investment and a press producing newspapers, magazines and books. At the time of his death his business interests had a turnover running into millions of naira.

He died peacefully on 9 May 1987, aged 76, at his country home at Ikenne. The University of Ife, where he had been made first Chancellor in May 1967, was renamed Obafemi Awolowo University after his death. It was a testimony to everything he had done for education in his country.

10. Modern Rulers

Scion of the North

AHMADOU BELLO
1909-1966

Sir Ahmadou Bello, the Sardauna of Sokoto, was the most powerful man in northern Nigeria, indeed in the whole Nigerian federation from the time of independence in 1960 until his assassination in 1966.

He was the great-great grandson of the founder of the Fulani empire, Othman dan Fodio (q.v.). Though honoured later with the title Sardauna (Captain of the horse) of Sokoto and always close to the traditional native government, he never became sultan. Often accused of feudalism, he proved remarkably adaptable to modern ideas and he changed his region beyond recognition during his relatively short stay in power. His achievement was to adapt rapidly to the change that was sweeping Nigeria and emerge as the dominant force in Nigerian politics.

He was a natural conservative and pragmatist who believed in his Muslim culture and historical tradition and he wanted time for his people to adjust to the pace of modern politics, but this he was not given.

A hmadou Bello was born on 12 June 1909, into the Sokoto royal family. His father Ibrahim gave him a good start. He was a devout Muslim, the district head of Rabah 20 miles north of Sokoto. He was sent to Sokoto provincial school until he was 16. He rode there on horseback. In his autobiography *My Life* he tells how there was no electricity, so he would read late into the night by the light of a lamp made of raw cotton dipped in groundnut oil.

All bright boys from the north at that time were sent to be trained as teachers. Katsina training college was even further away and as there was no transport he would have to walk for seven days with bearers carrying his possessions.

The college was run as a British public school and reinforced his traditional values. He became good at cricket and fives, while never neglecting his academic studies.

He graduated as a teacher and returned home to teach in Sokoto Middle School in 1931. At the age of 24 he was appointed district head of Rabah (like his father before him) in the "native administration." One of his main functions was the collection of local taxes, but he also found time to start a voluntary school which was to be the forerunner of adult education in the district. He stayed in this post from 1934-38.

The Sultan of Sokoto died in 1938 and though Ahmadou was considered to be the most modern and reformist candidate, the British authorities decided that the succession should go to the son of the old sultan, Abubakar. Ahmadou accepted this gracefully and was compensated by being appointed Sardauna, an honorary title showing that he was considered to be next in line for the succession - something that encouraged him for the rest of his life.

Blocked in the traditional succession, he spent the rest of his career achieving political mastery of the new world of national politics.

After a course studying local politics in Britain in 1948, he returned home to find the British trying to establish a primitive form of representative government.

In 1949 he was chosen by the Sultan of Sokoto to represent his area in the newly created Northern House of Assembly in Kaduna, which had been established under a new constitution largely devised by the Governor, Sir Arthur Richards.

By this time he had become a local figure of substance as a member of the Northern Region Production and Development Board, the Northern Regional Loans Board and the Nigerian Forests Inspection Board. Soon he found himself one of three chosen to represent the north on the drafting committee for a new constitution, which came into effect in 1951.

It was at this time that he saw the necessity for northeners to organise themselves in their first political party, to safeguard the interests of the north and to play a greater part in national affairs. He was not the instigator of the Northern Peoples Congress (NPC) but helped relaunch it as a modern party, when he joined in October 1951.

During the constitutional discussions he made his first visit to Lagos and found himself in an alien world which he never came to terms with. But his eyes were opened to the far more sophisticated level of political development in the south and the need for the north to have time to catch up as the scramble for independence gathered momentum.

Back in Kaduna he became Minister of Works in the local government of 1952, where he complained interminably about the lack of materials for construction projects. In 1953 he was given a new portfolio - as Minister of Local Government and Community Development where he could indulge his keen interest in the intricacies of local administration.

In April 1954, at the national convention of the NPC he was elected President General of the party. Later in the regional elections which followed the NPC swept to power in the Northern House of Assembly.

Ahmadou emerged on 1 October 1954 as Prime Minister of the new northern government as Nigeria became a federation.

His position as leader of the party and Prime Minister of the Northern Assembly gave him a central role in the constitutional future of Nigeria.

The Sardauna found himself leading united Nigerian delegations in the constitutional conferences with Britain about independence, over the period 1953-57.

He made his first *hadj* to Mecca in 1955 and every year thereafter. He also travelled widely in the world and was much honoured, being granted a KBE by the Queen of England in 1959. The Queen herself visited northern Nigeria in January 1956 and was received with much pomp and ceremony.

The north only had a handful of university graduates, and not many more than 2,000 holding school certificates and few trained personnel ready to take over regional government, so the Sardauna was not prepared to be rushed into independence.

In the May 1957 conference it seemed as if northern hesitations might delay self government, but realising that his region might be left behind he finally gave way. In the elections that followed the NPC gained a huge majority over two small opposition groups and a new house was sworn in by December 1957.

In the federal elections of March 1959, the NPC won all 148 seats in the north. At the same time the Northern region achieved self government.

It was at this point that the Sardauna could have chosen to lead the Federation of Nigeria as Prime Minister in Lagos or continue as before as Premier of the North. Throughout his career he had shown his active dislike for life in the south.

He talked of Lagos as an "alien world" and of his abhorrence of the atmosphere and "the habits of the Lagos crowd." But he might yet have overcome his personal antipathy was it not for the fact that Sir Abubakar Tafawa Balewa (q.v.), always his deputy since the founding of the NPC, was prepared to take on the federal challenge. The Sardauna was quite prepared to allow Balewa to be his front man while he pulled the strings behind the scenes. "I would rather be called the Sultan of Sokoto (which he never was) than the President of Nigeria, " he once said.

Balewa became Federal Premier at independence on 1 October 1960, but throughout his term of office he would have frequent consultations with the Sardauna. Balewa formed alliances with the southern parties, first with the National Council of Nigeria and the Cameroons (NCNC) of the East and later with a faction of the Action Group in the West, led by Chief Samuel Akintola.

Throughout the period between independence in 1960 and the military coup in 1966, the NPC and indirectly the Sardauna through Balewa, controlled the Federal Assembly. It was when the NPC wanted to extend its dominance to the West through the minority faction of Chief Akintola against Chief Awolowo (q.v.), the Yoruba people's choice, that real trouble started.

After a series of violent regional elections in the West, marred by extensive rigging and electoral malpractice, Akintola was declared the winner. But the majority of the Yorubas felt cheated and three months of arson rioting and disorder followed.

This total breakdown of law and order gave a new generation of young soldiers the perfect pretext to stage Nigeria's first military coup in January 1966.

The Sardauna who symbolised the whole power structure of the old regime was marked out as a priority target of the young coup makers. In the early hours of 15 January 1966 a group of soldiers under Major Patrick Nzeogwu, the chief instructor at the military training centre in Kaduna, took a group of troops to the Sardauna's house. After killing two policemen and his chief of security, the soldiers confronted him as he was saying his prayers with his senior wife and shot them both dead.

Two other leaders identified with northern dominance, Sir Abubakar Balewa and Chief Akintola were also murdered elsewhere in the country. One of the coup makers tried to justify his action by accusing the Sardauna of being an "arch tribalist...directing national affairs from Kaduna," of being a "fanatic-muslim" and the "chief architect of the *jihad*... running a repressive regime." Other justifications such as corruption and extravagant spending were heaped upon him. But the main rationale for the coup was the fear by southerners that the Sardauna had been manipulating the whole political system against their interests.

The coup was often interpreted as the work of idealistic fanatics who wanted to free Nigeria from the Sardauna's control. It was true that he had exerted extensive indirect control over the power structure during the whole of the First republic. This made him very unpopular with southerners whose own quarreling politicians had let them down. But in the disciplined, Muslim society of the north, he had ruled with the broad consent of the people who returned him and his party in successive elections.

A Sacrificial Lamb

ABUBAKAR BALEWA
1912-1966

Alhaji Abubakar Tafawa Balewa was a modest, unassuming Nigerian and a devout Muslim, who could have happily spent his life as a schoolteacher or local official, instead he had greatness thrust upon him. Under the patronage of his feudal mentor, Ahmadou Bello, the Sardauna of Sokoto (q.v.), he became Prime Minister in Nigeria's first government of independence.

He was a gentle man of tolerance and compromise who realised that Nigerian unity had to be nurtured as ethnic politicians struggled for power in the new nation. But he was always under pressure from his northern overlords to put the interests of his party first. At no stage in his premiership could he reconcile the conflicting needs of national unity and party supremacy.

He underestimated the ethnic forces that were tearing Nigeria apart and found himself unable to control them. Electoral malpractice, ballot rigging, corruption and violence escalated so much that no single man, not even the Prime Minister, could deal with them. When the inevitable military coup came, he was swept away with the old regime he represented. A lamb was sacrificed as the soldiers took their bloody revenge.

He was born in 1912 in the small town of Tafawa Balewa, in Bauchi state, north east Nigeria. He had the humblest of backgrounds. He was the son of an unimportant district head, of the Jere branch of the Hausa tribe – a commoner in a feudal society. His early story was one of any other modest, humble schoolteacher.

He did his elementary education at Bauchi provincial school, going on to Katsina Higher College in 1928. At Katsina he studied in his spare time for the senior teacher's certificate, qualifying as a teacher in 1933. He started teaching at Bauchi Middle School. It was not until 1945, when he was already 33, that he finally won a scholarship for a year at the

Institute of Education at the University of London.

On his return, as one of the very few educated northerners, he was inevitably drawn into politics. He joined the Bauchi Improvement Association, with a handful of other companions, such as Aminu Kano, who later made names for themselves politically. Young northerners realised that constitutional change was coming and that they should not allow themselves to be dominated by the better educated and politically advanced southerners. Meanwhile he worked as an education officer to the local Native Authority.

His conservatism, caution and humility had already impressed the traditional rulers who appointed him in 1947 to the Northern House of Assembly. From there he was elected to the legislative assembly in Lagos. Before he left for the national arena, in 1949, he and a handful of other aspiring politicians formed the Northern People's Congress (NPC). In the 1949-50 constitutional talks he championed the interests of the north with unexpected debating skill.

The new constitution introduced by the Governor, Sir John Macpherson, brought the appointment of the first Nigerian ministers in the national government. Balewa was among the first group of African ministers when he was appointed Minister of Works in 1952 and then Minister of Transport in 1954. His unassuming manner belied his organisational ability and he soon made his mark, reorganising ministerial departments and setting up new agencies for the coasts and waterways.

Under the new constitution in 1957, he became the first Prime Minister of Nigeria, as parliamentary leader of the NPC, the largest party in the national assembly. He thought national unity and co-operation were essential if independence was to be secured from the British in the shortest time span, so he included representatives of all the major parties in his government.

In the 1959 national elections the NPC again won a majority, securing 148 seats, with 89 for Dr Azikiwe's National Council of Nigeria and the Cameroons (NCNC) and 75 for Chief Awolowo's Action Group. An uneasy coalition was formed with the NCNC in the first government of independence which followed.

On 1 October 1960 Balewa became the first Prime Minister of independent Nigeria. He got the job because his mentor, the Sardauna of Sokoto, Sir Ahmadou Bello did not want it for himself. Sir Ahmadou hated Lagos and preferred to remain in the north, with "his lieutenant" in the capital, as he once boasted.

The Sardauna influenced Balewa throughout his term of office, though he probably did not control him to the extent that some southern critics believe. Balewa acquired a mind and style of his own as he grew into office.

He was knighted by the Queen as he became Prime Minister and in the early years things went smoothly, but a row soon blew up over the defence agreement signed with Britain at the time of independence. His opponents stirred up protest with exaggerated claims that he had signed a secret agreement for a British base. This was untrue, but protest grew to the extent that he had to abrogate the agreement in December 1982.

Balewa suspected that the opposition leader Chief Awolowo (q.v.) had inflamed this defence row and a lack of trust between the two men began to grow from this point.

National peace and unity were always foremost in the mind of the soft-spoken conciliator, but tensions were growing in the Federation. Awolowo and his Action group were frustrated in opposition and the power-brokers in the NPC were determined to take advantage by splitting his party. They did this by backing Awolowo's deputy, Chief Samuel Akintola.

Balewa watched the growing troubles in the Western region with mixed feelings. He was glad to see his political opponents in disarray but unhappy when the chaos in the West began to threaten national stability.

When fighting broke out between members, on the floor of the Western House of Assembly in May 1962, Balewa declared a state of emergency and suspended the Western government. This allowed the Federal government to intervene with troops, set up commissions of inquiry into the regional government and finally charge Awolowo with treason.

This simply inflamed feelings still further in the West, while a major row blew up with their allies in the NCNC over a census that gave the north a larger population than the south.

The campaign for the 1964 elections was long, bitter and abusive. There were allegations of rigging even before the elections were held. Opposition candidates complained that their men were not allowed to register. In Balewa's own Bauchi South West constituency no opposition candidate was allowed to stand. This brought Balewa into direct conflict with the President Dr Nnamdi Azikiwe (the founding father of the NCNC) who eventually tried to prevent the elections taking place on the grounds that law and order had broken down. Balewa cooly countered by saying that all the trouble was in the south, the north was calm and wanted the elections to take place.

In the upshot the southerners partly boycotted the elections while the NPC and its allies voted monolithically and secured an even greater majority over their divided southern opponents.

Balewa had won a battle, but only at the expense of deeper resentment and bitterness.

The Western regional elections which followed in November 1965 were even dirtier and more violent. They were, both literally and metaphorically, the "elections to end all elections." The rigging was so obvious and shameless and the minority Akintola regime so determined to cling to power, that the election campaign sparked months of violence, murder and unrest which showed no sign of abating.

Balewa said he was powerless to intervene, though he had already set a precedent when he declared an emergency and sent in the troops to suppress the lesser troubles in the West in 1962.

In the early days of January 1966 Balewa was proudly chairing the first ever Commonwealth Conference on Nigerian soil. Other African heads of state were quietly arriving and conferring as violence spread from the West to Lagos, where the conference was being held.

Balewa was warned by his intelligence services that a coup was being planned, but he was by nature fatalistic and he had heard it all so many times before.

On the night of 14 January 1966, a group of hot-headed and idealistic younger officers decided to sweep away the old regime. All over the federation the leaders identified with the First Republic were assassinated, among them was the man they considered to be the real villain of the piece: Ahmadou Bello the Sardauna of Sokoto. He was shot dead in his lodge in Kaduna.

The group who came for Balewa at his house in Lagos was led by Major Emmanuel Ifeajuna, a former Commonwealth high jump gold medallist. He kicked in Balewa's bedroom door. Balewa remained calm apparently resigned to his fate. He was allowed to say his prayers before being driven away. Several days later his body, riddled with bullet wounds, was found in a ditch on the Abeokuta- Lagos road.

Few Nigerians except the coup-plotters thought that he had deserved to die. He was regarded as a decent honourable man who had been trying to do his best in impossible circumstances to hold the disintegrating nation together. After him came revenge – massacres in the north, another coup, military rule and a bitter civil war.

Not Just a Showman

WILLIAM TUBMAN
1895-1971

William (nicknamed Shad) Tubman is regarded as a great Liberian character. He was described by his predecessor President Edwin Barclay as "a jolly, backslapping, finger-snapping fellow, who could carry his liquor well, popular with women of a certain type and a careless spender of his own and other people's money." At official functions he always appeared in a top hat and morning coat.

But he was not just a showman. He was the man who over his 27-year rule pushed Liberia into the modern era. He gave all Liberians the vote for the first time and began to erode the distinctions between the small colony of Afro-Americans of Monrovia and the hinterland Africans. He also brought rapid economic growth and increase in government revenues under his "open door policies."

He imposed one man rule, but he had regard for the checks and balances of the constitutional system. Opposition against him was weak and disorganised and it was not until his declining years that he became overly suspicious and repressive. By the time of his death Liberia was ready for change, but he had already brought his country a long way down the road of modernisation.

William Vacanarat Shadrach Tubman was born on 29 November 1895 at Harper, Cape Palmas in Maryland County, in the remote south east of the country. His birthplace was nearer to the neighbouring Ivory Coast than the capital Monrovia, which was hundreds of miles away and accessible only by sea.

His family descended from American negro slaves who immigrated from Georgia in the 19th century. His mother, Elizabeth Barnes, was one of the few negroes to have emigrated to Liberia after the American Civil War, arriving in 1872.

But the Tubmans were well established as one of Liberia's leading families when he was born in 1895. His father Rev. Alexander Tubman had been a former Speaker in the Liberian House of Assembly, a senator and a minister in the Methodist church.

He grew up in a strongly Christian environment and throughout his life he peppered his speeches with quotations from the Bible.

He was educated at Cape Palmas Methodist Seminary and Cuttington College Divinity School until 1913. He might have become a pastor, but instead he plunged into a variety of temporary jobs: teaching; working as a tailor and briefly joining the Liberian frontier force where he helped put down a number of native uprisings. He also studied law privately under a brilliant tutor who saw him called to the bar in 1917.

He practised law in his home town Harper, where he gained a reputation as a poor man's lawyer, taking cases for virtually no financial recompense. He entered government service first as a recorder in the probate court, then he was appointed a county attorney in 1919, at the age of 24.

Ever ambitious and industrious, he took up politics and joined the ruling True Whig Party. Soon the confident, charming, happy- go-lucky young man was rapidly ascending the political ladder. In 1923, though scarcely 28 years old, he had won enough influence to become senator for Maryland, the youngest senator in Liberia's history.

He continued until 1929 when he resigned to defend Vice President Allen Yancy who was accused by a commission of the League of Nations of using forced labour at home and exporting slaves from Liberia to foreign colonies. The scandal brought the resignation of the President and the Vice President and when Tubman tried to stand again as senator, much of the dirt had stuck and the party chose another candidate.

His constituents re-elected him as a senator in 1934. He continued until 1937 when the new President Edwin Barclay appointed him associate justice in the Supreme Court of Liberia.

When Barclay's term of office came to an end in 1943, he gave Tubman his backing for the presidency. He duly won the party nomination and was elected President on 3 January 1944, becoming the 18th President of his country.

Many of the 19th-century Liberian presidents had come direct from the USA. He was one of the new breed, not only Liberian born, but the first "provincial" to assume the supreme office.

He inherited a desperately poor, backward nation. Though it had been proudly founded in 1822 by the American Colonisation Society as a refuge for freed slaves, it was still recovering from its internationally ostracisation for exporting native Liberians as slave labour.

It had a reputation as a corrupt country with a bad record for debt repayment. Successive governments were virtually bankrupt and borrowed extravagantly at usurious rates of interest on the London money markets. They incurred huge foreign debts simply to survive.

The national wealth of the country was almost entirely in the hands of the 25 leading Liberian families. These descendants of the freed slaves formed scarcely one per cent of the total population. And the nation was almost totally undeveloped. Outside Monrovia there were just a few miles of tarred roads, leading in the direction of the Firestone rubber plantation at Harbel, which had provided the nation with most of its budget and export revenue since its foundation in 1926.

On taking power Tubman wanted to show that he was more than just a stand in for Barclay. He saw he could gain international approval for his demoralised nation in one brilliant gesture. One of his first acts on assuming office was to declare war on Germany, thus pleasing his American allies.

Internally he was determined to consolidate his power. He was elected for eight years and ruled skilfully, using a mixture of patronage and rough treatment for the few political opponents who occasionally surfaced.

As his term of office neared its end he had the constitution amended which allowed him to be re-elected for further four-year terms. Ultimately he was able to extend his rule to more than 27 unbroken years.

He had a highly personal style. Though charming and jovial in private, in public he was a stickler for formality always wearing morning dress and a top hat on formal occasions regardless of the tropical heat. When his presidential cavalcade swept past, all other traffic was forced to halt. Once a car took too long to stop. He leapt out of his own limousine, drew the revolver that he regularly carried and shot the back wheels of the offending vehicle. When he discovered that two white strangers were in the vehicle, he made a joke of the incident and offered them a lift to their destination.

He had an appetite for hard work and regular routine that allowed him to monitor government in detail. He personally appointed all civil servants. No payment of more than $100 could be made by any government department without his personal approval. He appropriated six per cent of the entire national budget for the administration of the presidential office.

On taking power he introduced a national unification programme which gave the same rights to the Africans of the hinterland to those already held by the Americo-Liberians in Monrovia. In 1945 he gave the vote for the first time to all male Liberians who paid taxes and in 1947 he extended the franchise to women.

In foreign affairs he was a staunchly anti-communist friend of the West.

He was also keen to play his part in the post war Africa which was marching towards independence. As other African countries became independent and sought a formula for African unity, he organised conferences for independent heads of state in the northern town of Sanequellie in July 1959 and, in 1961, in Monrovia. The conference attended by 21 out of 28 African heads of state gave its name to the

"Monrovia group." These were the pragmatic, moderate leaders who wanted co-operation in all practicable fields by voluntary association, but not outright political union as proposed by Kwame Nkrumah and Sekou Toure (q.v.)

Ultimately it was the moderates led by Tubman and Haile Selassie of Ethiopia (q.v.) who formulated the principles of the Organisation of African Unity in 1963. They ensured that the OAU safeguarded established frontiers and the principle of non-interference in neighbours' affairs.

When Tubman came to power he found that previous regimes had barely scratched the surface of economic development. His answer was to introduce a series of, then fashionable, five-year economic plans and to throw his country open to foreign investment by an "open door policy." This gave liberal conditions to foreign investors, who took advantage by investing in new iron ore mines and in more rubber plantations.

As a result government revenue rose from $2m in 1944 to nearly $200m at the time of his death in 1971, while exports increased even faster. Under him the first national deepwater port, the Freeport of Monrovia and the iron ore port at Buchanan were established. Arterial roads were macadamised, a power grid was extended nationally and the state spent money on schools and medical services.

But towards the end of Tubman's rule iron ore and rubber prices declined and earnings fell, exposing Liberia's dependence on just two exports. It was also apparent that the enclave development by international companies had improved government revenues and export earnings, but had done little to improve the lot of ordinary Liberians.

As he was returned for successive presidential terms, opposition to him gradually took shape; but it was badly organised and found no real leadership. A break away group formed the Independent True Whig Party in 1955. It lost the 1955 presidential elections and was then accused of being involved in a plot on Tubman's life. The plotters were found guilty and sentenced to death, but Tubman refused to sign their death warrants - indeed he never imposed the death penalty on anyone during his rule.

In September 1961 a strike flared in Monrovia in which most of the city work force marched on the Presidential Palace. Tubman, who had tried hard to improve workers pay and conditions in earlier years, was so rattled that he got the legislature to pass emergency powers to deal with further threats to security.

Another alleged assassination plot was discovered in 1963 involving Colonel David Thompson, a former commanding officer of the National Guard. A few years after this, on his 71st birthday in 1966, Tubman expressed his willingness to stand down for another candidate at the next presidential elections but the party organised huge demonstrations that persuaded him to stand and win re-election.

As he grew older he became increasingly suspicious that people were plotting against him. Coups were in fashion in Africa. (Nkrumah had been toppled in Ghana in 1966 and there had been two military coups in Nigeria). In 1968 he turned on Henry Fahnbulleh, his ambassador to the distant East African Community, and accused him of plotting. Fahnbulleh was found guilty, still protesting his innocence, after a prejudiced trial. Within a few years, in 1971 Tubman's successor William Tolbert released him and gave him a post as a minister.

Towards the end Tubman was tired and suffering from progressive blindness in one eye. But his health was as good as could be expected when he went to London for a prostate operation. Everything seemed to have gone well when a haemorrhage developed on 23 July 1971 and he died unexpectedly, leaving a nation grieving the leader who had brought his country into a new era.

Victim of Circumstance

KOFI BUSIA
1913-1978

Dr Kofi Busia was a brilliant academic who blazed a trail among his talented peers in scholarly distinction and authorship. He was also the chosen son of his own Asante people and the worthy colleague and successor of Dr J B Danquah (q.v.). Still today the "Busia-Danquah tradition" is a way of describing the conservative, economically liberal, middle class constituency that they represented.

Busia was a dedicated Methodist, a cautious, bookish intellectual. He was thrust into politics in reaction to Nkrumah's socialism and authoritarianism. But when he finally came to power he had neither the charisma and charm of his great rival, nor the authority to impose his will on a quarrelling cabinet. A clever theorist rather than a decisive politician, he was unable to meet the people's high expectations that had been frustrated by more than a decade of rule under Nkrumah and the military. He failed to cope with a tottering economy and divisive forces unleashed by the new democracy. His 27 months in office were disastrous, but scarcely any leader could have done much better in the impossible circumstances of that time.

Kofi Abrefa Busia was born on 11 July 1913 into the Royal House of Wenchi, in Brong Ahafo, north west of the Asante region. He was educated at the Kumasi Methodist School, the Mfantsipim Secondary School in Cape Coast. He then trained as a teacher at Wesley College, Kumasi, before joining the staff of Achimota College, Accra in 1936.

In 1939 he took an external degree in history at London and later went to University College, Oxford where he won a BA in Politics, Philosophy and Economics. During that period Harold Wilson, who later became the Prime Minister in Britain's Labour government in the 1960s, was his tutor. He went on to get an MA and DPhil in Social Anthropology.

He returned to Ghana in 1942 and became one of the first Africans to be appointed an administrative officer. A Carnegie scholarship took him back to Oxford in 1946 to write a doctorate thesis entitled, "The position of the Chief in the modern political system of the Ashanti (Asante)."

He returned to Ghana in 1947 to take charge of social surveys, producing a book *Social Survey of Sekondi-Takoradi*. In 1949 he became the first lecturer in African studies at the newly styled Ghana University College, Legon. In 1954 he was the head of the sociology department and the first African to hold a chair as a professor.

His political career started in 1951 when he was indirectly elected by the Asante Confederacy Council for his home constituency Wenchi.

In the early 1950s Kwame Nkrumah (q.v.) was the rising star in the political firmament. Recently released from prison and preaching the message of nationalism and socialism, he swept all before him in the elections of 1951. J. B. Danquah, the leader of the Asante and the conservative middle class was heavily defeated and demoralised. This gave Busia an opportunity in 1952 to form the Ghana Congress Party out of the rump of the old conservative forces of the United Gold Coast Convention.

In 1956 Busia gave up his professorship at Legon for full-time politics. But in the elections of 1956 Nkrumah's political steamroller crushed the disunited opposition. Ghana became independent on 6 March 1957.

While Danquah became leader of the opposition, Busia tried to pick up the pieces. In October 1957 he managed to merge all the main opposition parties into the United Party, giving a voice to the discontented intellectuals, Asante cocoa farmers, and the traditional middle class. But as Nkrumah's rule became increasingly repressive and intolerant, opposition figures were regularly detained and Busia became genuinely afraid. He slipped out of the country. A few days later police, with warrants for his arrest, searched the boat on which he had originally booked his passage.

Safe in Europe, he returned to academia by becoming a Professor of Sociology and Culture at the University of Leiden, at the Hague.

He preached and wrote voluminously against the Nkrumah regime while abroad. He became director of studies for the World Council of Churches where he wrote a book entitled, *The Urban Churches in Britain*. He wrote at least five major books over his long academic career, giving him a prominent place in the world of scholarship, quite apart from politics.

By 1967 he had published another book, *Africa in Search of Democracy* criticising the fashionable African rejection of western style democracies of the time. He noted that democracy was "not for the European only, it has a moral language which is universal."

While he was abroad he and other opposition leaders were accused of plotting to kill President Nkrumah. He dismissed the charges saying that he would be quite prepared to be tried by international jurists anywhere in the world but, "I shall not foolishly sign my death warrant by agreeing to go to Ghana."

At the time of the coup against Nkrumah on 24 February 1966, he was a senior member of St Antony's College, Oxford. He returned home immediately to scenes of jubilation at Accra airport. The soldiers who had taken power were glad to have his intellectual and moral support and he was keen to use them as a stepping stone to a political career under the civilian rule which they had promised.

He was appointed to the political committee of the National Liberation Council, to the National Advisory Committee and to the Centre of Civic Education. In these capacities he was able to wield considerable political influence during the three and a half years of military rule. He travelled the country to build a political following on the popular reaction to Nkrumah's dictatorship. In the words of one commentator, "He preached democracy so much that when the time came they gave him the task of government."

He was automatically chosen as member of the Constituent Assembly whose task was to draw up a new constitution to return Ghana to civilian rule.

Nkrumahism was totally rejected, but he was opposed by Komla Gbedemah, a former Nkrumah minister who had quarrelled violently with his master and been forced to flee Ghana in 1964. Gbedemah was the leader of the National Alliance of Liberals (NAL), grouping all those not of the Danquah/Busia persuasion. It was thought that the election of 29 August 1969 would be close, but in the event Busia's new Progress Party won 105 seats to the NAL's 35. Busia became Prime Minister under the watchful eye of a Presidential Commission composed of the three military rulers of the previous regime.

Busia came to power with fine ideals - the preservation of democracy and a determination not to repeat the mistakes of the past. But he soon showed that a clever academic does not necessarily make a good, decisive politician. He lacked sufficient personal authority to discipline a team of quarrelling ministers.

The realities were harsh. After a decade of Nkrumahism and military rule the people's expectations were high, with everyone wanting an economic miracle to benefit them personally. Yet the economy, foundering on mounting foreign debt and an acute balance of payments crisis was also hit by falling cocoa prices, soaring imports and rapidly increasing unemployment.

Busia tried to divert mounting unpopularity by expelling alien workers and dismissing civil servants simply because they had worked under the Nkrumah government. Because he could not deliver material progress he offended the very groups that had brought him to power - the rural people, the civil servants, the business community, the unions, students and finally the army itself. Opposition sprang up everywhere and was vociferously expressed in the newly freed press. When some opponents dared whisper that things had been better under Nkrumah, Busia promptly legislated to prevent the use of Nkrumahist symbols.

Busia found there were insufficient funds to pay the cocoa farmers.

He imposed new taxes and tried to curb the trade unions, while a massive crisis of confidence mounted over Ghana's debts. When he sharply devalued the cedi, it brought an explosion of inflation and gave the soldiers the excuse to mount another military coup. Busia was in Britain having treatment for eye trouble and his recurring diabetes on 13 January 1972 when the military took power, under Lt.Colonel Ignatius Acheampong, a man he had recently promoted.

Busia's brief 27 months in power had been an unmitigated disaster. He retired to his modest house at Standlake in Oxfordshire and went back to St Antony's College. His political failure haunted him. Little was heard of him in his later years. He died of a heart attack, at the Radcliffe Infirmary in Oxford on 28 August 1978.

Victim of the Revolution

WILLIAM TOLBERT
1913-1980

William Tolbert was the last Liberian President before the revolution in 1980 and all the troubles that followed. He was a representative of the *ancien regime*, the small class of Americo-Liberians who had ruled the country since independence on 27 July 1847. His power base was the True Whig Party, the Masonic orders, the Baptist church and the officer class in the army.

Yet like many others before their revolutions, Tolbert had been a reformer, a well meaning idealist struggling to bring change and development to his backward country.

Shortly before he was assassinated by Sergeant Samuel Doe and his men, he had been trying to persuade his parliament to extend the vote to all Liberians regardless of income or property qualifications.

Curiously it was his own good intentions that provoked the revolution. It was his decision to encourage farmers to produce more rice by increasing rice prices that brought the urban workers onto the streets and gave the radical politicians a stick to beat him with. By trying to be conciliatory he appeared to be weak. He paid with his life, while his opponents exploited the situation and brought a bloody revolution, pushing Liberia down the road to chaos.

William Richard Tolbert was born on 13 May 1913 in Bensonville, Montserrado County. His father William R. Tolbert and his mother Charlotte A Hoff, both came from well known settler families. His grandparents had emigrated from South Carolina, USA in 1877 to start farming in Bensonville.

His father married a native Kpelle girl and acquired extensive farming land integrating himself into local African society. Later, after divorcing his first wife, he married the Americo- Liberian Charlotte Hoff in 1908, whom he met through the local Baptist church. William was the fourth of five children.

He was educated at Mr Padmore's elementary school in Bensonville, then at Crummel Hall, an episcopal high school and finally at Liberia College, which he later upgraded, under his vice- presidency to become the University of Liberia. He took a BA there in 1934.

An industrious and imaginative child, he earned pocket money wherever he could, doing washing (which was then considered to be women's work), selling palm kernels, and teaching his friends how to set traps to catch rodents and birds.

He joined the local militia and rose to the rank of captain. The Zion Praise Baptist Church was ever important in his life. He became a deacon in 1933 and licentiate in 1952, being ordained later as an elder. In 1960 he was elected Vice-President and in 1965 President, of the Baptist World Alliance – the first African to be elected to the post.

He built a church locally and preached there every Sunday. He often said later that he had been asked by the Lord to preach the gospel and his political speeches in later life were peppered with Biblical quotations.

He started work in 1935 as a clerk, then typist in the bureau of supplies, a treasury department. In 1936 he became a disbursing officer, a post he held until 1943, when he launched his political career.

He was always a supremely confident young man and admitted that he formed the ambition to be President of Liberia in his youth. He had privileged access; his father was still a member of the legislature and chairman of the True Whig Party. An elder brother was chosen, by the family, to stand in the 1943 House of Representative elections for his home constituency Montserrado. But William was even more keen and forceful. He started campaigning and persuaded the electorate to chose him instead.

He was duly returned. Only 30, his enthusiasm and application were soon noted. He became chairman of a number of parliamentary committees. In the house he sponsored over 400 pieces of legislation including the women's suffrage bill of 1947.

President William Tubman (q.v.) was on the look out for a younger progressive man to replace his deputy who had died. He ignored other senior contenders and chose Tolbert as his running mate and triumphed in the elections of 1951. Both men were inaugurated in January 1952. Tolbert stayed as Tubman's vice-president for the next 19 years, being regularly re-elected every presidential election until Tubman's death.

The two men formed a good team. Tolbert was a loyal lieutenant agreeing with Tubman's broad policies both at home and in foreign affairs. Tubman sent him abroad frequently as his representative and used him at home to supervise development projects in the interior. In 1969 he made a courageous flight to Biafra to try and mediate in the Nigerian civil war.

When President Tubman died in a London clinic on 23 July 1971, his reign came to an end without the expected political upheaval. No challengers emerged and Tolbert automatically became President to serve the remainder of the unexpired, four year term of office.

After being sworn in he went back to his home church and prostrated himself full length before the altar as he pledged himself to the future of his country.

Just as Tubman needed to make dramatic reforms when he first came to power in 1943, Tolbert needed to revitalise the country, purge corruption and push change forward. He inherited an economy that was rapidly running out of steam as it was hit by declining commodity prices for Liberia's main exports, iron ore and rubber. Inflation began to surge after a sudden increase in oil prices. This hit the vulnerable Liberian economy hard.

Tolbert made extensive changes in his administration, cutting out the deadwood and bringing in new blood. He wanted a new team keen on his own goals of liberalisation, adherence to the rule of law and attention to development.

He rationalised and cut back the security services, gave more freedom to the media, and threw himself into national development.

His development schemes were real enough, but he publicised them with fine sounding slogans for which he became famous – the "Wholesome functioning society" (meaning industriousness without corruption), "Rally time" (appealing to all individuals to contribute and help each other, in building local projects).

His style was rhetorical as he tried to motivate his people in self-help projects with calls for "Total involvement", "Higher heights", "From mats to mattresses."

He was elected President in 1975, but then he had the constitution specially amended so that no president could enjoy more than two terms of office (eight years). He explained that he was prepared to serve his country in any capacity, he did not have to be president.

In foreign affairs Tolbert maintained Tubman's policies of friendship with the West and an "open door" policy towards foreign investors, but he also extended the hand of friendship to the Soviet Union and the Eastern bloc by establishing diplomatic relations.

He brought Guinea and Sierra Leone into a new sub-regional economic organisation - the Mano River Union. Its formation spanned his presidency from the first meeting in May 1971, the establishment of a secretariat in January 1974, to the initiation of a tariff union in April 1977.

While being resolutely anti-apartheid, he courted unpopularity by allowing the South African Prime Minister John Vorster to come to Monrovia in February 1975, to try and persuade him to reverse his race policies.

He also participated fully in all intra-African organisations. In 1975 he signed the treaty setting up the Economic Community of West African States (ECOWAS), grouping 16 West African countries.

He was keen to end the divisions among his own neighbours and played a great part in getting the Guinean President, Sekou Toure (q.v.) to drop his quarrel with Senegal and the Ivory Coast. The three states signed a peace agreement in Monrovia in May 1978.

Recognition as a major statesman came in July 1979 when he was elected chairman of the Organisation of African Unity, which was due to hold its annual Heads of State meeting in Monrovia that year.

He was fully involved in preparations for that important meeting when trouble started at home. The clouds gathered slowly. At first they were just dark spots in a seemingly clear sky.

One major problem afflicting the economy was a shortage of rice. Tolbert decided the best policy was to put the price up to encourage farmers to produce more and make Liberia self sufficient. But this meant increasing the rice price for the consumer.

This apparently unimportant technicality was to bring a national crisis. Immediately after he threatened to increase the rice price in Easter of 1979 the urban workers came onto the streets of Monrovia to demonstrate. The government tried to ban the demonstration provoking a serious riot and the police, totally unprepared for such violence, shot hundreds dead.

The riots seemed to spark all the pent up feelings of the indigenous people against the Americo-Liberians who had ruled without challenge since independence in 1847. It unleashed unknown and incoherent political forces expressing the indigenous people's resentments against the ruling caste.

Tolbert was shaken, but his immediate reaction was conciliatory, not repressive. He arrested the leaders of the small urban parties who were exploiting the situation, but quickly released them. His attitude was to forgive and forget and preach national unity and reconciliation.

He had long recognised that political change was necessary. For years he had been trying to persuade his own legislature to pass laws allowing all Liberians to vote regardless of property or income qualifications. Now he began to recognise and register the emergent, but as yet unrepresentative, opposition parties. For a time he appeared to have persuaded the opposition leaders to limit their protest to constitutional action.

But early in March 1980 trouble erupted again. The opposition held a huge, emotional rally and called a general strike. This time the government was ready. It clamped down on all trouble makers, arresting 100 of them and threatening to put them on trial for sedition.

In the tense days that followed the army, hitherto considered to be totally loyal, decided to act. A group of ordinary soldiers led by the 28-year-old Sergeant Samuel Doe mutinied against their Americo-Liberian officers.

At 1am on the morning of 12 April 1980 Doe stormed the Executive Mansion. (Tolbert had been sleeping there rather than at his home, in order to keep on top of the crisis).

The rebels overpowered the guards and found Tolbert in one of the upstairs corridors of the huge block. According to some reports Doe himself shot Tolbert dead. A doctor found later that he had been shot three times in the head.

His body and those of 27 of his aides were put in a truck and dumped in a common grave in the swamps near the capital on 15 April.

The international outcry was deafening. Tolbert had made friends everywhere in the world, particularly among African heads of state. A decent, tolerant, well-meaning man had become a victim of the revolution.

Triumphant Traditionalist

SOBHUZA II
1899-1982

Sobhuza II reigned for 60 years. He had been the world's longest reigning monarch. He was a traditionalist who encouraged his people's conservative nature and semi-mystical pride in the monarchy as a means of building his own power. His long career was dedicated to ensuring that when the British finally left Swaziland the monarchy would be in full political control.

His public image as a warrior king, dressed in skins and feathers like one of his own *impis* (warriors), belied a shrewd, cunning operator. Always courteous and diplomatic, he had a clear head and total dedication when pursuing his political objectives and personal power.

In many things he was a modernist. He encouraged modern economic development and agricultural techniques, while encouraging foreign investment in a liberal economy. He fostered scientific progress and the latest advances of medical science.

But he saw modern political systems and parties as a threat to his authority. When the opposition showed the first glimmerings of political success he clamped down and went back to a system of traditional rule that left him in total control. He created a system, unique in Africa, which was largely accepted by his people. He left the political modernisation of his country to his successors.

Sobhuza, then called Nkhotfotjeni, was born on 22 July 1899, into the Dlamini house that had ruled his country for four centuries. Only five months later his father, King Bhunu (Ngwane V), died. He was named as his father's heir, but as he was still a baby, his grandmother Queen Labotsibeni became regent. She was keen that he would not be educated by the missionaries and had a national school specially built at Zombodze so that he could be educated there. She also hired Robert Grendon, a

Eurafrican from Natal to be his personal tutor.

In 1916 he was sent to the Lovedale Institute in Cape Province, South Africa for his secondary education. After two years, when he was only 19 years old, he was brought home to prepare for the kingship.

On 22 December 1921 he was crowned *Ngwenyama*, the lion, and King of Swaziland, according to traditional ceremony and took the name Sobhuza II.

The main problem for his predecessors had been the preservation of Swaziland's independence. For some time his tiny, landlocked country had actually been ruled by the Boers of Transvaal and whites had seized land and settled permanently. The Anglo-Boer agreement of 1898 had actually reduced the Swazi King to a paramount chief, subject to European control. There had also been a long dispute over the precise demarcation of Swazi frontiers. But when the Afrikaners were defeated in the Boer war Swaziland was confirmed as a British protectorate in 1903.

At the time of his accession Sobhuza found that two-thirds of his traditional lands had been ceded to European concession holders by his father, who had said,"If I do not give the whites rights here, they will take them. Therefore I give them when they pay."

Immediately after his accession the 22-year-old king began a long campaign to regain his people's lost lands. He led a delegation to London in 1922 where he lobbied both the Commonwealth Secretary and King George V. His pleas were rejected, so in 1924 he appealed to the Special Court of Swaziland and then to the Privy Council in March 1926. No court was prepared to overturn the claims of the white settlers no matter how dubious the circumstances in which they had acquired their land.

Sobhuza continued with his campaign for the next 15 years until he was able to petition the new British King, George VI in 1941. Britain wanted Swaziland's assistance in the World War and Sobhuza was only too willing to help. He sent an *impi* of Swazi warriors to join the allies and in return a native land settlement scheme was set up, originally financed by Britain, to buy land from Europeans and resettle Swazis. Later Sobhuza established the special *Lifa* fund. All Swazis had to contribute annually in order to generate more capital and buy back land. At the time of his death nearly two-thirds of all European lands had been reclaimed. No foreigner can now buy land without the approval of the land board.

Though he is often thought of as a total traditionalist, fond of dressing in native costume and dancing with his *impis*, he believed strongly in economic modernisation. He put down much of the land he acquired from the Europeans to modern agriculture, farmed by large estates or producer cooperatives. He also carried out extensive reforestation in huge schemes such as the Usutu plantations which became one of the largest man-made forests on the continent of Africa.

After a long political campaign to gain more recognition for the monarchy, the Swaziland Native Administration Proclamation was passed by Britain, in 1950. His position was also recognised in the independence constitution drawn up in the early 1960's. Britain may have believed that Swaziland would follow the same course towards independence as any of its other colonies, but Sobhuza during the negotiations was determined to safeguard as much royal power as possible and frustrate the growth of political parties.

When the Colonial Secretary, Duncan Sandys, produced a pre-independence constitution in 1963 which encouraged the growth of modern political parties, Sobhuza countered by forming his own party, the Imbokodvo (grindstone). One of the princes of the royal family Prince Makhosini Dlamini was chosen as the party leader, but he soon revealed where the real power lay, "It is the king not I, who leads his people."

In alliance with one urban party Imbokodvo swept the 1964 elections, taking all the seats. Sobhuza was then able to demand immediate independence from Britain knowing that his power was confirmed.

In the pre-independence elections in April 1967 it again won all 24 seats in a new house of assembly. The curious winner-takes-all constituency system had excluded the only modern party which had a following in urban areas.

In the run up to independence Sobhuza allayed white fears by revealing that he believed in free enterprise and that he would safeguard foreign investment. Britain finally granted him exclusive control over mineral rights and independence was declared on 6 September 1968.

In the new parliament he not only controlled the 24 elected members through his Imbokodvo party but was able to nominate an additional fifth of the assembly and half of the senate from his own men.

Sobhuza grappled enthusiastically with economic development. He relied heavily on foreign capital, particularly from South Africa, in mineral and agricultural projects. He also set up royal corporations, financed by mineral royalties, which invested in major projects.

Though financially successful, foreign economic domination and the lack of opportunity for younger educated Swazis resulted in considerable resentment. In the elections of 1972 Imbokodvo lost three seats.

Sobhuza appeared to take this as a personal affront. After a messy attempt to deport one of the opposition MPs which was not upheld in the courts, he declared a state of emergency, revoked the constitution, banned all political parties (including Imbokodvo) and closed parliament. He then announced that he would form a national army with its men trained by South Africans.

Why he should have taken such extreme measures, when he appeared to be in total control, remains obscure. Perhaps he saw the minor success of the opposition as the beginning of a sustained challenge to his personal authority.

He ruled by decree and harassed all suspected dissidents, until in March 1977, he announced that the parliamentary system had been formally abolished. In its place he instituted a traditional tribal system called *Tikhundla*. It established a parliament of members nominated by the king, which could debate and advise, but not legislate. Sobhuza nominated the Prime Minister and his cabinet and had power of veto over parliament, thus retaining full control of all executive decisions.

In foreign policy, living under the shadow of South Africa, he always maintained strict neutrality. Though strictly non-racial at home and opposed to South African apartheid, he recognised political realities and could not afford to offend his powerful neighbour. Swaziland was finally forced to sign a non-aggression treaty with South Africa in February 1982 which ruled out further support for African National Congress refugees.

By the time of the diamond jubilee celebrations in September 1981, his power was absolute. Twenty-two foreign heads of state attended and saw the 83-year-old king, dressed in skins and feathers, joining the celebratory dancing, while a modern trade fair opened its doors nearby.

The next year on 21 August 1982, he died, frail and suffering from leukaemia. After more than 60 years on the throne, he had been the world's longest reigning monarch. At his funeral his embalmed body was carried upright in a sedan chair to create the illusion that he was still alive.

After his death the political system he had erected, which depended so much on his personal authority, came under severe strain. A regency was established as rival members of the royal Dlamini family tussled for power. During his long reign he had dozens of wives and hundreds of children and grandchildren. Eventually the succession was handed over to one of the youngest of his many children, Prince Makhosetive, still studying at Sherborne College in Britain. It was left to him to see whether he could take Swaziland into another age.

Martyr of the Revolution

THOMAS SANKARA
1949-1987

Thomas Sankara was a Marxist idealist who tried to establish government of the people, by the people, for the people during his short rule (1984-87) in Burkina Faso. He led a revolution that achieved significant political, social and economic success. He put his populist, communalist policies into practice and began to improve the economy by relying on the efforts of his own people rather than foreign aid. In foreign affairs he pursued an anti-imperialist and by necessity anti-Western line, establishing good relations with militant Third World states.

But he was too young and politically immature to appreciate the forces that were building against him both externally and internally among his closest comrades. In the words of one of his chiefs, "Sankara was too tall and too far sighted to see his own feet."

Ultimately the Burkina revolution began to devour its own leaders. His life-long colleague, Blaise Compaore proved himself more cunning and ruthless in the struggle for survival. Sankara was cynically murdered and became a martyr of the revolution, that he more than any other, had created.

Thomas Sankara was born on 21 December 1949 into a poor peasant Catholic family, near Yako, just over 100 kilometres north west of the capital of Upper Volta, Ouagadougou. He lived as a child at Kaya.

His family was determined to give him a solid career and sent him to do his secondary schooling at the military school at Kadiogo from 1966-69. He then went abroad to continue his military studies at the military academy at Antsirabe in Madagascar, where his colleagues remember him as a very serious student – idealistic, interested in politics and a non-drinker and non-smoker. While in Madagascar he became more politically aware. He witnessed the demonstrations by students that led to the overthrow of President Tsiranana. He passed out as a 2nd Lieutenant in 1972 and was soon sent to the parachute school at Pau in France and then to Rabat in Morocco for further courses.

When he returned he was one of the most highly trained soldiers in the minuscule Voltaic army. He soon found himself plunged into a border war, that he later regretted, with the neighbouring state of Mali. He was given command of a large body of troops and though he had political misgivings, his training triumphed over his instincts and he won glory in a number of engagements, once triumphing over a larger force and taking a number of prisoners.

Sankara had all the credentials of a solid, professional, apolitical soldier, but he was far from that. He had been left-inclined from his student days and took a prominent part in the politics whenever he was in the capital. He watched with interest as a two-day general strike in December 1975 resulted in wage increases for workers.

He was rewarded for his achievements during the war by being given command of the National Training Centre for commandos at Po, 150 km south west of Ouagadougou.

Sankara's smooth professional career contrasted with the political ferment in the nation as a whole. Throughout 1979 and most of 1980 the teachers, workers and unionists incited by left wing political parties, ran a succession of strikes. The government of President Lamizana was weary and bereft of ideas. Indeed Lamizania may well have connived in his own deposition when he was removed from power by the bloodless military coup of Colonel Saye Zerbo on 25 November 1980.

Zerbo wanted the popular young officer in his new team but, at first, Sankara publicly refused to join the new government. Later he agreed to be appointed secretary to the President in charge of information, "on a temporary basis." There he encouraged the press to be critical and independent and not the slavish voice of government. Unlike others of ministerial rank he eschewed material rewards for himself. He lived in a humble house and cycled to his office every day for work.

Sankara was totally out of sympathy with Zerbo's military government. He and other young officers such as his friends Blaise Compaore, Jean Baptiste Lingani and Henry Zongo were young, leftist rebels who wanted no truck with the old order.

In April 1982 he resigned from government and called a news conference to say it was corrupt and incompetent. He was immediately arrested and sent to Dedougou to await court martial along with Compaore and Zongo.

While he was still under detention a group of senior officers led by an army doctor, Major Jean-Baptiste Ouedraogo mounted another military coup on 7 November 1982. Sankara was offered a place on the 120-man military council. At first he refused on the grounds that it was yet one more reshuffle of the old guard, but eventually he was prevailed upon to take the post of Prime Minister on 10 January 1983. Still only 33 he had virtually been thrust into the exalted post.

The Ouedraogo government gave the unions the right to strike and promised that it would bring military rule to an end by 1984, but such was the political ferment that Sankara was never able to go far enough to appease the many voices of the opposition. There were a myriad of political parties, different workers' unions and even the Military Revolutionary Organisation which represented the radicalised soldiers. The country was becoming distinctly unstable.

Thomas Sankara took full advantage of his position by seeking the company of radical leaders abroad. He attended the Non-Aligned Summit Conference in New Delhi in March and returned home to give a major speech at a mass rally.

He was then responsible for the flamboyant, symbolic gesture of inviting the Libyan leader Muammar Gadaffi, to visit Ouagadougou in April. This worried the French who sent Guy Penne, President Mitterrand's adviser on African Affairs to try and restore French influence.

Major differences were now showing between the conservative, pro-Western Head of State, Ouedraogo and the young, revolutionary Sankara. Less than two weeks after Gadaffi's departure, the conservatives struck.

Sankara and his militant associates were arrested and imprisoned at the military camp at Ouahigouya after being accused by Ouedragogo of "dangerously threatening national unity." But significantly Sankara's friend, Blaise Compaore remained free as commander of Sankara's old parachute regiment at Po.

Compaore led a revolt by the paratroops as the students and workers demonstrated in the streets of the capital. Ouedraogo tried to temporise by releasing Sankara while keeping him under house arrest in Ouagadougou. But Compaore maintained his rebellion and by 4 August was strong enough to overthrow the Ouedraogo regime and free Sankara.

A few days fighting followed in which the leader of the conservative faction in the army, Colonel Gabriel Some, was killed. Sankara emerged as the new leader at the head of the National Council of the Revolution (CNR).

In his inaugural speech he declared the August revolution to be democratic, anti-imperialist and designed to take the power away from the petty bourgeoisie and put it into the hands of the people. He said mass Committees for the Defence of the Revolution (CDRs) would be established in villages and communities throughout the country.

On the first anniversary of the revolution on 4 August 1984, in a symbolic gesture, he changed the colonial name of the country from Upper Volta to Burkina Faso. This caused considerable mirth in sophisticated circles as the new name meant "the land of the incorruptible men." Yet already, in the first year of the revolution, the peoples tribunals had been hard at work trying the old guard for economic crimes. Many ministers and dozens of top officials were found guilty of embezzlement and sentenced to long terms of imprisonment.

Sankara then threw himself into bringing the socialist millennia to his country. He reorganised the administration, deprived the traditional chiefs of their powers while boosting the powers of the CDRs.

On the plus side a crash development programme was introduced which brought mass vaccination, a major literacy drive, tree planting on the fringes of the Sahara and water conservation. The CNR nationalised all land, suspended residential rents in 1985 and tried to collectivise agriculture and industry.

In foreign policy there were other radical initiatives. Sankara talked of union with Jerry Rawlings' Ghana, but the Ghanaians were not ready to be swept off their feet. A cooperation agreement was signed with Cuba.

But by March 1984, nine months after he had assumed power, there was a major reaction from those who thought the revolution had gone too far.

The lawyers were complaining about the revolutionary tribunals, the teachers were striking against the arrest of some of their leaders and internal discord within the CNR began to show.

Sankara was welcome in revolutionary capitals abroad, but he was snubbed by President Houphouet Boigny of the Cote d'Ivoire when Sankara insisted that he would only make a visit if he was allowed to speak to his students and workers living in Abidjan.

Left wing visitors were encouraged. Daniel Ortega, the revolutionary Nicaraguan leader, arrived in August 1986 and Sankara visited Cuba en route to Nicaragua, on a return visit. The month before he had been in the Soviet Union.

He then plunged his country into a headlong confrontation with France by embarassing President Mitterrand publicly, at a formal dinner party, by accusing France of helping the apartheid regime in South Africa.

But it was internal politicking that finally brought Sankara's downfall. Years before Sankara came to power national politics had acquired the characteristics of a permanent student debating society. Dozens of communist, neo-Marxist, Trotskyist, socialist and allied groups in the trade unions spent their time jockeying for power and trying to impose their ideologies.

At the top the CNR was itself composed of disparate groups though it was ruled by the four *Chefs historiques de la revolution*: Sankara, Compaore, Lignani and Zongo. Soon stresses and strains began to show even between these life long comrades.

Sankara became so estranged from the others that he decided he would have to set up his own security force to counter that of Compaore who had the backing of the redoutable parachute regiment.

Compaore meanwhile feared that Sankara might try and topple him and his colleagues. Suspicion mounted between the top leaders, yet shortly before the dramatic events of 15 October 1987, it appeared that Sankara and Compaore had patched things up. They were seen in amicable discussions with each other and neither of their wives had been given any indication of what might happen.

On that fateful morning, Sankara was mown down together with six members of his cabinet, his chauffeurs and bodyguards, and dozens of others in a hail of Kalashnikov bullets outside the conference hall of the Entente Council. Compaore emerged, one and a half hours after the shooting, pretending that he knew nothing about the firing in the middle of town which had wiped out nearly 100 innocent people.

The killing was by Compaore's commandos but he claimed that he had given no orders and knew nothing about it. Later he told *Reuters* that it was to pre-empt a meeting at 8pm when Sankara would have arrested him and his colleagues. Later still Lignani and Songo called the diplomatic corps to say that Sankara's methods of economic management showed "eccentricity and immaturity. Changes were necessary to put an end to internal battles and economic ruin."

Since the killings no judicial inquiry has ever been held. A government explanation was published, entitled *A Memorandum on the Events of 15 October 1987* which claimed that Sankara was planning to eliminate his opponents who had carried out a pre-emptive strike, but again no evidence was produced to support this thesis.

The Burkina revolution was devouring its own children. Significantly Lignani and Zongo were in turn summarily executed following the alleged discovery of a plot to overthrow Compaore in September 1989. This left Compaore as the sole survivor from the *"Chefs historiques de la revolution."*

Sankara's death was widely mourned throughout Africa and the Third World. He was seen as the representative of a new generation of young leaders who had been brought down by the forces of reaction.

One Fatal Mistake

AHMADOU AHIDJO
1924-1989

Alhaji Ahmadou Ahidjo built a powerful, single party state, and gave himself unchallenged authority as President of the Cameroon. When he handed over power in November 1982, even his critics hailed him for unifying the nation, revitalising a poor economy, and creating an aura of stable tranquillity. But he was never content to rest on his achievements. He interfered in the affairs of his successor, Paul Biya and reintroduced ethnic division.

Within a few years he had undone the stability that he created. Biya regained control, but the seeds of change had been planted and he had to reap the harvest of change. Within a few years single party authoritarianism was under challenge as Cameroonians began to demand basic liberties and multi-party government. Ahidjo had been a man of his time, the prime example of the authoritarian ruler of the 1960s and 1970s, that was swept aside in the new multi-party Africa.

Ahmadou Ahidjo was born in August 1924 in Garoua, northern Cameroon. He was a Muslim, northerner and son of a Fulani chief, estranged from his wife. The brunt of Ahmadou's early upbringing fell on his mother who had to provide for him.

He did not get much of an education but completed his studies at the *Ecole Primaire Superieur* at the capital Yaounde. He then started work in 1941, as a middle-grade technician, a radio operator in the post office.

An interest in politics made him join the *Jeunes Musulmans* and he came to the attention of the Muslim chiefs in his home area.

His political career was launched when in January 1947 he was elected to the Cameroon Representative Assembly as the member for the Adamoua circle in the north. He was re-elected again in 1952 to the renamed Territorial Assembly and again in December 1956 and January 1957. In October 1953 he was also elected to represent his country at the

Assembly of the French Union in Paris. There he was elected unanimously as President of the Union Assembly in December 1956.

At home he was not the leading figure in Cameroon politics – Andre-Marie Mbida, a southern lawyer, was the pioneer of Cameroon nationalism. It was he who became Prime Minister in the first African government formed in May 1957. Ahidjo had been in the same party for several years and by becoming his deputy as Vice Prime Minister he provided a good regional balance between north and south.

Mbida was fully occupied in trying to suppress a rebellion by the opposition *Union des Populations Camerounaises* UPC which had converted its demand for immediate independence and unification with West Cameroon, into a bloody armed uprising in the Bamileke mountains under the legendary rebel leader Ruben um Nyobe.

Mbida's policy of total repression was not working and he was disliked for his authoritarianism. He also had enemies in his own cabinet and finally turned the French colonial authorities against him. The French forced Mbida to resign and Ahmadou Ahidjo became Prime Minister in February 1958.

Ironically though, one major reason for Mbida's downfall was his violent repression of the UPC revolt, Ahidjo was equally severe. He used French troops and tough tactics but he also offered a political solution and an amnesty.

Within a month of his succession, as the rebellion fizzled out, he began negotiations with France for progress towards independence. By May 1958 he was asking for full independence and soon he and his ruling party the *Union Camerounaise* were pressing for reunification with British Cameroons. Within a few months of acceding to power he had endorsed the former demands of the rebels.

Meanwhile General De Gaulle, who had developed a friendship for the young Cameroonian, came to power in France. This smoothed the transition as Cameroon became independent on 1 January 1960 with Ahidjo as President.

To further his policy of reunification, he encouraged the United Nations to hold a plebiscite on 11 February 1961 in British Cameroons. The south voted overwhelmingly for union and was integrated into a federation as West Cameroon, while the north voted to join Nigeria.

Ahidjo inherited a nation divided racially, ethnically and on language lines. His answer was to centralise and unify. For the first two decades of his career he concentrated on securing control by centralisation and boosting the importance of the party and his own personal power at the expense of civil liberties, individual rights and the freedom of the press.

In foreign policy he pursued a pro-Western and particularly pro-French line and a liberal, mixed economy designed to attract foreign investment.

In September 1966 he was sufficiently powerful to merge all the opposition parties (including the party which represented the interests of the English speakers in the West) into the ruling party that was renamed the *Union Nationale Camerounaise* (UNC). He was declared President of the new party, which was to control all political life in the country by persuasion or intimidation. He created a quiescent "stable" state in which private enterprise, foreign capital and the economy as a whole was able to flourish.

He was re-elected President of the country in 1970 and again in 1975. By 1972 he was strong enough to change the constitution, abolish the federal system altogether and increase his own powers by dropping the posts of vice president and prime minister.

As his rule proceeded his policies became more authoritarian and intimidatory and all resistance was totally cowed. Yet Ahidjo, who had fought so long and cleverly for supreme power, was curiously reluctant to enjoy it. In a number of statements after 1975 he said that he would not hold onto power permanently.

But when he finally resigned the Presidency on 6 November 1982 he caught everyone by surprise. Commentators eulogised his surrender of power after 24 years of successful rule. But it is still not clear why he chose to go. Perhaps his reticence was because he soon came to the conclusion that he had made a mistake. One theory is that his French doctors had told him (wrongly) that he would not have long to live if he continued to carry the cares of office. So he resigned, only to regret it later.

He handed over the presidency of the nation, but not the party, to Paul Biya, a Christian southerner who had been his deputy virtually since independence. Ahidjo may have felt that by retaining control of the party he could stop Biya from departing too far from his policies.

But Biya soon began to show that he had a mind of his own. Stealthily he began to rid himself of Ahidjo's closest lieutenants and favourite ministers, replacing them with his own men.

Then on 27 August 1983 he announced the discovery of an attempted coup, which was interpreted as a northern plot possibly to allow Ahidjo to regain power. Biya took the opportunity to dismiss the Prime Minister and the minister for the armed forces, both northerners who were considered to be pro-Ahidjo.

At the extraordinary UNC party congress of 27 August 1983 Biya then stripped Ahidjo of the chairmanship of the party and assumed it himself.

By this time Ahidjo had already taken refuge in Paris and began making statments and giving interviews that were highly critical of Biya. In January 1984 he was tried in absentia for taking part in the attempted coup. He was said to have given instructions to his aides to eliminate Biya by assassination. He was found guilty and sentenced to death.

A much more serious coup attempt followed on 6 April 1984 when rebel elements of the presidential guard (who had been originally recruited by Ahidjo) attempted to seize Paul Biya's palace. Fighting raged for three days and the streets were littered with the bodies of fallen soldiers, though the government admitted to only 73 dead. This time there was even more evidence that it had been a pro-Ahidjo, northern plot.

The irony of the situation was that the man who for 24 years had given his country an enviable reputation for stability and unity had undone everything because he regretted handing over power. Biya inherited a precarious situation in which the monolithic rule of the party and the deprivation of individual rights would be increasingly challenged.

Ahidjo spent his remaining years in exile, either in Senegal or in France. He died in Dakar, Senegal on 30 November 1989 still complaining about the vicissitudes of fate.

Federation First

ROY WELENSKY
1907-1991

Roy Welensky rose from a poor white background to become, for more than a decade (1953-63), the leading figure in central African politics. He was a train driver, ex-heavyweight boxer and trade unionist with few social connections, who emerged by his abundant charm and the sheer force of his personality as a leading white politician. He became the father of a novel political experiment, the attempted union of three countries (Northern and Southern Rhodesia and Nyasaland) into the Central African Federation. Welensky was totally obsessed with his federal ideal, but he found it was unsustainable against the rising tide of African nationalism in the 1960s.

He always professed his non-racialism, but it was his failure to win the trust and friendship of the emerging African nationalist leaders, as much as his failure to convince the Rhodesian whites, that finally undermined his federal dream. When it collapsed, his political career was also at an end. He abandoned Rhodesia and retired to Britain where he spurned all political honours and every offer to start a new career.

Roy Raphael Welensky was born on 20 January 1907, in Salisbury, Rhodesia (Zimbabwe) the son of poor white immigrant parents. He was the thirteenth child of a half-Jewish, Lithuanian married to an Afrikaner girl who had trekked by ox wagon from South Africa. They had arrived in Rhodesia in the 1890s.

His mother died when he was only 11 so he lived with his father who had been a horse smuggler in the Franco-Prussian war and a bar keeper in the American Mid-West, before trekking to Rhodesia in time to fight the Matabele war in 1896.

His father made and lost several fortunes along the way and acquired a huge family, so he could only afford to give Roy a primary education, up to standard four.

He left school at the age of 14 and got work wherever he could find it as a barman, storekeeper and a miner before getting a job in 1924 as a fireman and later as an engine driver on Rhodesia railways, where he furthered his education by reading Marx and John Stuart Mill on the footplate.

Few would have guessed that he was destined for a major political career as he became the national heavyweight boxing champion in 1925, a title he held for two years. He was an exceptionally large man weighing over 20 stone and found it difficult to find clothes to fit him in the local shops; they had to be custom made for him by his wife.

His tastes were simple. He liked to work about the house and garden, being particularly fond of growing roses. He was a teetotaller and non-smoker. In his early years he carried much of the colour prejudice of the other settlers. He once revealed that he thought that all great black athletes must be at least partly white to have achieved success.

In 1933 he moved to Broken Hill, the railway headquarters in Northern Rhodesia (now Kabwe, Zambia), where he set about rebuilding the railway union which had lost its influence after losing a strike in 1930. He was soon national chairman of the all-white railway workers union.

It was trade unionism that led him into politics. In 1938 he was elected member for the Northern Rhodesia legislative council for Broken Hill. So great was his local popularity that he was seldom opposed thereafter. In 1941 he formed the all white Labour party, with the twin aims of amalgamating the two Rhodesias and of wresting the mineral rights away from the British South Africa Company (BSAC), originally founded by Cecil Rhodes (q.v.). After eight years of pressure he did get a compromise agreement from the BSAC which brought considerable financial benefit to the Northern Rhodesia government; even Kenneth Kaunda, the Zambian President, later acknowledged this.

On the resignation of Sir Stewart Gore Brown in 1947, he became chairman of the unofficial (i.e. elected) members of the legislative council. As the elected members in Northern Rhodesia virtually ran their own legislature this made him prime minister in all but name.

At the time the objective of the whites was to achieve amalgamation of the two Rhodesias thus perpetuating white rule and ensuring the sharing of Northern Rhodesia's copper wealth. Under pressure from the British colonial government which was determined to afford some protection of African interests, he and his associate Sir Godfrey Huggins (later Lord Malvern) of Southern Rhodesia modified their stance to one of federation rather than outright amalgamation.

Welensky called a federation conference at Victoria Falls in February 1949 to which neither the colonial authorities nor African representatives were invited. This alienated African opinion, but Welensky and Huggins continued to lobby strongly for Federation at a conference in London in March 1951.

Welensky stated his paternalist position, "Europeans in Central

Africa cannot ignore the march of African nationalism, but they still have an opportunity to guide it on sane lines."

At a second Victoria Falls conference in 1951 he finally persuaded the new Conservative government to put Federation to a referendum in Southern Rhodesia and to a vote in the Northern Rhodesia legislature. Africans were not consulted so both proposals were overwhelmingly carried.

Federation was declared in June 1953 and on 7 September Sir Godfrey Huggins resigned the Rhodesian premiership and became the new Federal Prime Minister. Welensky first became transport minister then deputy prime minister. The Federation professed to be a multi-racial partnership, but Welensky saw it as a means of perpetuation, into the foreseeable future of white, Southern Rhodesian dominance.

He took over as Prime Minister when Huggins retired in November 1956. The train driver had become Prime Minister of the Central African Federation, which also included Nyasaland (Malawi). It was a highly complex organisation with three territorial governments as well as the federal government, and it was not independent. Britain had its own agenda and continually interfered through the Colonial and the Commonwealth office.

But Welensky set himself the goal of achieving independence under dominion status for the federation. Worried about Britain's plans to extend the franchise in Northern Rhodesia he said, "Adult suffrage is a myth and as long as I am head of the federal government it will never be given any consideration whatsoever."

But African opposition was growing apace and in 1959 he fully backed the national governments in declaring a state of emergency in Southern Rhodesia and Nyasaland. He frequently claimed that African opposition to the Federation was the result of professional agitators or communists, though he was intelligent enough to know that it was the product of the African nationalism that was sweeping the continent.

He felt betrayed when a commission headed by Lord Monckton in 1960 recommended that the right of secession should be granted to individual territories after a fixed period of time. He threatened that the Federation might be forced to "go it alone" without British approval.

In 1960 violence broke out in Northern Rhodesia as trouble erupted in Katanga in the neighbouring Congo. Britain revised the constitution for Northern Rhodesia, making it easier for Africans to win seats, and establish an anti-federal majority there. Welensky flew to London in March 1962 and blustered about using force if necessary to preserve the federation.

But Northern Rhodesia and Nyasaland were pushing ever harder for self- determination. Hastings Banda returned to fight for the freedom of Nyasaland and in December 1962 it was allowed to secede. Nationalist pressure was building in Northern Rhodesia too. By the end of 1963 the federal experiment became untenable and on 31 December ironically again at Victoria Falls, Welensky watched with quiet dignity as it was formally wound up.

Welensky was bitterly disappointed. His major political ambition to create a successful Federation had been destroyed. His ideal of gradual African evolution under white civilisation was swept away. He had tried to stand unbending in the full flood of African nationalism as one African country after another became independent, but he was forced to give ground.

He was also undermined by the wily Conservative politicians in Britain who had long since decided that each nation should choose its own destiny. He had even lost the support of white extremists in Rhodesia who now wanted their own independence to secure their dominance in Southern Rhodesia, even if the game was lost in the north and Nyasaland.

He was never prepared to take the final step towards a Unilateral Declaration of Independence (UDI), as advocated by a succession of militant opponents in the right-wing Rhodesian Front. When he tried to fight for a seat in the Rhodesian legislature on an anti-secessionist platform against Clifford Dupont in 1964 he was heavily and humiliatingly defeated.

Utterly dispirited, he turned on Britain in his book *4,000 days* and accused the government of bad faith and treachery. He retired to his farm to brood and grumble to visitors as he tended his roses.

Still more extreme figures were to rule Rhodesia until Zimbabwe finally gained its independence in 1980. Welensky never condoned Ian Smith's UDI in 1965, but he was powerless and out of office.

In 1981 he left Zimbabwe with his family and went to live in England. The British were sorry for him and offered him safe Conservative seats, even a peerage which would have brought a seat in the House of Lords. But Welensky the ex-railwayman, and ex-unionist refused all honours. He settled near Shaftesbury in Dorset and kept a large turtle in a kennel instead. He died at Blandford Forum on 5 December 1991.

Pater Familias

FELIX HOUPHOUET-BOIGNY
c.1905-1993

Houphouet-Boigny ruled longer than any other African head of state. He was president from 1960-93 and the acknowledged leader of his people, the *pater familias* of the Ivorian family, from the birth of Ivorian nationalism in the 1940s. He had the sophisticated self assurance of a man who was in command for the whole of his political life. He was a French cabinet minister for 13 years, saturated in French culture, as much at ease in Paris as Abidjan or his birthplace, turned capital, Yamoussoukro.

Ever tactful, pragmatic and tolerant, he was conservative, intensely cautious and unwilling to risk national interest for any great African design. From the time he turned his back on the communists in the 1950s he was *"un homme sage"*, the best African friend of France, outliving de Gaulle and the French leaders who were his early colleagues.

Short, stocky with a smiling, gnome-like face, masking his political cunning and his peasant instincts, he delivered an economic miracle in the 1970s, though this faltered in the harsher economic environment that followed. In politics he was subtle, devious and always prepared to reform and absorb the opposition. He adopted "dialogue" as one of his key words. He was significantly the first of the African heads of state to adapt successfully to multi-party democracy. Indeed he had started to adapt before it became a requirement to do so and he ensured that his political hegemony remained intact against the opposition challenge. His political judgement and gentle persuasive power ensured steady rule for nearly 40 years, without parallel in Africa.

Felix Houphouet-Boigny was officially born on 18 October 1905 at Yamoussoukro, a rich coffee-growing area. His father was a chief of the Akuwe sub-group of the Baoule tribe. Some sources say that his birthday was probably much earlier, nearer to 1900, but this has never been established.

He was educated at Bingerville Higher Primary School, before entering *Ecole Ponty*, the Dakar School of Medicine and Pharmacy where he graduated in 1925. He served in the colonial medical service and became a well off planter for almost 20 years, gaining a reputation as a famous *guerrisseur* (healer).

When his maternal uncle died in 1940 he inherited much land at Yamoussoukro and was appointed a canton chief of the Akuwe. He organised the Confraternal Association of Customary Chiefs and became well known for his charm, persuasive powers and organisational abilities.

In 1944 he formed the African Agricultural Union, an association of small planters set up to fight the favoured treatment given to the large white planters and to combat the *indigenat* (forced labour).

In 1945 he converted this union, with a membership of some 20,000, into the *Parti Democratique de la Cote d'Ivoire* (PDCI). He organised the first multi-ethnic list of candidates to fight the Abidjan municipal elections, under the name the *Bloc Africain* and won an overwhelming victory.

His political reputation soared when he became one of the first Africans to be elected to the French National Assembly in November 1945. There he tried unsuccessfully to introduce a bill calling for the abolition of forced labour throughout the French colonies.

It was a militant phase of his life. He added 'Houphouet' to his name, meaning "battering ram." In June 1946 he was re-elected to the French Assembly under a new constitution. It was customary for African parties to associate with a metropolitan party, so he put the PDCI into an alliance with the French Communist Party.

In October 1946 he helped found the *Rassemblement Democratique Africain* (RDA), a pan-African movement for the French territories with the PDCI as the Ivorian branch. Prompted by the French communists, the party became involved in a series of strikes, boycotts and demonstrations, reaching a climax on 24 January 1950 when a warrant was issued for his arrest. If he had not been a privileged member of the French Assembly he would have been imprisoned.

Houphouet saw that violence was leading him nowhere and became suspicious of the intentions of the French communists, so he transferred his alliance to the French socialists, under the leadership of the up-and-coming Francois Mitterrand. But the move did not come soon enough to rescue the PDCI from a severe defeat in the 1951 elections.

The French sent a new, sympathetic Governor-General to Abidjan and Houphouet took advantage to rebuild the party, turning his back on Communism for ever. The PDCI-RDA won seven seats in the January 1956 elections and Houphouet became a French cabinet minister.

As Minister-Delegate to Guy Mollet, the French Prime Minister, he played a leading part in drawing up the *loi cadre* for the French colonies, a blueprint for internal autonomy within the French community.

In the 1957 elections under the new constitution, the PDCI took 95% of the votes. He continued as a minister in Paris. He was Minister of State under the Prime Minister Bourges Manoury (June- November 1957); Minister of Public Health and Population under Felix Gaillard (November 1957-April 1958); Minister of State under Pierre Pfimlin (May 1958); Minister of State under Charles de Gaulle (June 1958-January 1959) and under Michel Debre until 23 May 1959.

The French colonies were given the choice of federation between themselves or autonomy and association with France. Houphouet was strongly anti-federal. He and de Gaulle designed a scheme for holding a referendum giving a choice between total independence or autonomy within the French community. The two men then toured Africa campaigning for a "Yes" in favour of association with the French community.

In April 1959 he became Prime Minister of the Cote d'Ivoire, while still retaining his French ministry. But when Mali persuaded de Gaulle to go one step further and allow "independence within the French community", he followed suit and led his country to independence on 7 August 1960.

Houphouet's relationship with France was strong even during the early rebellious days. Now he was to become *"un homme sage"*. He married a French lady, Therese Brou. He employed French ministers in his government. His ministries were stuffed with French expatriates and the tens of thousands of French settlers actually increased in number in the years after independence.

On 27 November 1960 he was elected President by 98% of the votes cast. He also retained the ministry of foreign affairs and from time to time the ministries of interior, defence, agriculture and education.

In January 1963 there were some serious plots against him, with over 100 arrested, including prominent ministers. Many were condemned but he commuted all their death sentences. He always felt that he could win his opponents round without pursuing vindictive policies. Once he described the detainees taken in the attempted coup in half-affectionate terms as his "little perverts."

Another plot was discovered in 1964, but by the end of the year the opposition had been thoroughly suppressed and he was able to embark on nation building, marked by liberal economic policies. He sought foreign investment and rewarded his farmers with high prices.

In 1965 he was elected President for another five years. Frequently he was the object of student protest, as in May 1969 when he ordered the closure of Abidjan university, but his response was always conciliatory. He would personally hold "dialogues" with the students and promise to tackle their grievances.

Throughout Houphouet saw himself as the father of a national extended family. Again and again his speeches return to the family analogy, with himself as the *pater familias* with the task of settling family squabbles among his children. One of his most famous election posters shows him hand in hand with a band of happy, smiling children.

In 1970 he celebrated the tenth anniversary of independence with a massive vote of confidence as he was re-elected President. The same year he announced a summit conference to have a dialogue with South Africa. Pan-African opinion was unprepared for this initiative, but he stuck with his attempts at dialogue, sending a delegation to South Africa in 1971 and receiving several South African premiers in the Cote d'Ivoire in the years that followed.

In 1975 he was re-elected President for a fourth five-year term and he had a constitutional amendment passed that would allow the President of the National Assembly to succeed him in the event of his death. Though he was almost 75, worries about the succession which recurred perenially, proved premature. He was to continue as President well into his nineties.

Throughout the 1970s he presided over a near miracle economy with staggering rates of growth and soaring exports. But bureaucratic inflexibility, misdirected investment, falling commodity prices and growing international debt caused the economy to suddenly collapse in the 1980s.

In September 1980, following a coup plot earlier in the year, the seventh congress of the PDCI was called and Houphouet announced democratisation in which the single party list would be abolished. He was elected for another term in October and, in February 1981, brought younger technocrats into his ministerial team. He also announced that he would appoint a Vice President who would take over from him in the event of his death, but fearing a succession struggle, he never filled this post. This was partly because he could see no one sufficiently outstanding to succeed him and because he did not want to be seen to be favouring one individual or faction.

The early 1980s were marked with rapidly deteriorating economic conditions and social unrest led by students, teachers and other sections of the urban middle class. Houphouet put the blame on his ministers, sacked those responsible and persuaded the militants that he was on their side. As always his philosophy was to forgive, forget and reconcile. This touch as a peace-maker never left him even in his dotage.

In the new style elections of October 1985 he was re-elected President for a sixth term but only 64 of the original 114 PDCI members were returned to the assembly.

In December 1985 he restored diplomatic relations with Israel which he had reluctantly broken off in 1973 and to prove his impartiality he also re-established diplomatic links with the Soviet Union.

In 1988 he began construction of a huge basilica at his home town, Yamoussoukro. It was a cathedral, standing taller than St Peter's in Rome and occupying an area greater than the Holy See. Its official cost was 40bn CFA ($115m). Unofficial estimates put it at twice that sum.

Houphouet insisted that the finance came entirely from himself and his family and yet he admitted that it was money that he had acquired by virtue of the offices that he had held during his long rule.

He was never ashamed of discussing his wealth. He once admitted, "The budget of the President of the Republic is two billion CFA (for personal expenses and political funds). I am not selfish. For me money only counts for the good use that can be made of it."

On another occasion he admitted that he had billions of CFA deposited in bank accounts in Switzerland, but even more billions banked at home. "My deposits account for more than a quarter of the deposits in one of the banks in Abidjan."

The wind of democratic change that was sweeping Africa caught the Cote d'Ivoire in its blast in the early 1990s. Three months of strikes and demonstrations, culminating an in in an army mutiny among junior ranks in May 1990, provoked an unprecedented crisis. Houphouet responded by suppressing the immediate trouble and by confirming the move that he had already made in April to allow opposition parties to register, thus creating the foundations for a multi-party democracy. He remained supremely confident knowing that he could get his party machine moving long before the opposition had time to organise itself.

In the presidential elections of 28 October 1990, Houphouet was challenged for the first time in his long career by a younger history professor, Laurent Gbagbo, but he still took 82% of the vote. This triumph was repeated when the PDCI won the parliamentary elections with 163 out of the 175 seats leaving the opposition without an effective voice.

Under the new constitution a prime minister was appointed for the first time. The new PM, Allasane Ouattara, selected a new cabinet and presented it to Houphouet for approval. He assumed the day to day running of government while the President adopted a more detached, symbolic role as Head of State.

As Houphouet became older and more frail he showed no willingness to abandon office. He would make increasingly frequent trips to Paris to have medical checkups and would stay in France in his various properties to recuperate. His public appearances became less frequent while his lieutenants jockeyed for position in the still unsolved succession stakes.

The confrontation with the opposition and the liberalisation of the press also brought a series of more vicious confrontations.

The giant billboards in Abidjan proclaiming; "We have everything to thank you for Felix Houphouet Boigny," were daubed with graffiti "Houphouet le voleur" (Houphouet the thief).

When France threatened to withold assistance from a corrupt regime, Houphouet defying logic, went on the local radio to say that even if France was richer than the Cote d'Ivoire, he was richer than President Mitterrand.

He died after a long course of treatment for cancer in France. He returned home so ill a total news black-out was imposed. On the morning of 7 December he finally died, leaving a genuinely grieving nation.

11. Living Greats

The Great Deceiver
HASTINGS BANDA
1898-

Banda will ever be remembered as a maverick figure in African nationalist politics. In his 40 years of exile overseas the strict, Scottish mission-educated puritan made himself into a caring, philanthrophic doctor. When he returned home in 1958 he seized power, eliminated his closest colleagues and set up one of the most autocratic systems ever seen on the African continent. He was not the orthodox socialist nationalist, like the other leaders of the first independence decade. He was a total individualist, who always went his own way.

He thought of himself as a super-chief who understood his own people. He was a man of the extreme right, a capitalist who enriched himself while claiming to be helping the state. He parleyed with the leaders of apartheid and befriended the destructive Renamo guerrilla movement. Only at the very last did he give way to the new democratic pressures that were sweeping the continent, as his Western friends turned against him. He was swept from power in the elections of May 1994. Why had he risked defeat? Was it the response of a befuddled old man, or was it a recognition of his ultimate failure to understand his own system?

Hastings Kamuzu Banda claimed that he was born on 14 May 1906 in order to make himself appear younger than he actually was, but most authorities and living testimonial put the real date at February 1898. His parents were poor subsistence farmers living near the trading centre of Kasungu in the centre of the country. He was called Kamuzu, meaning "little root" in Chewa, which is said to have cured his mother's barren condition.

It was a time of transition. The slave traders had been replaced by the Christian missionaries and Britain had declared a protectorate over the area known as Trans-Zambezia only seven years before.

He started school in 1905 at the Livingstonia Church of Scotland School where he was quickly converted to Christianity and took on the name of Hastings from one of the missionaries.

He continued his schooling at Chilanga primary school under instruction from his uncle Hanock Phiri, who took a great interest in his education. In 1914 he passed standard three.

Two years later he and his uncle set off on foot for South Africa. They broke their journey at Hartley, near Salisbury (Harare) where he worked as a hospital orderly and vowed to become a doctor.

After a spell at a Natal colliery he eventually reached Johannesburg and became a clerk-interpreter at the Rand gold mines. It was there he heard the Ghanaian educationist J E K Aggrey (q.v.) who fired him with the desire to go to the USA for further education. He continued his studies at night school in Johannesburg, passed standard eight and became a member of the African Methodist Episcopal Church which financed his further education in the US.

In July 1925 Banda, then 27 years old, arrived in America and started at the AME Church, Wilberforce Institute, Ohio, where he completed his diploma in three years before going on to study political science at Indiana University. He graduated as a bachelor of philosophy at the University College of Chicago before going on to the Meharry Medical College, in Nashville, Tennessee. He qualified as a doctor in 1937 and went to Scotland to complete his medical studies at Glasgow and Edinburgh in 1941.

It was wartime and the Church of Scotland refused to give him a post because its nurses said they would not serve under a black doctor. When he applied to the Colonial Office, he was told that he could only be given a post if he agreed "not to seek social contacts with white doctors." Naturally he refused and instead he established a "panel", a National Health Scheme practice, for poorer patients in Liverpool.

Later he moved to South Shields and then London in 1945 where he ran a practice in Harlesden, tending thousands of patients and sponsoring dozens of scholarships for young Malawians.

His house became a meeting place for African nationalists such as Nkrumah, Kenyatta (q.v.) and Harry Nkumbula, of Zambia. He became a determined opponent of the creation of a Central African Federation and consistently campaigned against it in Britain. But the Federation was created regardless in 1953 and a disillusioned Banda, feeling let down both personally and politically by the British government, left to become a doctor in Ghana. Kwame Nkrumah offered him a government post, but he preferred private practice in Kumasi where he lived with a white woman, Margaret French.

Banda's personal life was in a mess. His political career seemed to have come to a halt while the need to divorce his wife conflicted with his strict puritanical nature.

Meanwhile in Malawi, the Nyasaland African Congress was floundering. In 1957 Thomas Dillon Banda (no relation) visited Banda in Kumasi and urged him to return home to head the NAC. Henry Chipembere also pleaded with him by letter, to return. Charges made against him in Ghana (which were later proved false and dropped) stopped him practising there. All this and the opportunity to assume the leadership of the nationalist struggle in Malawi finally convinced him. He and Margaret French passed briefly through London before flying to Chileka airport on 6 July 1958 to a tumultuous welcome. He spoke to the thousands that greeted him in English, being lost for words in his native Nyanja.

He was elected President-General of the NAC on 1 August 1958 and made a series of inflammatory speeches against the "stupid Federation," while stressing non-violence. His campaign was so virulent that a state of emergency was declared by the Nyasaland authorities on 9 March 1959.

Banda was arrested in the middle of the night and taken in his pyjamas to prison in Gwelo, Southern Rhodesia, with other leaders of the NAC. There he, Henry Chipembere, Dunduzu Chisiza and Yatuta Chisiza planned future strategy. Banda wrote an autobiography also (which remains unpublished).

On 1 April 1960 after 395 days in detention he was freed and set off on a speaking tour of Britain and the US. The new British Colonial Secretary, Iain Macleod, was prepared to be flexible and called a Lancaster House conference in July 1960, where Banda led the Malawi Congress Party, the successor to the NAC.

On 5 August 1960 a new constitution was agreed, introducing a ministerial system, leading to direct elections of Africans to the Legislative Council.

Shortly afterwards a report by Lord Monckton indicated that secession from the Federation could be permitted. Banda together with Kenneth Kaunda (q.v.) and Joshua Nkomo from Southern Rhodesia attended a Federal Review Conference in London in December 1960. The conference accomplished little but when Banda returned home he announced that the Federation was dead (though in fact it dragged on until 31 December 1963).

Banda concentrated on the Malawi elections. He fought such a successful campaign that the MCP swept the polls. On 3 September 1961 the Governor Glyn Jones appointed him Minister of Natural Resources and Local Government, then Prime Minister on 1 February 1963. Meanwhile Britain gave Nyasaland the right to withdraw from the Federation in December 1962. In the elections of April 1963 all the 50 MCP candidates were elected unopposed. Complete independence came on 6 July 1964, six years to the day after his return from exile.

Almost immediately he faced a cabinet crisis. On 7 September 1964 he dismissed three of his colleagues including Orton Chirwa, the Minister of Justice who had helped him to power. Three other fathers of Malawi nationalism also resigned. Banda ousted them from the MCP and began his regime of authoritarian, one-man rule.

Malawi became a one-party state in mid-1965. He adopted a system of government similar to a pre-colonial chieftainship. He revived or manufactured African traditions and exercised control over morality, even styles of dress.

He was elected President on 6 July 1966, when Malawi became a republic. A weak attempt at an invasion was mounted in October 1967 in which Yatuta Chisiza, the former Minister of Home Affairs was killed, but afterwards there was little open opposition to his rule. On 6 July 1971 he had himself voted life president and brought his ministers, parliament and the party totally under his personal control.

For all his militant nationalist origins, Banda was at the best a benevolent despot who insisted that authoriarian government was the only way to bring stability and foreign investment. In the early days he succeeded in this objective and foreign investment flowed in. He also ploughed his rapidly growing personal fortune into projects and companies, such as ADMARC and Press Holdings, through which he enriched himself while claiming to be helping the state.

Banda recognised that Malawi was primarily an agricultural country. In the early days he depended to some extent on communal effort and co-operatives as well as private plantations, but after the death of Dunduzu Chisiza he concentrated almost entirely on capitalist ventures.

In foreign affairs he rejected the socialist, African nationalist line adopted by the Organisation of African Unity and his closest neighbours and pursued alliances with Portugal and South Africa. In May 1970 he invited the South African premier John Vorster to visit Malawi. Then came President Fouche in March 1972. In August 1971 he became the first black African head of state to visit South Africa, then at the apogee of apartheid.

In the 1970s the economy began to turn down as foreign investment dried up and Malawi was dragged into the Mozambican war. The main ports of Beira and Nacala became increasingly unreliable and Malawi was hit by drought in 1979-81.

In February 1977 after suppressing another coup attempt, Banda felt that he had consolidated his position sufficiently to allow the release of up to 2,000 detainees. By then most of his critics were abroad, joining thousands of exiles who had already left the country.

He called the first elections in 17 years in June 1978. All the candidates were MCP. During the 1980s Banda continued to remove anyone who might conceivably threaten his own supreme power. In January 1980 Aleke Banda, once considered a likely successor, was expelled from the MCP for a gross breach of party discipline. Gwanda Chakuamba was sentenced to 22 years of imprisonment in March 1981. On Christmas Eve 1982, Orton Chirwa and his wife and son were seized across the border, on what they claim was Zambian soil and were taken into captivity.

Another opponent Dr Attati Mpakati, who was beginning to organise an efficient opposition movement, was murdered in Harare in March 1983. In May 1983 other possible successors to Banda - Dick Matenje, the Secretary General of the MCP, and Aaron Gadama, Minister for the

Central Region, were killed in a mysterious car crash. Even John Tembo who appeared to be Banda's choice as his successor was stripped of his post as Governor of the Central Bank in April 1984, just to show him that Banda was still in charge, though he later bounced back as the power behind the scenes.

During the mid-1980s Banda drew closer to his African neighbours whom he had earlier spurned. In October 1984 he signed a general co-operation agreement with Mozambique and hestitatingly reversed his earlier policy of supporting the Mozambique National Resistance Movement (Renamo). By April 1987 Malawi troops were sent to Mozambique to help protect the Nacala railway against guerrilla attack and the Mozambican refugees who had become a heavy strain on the economy were gradually sent home.

Banda pursued the policy of frequent cabinet reshuffles so that no minister could build a personal following. In the April 1987 elections all candidates were selected by the MCP but Banda insisted on making further nominations of his own. Two months later he removed three ministers in a major reshuffle. In January 1988 he dismissed the whole cabinet and reappointed a new one two weeks later.

By 1992 Banda's problems were multiplying fast. Amnesty International published a damning report alleging torture of hundreds of people in Malawi prisons. Church groups also openly challenged Banda's style of government.

Following the collapse of Communism and other authoritarian regimes in Africa, a new wind of multi-party democracy was blowing through the continent. Taking advantage of the international climate of opinion, the democracy campaigner Chakufwa Chihana returned home and vowed to campaign openly for democratisation. He was promptly arrested and put on trial.

At first Banda refused even to discuss change but in September the British Overseas Aid Minister, Baroness Chalker, said that Western donors would stop aid and not renew it until political changes were made.

Banda was 95 years old, frequently ill, and criticism was coming at him from all quarters. Many decisions were being made in his name by the *eminence grise*, John Tembo. Banda was clearly very worried that he was losing the support of his Western allies. His response, in November 1992, was to call a referendum on whether Malawi should continue as a one-party state or not. He genuinely thought his people would show the faith they had in him by rejecting the calls for multi-partyism voiced by a few disgruntled intellectuals.

The people gave an early indication of their feelings when in November an estimated 40,000 people marched to the funeral of Orton Chirwa, Banda's close colleague, who had died almost immediately after his release from detention. Banda released his widow Vera who had also been held separately in jail for 11 years.

When the referendum was held in June (after an earlier postponement) two thirds of the country's 25 districts gave 80% approval to multi-partyism. Hundreds of thousands, who had seen no point in voting under a one-party regime, turned out to show Banda that he was wrong. They wanted change. In urban areas his defeat was total and huge crowds poured onto the streets to celebrate.

Chakufwa Chihana who was released from prison after serving six months for sedition, said, "Dr Banda has two options either to be a figure-head, or to be a disgrace."

Banda riposted, "The suggestion that I should resign and be replaced by an interim government is out of the question and unacceptable." But he did promise elections under the new system in 1994.

Parliament repealed those parts of the constitution that had made Malawi a one-party state. New parties were able to register and for the first time under Banda's rule the press was allowed to function free of central directives. A new democratic constitution and bill of rights were prepared.

Banda became seriously ill with a brain haemorrage in September 1993 and was admitted to a Johannesburg hospital for an emergency operation. The operation was successful and he returned within a month to Malawi to prepare the country for the elections which he had been forced to accept.

He was persuaded to stand for the presidency despite his advancing years, but when the contest came, he revealed himself to be an old buffoon desperately appealing to past loyalties of an electorate that ridiculed him.

In the presidential election of 17 May he was soundly defeated by Bakili Muluzi who scored about 1.2 million votes to Banda's 800,000 and Chakufwa Chihana's 600,000. The voting had been almost entirely on regional and ethnic lines.

Banda, in a calm but shaky voice accepted the inevitable, "Muluzi is the clear winner. I wish to congratulate him wholeheartedly for his win...I wish to assure him that the MCP will work with him in building a better and democratic Malawi."

Were these the words of a befuddled old man too old to care, or had he experienced a sudden political conversion? He remains an enigma.

The Supreme Combatant

HABIB BOURGUIBA
1903-

Habib Bourguiba ruled Tunisia for more than 30 years and was the most outstanding Tunisian leader for more than half a century. He started with all the radical credentials of a young nationalist in the struggle against French colonialism and emerged as the leader of an independent country in 1956.

In the early years of his rule he was a secular moderniser, advancing women's rights and curbing the powers of the Islamic fundamentalists, but he was never able to find the right economic balance to make his country grow and prosper and entered a long struggle with the unions.

This led to recurrent strikes and riots as he shuffled his ministers and blamed others for his own mistakes. For a brief period he did try democratisation, but as he grew older he reverted to authoritarian paternalism. Eventually he paid the price for not keeping pace with his people's readiness for democratic change. And when he picked Zine el-Abidine Ben Ali as his right hand man, he chose someone who was ready to outmanoeuvre him. Too tired and ill to resist, he was "forcibly retired" in 1987. The "supreme combatant" had met his match.

Habib Bourguiba was born on 3 August 1903 at Monastir. He was the youngest of eight children in a small-town, upper middle class, property owning family. His father had been a soldier in the Bey's army, before becoming a government official. He was more concerned by the demands the Bey exerted over his people than occupation by the French.

He claims that as the youngest child he had a miserable childhood. His mother died when he was only 10 years old. He started studies at Sadiki college and then the *Lycee Carnot,* a school mainly for the French *colons.* He claims that he left school in 1913, because he contracted tuberculosis caused by poor conditions. But this may just have been the romantic nostalgia of a young man as he secretly read *La Tunisie Martyre* by Sheikh ath-Thaa'lbi, under the blankets of his bed.

The destruction of the Ottoman empire in the first World War and the achievement of independence of many eastern Arab countries had a profound influence on him, as did the formation of the Destour (Constitution) movement under the leadership of Sheikh ath-Thaa'lbi. In 1922 Bourguiba joined the Destour which was calling for reform under the Bey, a self-governing constitution and a local legislative assembly. It was the only serious, early nationalist party, fiercely opposed by the French in the late 1920s.

Bourguiba meanwhile was proving a brilliant pupil. He passed first in his philosophy baccalaureat at Carnot and became ever more interested in the world of books and ideas.

He won a scholarship to the University of Paris and travelled there in November 1924. He lived in the heart of the Latin Quarter, became a passionate theatre goer and even learnt to dance the Charleston.

He claims to have "absorbed French culture to the tip of his nails," yet he "clung on to his Tunisian soul." He became a fierce campaigner for the Arab-Muslim cause. Before he finished his course and left for home, he married Mathilde Louvain, a French widow, some years older than himself.

He returned to Tunisia in August 1927 to practice law, but his legal activities gradually gave way to a new love of journalism.

He began writing for *Le Voix Tunisien* where he attacked the French protectorate government and the ageing, conservative leadership of the Destour party.

At the time a bizarre, but all absorbing, controversy, raged over whether Tunisians who had opted for French citizenship should be allowed to be buried in Muslim cemeteries. He vigorously opposed the French government which wanted to change the law and force the cemeteries to accept French citizens. He also took up other issues with such passion that he was accused of stirring race hatred.

In 1928 he went too far even for *Le Voix Tunisien*, the paper that had given him a platform, so he broke away to found *Action Tunisienne* where he continued his campaign in a series of clear, didactic articles.

In 1933 the French governor offered to lift the ban on the Destour party if it would agree to moderate its demands. Bourguiba refused to compromise and was expelled from the party along with a number of younger comrades.

In March 1934, he and his fellow dissidents, formed the Neo-Destour party committed to a much more militant brand of nationalism, using widespread political agitation. He organised the party on the marxist cell-system in anticipation of action against the leadership. His fears were well founded. By the end of the year he and his colleagues were arrested and banished to Bordj le Boeuf in the Sahara.

A new French Governor and the victory of the Popular Front in France brought his release in 1936 and his resumption of the leadership of the Neo-Destour. Bourguiba was still in favour of a strong Tunisian association with France, but he wanted independence. He was opposed by the French *colons* and the local administration and no progress was made in direct negotiations with the French government.

The Popular Front fell in mid-1937 and the new government, preoccupied with the looming dangers of war, was far less sympathetic, particularly after Bourguiba organised a successful general strike in 1938. Widespread clashes with the police followed, martial law was proclaimed and both the Destour and Neo-Destour parties were banned.

Bourguiba was also challenged in mid-1937 by the return from exile of his boyhood hero Sheikh ath-Thaa'lbi who wanted to take control of the nationalist movement. A bitter power struggle developed.

Bourguiba emerged triumphant only to be re-arrested as his party was banned again. The French aimed to try him in France to avoid inflaming nationalist passions locally. After several months he was transferred to France in the spring of 1940, as the republic was about to be invaded by Germany. His trial never took place.

When the Germans pushed into the unoccupied regions of southern France in November 1942, they freed Bourguiba and other Tunisian nationalists in the hope of winning them over to the Axis.

Bourguiba spent the early months of 1943 in Rome where he made propaganda broadcasts attacking French colonialism, but he never went so far as to support the Axis powers. Bourguiba had an instinctive dislike of Fascism, and in any case the Axis powers would not guarantee Tunisian independence after the war.

In April 1943 he was allowed to return to Tunisia, then under the Vichy government. As the Allied forces closed in, Bourguiba refused German offers of evacuation.

After the end of the war in Europe he hoped Tunisian nationalists would be rewarded for their anti-German stance in the war, but again his demands met resistance from the *colons* and the local administration and no progress was made.

He came to the conclusion that the only way forward was to rouse international opinion and pressure the government from the outside. In April 1945 he secretly left the country to begin a four-year campaign to publicise Tunisian grievances. He took up exile in Cairo and worked through the Arab League.

In March 1947 he established the Committee for the Liberation of the Arab Mahgreb with other North African leaders. He also visited the USA and attended an early session of the UN in December 1946.

But while he was away a new, younger leadership under Salah Ben Yousuf was becoming disillusioned with Bourguiba's slow-moving international diplomacy and was demanding a still more rapid transition to independence.

In September 1949, the French protectorate authorities invited Bourguiba home in the hope that he would be a moderating influence, who might anyway help divide the nationalist movement still further.

Bourguiba accepted and was immediately restored to his place as leader of the party, although Ben Yousuf continued as Secretary General. Bourguiba revitalised the party and introduced special interest groups such as farmers, women, students into affiliated organisations. He also gave more influence to the *Union Generale des Travailleurs Tunisiens* the union that he had encouraged since its formation in 1946.

The French were at last ready for constitutional talks and prepared to accept internal autonomy. Bourguiba did not become directly involved but allowed Ben Yousuf to negotiate. By the end of 1950 the talks broke down in the teeth of strong opposition by the *colons*. A wave of protest strikes swept the country. Bourguiba again hoped that he could whip up international pressure and left on an extended trip, going to Paris at the end of 1951, just too late to break the deadlock in the talks.

He returned home to organise another round of protest and strikes. He was arrested in January 1952 along with the main activists and was imprisoned, first in the Sahara then on the island of Galit near Tabarka.

The breakdown of constitutional talks and the arrest of the nationalist leadership brought a classic response as the men of terror - the *fellagah* took up the armed struggle against government and settler targets.

The situation deteriorated until a new government under Pierre Mendes France declared itself ready to re-start talks. Bourguiba was invited to France to negotiate. Negotiations lasted almost a year while Bourguiba tried to raise the stakes to full independence rather than autonomy, but he recognised that Mendes France would not be allowed to concede more. Indeed, when the Mendes France government fell in February 1955, Bourguiba decided to seize what he had been offered. An agreement was finally signed in Paris on 2 June 1955, giving internal autonomy while preserving French responsibility for foreign affairs, defence and internal security.

But for the first time Bourguiba found himself in the camp of the moderates. The agreement was rejected by the exiled Salah Ben Yousuf, the old Destour and the Communists and by the right-wing colons.

Bourguiba nevertheless returned home in June to a hero's welcome. At the Neo-Destour Congress in October, Ben Yousuf mounted an unsuccessful challenge to Bourguiba's leadership and was expelled from the party. Later some of his supporters were shown to have set up a terrorist organisation to oppose the agreement. Ben Yousuf fled to Tripoli and many of his men were detained.

When France granted Morocco its independence, Bourguiba was quick to demand the same for Tunisia. After comparatively brief negotiations which ended on 20 March 1956, France recognised Tunisan independence and agreed to gradually withdraw French troops from Bizerta.

Bourguiba called elections and on 25 March saw his Neo-Destour party and its sympathisers win all 98 seats. On 11 April 1956, he became Prime Minister in the first government of independence and chose his own cabinet.

The first issue of substance was the withdrawal of French forces from Bizerta. France was reluctant to evacuate its troops because of the deteriorating situation in Algeria. Bourguiba tried to help negotiate a settlement, but his efforts were brought to an abrupt end when the Algerian leadership was kidnapped.

Tunisia immediately broke off diplomatic relations with the French and clashes broke out between Tunisians and French troops. He then set about creating alliances with neighbouring Arab states, experimenting with various forms of closer union with Libya. Diplomatic relations were restored with France and despite clashes over the Algerian war, negotiations finally resulted in the agreement of 15 April 1958 acknowledging Tunisian sovereignty over Bizerta.

Bourguiba took warmly to General de Gaulle when he assumed power in June 1958 and negotiated the final withdrawal of French troops.

Meanwhile he had been taking steps to strengthen his own position. In 1957 the last traditional ruler Amin Bey, was deposed and Bourguiba became nominal president. This title was confirmed on 1 June 1959 when a new constitution provided for the election of a president with a five-year mandate (renewable three times). He was empowered to lay down general policy, appoint members of the government and hold supreme command of the armed forces.

In the elections of 8 November 1959 he was elected unopposed and Neo-Destour won all 90 seats to the National Assembly. He was re-elected in 1964 and 1969 and in 1974 the National Assembly made him Life President.

He consolidated his position further in the late 1950s by turning on the Yousufists (Ben Yousuf himself had taken refuge in Cairo), putting them on trial for crimes such as misuse of funds and collaboration with the French.

Bourguiba was becoming increasingly autocratic and confident. He threw himself into an extensive programme of internal reform. His aim was to modernise and he started by tackling traditional Islamic institutions and practices. He eliminated *habus*, the Islamic system of putting land in trust, and the *sharia* courts. He gave women greater rights and brought all education under state control. He revealed his own stance by breaking the fast of Ramadan, saying that his country could not afford the loss of production involved in the month of fasting.

Within five years he brought virtually the entire religious establishment under state control, something he was to pay for later as the reaction set in and extreme Islamic groups began to confront him.

At first Bourguiba pursued laissez-faire economic policies, but hoping for a quicker breakthrough he appointed a young militant socialist Ahmed Ben Salah as Minister of Planning. On 11 May 1964 the Assembly passed legislation allowing the expropriation of all white settler land and Ben Salah was given Bourguiba's full support in his drive towards collectivisation.

His programme generated massive opposition and achieved little practical success. Bourguiba recognised the failure of the experiment and had no compunction in sacking his erstwhile protege, accusing him of corruption and putting him on trial for treason. He was found guilty and sentenced to 10 years imprisonment in 1969.

Bourguiba, by then known as the "*Supreme Combatant*", reversed Ben Salah's policies and introduced a free market. He appointed a new Prime Minister Hedi Nouira whom he designated as his successor. The new policies did stimulate foreign investment, but mostly of export oriented industries where employment opportunities were limited.

Bourguiba was becoming increasingly intolerant, unhesitatingly reshuffling ministers whom he suspected of opposition. In September 1974 at the 11th congress of the *Parti Socialiste Destourien* (PSD) he had himself elected President for life and appointed a cabinet almost entirely from party members. The New Assembly passed resolutions strengthening presidential power still further.

During the late 1970s Bourguiba was frequently ill, often travelling abroad for medical treatment. When he was absent Hedi Nouira lacked the dominant presence to keep control over increasing demands for democratisation and better pay and conditions for the workers. A gradual build up of tensions spilled over into the general strike of January 1978. There was serious rioting and over 50 people were killed.

Bourguiba reasserted control, put the trade union leadership on trial and broke the power of the unions. When Nouira died in March 1980 Bourguiba picked Mohammed Mzali as the new Prime Minister with instructions to liberalise the political environment and work out a new economic strategy.

Pardon was granted to 1,000 trade unionists who had been imprisoned in the 1978 riots and Bourguiba declared that he had no objection to the emergence of new political parties provided they were not dependent on foreign finance. He then called elections for November 1981. In the November elections the PSD and the reconciled trade unionists between them won all the 136 seats in the new assembly.

But further unrest and rioting broke out in January 1984 when the government, under pressure from foreign creditors, lifted food subsidies on bread and other staple foods. The government declared a state of emergency and Bourguiba considered the situation serious enough to restore subsidies. This undermined Mzali's position as Prime Minister and made it more difficult for him to handle social discontent in the years that followed.

By 1986 Bourguiba appeared to have been convinced by his right wing that the experiment in democratisation and in handling the unions gently had failed. He dismissed Mzali in July despite the opposition both of his son Habib and his wife, Wassila, whom he subsequently divorced. Mzali felt his position was serious enough to flee across the border to Algeria. The elections of November 1986 were boycotted by all the oppostion parties.

Bourgiba's preoccupation for the remainder of his rule was with the growing power of his old enemies, the Islamic fundamentalists. He became obsessed with the dangers of fundamentalism, supported by foreign powers, particularly Iran. To help deal with the perceived Islamic threat, he relied heavily on the Interior Minister Zine el-Abdidine Ben Ali, whom he made Prime Minister in October 1987.

Bourguiba appeared to have reached an age (84) where his good judgement and political acumen were deserting him. His mental facilities appeared to be deteriorating fast. He made appointments to top cabinet and state offices, then for no apparent reason revoked them within a few weeks. He claimed that plots were being hatched to overthrow him. He demanded a retrial of the Islamic fundamentalists, demanding death sentences rather than the prison sentences awarded by the courts in September. As his faculties deteriorated, he became both more dependent, yet more suspicious, of Ben Ali.

A recurrent bout of illness on 7 November 1987 gave Ben Ali the opportunity to intervene. Seven doctors were sent to his bedside to declare him senile and incapable of executing his presidential duties. He was indeed too ill to resist and Ben Ali was sworn in as President with the connivance of the majority of ministers and senior military officers.

Bourguiba, though unpopular, was treated with respect and allowed to retire to one of his residences at Mornaghia, near Tunis.

Within a few years the many holidays associated with his name were removed from the calendar, his statues were taken down and many streets and towns honouring him were renamed. It was as if his people wanted to obliterate the memory of his 30-year rule and his leadership of Tunisian nationalism over more than half a century.

Ambition Unfulfilled

NNAMDI AZIKIWE
1904-

Like many other great Nigerian leaders, Nnamdi Azikiwe was never able to emerge as the unquestioned ruler of his great country, competition from his peers and ethnic politics proved insurmountable. For a brief period from independence in 1960 he was Governor General and then President after the republic in 1963. These posts, held for only six years, brought prestige but no real power. He was deposed after the military coup of 1966 and was never able to make a come-back. Like many of his fellow Ibos, events forced him to change sides during the Biafran war and this further eroded his political credibility.

After the war, though he had immense international prestige and tried to reassert himself as an elder statesman, he found that a younger generation had taken over.

Flamboyant, irascible, sensitive of criticism, he was an idealist whose vision of national unity was dashed on the rocks of ethnic conflict leaving him unfulfilled, with memories of what might have been.

Nnamdi Azikiwe was born under a shooting star on 16 November 1904, in the Zungeru military camp of one of Britain's greatest colonial administrators, Lord Lugard. The comet that heralded his birth seemed to symbolically anticipate his meteoric life.

His father was a clerk serving the Nigerian Regiment. He followed a British administrator, Major Leonard, up the River Niger opening new administrative areas as Britain carved its Nigerian empire out of the bush.

Both his parents were Ibos, but he was brought up speaking fluent Hausa until he was sent back to his home town Onitsha, the gateway to his Ibo homeland, on the east bank of the Niger.

He was sent to Lagos in 1915, where his father was living at 189 Bamgbose Street. He won a place at the Wesleyan Boys' High School. His parents had just enough money to educate him, but nothing for luxuries. He was allowed to wear his only pair of shoes at Christmas time!

His parents moved back north, to Kaduna where he was summoned one holiday. He found his father had taken on a second wife. His parents quarrelled so much over this that he vowed to have one wife only and never succumb to polygamous temptations.

In 1921 he became a clerk in the Treasury office in Lagos and began to dream of a new life in America. He bribed some sailors and stowed away, but one of his companions became so seasick that they disembarked in Accra and he found a job with the Gold Coast police, before being persuaded to return home by his mother. His father admired his ambition to go to the USA and on retirement gave him his entire life savings of £300, enabling the young lad to set sail for the promised land in 1925.

He gained a place at Storer College, West Virginia and later transferred to Lincoln University earning his keep as a miner, dishwasher and gardener. His life in the US became a desperate struggle to survive. On one occasion he earned $10 fighting as a sparring partner against a professional boxer. Another time he attempted suicide, only to be dragged off the railway track at the last minute by a passer-by. He was eventually rescued by Dr. Locke of Howard University who gave him a job as a secretary. He went on as a graduate assistant to Lincoln University, where he wrote the much acclaimed book *Liberia in World Affairs* and later went to the University of Pennsylvania to do two years postgraduate studies for a Master of Science degree.

After nine years in the US he returned to a hero's welcome in Nigeria in November 1934. After a brief sojourn he moved to Accra, Ghana where he had been offered the editorship of the *Accra Morning Post*. He was charged with sedition and convicted, but escaped imprisonment on a legal technicality.

He returned home permanently in 1937 and founded the Zik Press which published the *West African Pilot* where he wrote editorials full of "long, technical and unusual words calculated to dazzle unsophisticated audiences."

Zik (the nickname which had stuck since his student days in the US) had spent the whole of the early part of his life fighting for financial solvency and advancing his career. His political involvement was far less calculated than that of other leaders such as Obafemi Awolowo (q.v.). In 1937 he joined the Nigerian Youth Movement (NYM) as a member of the executive committee, but not as an officer. And he insisted that the *Pilot* should give fair treatment to Herbert Macaulay's (q.v.) Nigerian National Democratic Party (NNDP) as well as the NYM. He supported the growing trade union movement and the break away African Church of Nigeria.

During the War in 1941 he sailed to Britain and there for the first time asked for self government and full responsible government within five years. On his return he left the NYM which was in its death throes.

In 1944 the National Council of Nigeria and the Cameroons (NCNC) was born out of Macaulay's National Council which had become an umbrella organisation for students, workers and the NNDP. Macaulay, the doyen of Nigerian politics became President and Zik the Secretary General of the new party. Zik took over when Macaulay died two years later.

In 1945 Sir Arthur Richards, a colonial governor of the old order, virtually imposed a new constitution without the consultation of nationalist leaders. Azikiwe began to campaign against its division of Nigeria into three federal states and the lack of provision for rapid Nigerianisation. This coincided with labour unrest and a prolonged general strike which Zik passionately supported. In July 1945 his paper was banned and he went into hiding in his home town, claiming that he had unearthed a plot to assassinate him.

But the government climbed down after the strike, promising an inquiry and no victimisation and Zik immediately became a hero. His stand during the crisis gave rise to the Zikist movement to protect him against the danger of attack and to act as a ginger group in nationalist politics. As time went on it became far more left-wing than Zik himself and he ultimately declared that he was "Not a Zikist!" But he did continue his agitation against the Richards constitution for the remainder of the 1940s.

A new federal constitution was introduced by the progressive governor, Sir John McPherson, in 1951. Though it had the broad agreement of most Nigerians, Zik did not like it because it introduced regional government rather than his grand design of a centralised country under nationwide NCNC leadership. Much power lay with the regional assemblies that elected delegates to the Federal Assembly. He felt he had been outsmarted by the British who had divided Nigeria.

But in the 1951 elections he stood for a Lagos seat in the Western House of Assembly and was duly elected. There he found himself as the opposition leader to a government led by his arch rival Obafemi Awolowo, whom he considered to be only a Yoruba leader, not a Nigerian nationalist like himself.

Zik had also miscalculated tactically because the Western House of Assembly, with its majority of Awolowo supporters, was not prepared to return him as one of their delegates to the Federal Assembly.

He began to agitate against the constitution and actually had some Federal ministers from his own NCNC party expelled for wanting to give the new deal a try. This caused chaos in the party leading to the dissolution of the Eastern Assembly. New elections were offered in May 1952 so Zik decided to move "back home" to assert his supremacy in the Eastern region. The NCNC won a sweeping victory and he became Chief Minister, then Premier.

But the McPherson constitution could not survive the struggle for power that ensued and Zik was one of those that hastened its downfall. He took part in fresh constitutional talks in London in July 1953 which resolved to achieve self government by 1956.

In 1956 the Foster Sutton tribunal was established to inquire into allegations that Zik had improperly invested regional government money in the African Continental Bank where he had a large interest. Zik's supporters claimed he had been victimised by the colonial government, but the impartial inquiry found that his conduct had "fallen short of expectations of honest, reasonable people." Afterwards Zik transferred his interests in the bank to the Eastern regional government.

He survived the scandal and further personality conflicts within the NCNC, while manoeuvreing to emerge in a stronger position on the Federal stage, even if this meant surrendering the Eastern region premiership which he had held since 1954. After the Federal elections of December 1959, he entered into coalition with the Northern People's Congress which had won the Federal elections. The new Federal Premier, Sir Abubakar Balewa (q.v.) offered him the Presidency of the Senate.

Zik had aimed higher. His objective since he returned to Nigeria in 1937 had been to emerge as the leader of a united country. Instead, when independence came in October 1960, the best he could get was the largely ceremonial office of Governor General, in charge of a country where ethnic factionalism was the prime political force.

He was honoured further by becoming President of Nigeria when Nigeria became a republic on 1 October 1963. Zik tried to rise above political conflict and establish himself as a national statesman. He worked well for a time with the continuing Prime Minister Balewa, but after the euphoria of independence tensions became more explicit.

In the elections of 1964 the NCNC decided to abandon its northern allies who had given it a grudging minority role in government and teamed up with Awolowo's Action Group. The two southern parties thought that by combining they could finally wrest power from the north, but in the heavily rigged and disputed elections they were bitterly defeated.

Zik could not remain impartial. He tried get the elections annulled and to postpone the appointment of Balewa as Prime Minister, but failed. Presidential powers under the independence constitution were proving to be strictly limited.

Zik was bitterly disappointed at having to preside powerlessly over a government that he felt had been fradulently elected. In October 1965 he left for England for treatment of a chest complaint as ethnic tensions exploded, with riots in the Western House of Assembly, plunging the nation into chaos.

While he was away in January 1966, the soldiers seized power in the first Nigerian military coup. He may have been lucky, as most of his colleagues in high office were murdered, but when he returned home he found he had been relieved of office.

He was identified with the old regime and withdrew to his country house at Nsukka. There he witnessed the trauma of his Ibo people who, after being violently driven out of the north, came flocking back to their homeland. As Nigeria slid remorselessly into civil war, Zik was driven to drop his ideal of national unity and to identify with the emotions of his people.

When civil war broke out he supported the Biafran cause and used his great influence internationally to seek diplomatic recognition and foreign support. He sat in the Biafran Consultative Assembly where he struggled with the Biafran militants and was frequently shouted down as a politician of the old order. They rewarded him by stripping him of the chancellorship of Nsukka University, an institution that he had done so much to found and foster. In 1968 he wrote a poem, "Be still my soul," which was later adoped as the Biafran national anthem.

He toured African capitals seeking diplomatic support for Biafra and attended peace talks in May 1968, in Kampala and in August 1968, in Addis Ababa.

When the war turned badly against Biafra, Zik urged the Biafran leader Odumegwu Ojukwu to seek a compromise solution with the Federal government, at peace talks in Paris. Ojukwu angrily ordered the Biafran delegation to return home. Zik decided that he had had enough and left for London. In 1969 he proposed a another peace plan in a speech at Oxford University.

His attempt to find a solution was matched by General Gowon the Federal ruler. Zik was able to take advantage of the improved atmosphere by returning to Lagos in August 1969. Gowon was at the airport to meet him.

He made an announcement on 28 August 1969, calling for a just settlement, "under the umbrella of One Nigeria." Zik toured the country repeating his message. Yet no official place was found for him. After the Federal victory another younger generation had taken over.

After the war in February 1972 he was installed as Chancellor of Lagos University.

He retired to his hometown and when the ban on politics was lifted in 1978 he was persuaded to join the Nigerian People's Party. He then fought the presidential elections of 11 August 1979, but came a poor third to Alhaji Shehu Shagari and Chief Awolowo, with only 2.8m votes to Shagari's 5.7m.

In 1983, as leader of the NPP, he threw his weight into yet another attempt by the southern parties to break the hegemony of the north. He combined with his old rival Awolowo and other smaller groups in the Progressive Parties Alliance, but neither man would give way on the question of overall leadership and another presidential challenge. As a result both he and Awolowo stood, split the southern vote and were again overwhelmed by the north united behind Shagari. Again Zik, with only 3.5m votes, came a poor third to Shagari with 12m votes and Awolowo with 7.9m.

Zik was nearly 80 and he virtually went into retirement after the 1983 elections and the military coup which followed shortly afterwards.

Man of All Cultures

LEOPOLD SENGHOR
1906-

Leopold Senghor is essentially a writer, poet and philosopher who turned himself into a politician and long-serving President of Senegal. He was one of the most outstanding prophets of "negritude" which was an assertion of African, or black, cultural values against French culture.

But the French culture of his upbringing never left him and as he grew older he became one of the most pro-French of all African leaders. He married a French wife and still spends much of his summers in France.

Politically he was disappointed because he failed to establish a strong federal system in West Africa and he had to spend a lifetime fighting against the deficiencies of an economy that depended on groundnuts and the social unrest that this created. His greatest achievement must be the way he overcame these disadvantages and successfully introduced democracy to his country, more than a decade before other African countries were swept in the same direction. He retired gracefully while still enjoying the respect and affection of his people.

Leopold Sedar Senghor was born into a prosperous Serer family, at Joal, a fishing village on the mouth of the Sine river, on 9 October 1906. His father was a middle-class planter-merchant and his mother a Catholic, in a predominantly Muslim country.

He was baptised and sent to a Catholic mission school in N'Gasobil, then to the Lycee Dakar, another mission school, where he continued his secondary education.

In 1928, at 22 years of age, he won a scholarship to Paris to continue his studies at the Lycee Louis-le-Grand where one of his schoolmates was Georges Pompidou, a future French President.

After obtaining his first degree there, he moved to the Sorbonne, to do his *aggregation* (a degree in more than one field) in African languages and literary studies.

He passed with distinction and went on to teach first in Tours (1935-39) and then in Paris. He was the first African to be appointed a professor at the Lycee of Tours.

In the 1930s he moved with a group of black intellectuals principally from the Caribbean, who frustrated with the French educational system and assimilationist ideas, were trying to establish a cultural base of their own. This was the period in which "negritude" was gestating. The word was first used by the Martiniquais Aime Cesaire in 1939. Starting as a typically French literary movement, it became a search for authentically African cultural values.

But for all this Senghor had drunk deep of French culture and had a fervent belief in democracy. On the outbreak of the World War he had no hesitation in joining the French infantry. He was taken prisoner and held in France until his release in 1942 when he worked with the resistance.

At the end of the war, the Brazzaville Conference of 1944 agreed to send African deputies to a Constituent Assembly in Paris. Senghor's political career began when he and another early nationalist leader, Lamine Gueye, formed the *Bloc Africain* and the two were returned as deputies from Senegal to the new chamber. He helped draft the constitution of the Fourth Republic, in November 1948, which gave Africans the right to sit in the National Assembly (Palais Bourbon). From November 1946 until November 1958 he was one of the deputies representing Senegal. The *Bloc Africain* aligned itself with the French Socialists (SFIO), but in 1948 Senghor took the key decision to leave the SFIO and join a new parliamentary group formed by those who had become disillusioned with their affiliation to French political parties. In the same year he formed the *Bloc Democratique Senegalais* (BDS) with its base in Senegal.

In the elections to the territorial assembly in 1951, Senghor's BDS, by appealing to the predominantly Muslim rural electorate, decisively beat Lamine Gueye, who still maintained links with the SFIO and drew his support mainly from the urban elite.

This was the beginning of the Senghor era. For the remainder of his political career Senghor, though frequently changing the name of his party, never lost control inside Senegal.

Unlike many of his contemporaries, Senghor also had wide interests outside politics. He and the poet Alioune Diop established the widely acclaimed cultural magazine *Presence Africaine* in Paris, to campaign for negritude and against cultural colonialism. Senghor contributed prolifically, writing poetry and articles about African art and culture.

Senghor was also politically active in Paris, ever campaigning for greater African autonomy. He became Secretary of State in the office of the Prime Minister Edgar Faure from March 1955 to February 1956.

During this period a struggle was developing between himself and Houphouet Boigny (q.v.) of the Cote d'Ivoire over the future shape of West

Africa. Houphouet wanted cautious advancement of autonomous states, while Senghor wanted the federation of all the Francophone states in West Africa. He claimed, "We must have an African community, before a Franco-African community."

To this end he formed the *Union Progressiste Senegalaise* (UPS) as the Senegal section of a wider Francophone *Parti du Regroupment Africain* (PRA). This wider federal grouping would, he hoped, counter Houphouet-Boigny's *Rassemblement Democratique Africaine* (RDA) that was then making all the running.

But, he had made no progress with his federal strategy, when in September 1958 de Gaulle asked all French African colonies to chose either autonomy within the French community, or complete independence. Senghor chose the lesser of two evils and got his people to endorse the French community by a huge majority.

He then rapidly organised a congress at Bamako for other pro-federal states which had made the same choice. The leaders of Senegal, Soudan, Dahomey and Upper Volta all discussed a federation that would be called Mali named after the great African empire of the 13th and 14th centuries.

But Senegal had hardly time to reorganise itself as a republic in January 1959, when the weaker federalists, under pressure from Houphouet-Boigny began to have second thoughts. When the Federation of Mali was finally formed in March, only Senegal and Soudan remained.

The flimsy structure, hastily cobbled together at a time of great political ferment could not take the strain. Soudan wanted to pursue far more radical policies, such as the expulsion of French troops and rapid Africanisation of the civil service and demanded greater autonomy. Senghor also had problems at home, so the federal experiment came to a sudden end in August 1960, after only just 18 months of existence. The two countries split and claimed their own independence. Senghor's federal dreams lay shattered and he had no alternative but to seek independence.

Senegal duly became independent on 20 August 1960 with Senghor as its President.

Senghor almost immediately began to repair his bridges with his fellow African heads of state, attending a series of meetings including one in January 1961 where the Brazzaville bloc was founded, grouping moderate Francophone states. They were later to form the backbone of the wider, pan-African Monrovia group which was to forge the Organisation of African Unity in 1963.

Meanwhile Senghor buried his differences with Houphouet Boigny and tried to encourage the maximum cooperation between Francophone states.

Internally Senghor became preoccupied in a power struggle with his brilliant young Prime Minister Mamadou Dia. Dia, in charge of the day-to-day running of government, soon proved to be far more leftist, authoritarian and ruthless than the President- philosopher.

After years of irritable tussling between them, Senghor in March 1962 announced the discovery of an alleged coup-plot which, he said aimed to overthrow the government by force. Dia was arrested, put on trial in May 1963 and condemned to prison for life. Senghor promptly held a referendum and won an overwhelming majority for a revision of the constitution. He then became Head of Government as well as President and swept to success in the elections of December.

But Senghor was too much of a democrat to insist on a one-party state. He always believed that it was best to allow a safety valve for opposition parties, while trying to absorb them into government whenever possible.

His problems in the mid-1960s were the decline in groundnut prices leading to economic hardship, wage freezes and union unrest. Students were also persistently troublesome. Following the Paris student's example, they started a major riot at Dakar University in May-June 1968. Only the firmness of the army prevented the government from being overthrown.

Senghor promised the students educational reforms and the promotion of a younger generation. He also revised the constitution re-creating the post of prime minister from 1970. His choice for the job was a young technocrat called Abdou Diouf who was given the task of restoring the economy.

In January 1973, elections returned both Senghor and the UPS with huge majorities but troubles recurred at the university. Students were expelled and the teachers' union was dissolved.

In March 1974 Mamadou Dia and his associates were released from detention. In the same year Senghor cautiously introduced political pluralism allowing the lawyer Abdoulaye Wade to register an opposition party. By 1976 he had decided on a three party system, calling his newly named *Parti Democratique Senegalais* (PDS) the "liberal and democratic party", Wade's PDS the "socialist democratic party" and even leaving room for a Marxist party.

Throughout his later years he showed that he had matured into a conservative reformer, wanting gradual change, but essentially within the existing structure of society. One of his major achievements was to gradually transform Senegal from a single-party into a multi-party state. He recognised that democratisation was inevitable more than a decade before the winds of democratic change swept Africa in the early 1990s.

Senghor scored an overwhelming victory under the new three party elections of February 1978 when he renamed his party yet again, the Parti Socialiste (PS).

In foreign policy he dreamt of a greater "Eurafrica", always maintaining good relations with France, while participating in all possible Francophone economic and political groupings. But relations with Guinea deteriorated particularly after the attempted invasion of Guinea by mercenaries in August 1970. In the recriminations which followed Sekou Toure (q.v.) called Senghor "a picturesque, negro Frenchman."

An irritant during his last years in power was the growth of a militant

Islamic movement financed by Libya and led by a prominent local firebrand, Ahmet Niasse, who went into exile in Libya and fomented trouble that eventually erupted in the Gambia, where Senghor had no hesitation in sending in troops to save the government of Sir Dawda Jawara from being overthrown.

At home the ever-worsening economic situation and the need for radical political change, led Senghor to announce in December 1980, that he would resign at the end of the month. Few thought he would do so as such a move was unprecedented by any African head of state in the two decades since independence. But he had reached his 75th year and had been shouldering the burdens of office since the 1950s. He wanted a well-earned rest, while demonstrating that an African head of state could hand over power in a democratic and civilised way.

Senghor had always said that he did not want to die in office. One of his famous aphorisms was, "In a democracy there must always be an after someone."

He maintained that when there was an excessive personality cult in dictatorial regimes, there was a danger of a coup and sudden change of policy. "A statesman must know when to retire," he said.

He was fortunate in being able to hand over early in January 1981 to Abdou Diouf, a man he had groomed as his successor for ten years, who was broadly in agreement with his policies. He also resigned the chairmanship of the party he had built from its earliest beginnings.

Senghor retired from public life, but remained an early riser and hard worker, writing extensively, attending international conferences and doing charity work. He spends much of the European summer living with his French wife in their house in Normandy.

Symbol of Reconciliation

NELSON MANDELA
1918-

Nelson Mandela became President of South Africa on 10 May 1994. By the time he was sworn in, as the first black president of this country, he had won the respect and love of all fair minded countrymen, regardless of their race or political persuasion. Though he had spent most of his active life in the prisons of apartheid he emerged unscathed, with no bitterness in his heart. Through 25 years of detention and harassment he remained a figurehead and a rallying force for everyone who wanted an end to apartheid in South Africa. On his release he assumed the role of a national leader determined to build a new South Africa, where there would be a place for all races, under a non-racial democracy.

Ever dignified, courteous, prepared to listen, he earned the adulation of his political friends and the profound respect of his rivals. Despite his advancing years he persuaded and negotiated, overcoming sorrow in his personal life - his divorce from Winnie and the loss of comrades in arms. He became a symbol of reconciliation, the leader of a new nation.

Nelson Rolihlaha Mandela was born on 18 July 1918, at Qunu near Umtata in the Transkei. His father was the chief councillor to the paramount chief of the Tembu (Xhosa), the largest single tribe in the Transkei, and was minor chief in his own right. Nelson's second name Rolihlala meant "One who stirs up trouble."

He spent his childhood at home near the Bashee river. His father died when he was only 12 and he came under the guardianship of his cousin, who tried to groom him for the chieftaincy.

Mandela was sent to Healdtown Methodist Boarding School, going on to Fort Hare University in 1938 to read law. He soon became involved in politics and met another keen young militant, Oliver Tambo, in the thick of a student strike which led to their expulsion from the university in 1940. Nelson refused to return permanently to the Transkei, where a tribal marriage was being arranged for him and took refuge in Johannesburg where he found work as a mine policeman. His relatives were still trying to persuade him to return home and inherit his father's chieftaincy, but he was resolved to make his way as an urban African, despite primitive living conditions, the pass laws and arrests and harassment by the apartheid police.

He met Walter Sisulu who helped him obtain his articles with a legal firm and encouraged him to continue his law studies by correspondence course. He gained a degree in 1941 then studied at Witwatersrand University for an LLB.

Tambo rembers Mandela as "passionate, emotional, sensitive, quickly stung to bitterness and retaliation by insult and patronage." But he had a natural air of authority. Tall and handsome, he was appealing to most women and worshipped by the politicised youth. He married his first wife Evelyn Mwase, a nurse, in 1944.

He and Tambo joined the ANC in 1944 and helped found the party's Youth League. In 1948 he was elected as the Youth League National Secretary. He helped draw up a programme of action to radicalise the party which was accepted by the ANC national conference in 1949.

In December 1952 he and Tambo established the first African law firm in Fox Street, Johannesburg. In the same year the ANC launched its defiance campaign against the race laws. Mandela was appointed the national "volunteer-in-chief" with the task of travelling South Africa to find others willing to defy the pass laws.

In December 1952 he and other colleagues including Sisulu were arrested and charged under the Suppression of Communism Act. He was sentenced to nine months imprisonment, suspended for two years and also served with a banning order preventing him from "belonging to any organisation," attending meetings or leaving the Johannesburg area.

These were impossible conditions and Nelson simply devised ways of getting round such repressive laws. He had become president of the Transvaal ANC and deputy national president and had added responsibilities because Chief Albert Lutuli (q.v.), the President of the ANC, had been banned to his home village.

The bans on Mandela himself were successively renewed so that he thought it better in September 1953 to resign officially from the ANC and exercise his leadership clandestinely.

On 5 December 1956 he and 156 other political activists were arrested and charged with high treason. The trial dragged on for nearly five years until he was acquitted on 29 March 1961. Mandela played an important part in the trial as many of the original defence lawyers, intimidated by the 1960 state of emergency, withdrew their services.

Immediately after his release Mandela defied the state of emergency and organised a massive stay-at-home protest as South Africa became a republic. He and over 1,800 activists were arrested and imprisoned without charge under the new regulations.

On his release he anticipated a renewal of his banning order, so he went into hiding and became known as the "black pimpernel" as he continued to rally and organise the ANC. Sometimes he dressed in a chauffeur's uniform and drove lesser personalities in his car to confuse the police. The regime's repression was so intense that Mandela came to the conclusion that the ANC needed its own armed wing. In June 1961 *umkhonto wa sizwe* (the spear of the nation), also known as MK, was formed as a guerrilla wing of the party. Though it was totally out of character for such a civilised and peace loving man, he became its first commander-in-chief.

He smuggled himself out of the country to address a conference of nationalist leaders at Addis Ababa in January 1962. He then went on to Algeria where he did guerrilla training.

On his return he was captured at a road block at Howick near Natal. He was tried at the old synagogue in Pretoria and on 5 August 1962 sentenced to five years' imprisonment. He began his sentence at Pretoria Central Prison, where he spent all his working hours in solitary confinement sewing mail bags.

While he was inside, the cream of the top ANC leaders were arrested at a clandestine meeting at their underground headquarters at Lilliesleaf farm, Rivonia, a suburb of Johannesburg. The police found documents concerning the manufacture of explosives, Mandela's diary of his African tour and a memorandum outlining a strategy in a future guerrilla struggle. He was brought from jail and put on trial with eight other ANC leaders and charged with plotting violent revolution. He was held in solitary confinement for three months between court sessions. His appearance shocked all those who saw him. He had lost weight and his skin had gained a prison pallor.

On 20 April 1964 he gave a memorable four and a half hour speech in his defence, extracts of which were later issued as a long-playing record. He said, "I do not deny that I planned sabotage. I did not plan it in a spirit of recklessness, nor because I have any love of violence. I planned it as a result of calm and sober assessment of the political situation that has arisen after many years of tyranny, exploitation and oppression of my people by the whites." His acts of sabotage had been directed against property not against people.

The trial lasted 11 months and on 12 June 1964, he along with eight others were sentenced to life imprisonment. They were sent to the notorious Robben Island prison where important political prisoners were detained. There, as prisoner No.466/64, he was subject to the harshest conditions being forced to break rocks with a hammer alongside his fellow prisoners. Yet his charisma was such that he continued to act as leader as he taught law to his fellow prisoners and educated himself.

Mandela was held on Robben island for 18 wasted years when he could have been making an important political contribution.

Visits from his new wife Winnie, a young social worker whom he had married during the treason trial, were heavily restricted. But as time went on his calm dignity, charisma and authority even gained the respect of some of his warders. Apartheid and repression were shown to have failed and world condemnation became ever more strident. A massive campaign for his release was launched in 1982. But President P. W. Botha was only prepared to release him providing he unconditionally renounced the use of violence. As outside pressure grew and doubts about apartheid policies were raised even in the ranks of government, Mandela, Walter Sisulu and others were transferred from Robben Island to Pollsmoor prison, Cape Town.

In August 1988 Mandela was diagnosed as having tuberculosis. Certainly his health was bad and this was the excuse given for transferring him from prison to Constantiaberg Clinic in September and then in December to a "suitable, comfortable and properly secured home," at Victor Verster prison near Paarl. By then the South African government was looking for a face-saving formula that would allow the release of Mandela so that political negotiations could be started with the most important African leader.

Contacts with government representatives had started in 1986 and continued, as the years went by, with increasingly senior ministers. In July 1989 Mandela was brought to the Tuynhuys, the residence of P. W. Botha for talks. When De Klerk assumed power in September, he made a meeting with Mandela a priority. The two met for the first time in December 1989.

Mandela was finally released, to scenes of great rejoicing and enthusiasm on 11 February 1990, after more than 25 years in detention. There was no bitterness in his heart, all he wanted to do was negotiate an end to apartheid and bring democracy to his people.

He adopted a pragmatic line in his first talks with government in May and the meetings which followed. He was able to negotiate a partial ending to the state of emergency and an amnesty of political exiles in return for a promise to abandon the armed struggle.

In June 1990 Mandela began a six-week tour of Europe, Britain, America and Africa explaining his case and bolstering his position as the voice of the South African people.

In addition to his political problems his personal life reached a crisis in May when his wife, Winnie, was sentenced to six months imprisonment on charges of kidnapping and being an accessory to the assault on four township youths and the death of one of them.

He was also faced with fighting between the supporters of the ANC and Chief Gatsha Buthelezi's Inkatha Freedom Movement.

The ANC held a national congress in Durban in July and Mandela had his leadership confirmed by being elected President. He also won the party's endorsement to continue negotiations with government and promised that all races would be protected in a future South Africa by a Bill of Rights guaranteed by an independent judiciary.

In December 1991, the long awaited all-party negotiations under the name of the Convention for a Democratic South Africa (CODESA) began at the Trade Centre outside Johannesburg. Mandela's ANC was pressing for a constituent assembly which it hoped would be in place by Christmas 1992. Mandela and de Klerk both clashed publicly so that they could begin negotiations from a position of strength, but both were resolved to keep the talks moving.

De Klerk showed his good faith by getting overwhelming endorsement in an all-white referendum in March 1992 for an end to minority rule.

Talks faltered for three months after the Boipatong massacre on 29 June when Inkatha supporters killed 42 people considered to be ANC supporters. The ANC complained of the lack of government protection. Mandela announced the suspension of further talks with the government and threatened to adopt the alternative strategy of "mass action." But too much was at stake and by September he was again in talks with de Klerk.

Negotiations stuttered forwards in 1993, despite bouts of fighting between the ANC and Inkatha and the suspicion of killings by an unidentified "third force" related to the security services.

Mandela remained remarkably well despite the strain on his health caused by long hours of work, ceaseless travelling, and tiring meetings. He survived the death of his old comrade Oliver Tambo, the assassination of the *Umkhonto* chief, Chris Hani, and divorce from his wife Winnie on the advice of the party.

He also suffered moments of black despair as his people were killed in seemingly pointless internecine conflict and clashes with the security forces. But negotiations inched forward. By May 1993 all parties adopted a declaration of intent and set a date for elections not later than April 1994.

As the year proceeded the ANC and government grew closer as the extreme right wing groups and Inkatha fought for more power for the regions and minority groups. Violence escalated and experienced analysts forecast the worst - even a prolonged and bloody civil war.

Mandela's vision was clear - he knew he must press ahead to hold the elections on schedule while using every effort to persuade even the most extreme sections of the community to take part. By making calculated concessions and extending deadlines he persuaded Inkatha to join the electoral process at the eleventh hour together with the most important extreme-right faction of the whites.

In April 1994 the elections went ahead on schedule in an atmosphere of almost total peace, calm and national reconciliation. The ANC swept 62.7% of the poll. Mandela's quiet confidence had paid off. A mood of relief and euphoria swept the country.

He was inaugurated as the first Black president of South Africa on 10 May 1994. All South Africans of goodwill recognised how fortunate they were to be blessed with so moderate and statesmanlike a leader. He had no bitterness in his heart. He called on his people to forget the past and build a new future; "Never, never and never again shall it be that this beautiful land will experience the oppression of one by another and suffer the indignity of being the skunk of the world. Let freedom reign."

The Eternal Idealist

JULIUS NYERERE
1922-

Julius Nyerere is highly regarded throughout Africa and the world as the father of his nation and as a humane and liberal-minded socialist and pan-Africanist. A handsome and intelligent man, he radiates charm and charisma that makes him one of the most beloved leaders in Africa. He is one of the few African presidents to have voluntarily stepped down from office.

He became leader of his country long before its independence in 1961. He ruled for 25 years and tried to involve all his people in his own homespun brand of do-it-yourself socialism. He was an idealist and his economic policies were hardly successful, but he did create a moral and social climate superior to the rest of Africa. He gave his people good educational standards and a pride in trying to do things the Tanzanian way.

Julius Kambarage Nyerere was born at Butiama near the eastern shore of Lake Victoria. His father, Chief Burito Nyerere, was a none too prosperous petty chief with 22 wives and 26 children. Julius was the son of the fourth wife.

His birthdate was in March 1922. The exact date is not known as no records were kept, but as it was raining he was named Kambarage after the rain spirit.

His tribe, the Zanaki, was one of the smallest among Tanzania's 113 tribes. He spent his youth helping the family as a herd boy, looking after his father's cattle. At the age of 12, wearing only an old piece of cloth, he was sent to primary school. He did exceptionally well and entered Tanganyika's only secondary school at Tabora, run on strict public school lines. He became a practising Catholic.

From 1943-45 he studied at Makerere, the University College of East Africa, where he gained a teaching diploma.

There were no political parties in Tanganyika at that time. The Tanganyika African Association (TAA) had been founded by a group of British colonial officers as a discussion forum for Africans, but African opinion was already demanding a more nationalist organisation. Nyerere became interested and organised a TAA branch while still a student at Makerere. After he qualified he did a spell teaching at St Mary's Mission School, Tabora which was run by the White Fathers.

The Fathers encouraged him to go to a British university. He was the first Tanganyikan student to go to Britain, studying for a general arts degree at Edinburgh University. There he had time to indulge his interest in politics, before returning home with a good degree. In Tanganyika he took up teaching again, but was resolved to start a political career.

In 1953 he became President of the Tanganyika African Association, though he saw this as only a stepping stone towards the formation of a new political party. On the seventh day of the seventh month of 1954 he founded the Tanganyika African National Union (TANU) and became its first President. He displayed an unusual talent for organisation and soon created one of the most united nationalist movements anywhere in Africa.

Tanganyika was a United Nations Trust Territory, administered by Britain since World War I, so Nyerere felt entitled in 1955 to take the anti-colonial case before the Trusteeship Council of the United Nations.

He returned home and using his huge charisma and persuasive charm, gradually built a strong following, organising TANU branches throughout the country.

In 1957 he was persuaded to serve as a member of the embryo Legislative Council but he resigned after four months' service, in December, because he felt insufficient political progress was being made. In 1958 he was convicted and fined for an article that he still denies writing in his party newspaper.

Despite his strong convictions he was always prepared to compromise and was persuaded to accept a "tripartite" election in which some seats would be reserved for Europeans and Asians.

There was no white settler tradition in Tanganyika and TANU swept to power in September 1958, helped by well-meaning whites and Asians who saw Nyerere as a moderate, straight talker, who could be trusted.

Nyerere campaigned on the slogan *Uhuru na kazi* – Freedom and Work and though he refused to take a ministry for himself he allowed members of TANU to take government posts.

At the time he was so keen that Tanganyika should share its independence with its neighbours Kenya and Uganda that he volunteered to delay Tanganyikan independence while the others caught up. But this was an idealistic dream. Kenya was still recovering from Mau Mau and Uganda was by no means united.

Further elections were called in August 1960 when TANU gained 58 of the 71 seats. In October the country was given self-government and Nyerere emerged from his party role to become Chief Minister. He remained in that post until Tanganyika won its full independence on 9 December 1961.

One month later he surprised everyone by resigning from the premiership to concentrate on reorganising the party and change it from battling against colonialism to becoming a force in building the new nation. He was ready to return to the centre of power as President on 9 December 1962.

In December 1963 the offshore island of Zanzibar was given its independence. One month later the inexperienced Afro-Arab government was overthrown. Coup hysteria spread rapidly throughout East Africa and affected Tanganyika when the Tanganyika Rifles mutinied and Nyerere came near to being deposed. He went into hiding and was forced to call in British troops to help put down the mutiny.

In April 1963 when the political leaders in Zanzibar had taken back the reins of power from the coup makers, he announced a union with the Zanzibar People's Republic to create the United Republic of Tanzania with himself as President. He thought it was the only way to control the politically tempestuous and racially divided islands just off the Tanzanian coast.

Internal opposition against him was almost non-existent and in June 1965, he was prepared to go along with the recommendations of a presidential commission to create a one-party state.

On 7 February 1967 he made his famous Arusha declaration speech in which he outlined an entirely revolutionary approach to African development. He announced the philosophy of *Ujamaa* (which means familyhood or sharing on a family basis). It was a philosophy of self-help, intended to tap the energies of his people rather than relying on foreign aid or assistance. He followed this initiative in 1970 with a policy of villagisation, a brand of rural socialism where people could come together in *Ujamaa* villages to co-operate in production and self-improvement. By the mid-1970s over two-thirds of the entire population was in *Ujamaa* villages. Some had been forced to move home.

Nyerere staked his whole future reputation on these initiatives which were unique in Africa. He tried to break away from conventional government and set up a form of socialism that would directly affect the lives of ordinary Africans.

He thought that the Tanzanian peasants, who form the vast majority of the population in his poor, undeveloped country would be happier living communally, sharing work, using common social services such as water, electricity, basic education and medical care. Meanwhile in the towns, he introduced state ownership by nationalisation of companies and financial institutions.

But this programme meant the total disruption of the way of life of Tanzania's peasants who were by nature conservative. They did not like being moved from their independent farms and landholdings to the villages where they were expected to spend a great deal of their time working for the common good rather than themselves.

They also found that the state marketing organisations, run as inefficient bureaucracies, resulted in worse farm prices than they were getting from the old free market system.

The economy was badly run. Food production actually fell despite massive, well-intentioned foreign assistance. Nationalisation did not work either. For the remainder of his career Nyerere was faced with the gradual realisation that his policies, though socially caring, had failed to build a growing economy.

In foreign policy his main concern during the 1970s was the coming to power of Idi Amin in Uganda and the ideological disagreements with capitalist-oriented Kenya. The twin strains led to the disintegration of the East African Community by the beginning of 1977.

Nyerere gave support to the former Premier, Milton Obote, and other Ugandan exiles and helped the attempted invasion of Uganda in September 1972. Later, following Ugandan provocations concerning the frontier, Tanzanian troops in support of Ugandan exiles successfully invaded Uganda in January 1979. Amin was toppled and Tanzanian troops remained behind until mid-1981 to preserve the peace.

Nyerere won the presidential elections of October 1980 with a mandate from 93% of the electorate. The 1980s were characterised by economic deterioration. Nyerere's *Ujamaa* and villagisation policies were not working, though he was not prepared to admit it. The bureaucracy had not been able to provide the basic support needed and Tanzania had been hit by drought and foreign exchange scarcity, leading to a shortage of even the most basic consumer goods in the shops.

Though Nyerere was still admired by the vast majority of his people he must have felt disappointed at the lack of practical achievement. In the mid-1980s he began to talk about stepping down from the presidency at the end of his term of office in 1985.

There were worries when his chosen successor Edward Sokoine was killed in a car crash, so efforts were made by the party to persuade him to stay in office. But when the presidential elections came on 15 August 1985 he did not stand and Ali Hassan Mwinyi, the Zanzibar President, was selected as the sole candidate and was sworn in on 27 October 1975.

Nyerere remained in the powerful position as chairman of the ruling party the *Chama cha Mapinduzi* (CCM) which he had fashioned out of TANU in 1977. Nyerere had always felt more at ease in the bosom of the party than as the leader of government. This reflected his strengths as a policy maker and ideologist rather than a leader of government.

Soon rifts between him and Mwinyi began to appear. He complained about Mwinyi's "unplanned retreats from socialism."

Though he originally intended to resign from national politics altogether, he became so worried at the course the new government was taking that, in October 1987, he was easily persuaded to accept the party chairmanship for another five years, in the hope that he could counter-balance Mwinyi's economic reforms.

He also gave himself more time for international activities such as the Chairmanship of the South Commission which tackles the urgent problems facing the Third World.

He began to express doubts about the efficacy of the one-party system early in 1990 and encouraged the debate which was to lead his country to multi-party democracy. He stood down from the Chairmanship of the CCM on 17 August 1990, allowing Hassan Mwinyi to assume full control.

But by 1993 he again emerged from semi-retirement this time desperately trying to defend the union that he had originally created between Zanzibar and Tanganyika. The move towards multi-party democracy had unleashed new nationalist forces, both on the islands and on the mainland and voices were raised for Tanzania to be divided. Nyerere resisted this trend vigorously in 1993, as if he was fighting his last major political battle.

Dignity in Defeat

KENNETH KAUNDA
1924-

For over 27 years Kaunda was one of Africa's longest serving heads of state. Throughout he wrestled with the problems of a small land-locked country heavily dependent on a single important export commodity, copper. He was an idealist, visionary, philosopher, almost a mystic. An emotional man, who often wept in public, fond of singing hymns and folk songs, he was conditioned by his Christian upbringing and faith. He attempted to introduce humanism and African socialism as his guiding philosophies, but he was not a consistent strategist and his grasp of economics and economic managment was minimal. Ultimately it was his failure to maintain the comparatively high living standards which Zambians enjoyed after independence, that brought discontent and his political downfall.

A tough political manipulator, for all his professed idealism, he survived by continually reshuffling his party stalwarts and ministers, but he was unable to cope with the criticism of a number of dissidents and the growing groundswell of unpopularity.

No rival of sufficient calibre was allowed to challenge him and he won his first six presidential elections without opposition. But he was not sufficiently aware of the wind of change that was sweeping Africa into multi-party government in the 1990s. He was insufficiently flexible to manipulate the political process so that he could retain power. Since his defeat in the elections of November 1991, he has retired and has won much sympathy for the dignity and graciousness with which he accepted defeat.

Kenneth David Kaunda was born on 28 April 1924 at Lubwa, near Chinsali in the north of the country. His Nyasa father was an ordained priest, who had become a teacher. His mother was one of the first African teachers in the territory. As the eighth child of a couple married for 20 years, he was called "*Buchizya*", the unexpected one. His family provided a strict moral background and he began his education in the Lubwa Church of Scotland Mission School, then Munali secondary school in Lusaka.

After teacher training, he returned in 1943, to the Lubwa Mission to teach. A brief spell of teaching in Tanzania followed before he became in 1947, the headmaster of his old school and the secretary of the Young Men's Farming Association, the political nursery of the Northern Rhodesia African National Congress.

He became the founder and the Secretary General of the ANC Lubwa, in 1948 and organising secretary of the whole party in 1950.

With tireless energy, he rose to become Secretary General of the movement and the deputy of the veteran nationalist leader, Harry Nkumbula.

He edited a militant ANC circular and had several brushes with the colonial authorities. He was passionately opposed to the proposed Federation of Rhodesia and Nyasaland, which came into being in 1953, regardless of African opposition.

In 1955 he was jailed by the colonial administration for possessing banned literature. Prison made him still more dedicated and ascetic. He gave up smoking and alcohol permanently, before his release.

In 1957 Kaunda visited England and then began a long tour of India, where he became ill for a time with tuberculosis.

He returned to find the party disillusioned with the leadership of Nkumbula who was vacillating over constitutional advancement. Kaunda broke with him in October 1958 and quit the ANC along with other young radicals. On 24 October 1958 he launched the Zambia African National Congress with himself as President.

In December 1958 he attended the first All African People's Conference in Accra, called by Kwame Nkrumah. He returned to continue his resistance to the new constitution. He won a reputation as a trouble maker as he ordered his party to boycott planned elections.

He was again arrested on 12 March 1959 and sentenced to nine months imprisonment for holding an illegal meeting. He was detained in a remote part of North West province where he became seriously ill with a recurrence of tuberculosis.

He was released on 9 January 1960 and setting his sights on independence, forged the United National Independence Party (UNIP) out of the old ZANC, on 31 January 1960.

He campaigned to break away from the Central African Federation and for immediate independence for Northern Rhodesia, through a massive campaign of civil disobedience.

He opposed Zambia's 1962 constitution, but when Nkumbula decided to contest the October elections, Kaunda also decided to compete. The election was inconclusive. UNIP did not win overall control, but joined in a coalition with Nkumbula's ANC to form, in October, the first government with an African majority. Kaunda became Minister for Local Government and Social Welfare.

By 1963 the Central African Federation had collapsed and a new constitution provided for self-government for the new state of Zambia. This time Kaunda campaigned vigorously and was rewarded with a landslide election victory. He emerged as the youngest Prime Minister in the Commonwealth on 22 January 1964.

After negotiating agreement on independence at talks in London in May 1964, Zambia became independent on 24 October 1964 with Kaunda as President. He had hardly assumed power, when he was forced to declare a state of emergency because white Rhodesia, under Ian Smith had unilaterally declared independence (UDI) on 11 November 1965. Britain consistently refused pleas to defend Zambia against possible Rhodesian attack.

Kaunda was also plagued with internal, tribal problems. Always an emotional person, who frequently wept in public, he reacted to the pressures on one occasion by resigning the presidency, but within nine hours he had reassumed office, commenting, "It was agonising for me. Party members were moaning and weeping."

Landlocked Zambia was almost cut off from the rest of the world by a blockade along the Rhodesian border and bad communications through other neighbouring countries.

Although Kaunda was re-elected President in 1968, he had lost much of the prestige and support he enjoyed in 1964.

By 1971 he was involved in a personality conflict with his talented Vice President, Simon Kapwepwe who broke with UNIP and formed the United People's Party. Kaunda arrested him and kept him in detention until the end of the year. He then made Zambia a one party state on 13 December 1972 and persuaded his old mentor Harry Nkumbula to join UNIP. Kapwepwe was released and eventually rejoined the party too, but he never fully regained Kaunda's confidence before he died following a stroke in 1980. Kaunda was duly returned for a third term as president in December 1973.

The fall in the price of copper and the closure of the economically important Benguela railway through Angola brought the first of a series of economic crises. Kaunda declared a nation-wide emergency in 1976 and put more power in the hands of the party.

Economic problems multiplied as Zambia failed to reduce its dependence on copper and the people fought to maintain their living standards. Kaunda took refuge in blaming external causes, particularly South African interference and rebutted his critics' accusations of economic mismanagement.

He was returned for a fourth term in 1978, though his election was a formality under the single-party, one-candidate system.

Zimbabwe gained its independence under Robert Mugabe in April 1980 and many of Kaunda's excuses for shortages of food and consumer goods were no longer valid.

In October 1980 there was an attempted coup in which several businessmen and UNIP colleagues were said to be involved. Kaunda blamed South African involvement, but tribal suspicion was at work, most of those arrested were Bemba, particularly from the mining areas.

Kaunda remained uneasy as further protest against economic deterioration came from universities, students and trade unionists. In December 1986 attempts to cure economic ills by introducing austerity measures and lifting food subsidies brought resistance from organised groups and rioting by the people. Kaunda claimed the trouble had been caused by his application of the International Monetary Fund's Structural Adjustment Programmes (SAP). He abandoned the SAP and tried to impose an alternative austerity programme of his own.

One of his greatest weaknesses was his failure to face up to economic realities. He had no clear strategy. Though he professed a nominal socialism, he experimented with mixed ownership, foreign ownership and state ownership according to the pressures of the moment. He went along with the IMF but then, in May 1987, dramatically broke with the organisation. He tried to cure Zambia's economic ills internally, but this style of readjustment was equally painful and foreign creditors refused to provide further assistance.

Kaunda played a leading part in the Organisation of African Unity (OAU) and among Front Line States. He also allowed the South African ANC to set up its headquarters in Lusaka. This brought reprisals and various attempts at destabilisation by South Africa. For many years he tried dialogue with South African leaders, but his initiatives were treated with suspicion by other African leaders, though he was senior and popular enough in Africa to be rewarded with the chairmanship of the OAU in 1987.

When he attempted again to eliminate food subsidies at the end of June 1990, three days of rioting and huge commercial damage followed, resulting in more than 29 deaths. Then came another attempted coup, easily suppressed, in which his people seemed to take a delight in the news (later proved false) that he had been toppled.

Opposition began to organise itself spontaneously, pressing for a multi-party system. Kaunda was reluctant to give way, but first his UNIP party and then the National Assembly declared themselves in favour of change. A serious opposition group, the Movement for Multi-Party Democracy (MMD), held massive rallies in different parts of the country at the end of 1990.

Reluctantly Kaunda set up a constitutional commission and on 7 December 1990 signed the bill to transform the nation to a multi-party democracy. The commission presented its findings in June 1991. It actually proposed a strengthening of presidential powers. The opposition saw this as a stratagem by Kaunda to take more power while allowing token democratisation lower down. It refused to attend talks on the new constitution and threatened to boycott the elections. Kaunda then compromised, talked to opposition leaders for the first time and agreed on a mutually acceptable constitution.

Kaunda's personal popularity was at an all-time low and reached its nadir at a soccer match in Lusaka, in July 1991, when he was pelted with oranges and empty beer cans.

Battle lines were then drawn for national and presidential elections in October 1991. The issues were multi-party democracy and mismanagement of the economy. UNIP was heavily defeated winning only 25 seats to MMD's 125. In the presidential elections of November, Kaunda himself was overwhelmed by the trade unionist Frederick Chiluba who won 972,753 votes to Kaunda's 310,761.

Kaunda had been in power for 27 years and never been defeated. It was a terrible blow to one of Africa's longest serving heads of state. It was the first time since independence that a president had been defeated at the polls, yet he retired gracefully, "My brother you have won convincingly," he told Chiluba, "and I accept the people's decision."

The new government claimed that it had inherited an empty treasury and that UNIP had paid out 50bn kwacha in a vain attempt to win the elections. Kaunda was even accused of salting away $4bn for himself in foreign bank accounts.

Kaunda denied the charges. He had never been personally corrupt and had always lived a modest and ascetic life, but during his long reign corruption had permeated the system, the state-owned companies and the civil servants determined to cling to power.

Kaunda was badly treated by the new regime. He was turfed out of State House without being able to retrieve all his personal effects. He was forced to rent a house in a Lusaka suburb. For more than two years he waited for the pension to which he was entitled under the constitution while the government carried out inquiries. He was even accused of having removed some books from his former library at State House.

Early in 1992 he announced that he was quitting politics altogether. He stepped down from the leadership of UNIP at the party congress in April. He decided to concentrate on the establishment of a Kenneth Kaunda Foundation. This would work for peace, democracy and the development of Africa, through an Institute of Peace and Democracy and a Kaunda Fellowship Programme, which would endow outstanding students.

Even his most implacable opponents acknowledged the way he bore his fate and his dignity in defeat.

Man Behind the Mask

ROBERT MUGABE
1924-

Robert Mugabe, a bespectacled intellectual, always gives the impression of being a university professor dragged reluctantly into the political limelight. He has little of the charisma and geniality of other great African leaders, yet he has proved himself a man of dedication and principle. He fought hard and long to emerge as the outstanding Zimbabwean nationalist leader. Hard work, political acumen and brilliant organisation as a guerrilla leader took him to the top. Since then he has never been seriously challenged.

Once in power he showed himself to be more of a pragmatist than the Marxist, that he insisted, he was. He wanted to maintain national unity and racial harmony while improving the economic lot of his people. At first he hoped to do this by eliminating tribalism and forging a one-party state. Later he put the emphasis on land redistribution, but at every stage he revealed his reluctance to force his will on his people. He proved remarkably hesitant and pragmatic over major issues. He was even prepared to change his mind over his ambition to achieve a single-party state. He has triumphed in successive elections and has remained faithful to a consistent ministerial team, but in recent years his popularity has waned. His people are beginning to say that he has been in power too long, but they cannot point to an obvious replacement.

Robert Mugabe was born at Kutama mission in Makonde district, in north-west Mashonaland. He was the son of Gabriel, the mission carpenter. He was educated at local mission schools and completed his secondary education and early university studies through correspondence courses, qualifying as a primary school teacher in 1941. He taught in Mpanzure, Dadaya and Empandeni mission schools (1942-45), before going to Fort Hare University, where he received his political awakening by learning of the South African peoples struggles and joining the African National Congress. He graduated with a BA in English and history in 1951.

He returned home in 1952, resolved to fight white rule. But he had to work within the system and earn a living, so he resumed teaching at Briefontein Mission, near Umvuna. He studied by correspondence course to get an education diploma while teaching at Mbizi government school at Highfield, Salisbury (Harare), then Mambo near Gwelo.

He was a quiet, intense, almost humourless character. A white liberal who knew him well described him as "rather a cold fish." In 1955 he moved to Northern Rhodesia to teach at Chalimbana Teacher Training College. He continued correspondence courses, winning a BSc from London University.

In the autumn of 1957 he went to Ghana, then on the threshold of independence, and taught at St Mary's College. It was an exciting time as he witnessed the first African country to gain independence from Britain and it was there that he met his future wife, Sally Hayfron. The example of Kwame Nkrumah (q.v.) and the Zambian leaders Harry Nkumbula and Kenneth Kaunda (q.v.), whom he had met earlier, spurred his interest in politics and gave him a new ambition in addition to his academic life.

He stayed in Ghana until May 1960, then returned to Salisbury to plunge into politics as publicity secretary and youth wing organiser of the National Democratic Party (NDP). He opposed the constitutional proposals initiated by the British for African representation in parliament. The Africans were only offered 15 of the 65 seats.

The NDP was banned on 9 December 1961 and he became deputy general secretary of the emerging Zimbabwe African People's Union. In 1962, ZAPU was also banned and he was arrested several times in 1962 and 1963. While he was released on bail, he and his wife Sally, escaped the country and travelled to Dar-es-Salaam, Tanganyika. There he broadcast regularly on Radio Tanzania's programmes beamed to Zimbabwe.

ZAPU split in 1963 and Mugabe joined the faction led by Ndabaningi Sithole, which formed the Zimbabwe African National Union (ZANU). He became the party's secretary general. On his return to Salisbury in August 1963 he was arrested for a broadcast that he had made in Dar-es-Salaam. Released on bail, he was rearrested in August 1964 for making a "subversive speech" and was again served with restriction orders.

He was to remain in detention for the next decade. He put his time to the best possible use, obtaining an LLB and BA (Admin) from London University by correspondence courses and spent much time teaching other prisoners. While he was still in detention he was elected by ZANU executive committee in November 1974, to replace Sithole as the leader of the party. The committee did not trust Sithole and had more faith in Mugabe's sharp and logical mind for the forthcoming constitutional talks.

International pressure eventually forced the Prime Minister, Ian Smith, to release the nationalist leaders in December. Mugabe was set free along with Sithole, Joshua Nkomo, and others but no settlement was reached and the guerrilla war continued. Smith tried to arrange an internal settlement with Bishop Abel Muzorewa, but Mugabe remained opposed.

Following factional fighting and an internal rebellion, a leading nationalist leader Herbert Chitepo was assassinated in March 1975. This caused considerable disruption in ZANU with Mugabe emerging as the unchallenged leader of the hard liners in the party who could see no possibility of an agreement with Smith.

Mugabe decided that the only way forward was to organise an armed struggle in exile. In April he went to Mozambique. His job was to reorganise the ZANU armed wing and make good some of the huge losses the guerrillas had been taking in the fight against the Rhodesians.

But international pressure for a settlement continued and Mugabe led the ZANU delegation to the Geneva peace conference in October 1976. In order to present a common front he also arranged for an alliance with Joshua Nkomo's ZAPU in the Patriotic Front. The talks dragged on for weeks before breaking down.

It was at this stage that Mugabe was elected ZANU President and the commander-in-chief of the Zimbabwe African National Liberation Army, (ZANLA) at a ZANU congress in Chimoio in 1977. Neighbouring African leaders who had been backing different guerrilla leaders also reconciled themselves to his leadership.

For the next three years he concentrated on the armed struggle, building international support and securing arms and training for his men in Mozambique. Meanwhile Smith and Muzorewa tried to achieve an internal settlement. But by now the guerrilla war was going Mugabe's way. He had proved himself the supreme nationalist leader and the best organiser and began seriously to sap the strength of the Rhodesian forces.

International pressure for a permanent solution intensified. Mugabe thought the time was right and led the ZANU delegation to the Lancaster House conference in London, in September 1979. The talks dragged on for three months but they were successful and on 27 January 1980 he returned to Zimbabwe to organise the pre-independence elections. The scale of his victory surprised observers. He took 63% of the votes and 57 seats, while Nkomo gained only 24% of the votes and 20 seats.

The following day Mugabe agreed to form a coalition government, appointing members of ZAPU in his cabinet, including Nkomo as Minister of Home Affairs. Mugabe was formally installed as Zimbabwe's Prime Minister at independence on 18 April 1980.

Mugabe the cool, prickly, pragmatist was overcome with emotion on taking power from Lord Soames after 89 years of white rule. Mugabe said of Soames, "I must admit that I was one of those who originally never trusted him. And yet I have ended up not only implicitly trusting him but also fondly loving him as well."

Mugabe was faced with an enormous task. He was still considered to be a hard line Marxist with commitment to land resettlement and rapid Africanisation. But he began cautiously, not wanting to wreck a viable economy. He urged the white farmers to stay and build the new country.

Political trouble came soon first from his old colleague in arms, Edgar Tekere, who felt that he was not being radical enough and later from Joshua Nkomo, who was still resentful that he had not emerged as the national leader. The Matabeles were also smarting from their electoral defeat at the hands of their despised rivals the Shona. Mugabe claimed that Nkomo was behind the terrorist groups that still operated in Matabeleland and arrested many of Nkomo's top lieutenants after the discovery of arms caches on their property.

Mugabe first demoted, then sacked Nkomo altogether on 17 February 1982. This sowed the seeds of trouble in Matabeleland and caused Nkomo's flight into exile in London. Mugabe crushed the Matabele discontent with unexpected ruthlessness and raised a storm of international criticism. He also curbed the excesses of the more radical of his own lieutenants and detained Bishop Muzorewa for suspected links with South Africa, in November 1983.

On 8 August 1984 ZANU held its first congress since it was first founded 20 years earlier. It adopted a new constitution which strengthened Mugabe's position and endorsed the aim of establishing a one-party state.

An election was held in June 1985. Mugabe triumphed again increasing ZANU's share of seats from 57 to 63 and reducing ZAPU's from 20 to 15. Nkomo returned from exile in August 1983 and Mugabe gradually developed dialogue with him to restore peace in Matabeleland and achieve political unity.

Mugabe wanted to establish single party government, but progress was slow and subject to many reverses; he wanted consensus first. In April 1987 he appeared to have lost heart and said that the unity talks had been abandoned. But they were revived and after two years a unity agreement was finally signed with Nkomo in which ZAPU was effectively absorbed into ZANU-PF (Patriotic Front).

Meanwhile Mugabe abolished the 20 seats that had been reserved for whites under the constitution, despite the fierce resistance of his old rival Ian Smith. ZANU's overwhelming victory had also given him a sufficient majority to change the constitution so that the post of prime minister could be absorbed into a new executive presidency. On 31 December 1987 he became Zimbabwe's first Executive President.

A major corruption scandal involving some of his top ministers occurred at the end of 1988 over the acquisition of vehicles from the Willowvale assembly plant. Mugabe appointed a judicial inquiry and sacked some ministers, but pardoned others and incurred vocal protest from students and trade unionists.

This stimulated the creation of Edgar Tekere's Zimbabwe Unity Movement when Mugabe was trying to finalise the creation of the one party state. This was passed at the ZANU-PF congress in December 1989, but only in the face of bitter opposition outside the ruling party.

Mugabe put the corruption issue to the electoral test in the elections of March 1990. Though there were allegations of intimidation and ballot rigging, he triumphed in the presidential elections by 2.03 million votes to 413,840 for his rival Tekere, while ZANU won even more convincingly taking all but four of the 120 parliamentary seats. The margin of victory underlined Mugabe's dominance and allowed him to resist the wind of change that was sweeping the rest of Africa in favour of multi-party democracy.

Opposition to a one-party state was growing even in the ranks of his own party. On 22 August 1990 the ZANU-PF politburo voted against formalising the single-party system. Mugabe, ever the pragmatist, let it be known that he was prepared to bow to majority opinion.

In January 1991, he went further, saying that he had accepted the wishes of the majority and that he now applauded those African governments that were embracing pluralism.

On 22 June 1991 ZANU also decided to abandon its theoretical attachment to Marxist-Leninism. Mugabe said that radical leftism was being cast aside all over the world so there was "no reason to continue to stick to it."

1992 started sadly when his Ghanaian wife, Sally, died of kidney failure in January. He took this badly and was not seen often in public. As the year continued a whole host of new opposition parties were formed but none had the leadership, financial resources or organisation to challenge ZANU-PF and Mugabe was able to continue to rule virtually unchallenged.

Despite Mugabe's rhetoric he had done very little in the way of transferring white-owned land to landless Africans. In March 1992 a tough bill was passed by parliament which opened the way to buying out about half of the land owned by white farmers, but real transfers were slow in coming. In July 1993, 27 farms were designated against the wishes of their owners and a wave of protest erupted. But Mugabe remained unrepentant: "If foreign investors do not like it, they should not come to Zimbabwe," he said. Later in the year he embarked on a round of speeches blaming Western interference, "How can those countries who have stolen land from the Red Indians, the Aborigines and the Eskimos dare to tell us what to do with our own land?" he said.

Further trouble came from students and trade unionists dissatisfied over state mismanagement, high level corruption in government and the need for economic reforms and stringent cuts in government spending.

As Mugabe headed towards the 1995 elections popular discontent with himself and his party was growing, but the opposition remained incapable of finding the unity, policies or leadership to provide the opposition required.

Surviving Tyrant

MOBUTU SESE SEKO
1930-

Mobutu has survived nearly three decades of violence, political chaos, guerrilla warfare and economic disintegration in his vast inpenetrable country. He is Africa's longest surviving tyrant.

A vain, acquisitive, despotic leader who has always identified himself with the state. He acted fast and ruthlessly to overcome successive crises including the wind of democratic change of the 1990s. He survived because of his control of the army and the national finances.

A hard worker, voracious reader and great traveller, he extended his power from army to government, from government to party, and from party back to the army, to resist every challenge. But he now presides over a country that is politically divided, unstable and economically bankrupt. Zaire has never known peace nor had sound government since he has been at the helm.

Joseph Desire Mobutu was born on 14 October 1930, at Lisala in Equateur province. It was near to Oubangui, then called Banzyville, from which he later took the journalistic pseudonym "Jose de Banzy".

His father died when he was eight years old and he was sent for primary and secondary education to Mbandaka, where he was expelled for throwing ink at a Belgian schoolmaster. He was then conscripted into the Force Publique on 14 February 1950.

He was trained as an accounts clerk and did six years' service, rising to the rank of sergeant. Secretly he dabbled in journalism under his pseudonym Jose de Banzy. He left the force in 1956 and went to the capital for a full-time journalistic career with the local newspapers *L'Avenir* and *Actualites Africaines* rising to become editor.

He went to Brussels to do a course in social studies and journalism, before going to work for the news agency, *Inforcongo*. Mobutu who was already a member of the *Mouvement National Congolais* (MNC) was glad to give hospitality to the party leader, Patrice Lumumba (q.v.), on his trips to Belgium. He organised the MNC office in Brussels and was the delegate, approved by Lumumba to the important round table conference in January, April and May that led to the Congo's independence. During this period he returned to Kinshasa as Lumumba's secretary of state.

At independence, in July 1960 he was appointed to the key position as Chief of Staff, second in command of the army. Army mutinies erupted a week after independence and he travelled round the country by plane trying to restore morale and discipline. He built a following in the army as the country disintegrated, Katanga declared secession and President Joseph Kasavubu and Lumumba struggled for power.

Early in September Kasavubu dismissed the army commander and announced that he was arresting Lumumba. Mobutu weighed his personal loyalty to Lumumba against doubts about growing national instability and decided to intervene, suspending both him and Kasavubu in his first military coup of 14 September 1960.

Mobutu was not ready to take power entirely for himself. Instead he set up a College of Commissioners, 15 young university graduates to run the machinery of government, but he retained effective control through the army. He concentrated on rebuilding the army and displayed great personal courage in dealing with mutinous troops. He solved the problem of dealing with Lumumba, who had escaped after being held under house arrest, by sending him on a plane to Katanga where he was killed.

Katanga secession was ended in January 1963, largely through the efforts of the United Nations, but immediately Mobutu was faced with widespread rebellions in Kwilu, Kivu and Stanleyville.

Mobutu was promoted to Lt.General on 11 November 1964, while Kasavubu struggled on with a minority government and a new rebellion in Katanga. This unstable situation prompted Mobutu and a group of officers to seize power on 23 November 1965. He found himself in charge of a country riven with violence, political chaos, armed rebellion and provincial secession. He started by centralising goverment, reducing parliament to a rubber stamp and extending his personal power to all important decision-making bodies.

He introduced a new constitution and started his own party, the *Mouvement Populaire de la Revolution* (MPR) which became the single authorised party, then the supreme organ of state.

Mobutu was the sole important survivor since independence and had shown his vanity, ambition, cool calculation and courage at every stage in the crisis. He began to impose himself as an authoritarian leader and deliberately developed a cult of personality around his name.

In October 1971 he came up with his policy of "authenticity" whose objective was to "decolonise" his people's minds and make them proud of their African origins. He started by renaming the Congo as Zaire and by getting all citizens to drop the missionary-given Christian names and take on authentic (traditional) African names.

Authenticity gave the people a major psychological boost, but Mobutu's headlong rush for Africanisation and nationalisation of industry and estates, as well as his dependence on a badly trained civil service and a poor party infrastructure, soon brought economic chaos. Bribery and corruption became rampant, government expenditure soared and Zaire became Africa's first major debt-crisis nation.

To rescue himself from this situation Mobutu turned to the International Monetary Fund which tried over the years to bring financial discipline to Zaire's economic affairs, but even though the IMF had resident experts running the economy and monitored appointments to the governorship of the central bank, it could not balance the books or restore financial propriety.

In this Mobutu was personally to blame. He used state funds as if they were his own and gradually made himself one of the richest men in the world with huge foreign bank accounts and properties in the choicest European sites.

In foreign policy Mobutu turned to the USA which saw him as a tough ruler who alone could maintain stability in his vast and impenetrable country. Mobutu was seen by the Americans as a bulwark against communism and a counter-poise to the leftist regimes.

Inside Africa he projected the position of Zaire as one of the most important and influential African countries, equalling Nigeria. He highlighted Zaire's comparatively small population and its huge, untapped economic resources. Mobutu retained close links with the Israelis, though he did break official diplomatic links between 1973-82 following pressure by fellow African heads of state. After the Camp David agreements he renewed relations and has since benefited by techincal and military assistance from Israel. He has also consistently supported UNITA in Angola and has provided the means by which Jonas Savimbi has maintained his battle against the Angolan government.

Opposition parties inside Zaire began to multiply by the mid-1970s and Mobutu was challenged by the rump of the old secessionist movements in the Katanga uprsisings of March 1977 and May 1978, which were only crushed with the assistance of French and Belgian paratroops. Other opposition groups continued jungle warfare in the extreme east of the country.

In April 1981 Nguza Karl I Bond, Mobutu's Prime Minister and most likely heir, went to Belgium, resigned and began to attack his master's corruption. It was not until June 1985 after lengthy negotiations that the dispute was settled and Nguza returned, soon to be brought back into government.

Meanwhile more logical political opposition was growing in the shape of the *Union pour la Democratie et le Progres Social (UDPS)* which actually dared to criticise Mobutu in the Assembly of March 1982. Mobutu detained his critics and only released them when Western nations began to criticise his human rights record.

In January 1988 the UDPS leader, Etienne Tshisekedi, was arrested and began a long struggle against Mobutu in which he emerged as the outstanding opposition leader from a new generation of critics.

Mobutu's love-hate relationship with Belgium, the former colonial power, exploded into a major row at the beginning of 1989. It started when Mobutu scornfully declined a Belgian offer for some debt remission. The quarrel blew into a major storm in which the Belgian press exposed the huge amounts of money that Mobutu had taken from the Bank of Zaire for his own use and the extent of his foreign properties.

With the wind of democratic change blowing through Africa in 1990, Mobutu came under intense pressure to change his tyrannical single-party system. The economy was plunging into chaos with inflation soaring. An international outcry erupted following the massacre of more than 100 demonstrating students by troops at Lubumbashi University in May.

Hoping to defuse the mounting tide of opposition, Mobutu decided to introduce a multi-party system and announced his resignation from the MPR so that he could "rise above" party politics. He set up a special commission to draft a new constitution by April 1991 and allowed opposition parties to operate freely.

These moves unleashed a wave of hitherto suppressed political activity. Opposition parties proliferated and personal attacks on him became ever more daring. Calls even came for him to resign. Mobutu set up a transitional government and desperately reshuffled his ministers, even trying to recruit Etienne Tshisekedi as his Prime Minister.

Finally a national conference was called on 7 August 1991 attended by over 200 political parties. The atmosphere was electric as Mobutu tried to pack the conference with MPR delegates. He failed and came under persistent personal attack with Tshisekedi threatening that he would be imprisoned if he lost power.

Mobutu had lost the sympathy of the West and the economy was disintegrating. Now he was being treated with contempt by the national conference. But the wily old fox was far more experienced than his opponents and soon learnt to play them off against each other.

He disregarded the resolutions of the conference and reshuffled his government bringing back his old opponent Nguza Karl I Bond as his new, tough-guy Prime Minister. He suspended the National Conference as riots and strikes rocked the country. But internal and foreign pressure forced the resumption of the conference which continued its efforts to overthrow him.

Mobutu used all his political wiles to ensure his survival. He even tried for a brief period to work with Tshisekedi as his Prime Minister, but when cooperation with his foremost challenger became impossible in October 1992, he sent in the troops to close and intimidate the Conference and won himself a further reprieve.

The national conference finally ended in December 1992 resolving to set up a new parliament under Tshisekedi and to reduce the powers of Mobutu to that of a purely constitutional figurehead.

But Mobutu refused to accept these changes, depending as a last resort on his control of the army and the central bank. He repeatedly demonstrated his power by encouraging his troops to go on the rampage, terrorising the population of the capital.

On 15 January 1993, the High Council found him guilty of high treason and called for a general strike and campaign of civil disobedience, but Mobutu simply absorbed the ensuing chaos and the continuing foreign criticism.

On 5 February Mobutu tried to dismiss Tshisekedi, blaming him for the riots and troubles, but Tshisekedi refused to surrender office claiming that he had been democratically appointed by the High Council.

Mobutu responded by appointing his own prime minister and cabinet to head a parallel government. This was not recognised by most Western governments, but Mobutu knew that as long as he could pay his army and maintain its loyalty he could cling to power and he did so for the whole of 1993.

Slayer of Apartheid

FREDERIK DE KLERK
1936-

Frederik de Klerk was the man who brought apartheid to an end in South Africa. Always a political realist, he overturned the apartheid policies that he had practised for the whole of his lifetime and his people had believed for generations.

It appeared to be a blinding and sudden conversion for this quiet, moderate, even tempered man. Once he recognised that a revolutionary change was needed, there was no going back. He released Nelson Mandela and resolved with him to achieve the smoothest possible change to majority rule. No task could have been more difficult in the face of generations of hatred and misunderstanding on both sides of the race barrier, but de Klerk was ideally suited to his new role.

Though a worrier and a chain smoker he developed a bland, smiling exterior in the face of the violence and bitter disagreements of the transition process. His calm dedication matched that of Nelson Mandela and the two irrevocably changed the course of South Africa.

Frederik Willem de Klerk was born on 18 March 1936 into a powerful, political family in Johannesburg. His great grandfather was a senator, his grandfather was a member of parliament and his aunt married Prime Minister J. G. Strydom.

His father, Jan de Klerk was the General Secretary of the Transvaal National Party from the watershed year in 1948, when the Nationalists took power and introduced apartheid. Jan became Minister of Labour and Public Works in 1955 and held other ministries before he became President of the Senate in 1968, a post he retained until his retirement in 1976.

At the time of Frederik's birth his father was a school principal living in Johannesburg. Frederik completed his matriculation at the Hoerskool Monument in Krugersdorp.

He became politically involved as a youngster, joining the youth section of the National Party (NP) while still in his teens. He later served on the executive of the *Afrikaanse Studentebond*, then the "finishing school" for future leaders of government. He became the editor of the campus newspaper at Potchefstroom University where he graduated in law in 1958 with a BA LLB (cum laude). He then travelled to England on the Abe Bailey Travel Scholarship.

He took his articles at Klerksdorp and Pretoria, then went on to practice as a small town attorney at Veereniging from 1961-72. There he also served as chairman of the local council of the National party. He also became chairman of the local Law Society and served on the council of the Vaal Triangle College for Advanced Technical Education.

He became chairman of Administrative Law at Potchefstroom University. When the local MP was posted abroad as an ambassador, de Klerk, at the age of 26, contested and won the Potchefstroom seat in November 1972.

He was returned again, unopposed, in 1974 and moved quickly through the party structures serving on a range of select committees and commissions.

On 3 April 1978 he was appointed Minister of Posts and Telecommunications by the Prime Minister P. W. Botha. Though he was repeatedly reshuffled, he remained a key member in the cabinet, holding many different ministries. As Minister of Home Affairs his progress towards scrapping the Group Areas Act and the Immorality Act was painfully slow. He laid great stress on "Community control" whereby residents would decide who should be admitted to live in their home areas.

As Education Minister (1984) he came under fire for a bill which proposed harsh controls over political activities on university campuses, with swingeing financial cuts for universities which did not apply them. His bill was challenged in the courts and he was finally forced to withdraw it.

The NP split in 1982 and some members defected to the right wing Conservative Party in reaction to Botha's introduction of a three-chamber parliament where coloureds and Indians were given seats for the first time. He did a lot to heal the divisions within his own party. His reward was to win the leadership of the party in the Transvaal on 6 March.

With the advent of the tri-cameral constitution he became chairman of the Council of Ministers in the House of Assembly on 1 December 1986, while retaining the National Education portfolio.

But he had by no means been converted to liberalism. In 1988 he came out strongly against the head of the South African rugby board Dr. Danie Craven, who held talks with the African National Congress in Harare. He said that he was shocked that Craven had by-passed the government and had "turned to a terrorist organisation." He said that the talks with the ANC were absolutely unacceptable.

His hour of triumph came when President P. W. Botha had a heart attack on 18 January 1989. Hurried elections were called on 2 February 1989 to find a new leader of the NP. De Klerk was widely liked in the party. He had charming manners and ready smile. A bland exterior masked a good political mind, yet he was respected rather than feared. There were several fancied candidates with brighter images in the party, but de Klerk easily won the first round of the elections, then narrowly beat Barend du Plessis in the final round. He emerged as the new leader of the NP.

Relations between himself and Botha became increasingly acrimonious as 1989 progressed. Whenever a quarrel loomed, he lined up with the party, and with the cabinet behind him, surprised everyone by confronting the "old crocodile." A furious row blew up over his proposed visit to Kenneth Kaunda in Zambia. Botha claimed that he should have been informed and resigned the presidency in a fit of rage on 15 August.

De Klerk was unanimously elected President by parliament on 14 September 1989, in an atmosphere of hope and goodwill from all races.

De Klerk's thinking on apartheid and the future of his country seemed to have undergone a total sea change in the space of a single year. Earlier his public statements had always expressed the party line on apartheid, but public opionion was expecting changes and he was prepared to be flexible in contrast with Botha who had significantly failed to deliver.

Perhaps it was a reaction to Botha's vacillation, but the moment he became President he affirmed his commitment to radical change without explaining how it would be effected. He took various measures to end petty apartheid and released seven senior veterans of the ANC including Walter Sisulu, but not at first, Nelson Mandela.

As time passed it became clear that he had abandoned apartheid as an official policy, but he was only cautiously edging towards discussions with a black leadership. He announced the unbanning of the ANC and other African parties on 2 February 1990 and finally released Nelson Mandela on 11 February to the plaudits of the world.

On 2 May 1990 he held the first negotiations ever between the government and the ANC since the party had been formed in 1912. De Klerk promised to lift the remaining apartheid legislation while the ANC agreed to end the armed struggle. In June the state of emergency was partially lifted and in September, de Klerk persuaded the National Party to open its ranks to people of all races.

In October he secured the repeal of the Separate Amenities Act, which for 37 years had been a pillar of apartheid legislation. This was followed in February 1991, by all the remaining apartheid laws. In March he tabled proposals for extensive land reform, aimed at immediately establishing a million black homeowners and releasing 1.25m acres of land for the purchase by black farmers.

These moves were interspersed with several tours abroad to explain to the world how apartheid was being abolished, while asking for new investment and the lifting of sanctions.

He developed a close affinity with Nelson Mandela as a man he could "do business with." At first he saw him as the black equivalent of himself, a moderate who would be ready to compromise in face of reality. For a considerable time he tried to foist the idea of power sharing on Mandela, but this was never an acceptable long term measure. He found the black leader, with his party behind him, were determined ultimately to win total democracy.

Occasionally there were heavy setbacks for their relationship as in July 1991 when it was revealed that the government had been secretly funding Chief Gatsha Buthelezi's Inkatha party. De Klerk climbed down and promised that there would not be any more covert political funding.

He remained true to his word; bit by bit the structure of apartheid was dismantled and was formally abolished in its entirety in June. In August he declared an amnesty for all political exiles.

In December 1991 talks between all political groups started over the constitution. De Klerk and Mandela clashed publicly over the ANC's refusal to end its guerrilla campaign. Mandela accused de Klerk of trickery and political immorality and yet this was mostly public posturing. Both men seemed resolved to achieve constitutional progress as soon as possible.

De Klerk wanted to seize public enthusiasm for a new deal by getting the endorsement of whites for his reform proposals. In the March 1992 referendum, there was a huge turnout of over 85% of white voters and nearly 70% voted "yes" to his reform proposals and the creation of a democratic non-racial South Africa.

But de Klerk had not been able to change the old attitudes and methods of the police. A series of incidents culminated in the Boipatong massacre of June 1992 in which Inkatha killed 42 people and injured many others while the police did little to intervene.

De Klerk tried to visit the township to show his sympathy, but was literally chased away by the enraged youth. Mandela was under pressure too from his own supporters and was forced to break off the bilateral talks.

Further massacres, examples of police indiscipline and inter-tribal fighting continued throughout most of 1992. De Klerk's popularity plummeted as he came under attack from all sides. Yet he and Mandela were sure there was no alternative but to pursue the constitutional course. By December, despite continuing violence, most parties were back at the conference table and determined to pursue the timetable of change.

Multi-party negotiations formally restarted in March 1993. The desire for a settlement overcame the assassination of the prominent ANC leader Chris Hani in April and an election date was established for April 1994.

For the remainder of 1993 De Klerk and Mandela found themselves thrown together, trying to negotiate a transitional process that would lead to democracy. They were under attack both from extreme whites and from the Inkatha party of Buthelezi. But neither the opposition, nor recurring violence, deflected them. For this they were jointly awarded the Nobel peace prize in Stockholm on 10 December.

In December a Transitional Executive Council was installed, parallel to government, to supervise the transition to the elections. De Klerk worked as hard as Mandela to persuade the right wingers and Inkatha to join the peace process. With a week to go Chief Buthelezi was finally persuaded to join the election campaign at the end of April.

De Klerk fought a tough, but clean, campaign as leader of the new-style National Party. He persuaded much of the electorate to forget the NP's image as the party of apartheid and to see him as the man who had been responsible for changing the face of South Africa.

He did surprisingly well. His party won a majority in the comparatively liberal Western Cape Province and secured 20.39 percent of the national vote. Under the constitution this was enough to secure his position as second deputy presidency under Nelson Mandela in the new government. De Klerk acknowledged defeat by the ANC graciously and wished Mandela every success as he took over the presidency, while Mandela referred to him as a man of honour.

The old team that had led South Africa to its first democratic government was still in power, though the captain and vice captain had switched roles. De Klerk was sworn in as Vice President on 10 May 1994.

New Style Ruler

JERRY RAWLINGS
1947-

Jerry Rawlings has emerged as the greatest Ghanaian ruler since
Kwame Nkrumah. Already he has ruled far longer than his much
admired predecessor, longer than any other Ghanaian head of
state. And he has succeeded economically in the harder
circumstances of the competitive modern world, while Nkrumah
failed miserably as an economic manager. Rawlings started as a
classical revolutionary leader – popular, young, handsome and
dashing. He hoped that leftist-populism would solve his nation's
problems, but ended by proscribing orthodox economic medicines
which made Ghana into one of the most successful of the new style
African economies.

Rawlings has also transformed himself, with consummate skill,
from a military ruler into a democratically elected President. He
has demonstrated his flexibility by adapting to changing
circumstance, by showing himself to be a superb political tactician
while still keeping the long-term interests of his people firmly in
mind.

Jerry John Rawlings was born on 22 June 1947 in Accra, the son of a
Ghanaian, Ewe mother and a Scottish father. His father had gone
back to Scotland before he was born. But he remained a bright and
popular boy, strongly attached to his mother. She was a civil servant and
sufficiently well off to arrange education for him at the prestigious
Achimota school, where he got a general certificate of education at O level
in 1966, before going on to the Ghana Military Academy at Teshie.

He joined the airforce as a flight cadet in Takoradi in August 1967 and
became commissioned as a pilot officer in January 1969, winning the
"Speed Bird Trophy" as the best cadet in flying and airmanship. He was
promoted Flight Lieutenant in April 1978.

Always highly politically conscious and idealistic, he became
associated with a group of young radicals, mostly young military officers

and NCOs, who planned a coup against General Fred Akuffo on 15 May 1979.

Rawlings had been highly critical of the political and economic bankruptcy of the old regime and demanded that all senior officers should first account for all their ill-gotten assets before the country was ready for the return to civilian rule in July 1979. Though Ghanaians were divided over the issue, he emerged as the voice of a new populism that was sweeping the country, which demanded complete change and an end to corruption.

He and his group of young officers were court martialled on 28 May, for leading a mutiny and forced to surrender the senior officers they had taken as hostages. In the turbulent weeks at the end of May, Rawlings had been greeted by the masses as a new Messiah and he took the opportunity in court, to denounce the corruption of previous regimes.

On 4 June, the junior officers and soldiers loyal to him, sprung him from military custody and took him direct to the radio station where, at 5.50am, he announced the setting up of the Armed Forces Revolutionary Council (AFRC), with himself as Chairman.

Fighting continued for some time afterwards, but he emerged triumphant and began to rule by decree in a populist regime which set about eradicating corruption and setting up a new order. The revolution was bloody. The army commander and many other senior officers died in battle. A number of past leaders and three former heads of state were summarily executed and people's courts imposed arbitrary punishments for corruption and other offences. The revolution soon expanded to engulf civilians who were routinely beaten and abused on being arbitrarily arrested. Rawlings frequently spoke out against the brutalities wrought on helpless victims, including women.

But Rawlings made it clear that he had no intention to hold onto power and said that the elections for the return to civilian rule would go ahead as planned. The elections were held one week early, Dr Hilla Limann's People's National Party triumphed and he was duly installed as President on 24 September 1979.

But Limann's government proved weak and indecisive and Rawlings, though holding no constitutional position, was continually breathing down his neck as the guardian of "the gains made on 4 June" (his revolution). Rawlings made several speeches warning the people about the dangers of the misuse of power by the Limann government, which responded by harrassing his closest associates.

On 1 December Rawlings was forced to resign his commission. He heard about his retirement on Radio Ghana after meeting Limann earlier that day, when the matter was not discussed. Ironically this actually strengthened his position by freeing him from his obligations to government as a serving officer.

On 22 October 1980 he was detained on the grounds that he was planning to train revolutionaries. He was freed but came under close surveillance as the government became paranoid about coup-plots.

Limann's rule became increasingly weak, while Rawlings chafed at the failure to fulfil the promise of his revolution.

His much discussed "second coming" came on 1 January 1982, when he seized power in a coup which started at 3am on New Year's Day.

Slight resistance by isolated military units had ended by the time he made his first broadcast at 11am.

He said that the armed forces had been forced to intervene again because of the failure of the Limann government to combat corruption and a deteriorating economy. He said he had come to restore democracy where the needs of the people would be heeded by government. He said this was not just a question of abstract liberties, "it involves above all, food, clothing, shelter and the basic necessities of life."

He set up a Provisional National Defence Council (PNDC), as the supreme ruling body, initially consisting mainly of soldiers. On 21 January 1982 he established a 16-member civilian government, with cabinet ministers called secretaries, who were told to see their appointments merely as "a chance to serve the people sacrificially."

He sought to implement leftist-populist policies and to decentralise power by setting up a People's Defence Committee in an attempt to create mass participation. He also tried to democratise the army. But this replacement of old institutions caused conflict and uncertainty. It also unleashed ethnic feelings with Rawlings relying increasingly on his own Ewe people, while PNDC leaders from other ethnic groups were forced out, often accused of plotting. A number of attempted coups were soon being reported.

Rawlings found that the Defence Committees often exceeded their powers and was forced gradually to clip their wings. In December 1984 he "restructured" the committees and their power dwindled thereafter. Students who had welcomed the second coming gradually became more estranged in the face of economic hardship and the need for austerity measures.

Rawlings may have wanted to run a Marxist economy and to lift it up by its own bootstraps with the help of Eastern bloc countries, but he was soon persuaded by his orthodox Finance Minister, Kwesi Botchwey, to realign towards the West and to adopt conventional cures. Harsh austerity budgets were passed from 1983 and Ghana accepted the tough International Monetary Fund conditions and heavy devaluation of the cedi. Rawlings decided to accept economic realities and run the economy on pragmatic lines. He succeeded in obtaining rapid expansion of local food production. Goods returned to the shops but only at a price.

In his early years Rawlings forged close relationships with a number of left-wing states including Libya and Burkina Faso, where he developed a particularly close relationship with its ruler, Thomas Sankara (q.v.). He also visited Burkina many times and there were tentative plans to create a common currency. Rawlings was devastated by Sankara's assassination in October 1987, although he made a point of maintaining good relations with his successor Blaise Compaore.

In December 1988 he instituted a programme of staggered local elections in different regions of the country. Voters were asked to vote for individuals (not parties) who could represent them in 18 district assemblies. Turnout was low, though this was a first hesitant step towards democratic rule.

On 10 May 1991, in response to massive international and internal pressure, he announced his acceptance of multi-party government. This *volte face* brought a burst of activity. On 17 May a law setting up a National Consultative Assembly to prepare a draft constitution was published. On 20 June conditional amnesty was granted to all political exiles asking them to return home.

The big question was whether or not Rawlings would retire and opt out of politics altogether, or whether he would try and contest the elections and turn himself into a democratically elected president.

On 28 April 1992 about half of Ghana's electors went to the polls and overwhelmingly approved the new constitution that would lead to civilian rule. In May Rawlings lifted the ban on political parties and unleashed a rush of frenzied electioneering. A plethora of new political parties made themselves known to the electorate, but Rawlings remained silent, giving no clue as to whether he would participate.

It was not until the last minute of the eleventh hour that Rawlings presented his own nomination papers and said that he would stand for the presidency. By then the opposition parties had split and divided themselves so often, that none of them seemed capable of providing clear leadership or stability in the new Ghana.

Rawlings had carefully managed the system to show that he was the only leader that could continue to deliver an improving economy and the stability in which democracy could thrive. He allowed proxy parties to campaign on his behalf and gave his opponents time to fragment and divide into meaningless smaller parties.

But the extent of his victory in the presidential elections of 3 November surprised everyone. He had won 60% of all the votes cast, far more than his four opponents taken together. The victory was repeated in the parliamentary elections which followed in December.

The opposition cried foul, but they had not protested about the elections beforehand. They had challenged Rawlings on a playing field of his own choosing and had been soundly trounced.

Rawlings was sworn in as President of Ghana on 7 January 1993 and smoothly transferred his style of government to the civilian system. He kept the key ministers who had transformed Ghana during his 11-year rule and concentrated still more specifically on maintaining the expansion of the economy.

Index

The index covers personalities in the book. For ease of reference it gives different appellations and spellings of African and Arab names.

About the Author

Alan Rake (BA, Politics, Philosophy and Economics, Brasenose College, Oxford) is Editor-in-Chief of the monthly London-based magazine *New African*. After working with *Drum* magazine from 1957, in East, West and South Africa for a nearly a decade, he returned to England to work with African publications and the newsletter *Africa Confidential* concerning the continent. He edited *African Development* until it was merged with *New African* in 1977. He founded and edited the magazine *African Business* in 1978. He has specialised in African affairs for the last 37 years.

He still travels in Africa regularly and is the author of a number of books and reference books on Africa including the *New African Yearbook*, and *Travellers' Guides to Africa* published by I.C. Publications, London. His first *Who's Who in Africa*, written jointly with John Dickie was published in 1973 and the *Who's Who in Africa* published by Scarecrow Press appeared in 1992. He is continuing to write and planning further books on African history and politics.